CONTRACTS

CONTRACTS
Second Edition

JOHN D. CALAMARI

Wilkinson Professor of Law, Fordham University

JOSEPH M. PERILLO

Cameron Professor of Law, Fordham University

BLACK LETTER SERIES®

WEST PUBLISHING CO.
ST. PAUL, MINN.
1990

COPYRIGHT © 1983 WEST PUBLISHING CO.
COPYRIGHT © 1990 By WEST PUBLISHING CO.
50 West Kellogg Boulevard
P.O. Box 64526
St. Paul, MN 55164–0526

Printed in the United States of America

Library of Congress Cataloging-in-Publication Data

Calamari, John D.
Contracts / John D. Calamari and Joseph M. Perillo.
p.   cm. — (Black letter series)
ISBN 0–314–73305–1
1. Contracts—United States—Outlines, syllabi, etc. I. Perillo,
Joseph M. II. Title. III. Series.
KF801.Z9C27 1990
346.73'02—dc20
[347.3062]
90–12470
CIP

ISBN 0–314–73305–1

PUBLISHER'S PREFACE

This "Black Letter" is designed to help a law student recognize and understand the basic principles and issues of law covered in a law school course. It can be used both as a study aid when preparing for classes and as a review of the subject matter when studying for an examination.

Each "Black Letter" is written by experienced law school teachers who are recognized national authorities in the subject covered.

The law is succinctly stated by the author of this "Black Letter." In addition, the exceptions to the rules are stated in the text. The rules and exceptions have purposely been condensed to facilitate quick review and easy recollection. For an in-depth study of a point of law, citations to major student texts are given. In addition, a **Text Correlation Chart** provides a convenient means of relating material contained in the Black Letter to appropriate sections of the casebook the student is using in his or her law school course.

If the subject covered by this text is a code or code-related course, the code section or rule is set forth and discussed wherever applicable.

FORMAT

The format of this "Black Letter" is specially designed for review. (1) **Text.** First, it is recommended that the entire text be studied, and, if deemed necessary, supplemented by the student texts cited. (2) **Capsule Summary.** The Capsule Summary is an abbreviated review of the subject matter which can be used both before and after studying the main body of the text. The headings in the Capsule Summary follow the main text of the "Black Letter." (3) **Table of Contents.** The Table of Contents is in outline form to help you organize the details of the subject and the Summary of Contents gives you a final overview of the materials. (4) **Practice Examination.** The Practice Examination in Appendix B gives you the opportunity of testing yourself with the type of question asked on an exam, and comparing your answer with a model answer.

In addition, a number of other features are included to help you understand the subject matter and prepare for examinations:

Short Questions and Answers: This feature is designed to help you spot and recognize issues in the examination. We feel that issue recognition is a major ingredient in successfully writing an examination.

Perspective: In this feature, the authors discuss their approach to the topic, the approach used in preparing the materials, and any tips on studying for and writing examinations.

Analysis: This feature, at the beginning of each section, is designed to give a quick summary of a particular section to help you recall the subject matter and to help you determine which areas need the most extensive review.

Examples: This feature is designed to illustrate, through fact situations, the law just stated. This, we believe, should help you analytically approach a question on the examination.

Glossary: This feature is designed to refamiliarize you with the meaning of a particular legal term. We believe that the recognition of words of art used in an examination helps you to better analyze the question. In addition, when writing an examination you should know the precise definition of a word of art you intend to use.

We believe that the materials in this "Black Letter" will facilitate your study of a law school course and assure success in writing examinations not only for the course but for the bar examination. We wish you success.

THE PUBLISHER

SUMMARY OF CONTENTS

	Page
CAPSULE SUMMARY	1
PERSPECTIVE	83
I. Mutual Assent—Offer and Acceptance	**87**
A. Mutual Assent	90
B. Offer	93
C. Acceptance	99
D. Termination of Revocable Offers	113
E. Option Contracts—Irrevocable Offers	126
F. U.C.C. Section 2–206	128
G. Certainty	131
Review Questions	138
II. Consideration And Its Equivalents	**145**
A. Introduction	148
B. Consideration	148
C. Moral Obligation	171
D. Promissory Estoppel	176
E. Sealed Instrument	181
Review Questions	181
III. Legal Capacity	**185**
A. Infants	187
B. The Mentally Infirm	190
Review Questions	192
IV. Proper Form (Writing) and Interpretation	**193**
A. Parol Evidence Rule	195

Page

IV. Proper Form (Writing) and Interpretation—Continued
    B. Interpretation _____ 202
    C. Statute of Frauds _____ 208
Review Questions _____ 223

V. Conditions, Performance and Breach _____ **229**
    A. Nature and Classification of Conditions _____ 232
    B. Conditions and Promises as Related to Substantial Performance and Material Breach 235
    C. Recovery Despite Material Breach or Failure to Perform Substantially _____ 240
    D. Excuse of Conditions _____ 242
    E. Prospective Unwillingness and Inability to Perform: Repudiation _____ 247
    F. Performance of the Sales Contract _____ 253
    G. Warranties in the Sales Contract _____ 259
Review Questions _____ 263

VI. Defenses _____ **267**
    A. Impracticability _____ 270
    B. Frustration _____ 275
    C. Risk of Casualty Losses _____ 277
    D. Illegality _____ 281
    E. Discharge of Contractual Duties _____ 288
Review Questions _____ 294

VII. Contract Remedies _____ **297**
    A. Damages _____ 299
    B. Restitution _____ 313
    C. Equitable Enforcement _____ 316
Review Questions _____ 323

VIII. Avoidance Or Reformation for Misconduct or Mistake _____ **327**
    A. Duress _____ 330
    B. Undue Influence _____ 333
    C. Misrepresentation _____ 334
    D. Mistake _____ 343
    E. Reformation for Mistake, Misrepresentation or Duress _____ 348
    F. Unconscionability _____ 351
    G. "Duty" to Read _____ 354
    H. Affirmance or Ratification _____ 356
Review Questions _____ 357

IX. Third Party Beneficiaries _____ **359**
    A. Types of Beneficiaries _____ 361
    B. Promisor's Defenses _____ 365
    C. Cumulative Rights of the Beneficiary _____ 368
    D. Rights of the Promisee Against the Promisor _____ 369
Review Questions _____ 369

X. Assignment and Delegation _____ **371**
    A. Assignment of Rights _____ 373
    B. Delegation of Duties _____ 384
Review Questions _____ 387

APPENDICIES

App.
A. Answers to Review Questions 389

B. Practice Examination 415

C. Correlation Chart 449

D. Glossary 451

E. Index 457

*

TABLE OF CONTENTS

		Page
CAPSULE SUMMARY		1
PERSPECTIVE		83

I.   Mutual Assent—Offer and Acceptance **87**
- A.   Mutual Assent 90
  - 1.   Nature of Mutual Assent 90
  - 2.   Objective Theory of Contracts 90
    - a.   Discussion 90
    - b.   Law and Fact 90
  - 3.   Must the Parties Intend to Be Bound or Intend Legal Consequences? 91
    - a.   Discussion 91
  - 4.   Intention That the Agreement Be Reduced to One Formalized Writing 92
- B.   Offer 93
  - 1.   Meaning of Offer 93
  - 2.   Meaning of Promise 93
  - 3.   Offers Distinguished From Statements That Are Not Offers 93
    - a.   Expressions of Opinions and Words of Reassurance 93
    - b.   Offers Distinguished From Statements of Intention, etc. 94
    - c.   Offers Distinguished From Inquiries or Invitations 95
    - d.   Offers Distinguished From Ads, Catalogues and Circular Letters 95
    - e.   Offers Distinguished From Price Quotations 96
    - f.   The Offer at Auction 97
    - g.   Offer v. Preliminary Negotiations 97
  - 4.   Distinction Between Unilateral and Bilateral Contracts 97
    - a.   Basis of Distinction 97
    - b.   Acceptance of Offer Looking to a Bilateral Contract 97

                                                                    Page

I.   **Mutual Assent—Offer and Acceptance**—Continued
            c. Acceptance of an Offer Looking to a Unilateral Contract 98
            d. Ambiguous Offer 98
            e. U.C.C. and Restatement, Second 98
      C. Acceptance 99
            1. General Requirements 99
                 a. Introduction 99
                 b. Acceptance by Authorized Party 99
                      1) Options 100
                      2) Undisclosed Principal 100
                 c. Knowledge of the Offer and Intent to Accept 100
                      1) Knowledge of the Offer 100
                      2) Intent to Accept 101
                 d. Necessity for Communication in a Bilateral Contract 102
                      1) Theory 102
                 e. Necessity for Notice of Performance in a Unilateral Contract 103
                      1) Introduction 103
                      2) Views 103
                      3) Discussion of View (a) 103
                 f. Acceptance of an Offer Looking to a Series of Contracts 104
            2. Acceptance of a Bilateral Contract 105
                 a. Acceptance by Silence 105
                 b. Acceptance by Conduct 107
                      1) Discussion 107
                      2) Statutory Exceptions 108
                 c. When Is an Acceptance Effective? 108
                      1) Introduction 108
                      2) Prescribed Method of Acceptance 108
                      3) Parties at a Distance 109
                           a) Use of Authorized Means of Acceptance (Mailbox Rule) 109
                           b) Unauthorized Means of Acceptance 109
                           c) U.C.C. and Restatement Second 109
                 d. Offeror's Power to Negate Mailbox Rule 110
                 e. When Offeree Sends Both Acceptance and Rejection 111
                      1) When a Rejection Is Sent First 111
                      2) When an Acceptance Is Sent First 111
                      3) Lost or Delayed Acceptance 111
                      4) Withdrawal of Acceptance 112
                      5) Parties in the Presence of One Another 112
                 f. Risk of Mistake in Transmission by an Intermediary 112
                      1) Introduction 112
                      2) Minority View 112
                      3) Liability of the Intermediary 113
      D. Termination of Revocable Offers 113
            1. Introduction 113
                 a. Lapse of Time 113
                      1) Time Specified in the Offer 113
                      2) Time not Specified in Offer 113
                           a) Face to Face Offer 114
                      3) Termination Upon the Happening of a Particular Event 114

I.   Mutual Assent—Offer and Acceptance—Continued

4) Effect of Late Acceptance 114
b. Death or Lack of Capacity 114
1) Death of Offeror 114
2) Incapacity of Offeror 115
a) Adjudication of Incapacity 115
b) No Adjudication of Incapacity 115
3) Death or Incapacity of the Offeree 115
c. Revocation 115
1) Direct Revocation 115
2) Equal Publicity 116
3) Indirect Revocation 116
a) Reliable Information 116
b) Limitations on the Doctrine 117
c) Special Problems Relating to Revocation of a Unilateral Offer 117
d) Additional Problems Under Third View 118
d. Death or Destruction 118
e. Supervening Illegality 118
f. Rejection or Counter Offer by Offeree 118
1) Common Law 118
a) Counter Offer Distinguished From Other Communicaticns 119
2) U.C.C. Section 2–207 120
a) Introduction 120
b) The Framework of the Statute 120
c) Subdivision 1 120
d) Subdivision 2 122
e) Subdivision 3 124
f) Confirmation 125
g) Restatement, Second 126
E. Option Contracts—Irrevocable Offers 126
1. Introduction 126
2. What Makes an Offer Irrevocable? 126
3. By Statute 127
4. The Nature of an Option Contract—Irrevocable Offer 127
5. Termination of Irrevocable Offers 127
6. When Is the Acceptance of an Irrevocable Offer Effective? 128
F. U.C.C. Section 2–206 128
1. U.C.C. § 2–206 128
a. Introduction 128
b. Subdivision 1(a) of U.C.C. § 2–206 129
1) Unilateral–Bilateral 129
2) Mailbox Rule 129
c. Subdivision 1(b) 129
1) Order to Buy Goods for Prompt or Current Shipment 129
2) The Unilateral Contract Trick—Subdivision 1(b) 130
3) Subdivision 2 130
2. The Restatement, Second 130
G. Certainty 131
1. Common Law 131
a. Introduction 131

Page

I. Mutual Assent—Offer and Acceptance—Continued

      b. What Are Material Terms? 131

      c. When Is a Material Term Reasonably Certain? 131

      d. Types of Indefiniteness 131

          1) Where the Parties Have Purported to Agree on a Material Term But Have Left It Indefinite 132

          2) Where the Parties Are Silent as to a Material Term 133

          3) Where the Parties Agree to Agree 135

             a) Traditional Rule 135

             b) Modern View 135

      e. Uniform Commercial Code 136

          1) Introduction 136

             a) Specific Provisions 136

             b) General Provision 137

Review Questions 138

II. Consideration and Its Equivalents **145**

  A. Introduction 148

  B. Consideration 148

    1. Elements of Consideration 148

      a. The Promisee Must Suffer Legal Detriment 148

      b. Detriment Must Induce the Promise 148

      c. The Promise Must Induce the Detriment 149

    2. Motive and Past Consideration 150

    3. Adequacy 150

    4. Sham and Nominal Consideration 151

    5. Invalid Claims 152

    6. The Pre-existing Duty Rule 153

      a. Introduction 153

      b. Duties Imposed by Law 154

      c. Modification in a Two Party Case 154

      d. The Three Party Cases 155

      e. Agreement to Accept Part Payment in Satisfaction of a Debt .. 156

    7. Accord and Satisfaction 157

      a. Liquidated and Unliquidated Claims 157

      b. Definition 157

      c. Problems Presented 157

    8. U.C.C. Inroads on Pre-existing Duty Rule and Foakes v. Beer ... 160

      a. U.C.C. § 2–209(1) 160

      b. U.C.C. §§ 2–209(2) and (3) 160

      c. U.C.C. § 2–209(2) 160

      d. Subdivision 4 160

      e. Subdivision 5 160

      f. Duress 161

      g. U.C.C. § 1–207 161

      h. U.C.C. § 1–107 162

      i. U.C.C. § 3–408 163

    9. Bilateral Contracts 163

    10. Mutuality of Obligation 163

      a. Introduction 163

      b. Unilateral Contracts 163

Page

II.   **Consideration and Its Equivalents**—Continued
             c. Voidable and Unenforceable Promises _____ 164
             d. Illusory Promises _____ 164
             e. Right to Terminate a Contract by Virtue of a Provision Contained Therein 165
             f. Conditional Promises _____ 166
             g. Aleatory Promises _____ 167
             h. Consideration Supplied by Implied Promise _____ 167
             i. Agreements Allowing a Party to Supply a Material Term _____ 167
             j. A Void Contract Is Not Necessarily a Nullity _____ 168
       11. Requirements and Output Contracts _____ 169
             a. Introduction _____ 169
             b. Validity of Requirements Contracts _____ 169
             c. U.C.C. § 2–306 _____ 169
             d. How Much Is a Requirements Buyer Entitled to Demand? _____ 169
             e. May a Requirements Buyer Diminish or Terminate Requirements? _____ 170
             f. Does a Requirements Buyer Have a Duty to Promote the Goods? _____ 170
       12. Must All of the Consideration Be Valid? _____ 170
       13. Conjunctive and Alternative Promises _____ 170
             a. Conjunctive Promises _____ 170
             b. Alternative Promises _____ 171
                   1) Where the Choice of Alternatives Is in the Promisor _____ 171
                   2) Where the Choice of Alternatives Is in the Promisee _____ 171
   C. Moral Obligation _____ 171
       1. Introduction _____ 171
       2. Exceptions _____ 172
             a. Promises to Pay a Liquidated Debt _____ 172
             b. Promises to Pay Fixed Amounts for Services Previously Requested _____ 172
             c. Promises to Pay a Fixed Amount for Services Not Requested _____ 172
                   1) Where Promisee Is Entitled to a Quasi–Contractual Recovery _____ 172
                   2) Where Promisee Is Not Entitled to a Quasi–Contractual Recovery _____ 172
             d. Promises to Pay Debts Discharged or Rendered Unenforceable by Operation
                   of Law _____ 173
                   1) Discharge in Bankruptcy _____ 173
                   2) Statute of Limitations _____ 173
             e. Promises to Perform a Voidable Duty _____ 174
             f. Statute of Frauds _____ 175
             g. Miscellaneous Promises Supported by Antecedent Events _____ 175
             h. To Whom the Promise Must Be Made _____ 176
   D. Promissory Estoppel _____ 176
       1. Introduction _____ 176
       2. The First Restatement _____ 176
       3. Restatement, Second _____ 177
       4. The Roots of the Doctrine of Promissory Estoppel _____ 177
       5. Present Approach to a Gift Promise _____ 179
       6. Doctrine Not Limited to Gratuitous Promises _____ 179
       7. Approach to a Problem _____ 181
   E. Sealed Instrument _____ 181
       1. Effect of a Seal _____ 181
Review Questions _____ 181

		Page
III.	**Legal Capacity**	**185**
	A. Infants	187
	1. Who Is an Infant?	187
	2. Is an Infant's Promise Void or Voidable?	187
	3. Avoidance Or Ratification	187
	a. Avoidance	187
	b. Ratification	187
	4. Restitution After Disaffirmance	188
	a. Infant as Defendant	188
	b. Infant as Plaintiff	188
	5. Necessaries	188
	6. Infant's Liability for Benefits Received	189
	7. Ignorance of Law and Fact	189
	8. Torts Connected With Contracts	189
	a. Infant's Torts Stemming From Contracts	189
	b. Effect of Misrepresentation of Age	190
	c. Torts and Agency Relationships	190
	B. The Mentally Infirm	190
	1. Is Promise of a Mentally Infirm Person Void or Voidable?	190
	2. Test of Mental Infirmity	190
	3. Requirement of Restitution	190
	4. Avoidance and Ratification	191
	5. Liability for Necessaries	191
	6. Intoxicated Persons and Drug Users	191
	7. Exploitation of Alcoholics and Weak Minded Persons	191
	Review Questions	192
IV.	**Proper Form (Writing) and Interpretation**	**193**
	A. Parol Evidence Rule	195
	1. The Nature and Meaning of the Rule	195
	a. What Type of Evidence May Be Excluded by the Parol Evidence Rule?	195
	b. Theory of the Rule	195
	2. How to Determine Finality	195
	3. How to Determine Completeness	195
	a. Four Corners Rule	196
	b. The Collateral Contract Rule	196
	c. Williston's Rules	196
	d. Corbin's View	196
	e. The U.C.C. Approach (U.C.C. § 2–202)	197
	1) U.C.C. § 2–202(b)	197
	2) U.C.C. § 2–202(a)	197
	3) Confirmations	197
	4) The Restatement, Second	198
	4. Approach of Trial Judge	198
	5. Separate Consideration	198
	6. Subsequent Agreement	198
	7. Is the Rule One of Substantive Law or Procedure?	198
	8. Is the Term Offered Consistent or Contradictory?	199
	9. Undercutting the Integration	201
	B. Interpretation	202
	1. Introduction	202

IV. **Proper Form (Writing) and Interpretation**—Continued
    2. Varying Views 202
        a. Plain Meaning Rule—Ambiguity 202
        b. Williston's Rules 203
            1) Integration 203
            2) Non–Integration 203
        c. Corbin's Rules—Restatement, Second 204
        d. U.C.C. on Interpretation 204
    3. The Relationship Between Parol Evidence and Interpretation 204
        a. Plain Meaning Rule 205
        b. Williston's Rules 205
        c. Corbin's Rules—Restatement, Second 205
        d. U.C.C. 205
    4. Course of Dealing, Course of Performance and Usage of Trade 205
        a. Introduction 205
        b. Meaning of Course of Dealing and Course of Performance 206
        c. Usage of Trade 206
        d. For What Purposes May They Be Used? 206
            1) Usage of Trade and Course of Dealing 206
            2) Course of Performance 206
    5. Other Rules of Interpretation 208
  C. Statute of Frauds 208
    1. Introduction 208
    2. Major Classes of Cases Covered by Writing Requirements 208
        a. Suretyship Agreements 209
            1) Cases Where There Is No Prior Obligation Owing From *TP* to *C* to Which *D*'s Promise Relates 209
            2) Cases Where There Is a Prior Obligation Owing From *TP* to *C* to which *D*'s Promise Relates 210
            3) Main Purpose Rule 210
            4) Promises of Indemnity 211
            5) Promise of the Del Credere Agent 212
            6) Promise of Assignor 212
            7) Promise to Buy a Claim 212
            8) Promise by Executor or Administrator 212
        b. Real Property 212
            1) What Is a Contract for Sale of Land? 212
            2) What Is an Interest in Land? 213
            3) What Is Real Property? 213
            4) Effect of Performance 213
        c. Contracts Not to Be Performed Within a Year 213
            1) Bilateral Contracts 213
                a) Promises of Uncertain Duration 214
                b) Contracts for Alternative Performances 215
                c) Contracts With Options to Terminate or Renew 215
                d) Effect of Performance Under One Year Section 216
                e) How Is the Year Measured? 216
                f) Unilateral Contracts 216
                g) Scope of One Year Section 217
                h) Is a Promise or a Contract Within the One Year Section? 217

Page

IV. **Proper Form (Writing) and Interpretation**—Continued
             d. Contracts in Consideration of Marriage _____ 217
             e. Contracts for the Sale of Goods _____ 217
                  1) What Is Covered? _____ 218
                  2) Other U.C.C. Provisions _____ 218
        3. Sufficiency of the Memorandum _____ 218
             a. Introduction _____ 218
             b. Contents of the Writing _____ 219
             c. What Is a Signature? _____ 219
             d. Who Is the Party to Be Charged? _____ 219
             e. Parol Evidence and the Memorandum _____ 219
                  1) Offered by Plaintiff _____ 219
                  2) Offered by Defendant _____ 219
                  3) Interpretation _____ 220
             f. Consideration _____ 220
             g. More Than One Writing _____ 220
        4. Provisions of the U.C.C. _____ 220
             a. Contents of the Memorandum _____ 220
             b. Written Confirmation Between Merchants _____ 220
        5. Auction Sales _____ 221
        6. Agent's Authority _____ 221
        7. Purpose of the Statute _____ 221
        8. Effect of Non-compliance With the Statute of Frauds _____ 221
        9. Part or Full Performance _____ 221
       10. Estoppel _____ 221
             a. Promissory Estoppel _____ 221
             b. Estoppel in Pais _____ 222
       11. Effect of Some Promises Being Within and Others Without the Statute of Frauds 222
       12. Oral Rescission or Modification of a Contract Within the Statute _____ 222
             a. Rescission _____ 222
             b. Modification _____ 222
       13. Relationship of Various Subdivisions _____ 223
Review Questions _____ 223

V. **Conditions, Performance and Breach** _____ **229**
   A. Nature and Classification of Conditions _____ 232
        1. Definition _____ 232
        2. Classifications of Conditions _____ 232
        3. Effect of Failure of Condition _____ 232
        4. Distinguishing Promises From Conditions _____ 232
   B. Conditions and Promises as Related to Substantial Performance and Material Breach 235
        1. Failure of Condition And Breach of Promise _____ 235
        2. Factors Used to Determine Materiality of Breach (May the Aggrieved Party
             Cancel?) _____ 237
        3. Factors Used to Determine Substantial Performance (May the Defaulting Party
             Recover?) _____ 237
        4. Effect of Delay _____ 238
        5. The Satisfaction Cases _____ 239
        6. Demand _____ 240
   C. Recovery Despite Material Breach or Failure to Perform Substantially _____ 240
        1. Divisibility _____ 240

Page

V. **Conditions, Performance and Breach**—Continued
    2. Independent Promises _____ 241
    3. Independent Promises in Leases _____ 241
    4. Independent Promises in Insurance _____ 241
    5. Quasi–Contractual Recovery _____ 242
    6. Statutory Relief _____ 242
  D. Excuse of Conditions _____ 242
    1. Prevention _____ 242
    2. Estoppel, Waiver and Election _____ 244
      a. Equitable Estoppel (Estoppel _in Pais_) _____ 244
      b. Waiver _____ 244
        1) Waiver Before Failure of Condition _____ 244
        2) Who Can Waive _____ 245
        3) Waiver After Failure of Condition _____ 245
        4) Repeated Waivers _____ 246
    3. Excuse of Conditions Involving Forfeitures _____ 246
      a. Discussion _____ 246
    4. Excuse of Conditions Because of Impossibility _____ 247
  E. Prospective Unwillingness and Inability to Perform: Repudiation _____ 247
    1. Repudiation as a Breach Creating a Cause of Action _____ 247
    2. Prospective Unwillingness and Inability as a Prospective Failure of Condition
       Creating a Defense _____ 247
    3. Role of Good Faith _____ 249
    4. Retraction of a Repudiation or Prospective Failure of Condition _____ 249
    5. Urging Retraction _____ 249
    6. Effect of Impossibility on a Prior Repudiation _____ 250
    7. Constructive Repudiation Under The U.C.C. and Restatement Second _____ 250
      a. Is the Common Law Displaced? _____ 250
      b. What Are Adequate Assurances? _____ 250
      c. The Restatement, Second _____ 250
    8. Insolvency _____ 251
      a. Insolvency Defined _____ 251
      b. The Effect of a Buyer's Insolvency _____ 251
      c. Effect of a Seller's Insolvency _____ 252
    9. Repudiation of a Debt _____ 252
    10. Repudiation and Right to Elect _____ 252
  F. Performance of the Sales Contract _____ 253
    1. Obligations of the Seller _____ 253
      a. Perspective _____ 253
      b. Qualification and Exceptions _____ 253
        1) "Unless Otherwise Agreed" _____ 253
        2) Cure (U.C.C. § 2–508(1)) _____ 253
          a) Within the Contract Time _____ 253
          b) A Further Reasonable Time (U.C.C. § 2–508(2)) _____ 254
        3) Acceptance (U.C.C. § 2–606) _____ 255
          a) Express Acceptance _____ 255
          b) Failure to Make an Effective Rejection _____ 255
          c) "Acts Inconsistent With the Seller's Ownership" _____ 255
        4) Revocation of Acceptance (U.C.C. § 2–608) _____ 256
          a) "Substantially Impairs the Value to the Buyer" _____ 256

V.   Conditions, Performance and Breach—Continued
              b)   Time Limitation 256
              c)   Effect 256
          5) Installment Contracts (U.C.C. § 2–612) 256
              a)   Presumption Against (U.C.C. § 2–307) 256
              b)   Effect 257
          6) Improper Shipment (U.C.C. § 2–504) 257
      2. Obligations of the Buyer 257
         a. How Much Must Be Tendered? 258
         b. Form of Tender 258
         c. Buyer's Duty to Accept Goods 258
          1) Perspective 258
          2) Right of Inspection (U.C.C. §§ 2–512, 2–513) 258
              a)   Exception 258
              b)   Place and Method of Inspection 258
         d. Buyer's Duties With Respect to the Rejected Goods (U.C.C. §§ 2–602—2–604) 259
          1) Extra Duties of Merchant Buyer 259
          2) The Seller is Silent 259
    G. Warranties in the Sales Contract 259
      1. Express Warranties (U.C.C. § 2–313) 259
         a. "Merely" Opinion 259
         b. Basis of the Bargain 259
      2. Implied Warranties 260
         a. Merchantability (U.C.C. § 2–314) 260
         b. Fitness for Particular Purpose (U.C.C. § 2–315) 260
         c. Free and Clear Title 261
         d. Infringement (U.C.C. § 2–313(3)) 261
      3. Disclaimer of Warranties 261
         a. Disclaimer of Express Warranties 261
         b. Disclaimer of Implied Warranties 262
          1) Merchantability 262
          2) Fitness 262
          3) Free and Clear Title 263
         c. Limitations Upon Remedies 263
Review Questions 263

VI.   Defenses **267**
    A. Impracticability 270
      1. Impracticability Is Not Necessarily a Defense 270
      2. When Impracticability Is a Defense 270
         a. Three Part Test 270
          1) The Basic Assumption 270
          2) Upon Whom Is the Burden of the Event Placed? 270
      3. Temporary and Partial Impracticability 273
      4. Temporary and Partial Impracticability Under The U.C.C. 273
         a. Temporary Impracticability Under the U.C.C. 273
         b. Partial Impracticability Under the U.C.C. 273
      5. Impracticability of Means of Delivery or Payment 274
         a. Delivery 274
         b. Payment Before Delivery 274

VI. **Defenses**—Continued

        c. Payment After Delivery 274

    6. Impracticability and Conditions 274

        a. Perspective 274

  B. Frustration 275

    1. What Constitutes Frustration 275

        a. Impracticability Compared 275

        b. Elements 275

        c. Perspective 275

        d. Restitution After Discharge for Impracticability or Frustration 276

  C. Risk of Casualty Losses 277

    1. Real Property 277

    2. Leases 277

    3. Sale of Goods 277

        a. Effect of Risk of Loss 277

        b. "Shipment" Versus "Destination" Contracts—Use of Common Carriers 277

            1) Factual Distinction 277

            2) Rule 278

        c. Distinguishing "Shipment" From "Destination" Contracts 278

        d. Delivery by Seller's Own Truck or on Seller's Premises 278

        e. Goods Held by a Bailee 279

        f. The Effect of Seller's Breach on Risk of Loss 279

        g. The Effect of the Buyer's Breach on Risk of Loss 279

    4. Risk of Loss and Impracticability 280

    5. Two Special Situations: Sale on Approval and Sale or Return 280

        a. Sale on Approval 280

        b. Sale or Return 280

    6. The Omnipotence of the Contract 280

  D. Illegality 281

    1. What is an Illegal Bargain? 281

        a. Generally 281

        b. Bribery Cases 282

        c. Licensing Cases 282

        d. Depositaries 283

        e. Knowledge of Illegal Purpose 283

    2. Effect of Illegal Bargain 284

        a. Illegal Executory Agreements 284

            1) Comment 284

            2) Exceptions 284

        b. Illegal Bargains Executed in Whole or In Part 285

            1) Reprise 286

            2) Divisibility 286

            3) Not in *Pari Delicto* 286

            4) *Locus Poenitentiae* (Place for Repentance) 287

        c. Change of Law 287

            1) Legalization of the Activity 287

            2) Supervening Illegality 287

            3) Supervening Illegality of an Offer 288

        d. Change of Facts 288

Page

VI. **Defenses**—Continued
   E. Discharge of Contractual Duties 288
      1. Mutual Rescission 288
         a. Rescission Requires a Mutual Agreement 288
         b. Distinctions 288
         c. Implied Rescission 289
         d. Cancellation Versus Rescission 289
      2. Executory Accord, Accord and Satisfaction, Substituted Agreement and Unilateral Accord 290
         a. Executory Bilateral Accord 290
         b. Unilateral Accord 290
         c. Accord and Satisfaction 291
         d. Substituted Contract 291
      3. Novation 292
      4. Account Stated 292
      5. Release and Covenant Not to Sue 293
         a. Release 293
            1) Generally 293
            2) U.C.C. 293
         b. Covenant Not to Sue 293
      6. Acquisition by the Debtor of the Correlative Right 293
      7. Alteration 293
            1) Waiver 294
            2) Negotiable Instruments 294
      8. Performance—To Which Debt Should Payment Be Applied? 294
Review Questions 294

VII. **Contract Remedies** **297**
   A. Damages 299
      1. Goal of Damages 299
      2. Foreseeability—General and Consequential Damages 299
         a. Application 299
         b. Particular Situations 300
            1) Sale of Goods 300
               a) Seller's Non-delivery 300
               b) Seller's Breach of Warranty 300
               c) Buyer's Breach 301
                d) Seller's Price Action 301
                e) Consequential and Incidental Damages in Sales Cases 302
            2) Employment Contracts 302
                a) Employer's Breach 302
                b) Employee's Breach 302
            3) Construction Contracts 302
                a) Contractor's Delay 302
                b) Contractor's Failure to Complete 303
                c) Defect in Construction 303
                d) Owner's Breach 303
                e) Consequential Damages in Construction Cases 304
            4) Contracts to Sell Realty 304
                a) Vendee's Total Breach 304
                b) Vendor's Total Breach 304

Page

VII. Contract Remedies—Continued
          c) Consequential Damages _____ 305
          d) Vendor's Delay _____ 305
    3. Certainty _____ 305
      a. Discussion _____ 306
      b. Alternatives Where Expectancy Is Uncertain _____ 306
        1) Protection of Reliance Interest _____ 306
        2) Rental Value of Profit–Making Property _____ 307
        3) Value of an Opportunity _____ 307
    4. Mitigation _____ 307
      a. Discussion _____ 308
      b. Exception _____ 308
      c. Non-exclusive Contracts _____ 308
    5. Present Worth Doctrine _____ 309
    6. Liquidated Damages _____ 309
      a. Penalties Distinguished _____ 309
      b. Formulas Are Acceptable _____ 309
      c. Shotgun Clauses Are Dangerous _____ 310
      d. Can't Have It Both Ways _____ 310
      e. Specific Performance Not Excluded _____ 310
      f. Additional Agreed Damages—Attorney's Fees _____ 310
    6. Limitations on Damages _____ 311
      a. Discussion _____ 311
      b. Failure of Essential Purpose _____ 311
        1) Discussion _____ 311
    7. Punitive Damages _____ 312
    8. Mental Distress _____ 312
    9. Nominal Damages _____ 313
  B. Restitution _____ 313
    1. Goal of Restitution _____ 313
    2. When Is Restitution Available? _____ 313
    3. The Party Avoiding Must Offer to Return Property _____ 313
      a. Equitable Action _____ 313
      b. Worthlessness _____ 314
      c. Consumption or Loss of Possession _____ 314
      d. Divisibility _____ 314
    4. Defendant's Refusal to Accept an Offered Return _____ 314
    5. Measure Of Recovery _____ 314
    6. No Restitution After Complete Performance _____ 315
    7. Election of Remedies _____ 315
    8. Specific Restitution _____ 315
  C. Equitable Enforcement _____ 316
    1. Inadequacy of the Legal Remedy _____ 316
      a. Uniqueness _____ 316
      b. Affirmative Rule of Mutuality _____ 316
      c. Conjectural Damages _____ 317
    2. Defenses to Specific Performance _____ 317
      a. Validity of the Contract and Value _____ 317
      b. Certainty of the Contract _____ 317
      c. Impossibility _____ 318

VII. Contract Remedies—Continued
       3. Equitable Discretion _____ 318
          a. Difficulty of Supervision _____ 318
          b. Personal Service Contracts _____ 318
          c. Undue Risk _____ 319
          d. Unconscionability _____ 319
          e. Unclean Hands _____ 319
          f. Laches _____ 320
          g. Balancing Hardships _____ 320
       4. Specific Performance With an Abatement _____ 320
       5. Relationship Between Specific Performance and Damages _____ 320
          a. Specific Performance Plus Damages _____ 320
          b. Specific Performance and Liquidated Damages _____ 321
          c. Effect of Denial of Specific Performance _____ 321
       6. Restraining Orders _____ 321
          a. Employment Contracts With Affirmative and Negative Duties _____ 321
          b. Trade Secrets _____ 321
          c. Covenants Not to Compete _____ 322
             1) Ancillary to Sale of Business _____ 322
             2) Ancillary to Employment _____ 322
Review Questions _____ 323

VIII. Avoidance Or Reformation for Misconduct or Mistake _____ **327**
    A. Duress _____ 330
       1. What Constitutes Wrongful Conduct _____ 330
          a. Violence or Threats of Violence _____ 330
          b. Imprisonment or Threat of Imprisonment _____ 330
          c. Wrongful Seizing or Withholding of Property, Including the Abuse of Liens or Attachments _____ 330
          d. The Abuse of Legal Rights or the Threat Thereof _____ 331
          e. Breach or Threat to Breach a Contract _____ 331
       2. Coercion by a Third Person _____ 332
       3. Voidable or Void? _____ 333
          a. Does It Make a Difference? _____ 333
          b. When Does Duress Make a Transaction Void? _____ 333
    B. Undue Influence _____ 333
       1. What is Undue Influence? _____ 333
    C. Misrepresentation _____ 334
       1. Requirements _____ 334
          a. Scienter Is Not a Requirement _____ 334
          b. Deception _____ 335
          c. Reliance _____ 335
          d. Justification _____ 335
          e. Injury Not Usually a Requisite _____ 336
          f. The Misrepresentation Must Be of Fact and Not Opinion or Law _____ 336
          g. Promissory Fraud and Statements of Intention _____ 338
          h. Non-disclosure _____ 339
          i. Misrepresentation by a Third Person _____ 341
       2. Cure of a Misrepresentation _____ 341
       3. Merger Clauses _____ 342
       4. Election of Remedies _____ 342

Page

VIII. Avoidance Or Reformation for Misconduct or Mistake—Continued

     5. Restoration of Status Quo Ante 342
     6. Fraud-in-the-Factum: A Rarity 343
  D. Mistake 343
     1. Perspective 343
     2. Mistake of Fact Versus Mistake in Judgment 343
     3. Mutual Mistake 344
     4. Mistake Versus Uncertainty 344
     5. Mutual Mistake as to Injuries 345
     6. Mutual Mistake as to Acreage 345
        a. Avoidance 345
        b. Restitution 345
        c. Perspective 346
     7. Unilateral Palpable Mistake 346
     8. Unilateral Impalpable Mistake 346
     9. Mistake of Law 347
    10. Mistake in Performance 347
    11. Defenses to Avoidance or Recovery for Mistake 348
  E. Reformation for Mistake, Misrepresentation or Duress 348
     1. Reformation for Mistake 348
        a. The Prior Agreement 349
        b. The Agreement to Reduce to Writing 349
        c. The Variance 349
     2. Reformation for Misrepresentation 350
     3. Reformation for Duress 350
     4. Reformation and the Parol Evidence Rule 350
     5. Defenses to Reformation 350
        a. Bona Fide Purchaser for Value 350
        b. Equitable Defenses 351
        c. The Effect of Negligence 351
  F. Unconscionability 351
     1. Unconscionability in Equity 351
     2. Unconscionability at Law 351
     3. What Constitutes Unconscionability 352
        a. Unfair Surprise (Procedural Unconscionability) 352
        b. Oppression (Substantive Unconscionability) 352
        c. The Hybrid—Surprise and Oppression 353
     4. Judge Versus Jury 353
     5. The Irrelevance of Hindsight 353
     6. Consumer Protection 353
     7. Termination Clauses and Sales of Goods 354
     8. Limitation on Consequential Damages—Personal Injuries 354
  G. "Duty" to Read 354
     1. Rule 354
     2. Exceptions 355
  H. Affirmance or Ratification 356
     1. Discussion 356
     2. Affirmance by Conduct 356
        a. Exercise of Dominion 356
        b. Delay 357

Page

VIII. Avoidance Or Reformation for Misconduct or Mistake—Continued
        3. The Party Avoiding Must Offer to Return Property Received 357
Review Questions 357

IX. Third Party Beneficiaries **359**
   A. Types of Beneficiaries 361
      1. Operative Concepts and Categories 361
         a. Privity 361
         b. Intended Beneficiary 361
         c. Who Is the Promisor? 361
         d. Incidental Beneficiary 361
         e. Creditor Beneficiary 362
         f. Donee Beneficiary 362
         g. Promises of Indemnity 362
         h. The Municipality Cases 362
         i. The Surety Bond Cases 362
   B. Promisor's Defenses 365
      1. Defenses From the Third Party Beneficiary Contract 365
      2. When Rights Vest 366
         a. Omnipotence of the Contract 366
         b. Creditor Beneficiaries 366
         c. Donee Beneficiaries 366
         d. Perspective 367
      3. Counterclaims 367
      4. Promisee's Defenses Against the Beneficiary 367
   C. Cumulative Rights of the Beneficiary 368
      1. Creditor Beneficiary 368
      2. Donee Beneficiary 368
   D. Rights of the Promisee Against the Promisor 369
Review Questions 369

X. Assignment and Delegation **371**
   A. Assignment of Rights 373
      1. What Is an Assignment? 373
      2. U.C.C. Coverage 373
      3. U.C.C. Exclusions 373
      4. Deviants From the Norm 374
         a. Gratuitous Assignment 374
         b. Voidable Assignment 374
         c. Assignment of Future Rights 374
      5. Formalities 375
      6. Attachment and Perfection of Security Interests in Accounts 375
         a. Attachment 375
         b. Perfection 375
      7. Priorities 376
         a. Comment 376
         b. Unperfected Assignments 376
         c. Non-code Cases 376
            1) Assignee Versus Attaching Creditor 376
            2) Successive Assignees 377
            3) Latent Equities 377

Page

X.   Assignment and Delegation—Continued
     8. Floating Lien _____ 377
       a. Comment _____ 377
       b. Prior Law _____ 377
     9. Non-assignable Rights _____ 378
       a. Standing to Complain _____ 379
       b. Contractual Prohibition of an Assignment _____ 379
         1) Common Law Rule _____ 379
         2) The U.C.C. Rule _____ 379
         3) Interpretation Under Article 2 _____ 379
       c. Contractual Authorization of an Assignment _____ 380
       d. Option Contracts _____ 380
    10. Defenses and Counterclaims of the Obligor Against the Assignor ____ 380
       a. Defenses _____ 380
       b. Counterclaims _____ 382
         1) Same Transaction (Recoupment) _____ 382
         2) Different Transactions (Set–Off) _____ 382
       c. Circumventing Rule _____ 382
         1) U.C.C. Rule _____ 383
         2) Exceptions for Consumer Paper _____ 383
    11. Rights of the Assignee Against the Assignor _____ 383
       a. Express Warranties or Disclaimers of Implied Warranties ___ 383
       b. Implied Warranties _____ 383
  B. Delegation of Duties _____ 384
     1. What is a Delegation? _____ 384
     2. Liability of the Delegant _____ 384
     3. Liability of the Delegate _____ 384
     4. Non-delegable Duties _____ 385
       a. What Duties Are Non-delegable? _____ 385
       b. Delegation in Sales Contracts _____ 386
       c. Effect of Improper Delegation _____ 387
Review Questions _____ 387

APPENDICIES

App.
A. Answers to Review Questions _____ 389
B. Practice Examination _____ 415
C. Correlation Chart _____ 449
D. Glossary _____ 451
E. Index _____ 457

CAPSULE SUMMARY

I. MUTUAL ASSENT—OFFER AND ACCEPTANCE

A. MUTUAL ASSENT

1. Objective Theory of Contracts

Mutual assent is ordinarily arrived at by a process of offer and acceptance. Under the objective theory, whether there is assent is determined by asking what a reasonable person in the position of one party would be led to believe by the words and conduct of the other party. This is usually a question of fact. However, if reasonable persons can reach only one reasonable conclusion, it is a question of law.

2. Intending Legal Consequences.

The parties needn't intend legal consequences to be legally bound, but if the objective evidence makes it clear that they do not intend to be bound there is no contract.

3. Intent to Formalize Agreement

If the parties agree that they are not to be bound unless and until they sign a formal agreement they will not be bound until that time. If they intend the future writing to be merely a convenient memorial of their prior agreement they are bound whether or not such a writing is executed. Intent is often a question of fact.

B.   OFFER
1.   What Constitutes an Offer?
Essentially an offer is a promise to do or to refrain from doing some specified thing in the future. To amount to an offer the promise, in the setting in which it was made, must justify the other party, as a reasonable person to conclude that his or her assent is invited and will conclude the process of offer and acceptance. It is possible, but unusual, to have a non-promissory offer.

2.   What Is a Promise?
A promise is a manifestation of intent that gives an assurance (commitment) that a thing will or will not be done.

3.   Offer Distinguished From Preliminary Negotiations
Preliminary negotiations are any communications prior to the operative offer in the case. Statements of opinion, statements of intention, hope or desire, inquiries or invitations to make offers, catalogs, circular letters, invitations to make bids, expressions of opinion and price quotations are not offers. An advertisement for the sale of goods is ordinarily not an offer. In an auction sale, the bidder is deemed to be the offeror. The situation is different in the case of an auction without reserve.

4.   Distinction Between an Offer Looking to a Unilateral Contract and a Bilateral Contract
An offer looking to a unilateral contract asks for an act; an offer looking to a bilateral contract invites a promise. The promise may be expressed in words or made by conduct. An offer looking to a unilateral contract may not be accepted by a promise. Conversely an offer looking to a bilateral contract may not, except under an unimportant exception, be accepted by performance. Under the orthodox common law rule, the offeree does not become bound when starting to perform the act requested by an offer looking to a unilateral contract. The changes made in these rules by the U.C.C. and the Restatement, Second, are discussed below.

C.   ACCEPTANCE
1.   Relationship to Offer
The offer creates the power of acceptance. The acceptance creates a contract and terminates the power of revocation that the offeror ordinarily has. The acceptance must be a voluntary act.

2.   Acceptance by Authorized Party
An offer may be accepted only by the person or persons to whom it is made. Thus, the offeree may not transfer the power of acceptance to another. But an irrevocable offer may be transferred if the transfer is consistent with the rules governing the assignment of contracts.

3. Knowledge of Offer

In the case of a unilateral contract, the offeree must know of the offer for a contract to arise. There is some dispute as to when this knowledge must occur. In the case of a bilateral contract, this rule may come into conflict with the objective theory of contracts. If so, the objective theory prevails.

4. Intent to Accept

For a unilateral contract to arise, the offeree must intend to accept. The offer need not, however, be the principal inducement for performing the act. It is possible to have a bilateral contract even though the offeree does not intend to accept, if there is an objective manifestation of intent to contract.

5. Necessity for Communication of Acceptance

To create a bilateral contract, the offeree's promise must be communicated to the offeror or his or her agent. However, the offeror may dispense with the necessity for communication by manifesting such an intent.

6. Necessity of Notice in Unilateral Contract

There are three views on the issue of whether the offeree must give notice of performance to the offeror. (1) Notice is not required unless requested by the offeror. (2) If the offeree has reason to know that the offeror has no adequate means of learning of performance with reasonable promptness and certitude, failure to exercise reasonable diligence in giving notice discharges the offeror from liability, unless the offeror otherwise learns of performance within a reasonable time or the offeror expressly or by implication indicates that notification is not necessary. (3) This view is the same as the second view except that no contract is consummated unless and until notice of performance has been sent. The second view is the prevailing view.

7. Acceptance of an Offer Looking to a Series of Contracts

If the offeror makes an offer looking to a series of contracts, a contract arises each time the offeree accepts. As to the future, the offer is revocable unless the offer is irrevocable. Whether an offer looks to one or a series of acceptances is a question to be determined under the reasonable person test. Care must be taken to distinguish an offer looking to a series of acceptances from an offer looking to one acceptance with a number of performances.

8. Acceptance by Silence

The general rule is that silence ordinarily does not give rise to an acceptance of an offer or a counteroffer. This rule does not apply: (1) Where the offeror has given the offeree reason to believe silence will act as an acceptance and the offeree intends by silence to accept; (2) Where the parties have mutually agreed that silence will operate as consent; (3) Where there is a course of dealing so that silence has come to mean assent; (4) Where the offeree accepts services with reasonable opportunity to reject them, and should reasonably understand that they are offered with expectation of payment.

9. Acceptance by Act of Dominion

At times an offeree takes possession of offered goods and indicates that the offered terms are not acceptable. This conduct constitutes the tort of conversion—the wrongful act of dominion over the personal property of another. Because the conduct could have been rightful and referable to the offered terms, the offeror has the option to treat the conduct as rightful, suing on a contract and estopping the offeree from claiming to be a wrongdoer. There is some authority, however, to the effect that this option is not available if the offered terms are manifestly unreasonable.

10. Unsolicited Sending of Goods

An exception exists to the rule stated above as a result of legislation providing that a person who receives unsolicited goods may treat them as a gift.

11. When Is an Acceptance in a Bilateral Contract Effective (Mailbox Rule)?

When the parties are at a distance from one another, is an acceptance effective when put out of the possession of the offeree or when it is received? This depends upon whether the method of acceptance is authorized or not. The medium is authorized if it is the one used by the offeror (unless the offeror specified otherwise) or it is customary in similar transactions at the time and place the offer is received. However a communication will not be effective when sent if proper care has not been taken in transmitting it (e.g. incorrectly addressed). The same rules apply to lost or delayed acceptances. Under the U.C.C. and the Restatement, Second, the question is not whether an authorized means was used, but whether it was "reasonable". Under the Restatement, Second, even if an unreasonable means is used or care is not taken in transmission, the acceptance nonetheless will be effective when sent, provided it is received within the time a seasonably dispatched acceptance sent in a reasonable manner would normally have arrived.

12. Prescribed Method of Acceptance

If the offer prescribes an exclusive method of acceptance, no contract arises if the offeree utilizes another means of acceptance even if the acceptance comes to the attention of the offeror. This is a qualification of the rules stated above.

13. Parties in the Presence of One Another

Contrary to the rule stated above for parties at a distance, when the parties are in the presence of one another, an acceptance is inoperative unless the offeror hears or was at fault in not hearing. Even if the offeror is at fault in not hearing, there is no contract if the offeree knows or has reason to know that the offeror has not heard.

14. Offeror's Power to Negate Mailbox Rule

An offeror may negate the mailbox rule by providing in the offer that the acceptance will be effective only when and if received.

15. Withdrawal of Acceptance
Even if the offeree is able to regain possession of the letter pursuant to postal regulations, the letter of acceptance is effective.

16. When Offeree Sends a Rejection First and Then an Acceptance
An acceptance dispatched after a rejection has been sent is not effective until received and then only if received prior to the rejection.

17. When Offeree Sends Acceptance First but Rejection Is Received Before Acceptance
The usual holding is that a contract is formed. But this view is sometimes qualified by saying that if the offeror relies on the rejection before receiving the acceptance, the offeree will be estopped from enforcing the agreement.

18. Risk of Mistake in Transmission by an Intermediary
The mistake discussed here is not made by a party or an agent, but by an intermediary; e.g. a telegraph company. It does not relate to a telegram that is lost. It relates to one that is received but is incorrectly transmitted. The majority view is that the message as transmitted is operative unless the other party knows or has reason to know of the mistake. The minority view is to the effect that there is no contract if the offer or acceptance is not the message authorized by the party.

D. TERMINATION OF REVOCABLE OFFERS
Introduction. A revocable offer may be terminated in a variety of ways.

1. Lapse of Time
An offer is terminated after the lapse of time specified in the offer. Usually this time is measured from the time the offer is received. If no time is specified, the offer is open for a reasonable time.

   a. Face to Face Offer
   Where an offer is made in any situation where there are direct negotiations (e.g. face to face, telephone) the offer is deemed, in the absence of a manifestation of a contrary intention, to be open only while the parties are conversing.

   b. Termination Upon Happening of a Particular Event
   If the offeror stipulates that the offer shall terminate upon the happening of a certain event and the event occurs before acceptance, the power of acceptance is terminated.

   c. Effect of a Late Acceptance
   There are three views with respect to a late acceptance. (1) The late acceptance is an offer which in turn can be accepted only by a communicated acceptance. (2) The original offeror may treat the late

acceptance as an acceptance by unilaterally waiving the lateness. (3) If the late acceptance is sent in what could plausibly be considered to be a reasonable time, the original offeror has a duty to reply within a reasonable time. Failure to do so creates a contract by silence.

2. Death of Offeror
If the offeror dies between the making of the offer and the acceptance, the offer is terminated even if the offeree is unaware of the offeror's death. Under a minority view, death terminates the offer only if the offeror is aware of it.

3. Incapacity of Offeror
a. Adjudication of Mental or Physical Incapacity
Where there is an adjudication of mental incapacity and the property of the mental defective is placed under guardianship, any unaccepted offer made by the mental defective is terminated. This is so, according to the majority view, even though the offeree is unaware of what has transpired.

b. Where There Is No Adjudication
If there is no adjudication of incompetency, the rule is that supervening mental incapacity in fact terminates the offer if the offeree is or should be aware of the incapacity.

4. Death or Incapacity of the Offeree
The supervening death or adjudication of incapacity of the offeree terminates the offer.

5. Revocation
a. Direct Revocation
A communicated revocation terminates the offeree's power of acceptance and is effective when it is received except in a few states where statutes provide that it is effective on dispatch. At common law, even if the offer says it is irrevocable it is still revocable unless consideration or the equivalent is given for the promise of irrevocability.

Special Situations:

b. Equal Publicity
When an offer is made to a number of persons whose identity is unknown to the offeror (e.g. a reward offer in a newspaper), the offer may be revoked by giving as much publicity to the revocation as was given to the offer. Even here if the offeror knows of the identity of a person who is taking action on the offer, the offeror must communicate the revocation to that person.

    c.   Indirect Revocation

Indirect revocation occurs when the offeree acquires reliable information from a third party that the offeror has engaged in conduct that would indicate to a reasonable person that the offeror no longer wishes to make the offer. Information is reliable only if it comes from a reliable source and is in fact true.

    d.   Special Rules Relating to the Revocation of an Offer Looking to a Unilateral Contract

There are three views with respect to the revocation of an offer looking to a unilateral contract. (1) The traditional rule is that the offer can be revoked at any time until the moment of complete performance. (2) A bilateral contract is formed upon the beginning of performance. (3) The prevailing view is that once the offeree starts to perform the offer becomes irrevocable. This rule requires the actual beginning of performance and not merely preparation. (An irrevocable offer is synonymous with an option contract. See below.)

6.   Death or Destruction

Death or destruction of a person or thing essential for the performance of the offered contract terminates the offer.

7.   Supervening Illegality

If, between the making of the offer and the acceptance, a change of law or regulations renders the proposed contract illegal the offer is terminated.

8.   Rejection or Counter–Offer

    a.   Common Law

An offeree's power of acceptance is terminated by a rejection or a counter-offer unless the offeror or the offeree manifests a contrary intention.

    b.   Nature of a Rejection or Counter–Offer

A rejection is a statement by the offeree that he or she does not wish to accept the offer. A counter-offer is a response to the offer that adds qualifications or conditions. A counter-offer acts as a rejection even if the qualification or condition relates to a trivial matter (ribbon matching or mirror-image rule). A counter-offer, in turn, can be accepted. A rejection is effective when it is received.

    c.   Counter–Offer Distinguished From Other Communications

A counter-offer must be distinguished from a counter-inquiry, a comment upon the terms, a request for a modification of the offer, an acceptance coupled with a request for a modification of the contract, a "grumbling assent" that falls short of dissent, an acceptance plus a separate offer, and a future acceptance. If an acceptance contains a term that is not expressly stated in the offer but is implied therein there is an acceptance and not a counter-offer.

    d.   U.C.C. § 2–207
This section is designed to negate the mirror image rule in cases involving the sale of goods. Under the U.C.C. "a definite and seasonable expression of acceptance . . . operates as an acceptance even though it states terms additional to or different from those offered, . . . unless acceptance is expressly made conditional on assent to the additional or different terms."

    e.   Additional Terms
If there is an effective acceptance under U.C.C. § 2–207(1), under U.C.C. § 2–207(2) additional terms in the acceptance are treated as proposals for addition to the contract. If the parties are both merchants these additional terms become part of the contract unless (1) the offer expressly limits acceptance to the terms of the offer; (2) the additional terms would materially alter the contract or (3) the offeror notifies the offeree in advance or within a reasonable time that he or she objects to the additional term.

    f.   Different Terms
The U.C.C. does not state a specific rule for different terms so it is difficult to know how they should be treated. Different terms are terms that contradict the offer.

    g.   Conduct of Parties
Even though a contract is not formed by virtue of the communications of the parties, a contract may arise by the conduct of the parties under subdivision 3 of U.C.C. § 2–207. In such a case the terms of the contract are those upon which the parties agree plus terms incorporated under other U.C.C. provisions.

E.   IRREVOCABLE OFFERS—OPTION CONTRACTS
1.   What Makes an Offer Irrevocable?
An offer can be made irrevocable (1) by consideration; (2) by statute; (3) under one of the special rules relating to the revocation of a unilateral contract (see above); (4) under the doctrine of promissory estoppel (see below); and (5) by virtue of a sealed instrument.

2.   Statute
The U.C.C. Sales article empowers an offeror to create an irrevocable offer without consideration. The requisites are: (1) a signed writing; (2) language assuring that the offer will be held open; (3) the offeror must be a merchant; (4) the period of irrevocability may not exceed three months; and (5) if the language of irrevocability appears on the offeree's form it must be separately signed by the offeror.

3. Terms Are Synonymous

For the most part the terms "irrevocable offer" and "option contract" are synonymous. In other words, an option contract is a contract that gives the offeree the choice of accepting or not accepting the offer of the offeror.

4. Termination of Irrevocable Offers

Irrevocable offers *are* terminated by: (1) lapse of time; (2) death or destruction of a person or thing essential for the performance of the offered contract; (3) supervening legal prohibition. They are *not* terminated by: (1) revocation, (2) death or supervening incapacity of the offeror or the offeree, (3) rejection (modern view).

5. When Is the Acceptance of an Irrevocable Offer Effective

Contrary to the "mailbox rule" employed in the case of revocable offers, in the case of irrevocable offers the weight of authority is that the acceptance is effective when received.

F. U.C.C. § 2–206
1. Introduction

This section de-emphasizes the common law distinction between a unilateral and a bilateral contract. It also has made changes in the "mailbox rule," the rule that is referred to as the "unilateral contract trick" and the rules on the effect of part performance.

2. Distinction Between a Unilateral and Bilateral Contract

At common-law, except in unusual cases, the offer looked either to a unilateral or a bilateral contract. If the offer was ambiguous as to the manner of acceptance it was presumed that the offer invited a promise. U.C.C. § 2–206 has substituted for this common-law presumption the notion that in the vast majority of cases the offeror is indifferent as to the manner of acceptance unless the offeror clearly insists upon a particular manner of acceptance. An illustration of this approach is found in subdivision (1)(b) which states that "an order or other offer to buy goods for prompt or current shipment shall be construed as inviting acceptance by a prompt promise to ship or by prompt or current shipment of the goods."

3. The Mailbox Rule

The "mailbox rule" states that, in the case of an offer looking to a bilateral contract, the acceptance (e.g. a letter) is effective when it is put out of the possession of the offeree provided it is sent in an authorized manner. The U.C.C. substitutes the words "by any manner reasonable in the circumstances" for the word "authorized". The concept of reasonableness is intended to be more flexible than the concept of an "authorized" means of transmission.

4. Beginning of Performance
Under U.C.C. § 2–206, "where the beginning of performance is a reasonable mode of acceptance" the offeree is bound when the offeree starts to perform (see the contrary common law rules on this point above), if "the beginning of performance unambiguously expresses the offeree's intention to engage himself." Even though the offeree is bound, the offeror is not bound to perform unless notice of beginning performance is given within a reasonable time. During the time between the beginning of performance and the reasonable time for giving notice, the offeror would be free to revoke except in a jurisdiction that follows the rule that the beginning of performance in the case of a unilateral contract makes the offer irrevocable. If timely notice is not given, the offeror, even though not bound to perform, may proceed as if there were a contract. The basic notion is that the offeror is not bound unless notified, but the offeree is bound on beginning performance.

5. Restatement, Second
The Restatement, Second, follows the lead of U.C.C. § 2–206 with some variations. Section 2–206 relates only to contracts for the sale of goods. The Restatement, Second, relates to all types of contracts.

G. INDEFINITENESS
1. Common Law
    a. Introduction
       Even though the parties have gone through a process of offer and acceptance so that there is mutual assent, the agreement is void if the content of their agreement is unduly uncertain. It is also true that the more terms that are indefinite the less likely it is that the parties intended to contract.

    b. Rule
       The offer must be so definite as to its *material* terms or require such definite terms in the acceptance that the promises and the performances to be rendered by each party are *reasonably* certain.

    c. What Are Material Terms?
       Material terms include subject matter, price, payment terms, quantity, quality, duration, and the work to be done. Given the infinite variety of contracts, it is obvious that no precise definition can be stated. Indefiniteness as to an immaterial term is not fatal.

    d. Reasonable Certainty
       To be reasonably certain a term need not be set forth with optimal specificity. It is enough that the agreement is sufficiently explicit so that the court can perceive their respective obligations. What is reasonably certain depends on subject matter, the purposes and relationship of the parties, and the circumstances under which the agreement was made.

e. Types of Indefiniteness Problems

(1) Where the parties have purported to agree upon a material term but have left it indefinite (not reasonably certain) there is no room for implication and the agreement is void. Indefiniteness, however, may be cured by the subsequent conduct or agreement of the parties.

(2) Where the parties are *silent* as to a material term or discuss it but do not purport to agree upon it, it is possible that the indefiniteness can be cured through the use of a gap-filler or from external sources including standard terms, usage, course of dealing and, according to some cases, by evidence of subjective intention. A gap-filler is a term supplied by the court because it feels that the parties would have agreed upon this term if it had been brought to their attention or because it is a term "which comports with community standards of fairness".

(3) Where the parties *agree to agree* as to a material term, under the traditional rule the agreement is fatally indefinite and the gap-filling mechanism, discussed above, may not be used. Some of the more modern cases (even without relying on the U.C.C. and the Restatement, Second, to be discussed below), have abandoned this rule and some have held that there is a duty to negotiate in good faith even though there is no such provision in the agreement. The U.C.C. and the Restatement, Second, are generally in accord with the modern view on questions of agreement to agree.

2. Uniform Commercial Code

a. Introduction

The provisions of the Uniform Commercial Code relating to indefiniteness are of two types. There are provisions relating to specific problems which can be generally categorized under the heading of gap-fillers. There is also a very important general provision.

b. Open–Term

The Code has specific provisions that supply reasonable terms in various circumstances. These include price, time for delivery, place of delivery, shipment, payment, duration of contract, and specification of assortment.

c. General Provision

Even if one or more terms are left open, a contract for sale does not fail for indefiniteness if the parties have intended to make a contract and there is a reasonably certain basis for giving an appropriate remedy. (U.C.C. § 2–204(3)). The test is not certainty as to what the parties were to do nor as to the exact amount of damages due to the plaintiff. Rather, commercial standards on the issue of indefiniteness are to be applied.

d.   Discussion of General Provision
      This provision is designed to prevent, where it is at all possible, a
      contracting party who is dissatisfied with the bargain from taking refuge
      in the doctrine of indefiniteness to renounce the agreement. This section
      is designed to change the traditional common law rule in all three types
      of cases discussed above. Thus a gap-filler would be available even though
      the parties purported to agree upon a term or made an agreement to
      agree with respect to it. But the section goes beyond gap-fillers and
      permits a court to use any reasonably certain basis for giving an
      appropriate remedy.

e.   Questions of Fact and Law
      Whether the parties intended to contract is a question of fact. Whether
      there is a reasonably certain basis for giving an appropriate remedy is a
      question of law.

3.   Restatement, Second
a.   Compared to U.C.C.
      The Restatement is in general accord with the Uniform Commercial Code,
      but it should be recalled that Article 2 of the U.C.C. by its terms applies
      only to a contract for the sale of goods. (Sometimes it is applied to other
      types of contracts by analogy.) The Restatement, Second, applies to all
      types of contracts.

b.   Trend
      The trend is toward the rules of the U.C.C. and the Restatement, Second.

II. CONSIDERATION AND ITS EQUIVALENTS

A.   INTRODUCTION
1.   What Promises Should Be Enforced
This section relates to the type of promises the law should enforce. Gratuitous
promises are not enforced. This is true of any promise not supported by
consideration, but such a promise may be enforced under the doctrine of
promissory estoppel or under certain statutes. In addition in certain instances
a moral obligation may make a promise enforceable. A delivered sealed
instrument is enforceable without consideration but this rule has been changed
in many states by statutes including the U.C.C.

B.   CONSIDERATION
1.   In General
For a promise to be supported by consideration (and therefore enforceable)
three elements must concur. (a) The promisee must suffer legal detriment—
that is do or promise to do what the promisee is not legally obligated to do;
or refrain from doing or promise to refrain from doing what the promisee is

legally privileged to do. (b) The detriment must induce the promise. In other words the promisor wishes to exchange the promise *at least in part* for the detriment to be suffered by the promisee. (c) The promise must induce the detriment. This means that the promisee must know of the offer and manifest an intent to accept.

2. Legal Benefit to Promisor
The rule above is stated in terms of legal detriment incurred by the promisee. Often, however, it is phrased in terms of either legal detriment to the promisee or legal benefit to the promisor. Because the result is invariably the same, the discussion here will be in terms of legal detriment.

3. Must Detriment Be Suffered by Promisee?
Although the rule is stated in terms of a legal detriment suffered by the promisee, it is nonetheless well settled that it does not matter from whom or to whom the detriment moves so long as it is bargained for and given in exchange for the promise.

4. Detriment Must Induce Promise
The promisor must have manifested an offering state of mind rather than a gift making state of mind. If the promisor manifests a gift making state of mind, any detriment has not induced the promise. Therefore, a promise to make a gift is not enforceable. Note that the promisor need only exchange the promise in part for the detriment to be suffered.

5. Past Consideration
Past consideration is not consideration because one does not make an exchange for something that has already occurred.

6. Motive
A promisor's motive in making a promise is not related to the question of detriment, but the motive of the promisor in making the promise is relevant on the issue of exchange.

7. Unilateral and Bilateral Contracts
The rule is set up in terms of a promise looking for an act (unilateral). If the arrangement is bilateral, there are two promisors and additional problems, to be discussed below, exist.

8. Adequacy of Detriment
Any detriment no matter how small or how economically inadequate will support a promise provided that the detriment is in fact bargained for. But economic inadequacy may constitute some circumstantial evidence of fraud, duress, overreaching, undue influence, mistake or that the detriment was not in fact bargained for. Adequacy of the detriment may also be considered under the doctrine of unconscionability.

9. Sham Consideration

This concept relates to an instrument that falsely recites that a consideration has been given. The majority view is that such a recital does not make a promise enforceable. There is a minority contrary view that relates only to option contracts and credit guaranties.

10. Nominal Consideration

As used here, nominal consideration assumes a case where the parties having learned that a gratuitous problem is not enforceable, attempt to make the promise of the promisor enforceable by cloaking a gratuitous promise with the form of a bargain and actually exchange or promise to exchange a peppercorn or small sum for the promise. One view is that the promise should not be enforced because the alleged bargain is a pretense. There is also a contrary view. The overwhelming majority of the cases involve option contracts in which the use of nominal (token) consideration has been upheld.

13. Invalid Claims

There are a number of views on the issue of whether the surrender of or forbearance to assert an invalid claim is detriment. (1) The earliest and now obsolete view is that the surrender of an invalid claim does not constitute detriment. (2) The surrender of the invalid claim serves as detriment if the claimant has asserted it in good faith and a reasonable person would believe that the claim was well founded. (3) Still other courts have held that the only requirement is good faith. (4) The new Restatement takes the position that either good faith or objective uncertainty as to the validity of the claim is sufficient.

14. Caveat

It should be noted that above we are discussing only whether the surrender of an invalid claim constitutes detriment. If it does, one must still confront the question of whether this is what is bargained for. For example, in a particular case is the promisor bargaining for the surrender of an invalid claim or the surrender of a worthless piece of paper?

The Pre–Existing Duty Rule

1. Introduction

A party who does or promises to do only what the party is legally obligated to do is not suffering a legal detriment because the party is not surrendering a legal right. The problem arises in three types of fact patterns. First, the rule applies even if the duty is imposed by law rather than by contract. Second, where the parties to a contract modify an existing agreement and one party does not suffer new detriment, usually the modification is not enforced, but there are cases that, on a wide variety of theories, have enforced such a modification. For example, The Restatement, Second, upholds such a modification if it "is fair and equitable in view of circumstances not anticipated when the contract is made." Third, where an outsider promises to compensate a party bound by a contract to perform a pre-existing duty under a contract, there are three views. (a) The promise is not enforceable; (b) the promise is enforceable if the promisee makes a return promise; (c) the promise is enforceable because there is less likelihood of coercion in the three party cases.

2. Foakes v. Beer

The rule of Foakes v. Beer is that part payment by the debtor of an amount here and now undisputedly due is not detriment to support a promise by the creditor to discharge the entire amount. The same is true if there is a present discharge (e.g. release) instead of a promise to discharge. The rule of Foakes v. Beer is another application of the pre-existing duty rule; the debtor, in making the part payment, is only performing part of a legal obligation. This rule is followed by the majority of jurisdictions with some exceptions in particular fact patterns. A minority of jurisdictions have rejected the rule completely. The rule does not apply if there is a detriment, in addition to the part payment, that is in fact bargained for.

Accord and Satisfaction

1. Liquidated and Unliquidated Claims

The rule of Foakes v. Beer (discussed above) applies only to liquidated claims; that is, claims that are undisputed as to their existence and where the amount due has been agreed upon or can be precisely determined. If there is a dispute as to liability or to the amount due or some other question, the claim is said to be unliquidated even if a party's assertion is incorrect, provided that the assertion is made in good faith and, according to some jurisdictions, if it is reasonably asserted (see Invalid Claims, supra.)

2. Problems Presented

When a question of accord and satisfaction is presented the discussion should be divided into three parts. (1) Have the parties gone through a process of offer and acceptance? The rule relating to an offer of accord is that the offeror must make it clear that the offeror seeks a total discharge otherwise any payment made and accepted will be treated as a part payment. (2) Has the accord been carried out? (3) Is there consideration to support the accord and satisfaction?

U.C.C. Inroads on Pre–Existing Duty Rule

1. U.C.C. § 2–209

a. Subdivisions 1, 2, 3

Under subdivision 1 of this Section, a modification of a contract is binding without consideration even if it is oral, but in two instances a writing is required. A writing is required under subdivision 3 if the contract as modified is within the Statute of Frauds provision of the U.C.C. (discussed below). The second situation where a writing is required is under subdivision 2 which is discussed immediately below.

b. Subd. 2
This section relates to a signed agreement that contains a provision that it cannot be modified or rescinded except by a signed writing. At common law, even if such a provision was in the original contract, a non-written modification was recognized. Under this subdivision such a provision will be honored if it is set forth in a signed writing. In this event a modification (or recission) will be enforced (except as stated below) only if the modifying agreement is in a signed writing. If the form containing the provision is prepared by a merchant, a non-merchant will be bound by it only if this provision is "separately signed".

c. Subd. 4 & 5
If a signed writing is required under the provisions of subdivisions 2 and 3, and the modifying agreement does not comply, it may nevertheless be enforced if there has been performance under the modifying agreement (subd. 4). Subdivision 5 provides that, despite performance, a party as to the unperformed part may reinstate the original agreement unless to do so "would be unjust in view of a material change of position" as a result of reliance upon the modification agreement.

d. Duress
U.C.C. § 2–209 also changes the common law rule with respect to duress. The traditional common law rule is that a threat to breach a contract does not constitute duress (see below). But under this provision of the Code the extortion of a modification without a legitimate commercial reason is ineffective as a violation of the "good faith" provisions of the Code. Conversely, a modification based upon a legitimate commercial reason does not constitute duress unless undue coercion is applied. Nor, under this provision, can a mere technical consideration support a modification extracted in bad faith.

2. **U.C.C. § 1–107**
e. Release
The pre-existing duty concept led to the rule that a release of a duty is ordinarily ineffectual without consideration. Section 1–107 of the U.C.C. provides, however, that: "any claim of right arising out of an alleged breach can be discharged in whole or in part by a written waiver or renunciation signed and delivered by the aggrieved party." Under this section a written signed and delivered release will be effective to discharge an alleged breach in whole or in part even though the release is not supported by consideration.

Special Problems In Bilateral Contracts

1. Is One Promise Consideration for the Other?

A promise in a bilateral contract is consideration for the counter-promise only if the performance that is promised would be consideration.

2. Mutuality of Obligation

a. Introduction

The doctrine of mutuality of obligation is commonly expressed in the phrase that in a bilateral contract "both parties must be bound or neither is bound." The doctrine is, however, really one of mutuality of consideration. The point is that if B's performance is not consideration B may not enforce A's promise. Conversely A may not enforce B's promise even though A's promised performance is consideration. Various aspects of the doctrine are discussed below.

b. Unilateral Contracts

The doctrine of mutuality does not apply to unilateral contracts.

c. Voidable and Unenforceable Promises

The doctrine of mutuality does not apply to a voidable or unenforceable promise because a voidable or unenforceable promise is deemed to be consideration for a counter-promise.

d. Illusory Promises

An illusory promise is an expression cloaked in promissory terms, but which, upon closer examination, reveals that the promisor has made no commitment. The modern decisional tendency is against finding a promise to be illusory and in general against defeating agreements on the technical ground of lack of mutuality. One method of circumventing the illusory promise problem is by interpolating into an agreement that otherwise seems illusory the requirement of good faith and/or reasonableness.

e. Right to Terminate in Contract

If a party reserves the right to terminate the arrangement by giving notice at any time or without giving notice at all, the older cases held that the party was not suffering detriment. The later cases lean to the view that there is detriment in giving notice. When the provision is for termination without notice, these cases ignore the provision by a process of interpretation and require reasonable notice. U.C.C. § 2–309(3) has a provision that bears on this problem. It states, "Termination of a contract by one party except on the happening of an agreed event requires that reasonable notification be received by the other party and an agreement dispensing with notification is invalid if its operation would be unconscionable."

f.   Conditional Promises

If a condition is attached to a promise, it does not render a promise illusory if the condition is outside the control of the party who makes it, or if it relates to an event that is outside of the promisor's unfettered discretion. At times an illusory promise problem is avoided by treating the express language of condition attached to a promise as implied language of promise.

g.   Aleatory Promises

An aleatory promise is one conditional on the happening of a fortuitous event, or an event supposed by the parties to be fortuitous. An aleatory promise is not illusory because the condition is based upon an event outside of the control of either party.

h.   Consideration Supplied by Implied Promise

At times, a party has made what amounts to an illusory promise, but the entire fact pattern shows an intention to be bound. In such a case a court may infer a promise (e.g. to use reasonable efforts) to eliminate the illusory promise problem. Sometimes, the promise inferred is called an implied promise. At other times, it is referred to as a constructive promise. Whichever conclusion is reached the result is the same.

i.   U.C.C. § 2–306(2)

The section relates to the problem discussed above. It provides: "a lawful agreement by either the seller or the buyer for exclusive dealing in the kind of goods concerned imposes unless otherwise agreed an obligation by the seller to use best efforts to supply the goods and by the buyer to promote their sale."

j.   Agreement Allowing Party to Supply Material Term

If a bilateral agreement permits a party to supply a material term, the promise at common law sometimes was deemed to be illusory and, therefore, the bilateral agreement void under the mutuality doctrine. The U.C.C., with its insistence on good faith, changes the common law rule relating to the right of a party to supply a term.

k.   Void Contract Is Not Always a Nullity

Although a wholly executory void contract is a nullity, if there is performance under a void bilateral contract, the case should be treated as if an offer looking to a unilateral contract or a series of unilateral contracts was made. If this cannot be done, a quasi-contractual action for reasonable value may be available.

Requirements and Output Contracts

1. **Introduction**
   The quantity term may be measured by the requirements of the buyer (requirements contract), or by the output of the seller (output contract). Since the rules are basically the same in the two situations, as a matter of convenience, emphasis will be on the topic of requirements contracts.

2. **Validity**
   Under the U.C.C. it is clear that these contracts are binding.

3. **How Much Is a Requirements Buyer Entitled to?**
   Under the Code the buyer under a requirements contract is entitled to good faith needs with two exceptions. (1) If there is a stated estimate, the buyer is not entitled to any quantity disproportionately greater than the estimate. (2) If there is no estimate or maximum or minimum stated in the contract, the buyer may demand only "any normal or otherwise comparable prior requirements."

4. **May a Requirements Buyer Diminish or Terminate Requirements?**
   Under the U.C.C. the buyer may go out of business or change methods of doing business in good faith. This is so even if the reductions are highly disproportionate to normal prior requirements or stated estimates.

Must All of the Considerations Be Valid?

1. **Rule**
   The general rule is that all of the purported considerations need not be valid.

2. **Conjunctive Promises**
   The rule stated above applies to conjunctive promises.

Alternative Promises

1. **Where the Choice of Alternatives Is in the Promisor**
   In this case each alternative must be detrimental unless, according to the Restatement, Second, there is a substantial possibility that events may eliminate the alternative which is not detrimental before the promisor exercises a choice.

2. **Where the Choice of Alternatives Is in Promisee**
   If the choice of alternatives is in the promisee, the alternative promises supply consideration for a counter-promise if any of the alternative promises is detrimental.

C. MORAL OBLIGATION
1. Introduction
Where a promisor makes a promise because of an antecedent moral or legal obligation, it is clear that the promise is not enforceable under the doctrine of consideration because of the rule that past consideration is not consideration.

2. Rule
A promise made in recognition of a prior moral or legal obligation is not enforceable.

3. Major Exceptions
a. **Promise To Pay Fixed Amount for Services Previously Requested Where No Price Fixed**
   In this case if the parties agree on a fixed price there is consideration for the new agreement, but most courts enforce a promise by a party to pay a fixed amount even though it is not accepted by the other party. Under a minority view the promise is enforced only to the extent that it is not disproportionate to the value of the services. However, if the services were rendered without expectation of payment, most cases hold that the promise is not enforceable.

b. **Promise To Pay When Services Not Requested**
   Under the majority view a promise to pay a fixed amount for services not requested is not enforceable. The Restatement, Second, states that the promise is enforceable "to the extent necessary to prevent injustice" if the promisee has conferred a material benefit on the promisor.

c. **Promises to Pay Debts Discharged by the Statute of Limitations**
   A promise to pay all or part of any antecedent contractual or quasi-contractual obligation for the payment of money causes the statute of limitations to run anew. An acknowledgment is ordinarily deemed the equivalent of a promise, as is a voluntary part payment of principal or interest. In most states, the promise or the acknowledgment must be in writing. The action is limited by the terms of the new promise.

d. **Promises to Perform a Voidable Duty**
   A promise to perform a voidable duty is enforceable despite the absence of consideration, as long as the new promise does not suffer from an infirmity that would in turn make it voidable. This rule does not generally apply to void contracts.

D. PROMISSORY ESTOPPEL
1. Introduction
The doctrine of promissory estoppel was created as a separate and specific doctrine in the Twentieth Century. Prior to that, the doctrine was employed, although not so labeled, in a limited number of cases. These included (1)

family promises; (2) a promise to make a gift of land; (3) gratuitous agencies and bailments; (4) charitable subscriptions, and (5) marriage settlements. There were specific rules for each category.

2. **Restatement, First**
Under the formulation of the First Restatement, the elements required for the doctrine to operate are: (1) A promise is required. (2) The promise must be one which the promisor should reasonably anticipate will lead the promisee to act or forbear. The same thought could be expressed by saying that the promisee must justifiably rely on the promise. (3) The reliance must be of a substantial character. (4) The promise will be enforced only if injustice can be avoided by the enforcement of the promise. (5) Although not stated, the notion is that the promise will be enforced as made or not at all.

3. **Restatement, Second**
The Restatement, Second, has made four important changes in the formulation of the doctrine. (1) In the text it has eliminated the requirement that the reliance be definite and substantial. However, a comment indicates that these are still factors to be considered except as indicated below. (2) It added a new sentence permitting flexibility of remedy. Thus the promise need not be enforced as made but may be enforced to the extent of reasonable reliance. (3) It provides for the contingency of reliance by a third party. (4) It contains a provision that a charitable subscription or a marriage settlement is binding without proof that the promise induced action or forbearance.

4. **Present Approach to Gift Promises**
Although initially the courts for the most part used promissory estoppel as a substitute for consideration in the types of cases mentioned in the introduction, with the impetus given to the doctrine by the two Restatements, it is fair to say that the present tendency is to use promissory estoppel in just about any case where the necessary elements are present.

5. **Doctrine Has Been Used in Business Context**
The doctrine has been used in some cases: (1) to make an offer irrevocable; (2) to enforce a promise that is part of an otherwise unenforceable defective contract; (3) to enforce a promise made during the course of preliminary negotiations.

III. LEGAL CAPACITY

A. **INFANTS**
1. **Who Is an Infant?**
Depending on the jurisdiction, a person remains an infant until the first moment of the day preceding his or her 21st or 18th birthday and remains an infant despite emancipation and despite marriage.

2. **Is Infant's Promise Void or Voidable?**
    According to the majority view the agreement is voidable at the option of the infant. However, the infant may not disaffirm certain contracts because public policy or a statute so provides or because the infant has done something or promised to do something which the law would compel even in the absence of contract (e.g. support his illegitimate child).

Avoidance and Ratification

3. **Avoidance**
    The infant may avoid (disaffirm) the contract at any time prior to ratification. The avoidance may be made during the period of infancy and once made is irrevocable. In the case of real property, however, the majority rule is that the infant's promise may be avoided only after majority.

4. **Ratification**
    The infant may ratify (affirm) the contract after reaching majority. This may take place in three ways: (a) express ratification, (b) conduct manifesting an intent to ratify (retention and enjoyment of benefits and services), and (c) failure to disaffirm within a reasonable time after majority.

Restitution After Disaffirmance

5. **Infant as Defendant**
    Although an infant has a right to disaffirm, the infant is liable for the return (or the value) of any tangible benefits the infant has received and still has.

6. **Infant as Plaintiff**
    If upon disaffirmance an infant sues for the return of the consideration the infant has supplied, under the now prevailing view the infant's recovery is offset by the value of use and depreciation of any property obtained from defendant. The more traditional view is that only property still retained need be returned.

7. **Necessaries**
    An infant is liable in quasi-contract for the reasonable value of necessaries supplied to the infant.

8. **Ignorance of Law and Fact**
    A ratification is ineffective if the former infant is unaware of the facts upon which the ratification depends. There is a split of authority as to whether the infant must know that the law gives a power of avoidance.

9. Tort Liability

An infant may avoid a contract, but is liable for torts. At times, it is difficult to distinguish tort liability from contractual liability, such as in the area of fraud and warranty.

10. Effect of Misrepresentation of Age

According to the majority view, infants may disaffirm even if they misrepresented their ages. The authorities are about evenly split on the question of whether infants are liable in tort for misrepresenting their ages.

11. Infants and Subsequent Purchasers for Value

If a minor disaffirms a conveyance of real property, the land may be reclaimed from a subsequent good faith purchaser for value without notice. The rule is different in the case of a sale of goods and a sale of securities.

B. MENTAL INCOMPETENTS
1. Tests of Mental Incompetency

Where there is no prior adjudication of incompetence, the great majority of the cases utilize the test of whether the party was able to understand the nature, purpose and consequences of the act at the time of the transaction. The more modern view adopts *in addition* the test of whether "by reason of mental illness or defect" a person "is unable to act in a reasonable manner in relation to the transaction, and the other party has reason to know of this condition." Under either test the promise of the incompetent is voidable.

2. Restrictions on Power of Avoidance

The promise of an unadjudicated incompetent that is still executory is voidable; but executed transactions are not voidable (contrary to infancy cases) unless the incompetent can restore the other party to the status quo ante. If the incompetence was obvious, however, the incompetent must make restitution only to the extent that tangible benefits remain.

3. Necessaries

As in the case of infants, incompetents are liable for the reasonable value of necessaries furnished them.

IV. PROPER FORM, WRITING, AND INTERPRETATION

A. PAROL EVIDENCE RULE
1. Rule

A total integration (a writing which the parties intend to be final and complete) may not be contradicted or supplemented. A partial integration (a writing which the parties intend to be final but not complete) may not be contradicted but may be supplemented by consistent additional terms.

2.   Focus of Rule
The rule relates to prior written or oral agreements entered into by the parties and, according to most authorities, contemporaneous oral agreements, but contemporaneous writings are normally deemed to be part of the integration.

3.   How to Determine Finality
Any relevant evidence is admissible on the question of finality. Most writings are intended to be final unless there is evidence of a contrary intent. The question of finality is one of law.

4.   How to Determine Completeness
There are a wide variety of views as to how completeness should be determined. These include: (1) The Four Corner's Rule; (2) The Collateral Contract Concept; (3) Williston's Rules; (4) Corbin's View; (5) The U.C.C. (§ 2–202) Approach; (6) That of the Restatement, Second.

5.   Subsequent Agreement
The parol evidence rule never excludes subsequent agreements.

6.   Rule of Substantive Law or Procedure?
The rule has both a procedural and a substantive aspect. It is procedural because it excludes evidence; it is substantive because it determines the terms of the contract.

7.   Is the Offered Term Contradictory or Consistent?
Under the modern view, to be contradictory the offered term must contradict an express term of the integration. It is not enough that it may contradict an implied or inferred term.

8.   Undercutting the Integration
The parol evidence rule is not applicable unless there is a contract. Thus, the rule does not exclude evidence offered to show that the agreement is void or voidable. For example, a party may show sham, illegality, mistake, duress and the existence of a condition precedent to the formation of the contract.

B.   INTERPRETATION
1.   What Is Interpretation?
Interpretation relates to the meaning of a communication or a document. In interpreting, there are two fundamental questions: (1) Whose meaning is to be given to the communication—in technical language, what standard of interpretation is to be used? (2) What evidence may be taken into account?

2. Variety of Views
As in the case of the parol evidence rule there are a wide variety of views on these two questions. These include (1) The Plain Meaning Rule; (2) Williston's Rules; (3) Corbin's View; (4) The U.C.C. Rule.

3. Rules of Construction
A rule of construction is an aid in interpreting contracts. For example, specific terms are given greater weight than general terms.

4. Course of Dealing
A course of dealing is based upon a sequence of *previous* conduct between the parties.

5. Course of Performance
A course of performance relates to conduct after the agreement.

6. Usage of Trade
A usage of the trade is "any practice or method of dealing having such regularity of observance in a place, vocation or trade as to justify an expectation that it will be observed with respect to the transaction in question."

7. Relationship Between Parol Evidence Rule and Interpretation
Again there are various views. For example, Corbin takes the position that the parol evidence rule does not apply to a question of interpretation. Williston, in general, follows the notion that an integrated writing may not be contradicted under the guise of interpretation.

C. STATUTE OF FRAUDS
Major Classes of Cases Covered by Writing Requirements. These include: (1) a promise to answer for the debt, default or miscarriage of another; (2) a contract to transfer an interest in real property or an actual transfer of real property; (3) a promise which by its terms is not to be performed within one year from the making thereof; (4) a promise in consideration of marriage; (5) contracts for the sale of goods (U.C.C.).

1. Suretyship Agreements

Where There Is No Prior Obligation Owing From the Third Party (TP) to the Creditor (C) to Which D's Promise Relates

In General. The promise of D is original (not within this subdivision of the Statute so that it is not a defense) unless (1) there is a principal-surety relationship between TP and D to the knowledge of C; (2) the promise is *not* joint; and (3) the main purpose rule does *not* apply. If all of these elements are present, D's promise is collateral (the Statute of Frauds is a defense).

Cases Where There Is a Prior Obligation Owing From TP to C to Which D's Promise Relates

In General. In such a case, the promise is collateral (the Statute is a defense). Exceptions: (1) where there is a novation; (2) where D's promise is made to TP; (3) where the main purpose rule applies.

a.   Main Purpose Rule
     Where the party promising (D) has for an object a benefit which D did not enjoy before the promise, which benefit accrues immediately to D, D's promise is original (enforceable) whether or not TP was obligated at the time of the promise, and even though the effect of the promise is to answer for the debt, default or miscarriage of another.

b.   Promise of Del Credere Agent
     An oral promise of a del credere agent is enforceable (original). A del credere agent (D) is one who receives possession of C's goods for sale upon commission and who guarantees to C that those to whom sales are made (TP) will perform.

c.   Promise of Assignor
     The promise of an assignor to the assignee guaranteeing performance by the obligor is original (enforceable).

d.   Promise to Buy a Claim
     If TP owes C $100 and C assigns this right to payment to D and D promises to pay a stated sum for the assignment, D's promise is enforceable because D's promise is a promise to buy a claim and not a promise to answer for the debt, default or miscarriage of another.

e.   Promise by Executor or Administrator
     The Statute applies only where the executor or administrator promises to pay out of *his or her own* pocket a debt of the deceased. Thus this provision is merely a particular application of the Suretyship Statute of Frauds.

2.   **Real Property**
     a.   In General
          A conveyance of land or of an estate in land, or a promise to transfer an interest in land, or a promise to pay for an interest in land are all required to be evidenced by a writing.

     b.   Interest in Land
          This includes the creation, transfer or assignment of a lease (except for a lease of short duration). It also includes an easement, rent and, according to the majority rule, a restriction on land. Also covered are equitable

interests in lands such as an assignment of a right to purchase land. An option to buy realty is also included. But the Statute of Frauds does not apply to an interest in land that arises by operation of law.

c. Liens
A promise to give a mortgage or other lien as security is within the Statute. However an assignment of a mortgage is not within the Statute because it is looked upon as a chose in action because it is connected to the debt it secures.

d. Products of the Soil—Timber—Unborn Animals
Products of the soil such as timber and annual crops obtained through labor or borne on perennial trunks (e.g. apples) are not considered to be interests in land.

e. Other Things Attached to Land
A contract for the sale of minerals or a building attached to land is considered to relate to an interest in land if they are to be severed by the buyer but not if they are to be severed by the seller.

f. Contracts Indirectly Relating to Land
Contracts that indirectly relate to land are not within this section of the Statute. For example a contract to build a building is not within this section of the Statute of Frauds.

g. Performance
If the *vendor* of the property conveys to the vendee the oral promise of the vendee is enforceable. Payment by the *vendee* does not make the promise of the vendor enforceable unless there is other conduct that is "unequivocally referable" to the agreement.

3. Contracts Not Performable Within a Year
a. In General
The Statute applies only to a promise which *by its terms* does not admit of *performance* within one year from the *making* thereof. If, by its terms, performance is possible within one year, however unlikely or improbable that may be, the promise is not within this section of the Statute of Frauds.

b. Promises of Uncertain Duration
Promises of uncertain duration are not generally deemed to be within the one year provision.

c. Contracts for Alternative Performances
Where a contracting party promises one of two or more performances in the alternative, the promises as a unit are not within the one year section

if any of the alternatives can be performed within one year from the time of the making thereof. It does not matter which party has the right to name the alternative.

d.   Agreement With Option to Terminate
In the case of a fixed term contract for more than a year where one or both of the parties has an option to terminate within a year, the majority view is that the Statute applies because termination is not performance. The minority view is contrary on the theory that alternative promises exist. The same two views exist in the case of a contract for less than a year where one or both parties have a right to extend or renew it beyond a year.

e.   Effect of Performance Under One Year Section
Under the majority view, full performance by one party makes the promise of the other party enforceable. A minority of jurisdictions restrict the performing party to a quasi-contractual remedy. Part performance does not generally permit a party to enforce the contract.

f.   How Year Is Measured
It is generally accepted that if A contracts to work for B for one year, the work to begin more than one day after making the agreement, the contract is within the one year section. If the work is to begin the very next day, however, the contract is not within the Statute on the theory that the law disregards fractions of a day.

g.   Restatement of Contract at Beginning of Performance
A subsequent restatement of the terms of the contract starts the one year period running again if the manifestation of mutual assent is such that it would be sufficient in the absence of prior agreement.

h.   Unilateral Contracts
There is substantial authority that unilateral contracts do not fall within this subdivision of the Statute of Frauds because full performance by one party in any event takes the case out of the one year provision of the Statute of Frauds. In jurisdictions where this is not true, it must be noted that a contract does not arise until there has been performance. Therefore the year should be measured from that time.

i.   Scope of One Year Section
The one year section applies to all contracts no matter what their subject matter except for a short term lease. However, it does not prevent specific performance of a land contract under the rules relating to specific performance set forth below.

j.   Is a Promise or a Contract Within the One Year Section?
Where any of the promises on either side of a bilateral contract (except for alternative promises) cannot be performed within a year from the formation of the contract, the entire contract is within the Statute. This means that none of the promises in the contract may be enforced in the absence of a sufficient memorandum, or performance, or the application of the doctrine of estoppel (see below).

4.   Contracts in Consideration of Marriage
a.   Consideration of Marriage
The Statute applies to any agreement made in consideration of marriage except mutual promises to marry between prospective spouses. It includes marriage settlements or prenuptial agreements even if the promise is made by a third party.

b.   Not in Consideration of Marriage
If the promise is made in contemplation, but not in consideration, of marriage, this subdivision of the Statute does not apply. The same is true if the marriage is merely an incident of the contract and not an end to be attained.

c.   Performance
A marriage ceremony does not take the case out of the Statute of Frauds, but additional performance may be sufficient to make the contract enforceable.

5.   Contracts for the Sale of Goods (U.C.C. § 2-201)
a.   Rule
A contract for the sale of goods for a price of $500 or more is within the Statute.

b.   Exceptions
(1) A contract for the sale of goods to be manufactured is not within the Statute if "[t]he goods are to be specially manufactured for the buyer and are not suitable for sale to others in the ordinary course of the seller's business and the seller, before notice of repudiation is received and under circumstances which reasonably indicate that the goods are for the buyer, has made either a substantial beginning or commitments for their procurement." The seller need not be the manufacturer.

(2) A contract is enforceable if the party against whom enforcement is sought admits that a contract for sale was made, but the contract is not enforceable beyond the quantity of goods admitted.

(3) No writing is necessary as to items which have been received and accepted.

(4) The writing requirement is also eliminated with respect to goods for which payment has been made and accepted.

c.   **What Is Covered?**
This section relates to a contract to sell or a sale of goods.

d.   **Choses in Action**
U.C.C. § 2–201 does not apply to choses in action. However U.C.C. § 1–206 applies to a sale of choses in actions as does § 8–319 which applies to securities.

Sufficiency of Memorandum

e.   **Introduction**
If the contract is within the Statute, a sufficient writing is required. The writing need not be formal or integrated. A note or a memorandum is sufficient.

f.   **Contents of Writing**
The writing should (1) indicate that a contract has been made or that the signer made an offer; (2) state with reasonable certainty (a) the identity of the contracting parties, (b) the subject matter, and (c) the essential terms in contrast to details or particulars; and (3) be signed by the party to be charged.

g.   **What Is a Signature?**
A signature is any mark, written, stamped or engraved, which is placed with intent to assent to and adopt (authenticate) the writing as one's own.

h.   **Who Is the Party to Be Charged?**
The party to be charged is the one against whom the claim is being made.

i.   **Agency**
A memorandum is sufficient if it is signed by an authorized agent of the party to be charged. The authority of the agent need not be expressed in writing, except in many jurisdictions under the real property provision.

j.   **Oral Evidence Offered by Defendant to Defeat Claim**
The party sued may show that the memorandum does not reflect the true agreement and thus defeat the claim except to the extent that the parol evidence rule excludes such evidence.

k. Oral Evidence Offered by Plaintiff
    Evidence of an essential term orally agreed to is not admissible on behalf
    of the party seeking to contradict or supplement the writing and this is
    true whether or not the writing is an integration.

l. Interpretation
    Oral evidence is admissible in aid of interpretation unless it is excluded
    under the rules of interpretation set forth above. For the purposes of
    interpretation, Williston treats a memorandum under the Statute of
    Frauds as if it were an integration.

m. Consideration
    If the plaintiff has fully performed, the plaintiff's consideration need not
    be stated in the writing. Any promise that is executory must be stated.

n. Form
    The memorandum may be in any form.

o. Time
    It may be made at any time.

p. Purpose
    It need not be prepared with the purpose of satisfying the Statute except
    in the case of a contract in consideration of marriage.

q. Delivery
    It need not be delivered.

r. More Than One Writing
    If the essential terms are in two writings, and only one is signed by the
    party to be charged, the Statute is satisfied if the unsigned document is
    physically attached to the signed document at the time it is signed or if
    one of the documents by its terms expressly refers to the other. Even
    when this is not true the better view is that the unsigned document is
    part of the memorandum if the documents by internal evidence refer to
    the same subject matter or transaction. In that event extrinsic evidence
    is admissible to help show the connection between the documents and the
    assent of the party to be charged.

Memorandum Provision of the U.C.C.

s. Contents of Memorandum
    Under the U.C.C. there are only three requirements: (1) the writing must
    evidence a contract for the sale of goods; (2) it must be signed by the
    party to be charged; and (3) it must specify a quantity.

t.   Written Confirmation Between Merchants
     If a merchant sends a signed memorandum to another merchant in
     confirmation of the agreement and the memorandum is sufficient against
     the sender, it is also sufficient against the receiver provided it is received
     and the party receiving it has reason to know of its contents, and fails to
     give notice of objection to its contents within 10 days after it is received.

u.   Auction Sales
     The auctioneer is authorized to sign a memorandum on behalf of both
     parties for a limited period after the sale.

Other Problems Under Statute of Frauds

v.   Purpose of Statute
     The statute is designed to prevent perjury and to promote deliberation and
     seriousness.

w.   Effect of Noncompliance
     Under the majority view, failure to comply with the statute renders the
     contract unenforceable. The minority view regards the contract as void.
     Under the majority rule, the oral promises are valid but they may not be
     sued upon at law.

x.   Promissory Estoppel
     Many recent cases have allowed recovery despite the fact that the Statute
     of Frauds was not satisfied when there was substantial reliance upon the
     oral promise by the plaintiff. The phrase that is often used is
     "unconscionable injury".

y.   Estoppel in Pais
     If a *representation* produces detrimental reliance as, for example, a party
     who represents that a memorandum of the contract has been signed will
     be estopped from relying upon the Statute of Frauds.

z.   Effect of Some Promises Within and Others Outside Statute
     The general rule, subject to limited exceptions, is that where one or more
     of the promises in a contract are within the Statute and others are not,
     no part of the contract is enforceable.

a.   Rescission of Contract Within Statute
     A written executory contract within the Statute may be rescinded orally
     except in the case of a contract to rescind a transfer of property.

b.   Modification of a Contract Within the Statute
     (a) If the new agreement is not within the Statute of Frauds, it is not
     only enforceable without a writing but also serves to discharge the prior

agreement. (b) If the new agreement is within the Statute and is not evidenced by a sufficient writing, the former written contract remains enforceable unless the new agreement is enforced under the doctrine of waiver or estoppel.

c.   Relationship of Various Subdivisions
A promise may contravene one or more of the subdivisions of the Statute of Frauds and not the others. If it falls within even one subdivision, a writing is required unless the case is taken out of the Statute under the theory of performance or estoppel. For example, a contract for the sale of goods that by its terms cannot be performed within one year from the making thereof must satisfy the more demanding one year provision as well as the U.C.C.

V. CONDITIONS, PERFORMANCE AND BREACH

A. CONDITIONS DEFINED
A condition is an act or event, other than a lapse of time which, unless the condition is excused, must occur before a performance under a contract becomes due, or which discharges a duty of immediate performance.

1. Classifications of Conditions
Conditions are either precedent, concurrent, or subsequent to the time when the other party's duty of performance becomes absolute. Any of these conditions can be created by agreement (express and implied-in-fact conditions) or imposed by the court (constructive condition).

2. Conditions Versus Promises
Failure of a condition imposes no liability on any party. A breach of promise creates a duty to pay damages. Note, however, that the same act may be both a condition and a promised event. In other words, a party may have promised that the event would occur and have conditioned his rights on the occurrence of the event. If it does not occur, there is both a breach of promise and a failure of condition.

B. CONDITIONS, SUBSTANTIAL PERFORMANCE, MATERIAL BREACH

1. Performance of Express and Constructive Conditions
Express conditions must be fully performed. Constructive conditions are satisfied by substantial performance. If a party has substantially performed, any breach is immaterial. A party who has materially breached cannot have rendered substantial performance.

2. Measuring the Materiality of Breach

The following factors help determine materiality: willfulness, the degree of harm, curability of the breach by a monetary allowance, hardship on the breaching party, and the type of transaction. The same and similar factors are used to determine the substantiality of the performance.

3. Effect of Delay

A reasonable delay is not a material breach unless the contract expressly makes time of the essence or the contract is for the sale of goods and there is a day or period certain for performance.

4. Effect of a Condition of Satisfaction

Where the contract expressly conditions performance upon the satisfaction or certification of a third person (e.g., an architect), the condition is treated as any other condition. If it is conditioned on the satisfaction of a contracting party, the same rule is applied if the performance is designed to gratify the taste or fancy of the party. However, if the performance is a matter of mechanical fitness, utility or marketability, the condition of satisfaction of a *party* is considered to be fulfilled if the performance is objectively satisfactory even if the party is not personally satisfied. In all cases, an expression of dissatisfaction must be made in good faith.

C. RECOVERY DESPITE MATERIAL BREACH

1. Divisibility

A contract is divisible if the performances of each party are divided into two or more parts and the performance of each part by one party is the agreed exchange for a corresponding part by the other party. If a divisible portion is substantially performed, recovery may be had for that portion despite a material breach of the overall contract.

2. Independent Promises

A promise is unconditional (independent) if it is unqualified or if nothing but a lapse of time is necessary to make the promise presently enforceable. The promisee may enforce an independent promise without rendering substantial performance.

3. Quasi–Contractual Recovery

Although the orthodox and still prevailing view is that a party who has materially breached may not recover from the other party in contract or quasi contract, the modern trend permits such recovery in quasi contract for benefits conferred in excess of damages caused by the breach.

4. Statutory Relief

A number of statutes permit recovery despite a material breach. Laborers, mechanics and clerical workers must be paid their wages despite the non-fulfillment of agreed conditions. The U.C.C. has a formula that permits a buyer in default to get partial restitution of a down payment.

D. EXCUSE OF CONDITIONS
1. Prevention
A condition is excused by prevention, hindrance, or failure to cooperate, provided the conduct is wrongful. When a condition is excused, recovery is permitted despite the non-occurrence of the condition.

2. Estoppel, Waiver and Election
A waiver is an intentional relinquishment of a known right. Not all waivers are effective, however.

    a. Waiver Before Failure of Condition
       (1) A waiver of a condition that constitutes a material part of an agreed exchange is ineffective in the absence of consideration, its equivalent, or an estoppel.

       (2) A waiver of a condition that is not a material part of the agreed exchange is effective but it may be reinstated by notice prior to any material change of position by the other party.

       (3) An effective waiver disables the party from cancelling the contract but does not discharge the waiving party's right to damages.

    b. Waiver After Failure of Condition
      A waiver after an express or constructive condition has failed is an election. An election may take place by conduct or by promise. No consideration is needed for an election and, according to the majority rule, an election once made cannot be withdrawn.

3. Excuse of Conditions Involving Forfeitures
A condition may be excused if it involves an extreme forfeiture, its occurrence is not a material part of the agreed exchange, and if one of the foundations for equitable jurisdiction exists.

4. Excuse of Condition Because of Impossibility
Impossibility excuses a condition, if the condition is not a material part of the agreed exchange and if a forfeiture would otherwise occur.

E. PROSPECTIVE UNWILLINGNESS AND INABILITY TO PERFORM: REPUDIATION
1. Repudiation
A repudiation is a material breach whether or not performance is due now or in the future. A party's unjustified statement positively indicating an inability

or unwillingness to substantially perform is a repudiation as is a voluntary act that renders one's own performance impossible or apparently impossible.

2. Prospective Failure of Condition

If a party repudiates or appears unwilling or unable to perform, the other party may possibly (1) continue performance; (2) suspend or withhold performance; (3) change position or cancel the contract. Which of the responses is permissible depends upon the degree of the prospective failure of condition. There is one firm rule. If the prospective unwillingness amounts to a repudiation, the first option is not available. Except in the rare case where continuation of performance would minimize damages, the aggrieved party has no right to continue performance after a repudiation.

3. Retraction

A repudiation may be retracted and a prospective unwillingness or inability to perform can be cured unless the aggrieved party has cancelled or materially changed position or otherwise indicated the contract is cancelled.

4. Urging Retraction

Rights are not prejudiced by the mere fact the aggrieved party has urged the other party to retract a repudiation.

5. Effect of Impossibility on a Prior Repudiation

Subsequent impossibility will discharge an anticipatory breach and partial impossibility will limit damages for the breach.

6. Failure to Give Assurances as a Repudiation

Under the U.C.C. a party who has reasonable grounds for insecurity may suspend performance and demand adequate assurance of the other's performance. Failure to give adequate assurance within a reasonable time, not exceeding 30 days, operates as a repudiation.

7. Insolvency

When a seller discovers that a buyer is insolvent the seller may: (a) refuse delivery except for cash, including payment for all goods previously delivered under the same contract; (b) stop delivery of goods in transit; (c) reclaim goods delivered on credit to a party while insolvent, provided that demand for their reclamation is made within ten days of receipt by the buyer; (d) reclaim goods delivered on credit to a party while insolvent irrespective of the ten day period, if the buyer has made a representation of solvency to the particular seller within three months before delivery.

8. Repudiation of a Debt

There is one important exception to the general rule that a repudiation operates as a total breach. No action lies for repudiation of a unilateral obligation to pay a sum of money at a fixed time or times in the future.

9. Repudiation and Right to Elect
As a general rule, the aggrieved party may elect to continue the obligations of the contract despite a material breach. Where, however, there is a repudiation, anticipatory or otherwise, the aggrieved party cannot elect to continue the contract.

F. PERFORMANCE OF THE SALES CONTRACT
1. Obligations of the Seller
The seller must make a tender conforming in every respect to the contract. If the tender is not perfect, the buyer may reject the whole, accept the whole, or accept any commercial unit or units and reject the rest. This drastic rule is eroded by the following qualifications.

a. **"Unless Otherwise Agreed"**
The contract may expressly limit the perfect tender rule or the rule may tacitly be limited by a trade usage.

b. **Cure Within the Contract Time**
If a non-conforming tender is made and the time for performance has not yet expired, the seller may seasonably notify the buyer of an intention to cure and may within the contract time make a conforming tender.

c. **Cure After the Contract Period**
When the buyer rejects a non-conforming tender which the seller had reasonable grounds to believe would be acceptable with or without a money allowance, the seller may, upon reasonable notification to the buyer, have a further reasonable time to substitute a conforming tender.

d. **Acceptance**
Once the goods have been accepted, rejection is no longer possible, although revocation of acceptance may be an available alternative. An acceptance may be express, or result from a failure to reject or to demand cure before a reasonable time to inspect the goods has passed.

e. **Revocation of Acceptance**
The buyer may revoke acceptance of a lot or commercial unit whose non-conformity substantially impairs its value to the buyer, provided (a) acceptance was on the reasonable assumption that seller would cure and has not seasonably cured; or (b) acceptance was reasonably induced by the difficulty of discovery or by the seller's assurances. Revocation must be made within a reasonable time after the buyer discovers or should have discovered the ground for it and before any substantial change in the condition of the goods which is not caused by their own defects. Note that the rule is one of substantial performance.

f.   Installment Contracts
     The perfect tender rule does not apply to installment contracts.

g.   Improper Shipment
     The perfect tender rule does not apply to breach of the duty of proper
     shipment. Failure to give prompt notice of shipment or to make a
     reasonable contract (in a shipment contract) with the carrier is grounds
     for rejection only if "material delay or loss ensues."

2.   Obligation of the Buyer
a.   Payment
     Absent an agreement to the contrary, receipt of the goods and tender of
     payment are concurrent conditions. Thus, even in a shipment contract
     (where the seller delivers the goods by placing them on board a carrier)
     payment is not due until the goods are received at their destination.

b.   Proper Tender of Payment
     Unless credit has been extended, the buyer must tender the entire
     amount. Tender need not be "legal tender" unless the seller demands it
     and grants the buyer sufficient additional time to procure cash.

c.   Acceptance of Conforming Goods
     Failure to accept conforming goods or wrongful revocation of acceptance
     constitutes a breach. Unless otherwise agreed, however, the buyer's duty
     to accept and pay for tendered goods is subject to a right to inspect them
     at any reasonable time and manner.

d.   Reasonable Care
     If the buyer properly rejects (or revokes acceptance of) goods in the
     buyer's possession, a duty is imposed to refrain from any acts of
     ownership over the goods, and to hold them with reasonable care at the
     seller's disposition for a time sufficient to permit a seller to remove them.
     A merchant buyer has additional responsibilities.

G.   WARRANTIES IN THE SALES CONTRACT
1.   Express Warranties
An express warranty is an affirmation of fact or promise with respect to the
quality or future performance of goods that becomes part of the basis of the
bargain. The affirmation may be in words or by sample or model. An
affirmation merely of the value of the goods or merely of the seller's opinion
of the goods is not a warranty.

2.   Implied Warranties
a.   Merchantability
     If a seller is a merchant with respect to the kinds of goods contracted for,
     unless effectively disclaimed, there is an implied warranty that the goods

be such as "pass in the trade under the contract description" and "are fit for the ordinary purposes for which such goods are used."

b. **Fitness for Particular Purpose**
If the seller has reason to know that the buyer wants the goods for a particular purpose and knows that the buyer is relying on the seller's skill and judgment, unless effectively disclaimed, there is an implied warranty that the goods shall be fit for that purpose.

c. **Free and Clear Title**
Unless effectively disclaimed, a seller impliedly warrants that the title conveyed is good, transfer is rightful, and the goods are free from any security interest or lien of which the buyer was unaware at the time of contracting. Note that this warranty applies also to nonmerchant sellers.

d. **Infringement**
A merchant who regularly deals in the kind of goods in question warrants, unless effectively disclaimed, that no patent or trademark is being infringed, but if the buyer furnishes the specifications, the buyer must hold the seller harmless against any third party claim if infringement arises out of the use of the specifications.

3. **Disclaimer of Warranties**
a. **Express Warranties**
If a contract contains express warranties as defined above, as well as a provision that states no express warranties are made, an attempt must be made to reconcile the two provisions. If consistency cannot be attained, the disclaimer is inoperative.

b. **Implied Warranties**
All implied warranties, except free and clear title, are disclaimed by language such as "as is." If other language is employed, the warranty of merchantability is the most difficult to exclude. If the exclusion is written, the language of exclusion must use the word "merchantability" and must be conspicuous. The warranty of fitness can be excluded only in writing and only if the exclusion is conspicuous.

c. **Implied Warranty of Free and Clear Title**
This warranty can be excluded only by specific language or circumstances that gives the buyer reason to know that the seller does not claim title or is only purporting to sell such right as the seller has.

d. **Limitation on Remedies**
Even if there is no disclaimer, remedies for breach of warranty may be limited pursuant to the provisions of U.C.C. §§ 2-718 and 2-719.

VI. DEFENSES

A. IMPRACTICABILITY

1. Impracticability is Not Necessarily a Defense

The general rule is that the promisor must perform or pay damages for failure to perform no matter how burdensome performance has become even if unforeseen changes have created the burden.

2. When Impracticability Is a Defense

When a performance becomes impracticable because of an event, the non-occurrence of which was a basic assumption on which the contract was made, the duty is discharged, unless the language or situation points to a contrary result.

3. What Assumptions Are Basic

There are certain understood risks assumed by the parties. These include market shifts, interruption of supplies (unless caused by war, embargo, or the like), and financial capability. Where, however, the difficulty in performing is caused by certain supervening events it is sometimes held that a basic assumption is violated. These events include (1) destruction of the subject matter or of the tangible means of performance; (2) death or illness of a person essential for performance; (3) supervening illegality or prevention by law; (4) reasonable apprehension of danger to life, health or property.

4. Temporary and Partial Impracticability

When the impracticability is temporary or partial, the general notion is that the promisor is obligated to perform to the extent practicable unless the burden of performance would be substantially increased. However, the promisee may reject any delayed or partial performance if the tendered performance is less than substantial.

    a.   **Temporary Impracticability Under the U.C.C.**
        If the seller expects to be late in tendering delivery and if the lateness is excusable because of impracticability, the seller must timely notify the buyer of the expected delay. The buyer may then cancel any non-installment contract. The buyer may cancel any installment delivery or installment contract under the criteria for cancellation discussed in connection with exceptions to the perfect tender rule. On the other hand, the buyer may within a reasonable time, not exceeding 30 days, agree to accept the delayed delivery or deliveries.

    b.   **Partial Impossibility Under the U.C.C.**
        "Allocation" is the key concept when the seller, on grounds of impracticability, can deliver only part of the promised goods. The seller must seasonably notify the buyer of the shortfall, and inform the buyer of the estimated quota allocated. The buyer has a reasonable time, not

exceeding 30 days, to accept the allocation. If the buyer does not accept, the seller's duties are discharged. If the contract is an installment contract, the buyer's right to cancel are subject to the criteria for cancelling installment contracts discussed in connection with exceptions to the perfect tender rule.

5.   Impracticability of Means of Delivery or Payment
   a.   Delivery
        The U.C.C. provision that deals with unavailability of an agreed type of carrier, docking facility, or manner of delivery focuses on the use of commercially reasonable substitutes. Although delivery modalities may be of serious concern, they are not usually at the core of the bargain. Consequently, if available, a commercially reasonable substitute must be employed and accepted.

   b.   Payment
        If the agreed manner of payment becomes unavailable, the seller's obligation to deliver is discharged but, if a commercially reasonable substitute manner of payment is available, the buyer has the option to use the substitute, thereby reinstating the seller's duty to deliver.

   c.   Payment After Delivery
        If the agreed manner of payment fails because of governmental regulations after the goods are delivered, the buyer may pay in the manner provided in the regulation. Even if this is not a commercially reasonable equivalent, the buyer is discharged unless the regulation is "discriminatory, oppressive or predatory."

B.   FRUSTRATION
1.   In General
   Where the object of one of the parties is the basis upon which both parties contract, the duties of performance are constructively conditioned upon the attainment of the object. Performance is practicable, but the performance one party contracted for has become valueless (or nearly so).

2.   Elements
   There must be: (1) an event that frustrates the purpose of one of the parties and the non-occurrence of this event must be the basis on which both parties entered into the contract; (2) the frustration must be total or nearly total; (3) the party who asserts the defense must not, expressly or impliedly, have assumed the risk of this occurrence nor be guilty of contributory fault.

3.   Restitution After Discharge for Impracticability or Frustration
   When a contract is discharged for impracticability or frustration, the executory duties are at an end. Compensation for part performance is available in the restitutionary action of quasi contract.

C. RISK OF CASUALTY LOSS
1. Perspective
When goods or real property are in the process of being sold or are under lease or bailment, the question frequently is, which of the parties must bear the risk of damage or destruction of the subject matter? For example, if Vendor and Purchaser enter into a contract for the purchase and sale of real property, which party should bear the loss caused by a fire that occurs after the contract was entered into and before closing of title?

2. Real Property
The majority rule places the risk of loss on the purchaser. This result is based on the theory of equitable conversion; once the contract is made, the purchaser is regarded by a court of equity as the owner. The minority view places the risk of loss on the seller until title closes. A third view, embodied in the Uniform Vendor and Purchaser Risk Act, enacted in about ten states, places the risk of loss upon a purchaser only if the purchaser is in possession or has legal title.

3. Leases
The orthodox common law rule placed the risk of loss on the lessee. Today, this view seems to have been largely abandoned in favor of the concepts of constructive eviction and implied warranties.

4. Sale of Goods
a. Effect of Risk of Loss
Assume goods have been damaged without fault of either party. If the risk of loss had shifted to the buyer, the buyer must pay the price. If the risk of loss is on the seller, the seller will be liable for breach of contract unless the breach is cured by tender of replacement conforming goods. In two limited situations the seller may have the risk of loss (seller won't be paid) but will not be liable for damages. These are situations (1) where impracticability can be invoked; and (2) where the contract expressly provides, "No Arrival No Sale." (U.C.C. § 2–324).

b. "Shipment" Versus "Destination" Contracts (Where Carrier Is Contemplated)
Most risk of loss cases involve injury to goods in transit. The Code seeks to provide clear and certain rules that usually work in tandem with normal insurance practices in commerce. Merchants have long thought in terms of contracts whereby the seller is responsible for "shipping" the goods—getting them aboard a common carrier in the seller's city, as opposed to the much less usual "destination" contract whereby the seller undertakes the responsibility of getting the goods to the buyer's city or plant. Under a "shipment" contract, the risk of loss passes to the buyer when the goods are delivered to the carrier, even if the seller reserves a security interest in the goods. Under a "destination" contract, risk of loss shifts when the goods are duly tendered to the buyer at destination.

c.   Distinguishing "Shipment" From "Destination" Contracts
      If the contract is unclear whether it is a "shipment" or "destination"
      contract, it is a "shipment" contract. It is not a "destination" contract
      unless it explicitly so provides. There are certain terms, intrenched in
      commercial usage, which are frequently used to indicate the parties'
      intent. These are: F.O.B., F.A.S., C.I.F., and Ex-ship.

d.   Delivery by Seller's Own Truck or on Seller's Premises
      Where a carrier is not used, as where the seller transports the goods in
      the seller's own vehicle or the buyer is to pick up the goods, the seller is
      in control of the goods and is likely to carry insurance on them. If the
      seller is a *merchant,* risk of loss shifts only if and when the buyer takes
      possession of the goods. If the seller is a *nonmerchant* the risk shifts
      when the seller tenders delivery.

e.   Goods Held by a Bailee
      At times goods in the hands of a bailee, such as a warehouseman, are
      sold with no expectation of a prompt transfer of possession. Risk of loss
      passes to the buyer in either of three eventualities. First, if the buyer
      receives a negotiable document of title that covers the goods; second, if
      the bailee acknowledges the buyer's ownership; third, if the seller gives
      the buyer a non-negotiable document of title or a written direction on the
      bailee, risk of loss passes after the buyer has had a reasonable time to
      present the document or direction to the bailee. If the buyer presents the
      document or direction to the bailee, risk of loss does not shift if the bailee
      refuses to honor it.

f.   The Effect of Seller's Breach on Risk of Loss
      The rules on risk of loss are suddenly made murky if it can be proved
      that the seller is in breach by tendering non-conforming goods. If the
      non-conformity is such that the buyer may reject (under the perfect tender
      rule or the installment contract rules), the risk of loss remains on the
      seller until the tender is cured or the buyer accepts the non-conforming
      goods. If the buyer revokes acceptance of the goods the seller is liable for
      any casualty to the goods to the extent that the buyer's insurance
      coverage is inadequate. The buyer, however, must have revoked prior to
      the casualty for this rule to apply.

g.   The Effect of the Buyer's Breach on Risk of Loss
      If the buyer breaches or repudiates prior to the shift of the risk of loss,
      the breach will itself shift the risk to the buyer provided that (a) the
      goods are conforming; (b) they have been identified to the contract; and
      (c) the loss occurs within a commercially reasonable time from the breach.
      However, the risk of loss passes to the buyer only to the extent that the
      seller's insurance is inadequate to cover the loss.

5.   Risk of Loss and Impracticability
The mere fact that the particular goods the seller intends to deliver are destroyed does not give the seller the defense of impracticability. The seller must offer replacement goods or be liable, although under appropriate circumstances the seller may be excused for any unavoidable delay under the doctrine of temporary impracticability. Under the provisions of U.C.C. § 2–613, however, if the contract dealt with identified goods (e.g., particular pieces of furniture rather than particular types), the seller is excused if the goods are totally destroyed, without the seller's fault, prior to the risk being shifted to the buyer. If the loss is partial, the buyer has the option to reject the goods or accept them with an allowance.

6.   Two Special Situations: Sale on Approval and Sale or Return
a.   Sale on Approval
      In a "sale of approval," the goods are sent to the buyer for the buyer's use with the understanding that the buyer may return the goods if they do not meet the standard of satisfaction. (See the material on conditions of satisfaction, supra). The risk of loss remains with the seller until the buyer "accepts" the goods. Failure to notify the seller of a rejection within a reasonable time is an acceptance. The expense of return is also thrust on the seller.

b.   Sale or Return
      In a "sale or return" (consignment) sale, the goods are sent to the buyer primarily for resale. Although the buyer may return conforming goods, the risk of loss passes to the buyer under the ordinary rules that govern the shifting of risk of loss. The risk remains with the buyer until the goods are returned to the seller at the buyer's expense.

7.   The Omnipotence of the Contract
All the rules governing risk of loss are gap fillers based in large part on the probable intention of the parties. The parties are perfectly at liberty, subject to the rule of conscionability, to provide for the allocation of risk of loss in any way they wish.

D.   ILLEGALITY
1.   In General
A bargain is illegal, if either its formation or its performance is criminal, tortious, or contrary to public policy. The difficult cases are those where the illegality is somewhat remote from the agreement. Remoteness will be illustrated by four kinds of situations: bribery, license violations, depositary cases, and instances where one party has knowledge of the illegal purpose of the other.

2. Bribery Cases

An agreement is illegal if it calls for the payment of a bribe, is procured by a bribe or is performed by bribery.

3. Licensing Cases

If a license is designed to control the skill or moral quality of persons engaged in a trade or profession, an agreement to practice that trade or profession by an unlicensed person is illegal. If the license is solely a revenue raising measure, the agreement is not illegal. If the license is required for other purposes, the courts will decide on a case by case basis.

4. Depositaries

A depositary of the fruits of a crime may not refuse to return the money or goods deposited, unless the depositary is a party to the illegal transaction.

5. Knowledge of Illegal Purpose

Knowledge by the seller of goods or services of the illegal purpose of the buyer taints the contract with illegality only if the intended purpose involves serious moral turpitude or if the seller does something to further the illegal purpose of the other. Some states, however, make criminal facilitation a crime. Under such a statute knowledge of the illegal purpose would make the contract criminally illegal.

6. Effect of Illegal Executory Agreements

An illegal executory bargain is void so that neither party to the agreement can enforce it.

7. Exceptions

a. If a party is justifiably ignorant of the facts creating the illegality and the other is not, the ignorant party may recover damages for breach.

b. If the illegality is minor and the party who is ignorant of the illegality justifiably relies upon an assumed special knowledge of the requirements of law by the other party, the contract may be enforced in an action for damages by the innocent party.

c. Certain statutes, enacted to protect a certain class, make only one party the wrongdoer. Contracts in violation of such statutes are enforceable by the protected party.

d. If an illegal provision does not involve serious moral turpitude and if the parties would have entered into the contract irrespective of the offending provision, the illegal portion of the agreement is disregarded and the balance of the agreement is enforceable. The illegal provision must not be central to the party's agreement.

e.   If an agreement can be interpreted so that either a legal or illegal meaning can be attributed to it, the interpretation giving the agreement a legal meaning will be preferred. An illegal contract can also be reformed to make it legal.

8.   Illegal Bargains Executed in Whole or in Part
Where there has been performance under an illegal bargain, the court will not aid either party and will leave the parties where it finds them.

9.   Exceptions
a.   Reprise
The exceptions under "Illegal Executory Agreements" also apply here.

b.   Divisibility
If a performance is illegal, but other performances are legal, recovery may be had for the legal performances provided that the illegal performance does not involve serious moral turpitude. "Divisibility" is not used in this context in the same sense as it is used in the chapter on performance. Divisibility is not determined according to fixed rules but by the judicial instinct for justice.

c.   Not in Pari Delicto
A party who has performed under an illegal bargain is entitled to a quasi-contractual recovery if this party is not guilty of serious moral turpitude and, although blameworthy, is not equally as guilty as the other party to the illegal bargain.

d.   Locus Poenitentiae (Place for Repentance)
Even if a plaintiff is in pari delicto and therefore as blameworthy or more blameworthy than the defendant, the plaintiff is entitled to avoid the bargain and obtain restitution if the attempted avoidance is in time to prevent the attainment of the illegal purpose for which the bargain was made, unless the mere making of the bargain involves serious moral turpitude. The plaintiff is generally not permitted to withdraw if any part of the illegal performance is consummated. Repentance comes too late if it comes only after the other party to the bargain has breached the illegal agreement or after attainment of the unlawful purpose is seen to be impossible.

10.   Change of Law
a.   Legalization of the Activity
If a contract is illegal when made and subsequently becomes legal because the law is changed, the change does not validate the contract except where the repealing statute so provides.

b. **Supervening Illegality**
If a contract is lawful when made, but the performance is outlawed prior to full performance, the case is governed by the doctrine of impracticability of performance.

c. **Supervening Illegality of an Offer**
If a lawful offer is made, but the making or performance of the proposed contract is subsequently outlawed, the power of acceptance is terminated.

11. Change of Facts
Where the bargain is illegal and a change of facts removes the cause of the illegality, the contract remains illegal. However, the parties, with full knowledge of the facts may subsequently ratify the agreement.

E. DISCHARGE OF CONTRACTUAL DUTIES
1. Perspective
Many methods of discharging a contractual duty are discussed elsewhere; for example, non-fulfillment of a condition, anticipatory repudiation, impossibility of performance, disaffirmance for lack of capacity, etc. In this chapter several kinds of consensual discharge will be discussed.

2. Mutual Rescission
Within limits, parties to a contract are free to end the obligations of the contract by agreement. The limits are imposed by the doctrine of consideration. One must distinguish three situations: (1) the rescission occurs before any performance; (2) the rescission occurs after part performance by one or both parties; (3) the rescission occurs after full performance by one party. In the first two situations, consideration is found in the surrender of rights under the original agreement by each party. In the third situation the rescission is void for want of consideration.

3. Implied Rescission
While rescissions are ordinarily expressed in words they can be implied from conduct. Some courts call an implied rescission an "abandonment."

4. Cancellation Versus Rescission
In the face of a material breach the injured party may properly cancel the contract. In cancelling, this party may inartfully use an expression such as "I rescind." According to U.C.C. § 2–720, which restates the sounder common law cases, "unless the contrary intention clearly appears, expressions of cancellation or 'rescission' of the contract or the like shall not be construed as a renunciation or discharge of any claim for damages for an antecedent breach."

5. Executory Bilateral Accord

An agreement, either express or implied, to render in the future a stipulated performance which will be accepted in satisfaction or discharge of a present claim is known as a bilateral executory accord. At common law, executory accords were unenforceable. Today, the executory accord is a binding contract. Prior to performance or breach, the existing claim is suspended. Upon performance, there is an accord and satisfaction that discharges the claim. If, however, the debtor breaches, the prior obligation revives and the creditor has the option of enforcing the original claim or the executory accord. If the creditor breaches, the debtor may ordinarily obtain specific performance of the accord. New York requires executory accords to be in writing.

6. Unilateral Accord

An offer by a creditor or claimant to accept a performance in satisfaction of a credit or claim is known as a unilateral accord. At early common law, the offeror could, with impunity, refuse the tender of performance. Under modern law, the debtor may, upon refusal of the tender, sue for damages for breach of the accord, or, in a proper case, for specific performance. New York requires that the offer be in writing.

7. Accord and Satisfaction

An accord and satisfaction is formed either by (1) performance of an executory bilateral accord or by acceptance of an offer to a unilateral accord; or (2) creation of a substituted contract.

8. Substituted Contract

A substituted contract resembles an executory bilateral accord. The distinction is that the claimant or creditor agrees that the claim or credit is immediately discharged in exchange for the promise of a future performance. The prior claim or credit is merged into the substituted contract. Consequently, in the event of its breach, it alone determines the rights of the parties. There would be no right to enforce the prior claim, unless the new agreement is void, voidable, or unenforceable.

9. Novation

A contract is a novation if it does three things: (a) discharges immediately a previous contractual duty or a duty to make compensation, and (b) creates a new contractual duty; and (c) includes as a party one who neither owed the previous duty nor was entitled to its performance. It is necessary to distinguish a three party executory accord from a novation. A novation is a substituted contract that operates immediately to discharge an obligation. If the discharge is to take place upon performance, the tripartite agreement is merely an executory accord.

10. Account Stated

An account stated arises where there have been transactions between debtor and creditor resulting in the creation of matured debts and the parties by agreement compute a balance which the debtor promises to pay and the creditor promises to accept in full payment of the items of the account.

11. Release

A release is a writing manifesting an intention to discharge another from an existing or asserted duty. A release supported by consideration discharges the duty. At common law, a release, without consideration, under seal, also effectively discharged a duty. Today, the effectiveness of a release, without consideration, is largely dependent upon local statutes. U.C.C. § 1–107 provides that: "Any claim or right arising out of an alleged breach can be discharged in whole or part without consideration by written waiver or renunciation signed and delivered by the aggrieved party."

12. Covenant Not to Sue

A covenant not to sue is a promise, supported by consideration, by a creditor not to sue, either permanently, or for a limited period of time. A release is an executed transaction, while a covenant not to sue is executory. The latter is sometimes used to circumvent the common law rule that the release of one joint obligor releases all of them.

13. Acquisition by the Debtor of the Correlative Right

Acquisition by the debtor of the correlative right in the same capacity in which the debtor owes the duty discharges it.

14. Alteration

A fraudulent alteration of a written contract, by one who asserts a right under it, extinguishes the right and discharges the other party's obligation. The aggrieved party may forgive the alteration, thus reinstating the contract according to its original tenor. A holder in due course of an instrument altered by a prior holder may enforce it according to its original tenor. U.C.C. § 3–407.

15. Performance—To Which Debt Should Payment Be Applied?

Where a person owes several debts to a creditor, payments are to be applied in the following sequence:

(a) in the manner manifested by the debtor, unless the manifestation violates a duty to a third person such as a surety;

(b) if the debtor manifests no intention, the payment may be applied at the discretion of the creditor, provided it is not applied to a disputed, unmatured, or illegal claim and also provided it is not applied so as to violate a duty of the debtor to a third person of which the creditor is aware, and is not applied as to cause a forfeiture;

(c)   if the creditor manifests no intent on receipt of payment, the law will allocate payment in the manner deemed most equitable.

VII.   REMEDIES

A.   DAMAGES
1.   Goal and Measurement of Damages
The basic goal of contract damages is to compensate the aggrieved party with enough money to attain the same economic position that would have been attained if the contract had been fully performed. The aggrieved party is entitled to the "benefit of the bargain," receiving "gains prevented" (expectancy interest) plus "losses sustained" (reliance and restitutionary interests), subject to the limitations imposed by the doctrines of foreseeability, certainty and mitigation.

2.   Foreseeability—General and Consequential Damages
Contract damages cannot be recovered unless they were foreseeable to the parties at the time of contracting. "General Damages" are those foreseeable to reasonable persons similarly situated and are calculated by the standardized rules discussed below. "Special" or "consequential" damages are those which are foreseeable because, at the time of contracting, the party in breach knows that in the event of breach no substitute performance will be available.

   a.   Sale of Goods
       (1)   Seller's Non–Delivery
           Purchaser recovers difference between market price and contract price or between cover price (price reasonably paid even if in excess of the "market") and contract price.

       (2)   Seller's Breach of Warranty
           Purchaser can recover the difference between the value the goods would have had if they had been as warranted and their actual value. Value is determined as of the time and place of acceptance.

       (3)   Buyer's Breach
           For total breach by the buyer as to goods that have not been accepted, the seller may recover the difference between the contract price and the market or resale price. If the seller has an unlimited supply of the goods involved, however, the seller has lost the profits on the sale, so the seller may instead recover the profit (including reasonable overhead) which would have been made from full performance. U.C.C. § 2–708(2).

(4) Buyer's Liability for the Price

If the buyer has accepted the goods, or if the goods are destroyed after risk of loss has passed to the buyer, the seller can recover the price. A price action is also available if the goods are identified to the contract and the seller cannot reasonably resell the goods.

(5) Consequential and Incidental Damages in Sales Cases

Consequential damages are available to a buyer if the foreseeability test is met. Sellers cannot claim consequential damages (U.C.C. § 1–106), but frequently can get incidental damages. Buyers can also claim incidental damages. These include brokerage commissions, storage charges, advertising costs, auctioneer's fees, etc., made necessary by the other's breach.

b. Employment Contracts

(1) Employer's Breach

An employee who has been discharged in breach of contract may recover the wages or salary that would have been payable during the contract term minus the income that the employee has earned, will earn or could with reasonable diligence earn during the contract term. In the case of a long term contract, the "present worth" doctrine will be applied.

(2) Employee's Breach

If an employee wrongfully quits, the employer recovers the difference between the market value of the employee's service minus the contract price.

c. Construction Contracts

(1) Contractor's Delay

Damages for delay are measured by the rental value of the completed premises for the period of delay.

(2) Contractor's Failure to Complete

Failure to complete is compensated by the additional cost of completion plus delay damages.

(3) Defect in Construction

If the breach consists of a defect in construction, the damages are the cost of remedying the defect, unless this would constitute unreasonable economic waste.

(4) Owner's Breach

If no work has been done, the contractor recovers the anticipated profit, that is, the contract price minus the projected cost of performance. If the work has been started, the contractor recovers the anticipated profit plus the cost of labor and supplies actually expended.

(5) **Consequential Damages in Construction Cases**
If foreseeability is shown, consequential damages are available against a breaching contractor. If an owner's breach is a failure to pay or a repudiation, consequential damages are *never* available to the contractor. (See "Failure to Pay" below).

d. **Contracts to Sell Realty**
(1) **Vendee's Breach**
If a contract vendee totally breaches, the vendor may recover the difference between the contract price and the value of the realty.

(2) **Vendor's Total Breach: Two Competing Rules**
(a) **English Rule**
For total breach, the vendee may recover only the down payment plus reasonable expenses of a survey and examination of title, unless the vendor was aware of the defects in title or refuses to convey.

(b) **American Rule**
Under the "American Rule", followed in a bare majority of jurisdictions, no matter what the reason for the breach, the vendor is liable for the difference between market value and contract price. This is the same as the primary rule of damages applicable where a seller of goods totally breaches.

(3) **Consequential Damages**
Consequential damages against a vendor in default is a strong possibility under both the American rule and the exceptions to the English rule.

(4) **Vendor's Delay**
If the breach consists of a delay in conveying, the vendee may recover for the rental value of the premises during the period of delay.

e. **Failure to Pay**
If the breach consists in the failure to pay a debt, consequential damages are not available. The aggrieved party is entitled only to recover the debt plus interest.

3. **Certainty**
a. **In General**
The fact of loss and its amount must be proved with certainty. The standard of certainty requires a higher quality of proof on the issue of

damages than on other issues in a lawsuit. It is rarely applied with stringency except as to lost profits, particularly lost profits as consequential damages.

b.   **Alternatives Where Expectancy Is Uncertain**
(1)   **Protection of Reliance Interest**
Where the aggrieved party cannot establish the lost expectancy interest with sufficient certainty, recovery is allowed for the expenses of preparation for and of part performance, as well as other foreseeable expenses incurred in reliance upon the contract. If it can be shown by the defendant that the contract was a losing proposition for the plaintiff, an appropriate deduction will be made for the loss that was not incurred.

(2)   **Rental Value of Profit-making Property**
If the breach disables the aggrieved party from utilizing profit-making property, recovery of the rental value of the property is permitted.

(3)   **Value of an Opportunity**
If a duty is conditioned upon a fortuitous event, and because of the breach it is uncertain whether the event would have occurred, the aggrieved party may recover the value of the chance that the event would have occurred.

4.   **Mitigation**
a.   **In General**
Damages that could have been avoided by reasonable efforts cannot be recovered. Conversely, the aggrieved party may recover reasonable costs incurred in an effort to minimize damages.

b.   **Exception**
One is not required to enter into another contract with the breaching party even if the offered contract would have minimized damages.

c.   **Non–Exclusive**
The principle of mitigation is not necessarily applicable in cases where the relationship between the parties is not exclusive. If the aggrieved party is free to enter into other similar contracts, entry into such a contract after breach does not reduce the damages that may be recovered.

5.   **Present Worth Doctrine**
Where damages include payments that were required to be made in the future, the value of the payments must be discounted to their present worth.

6. Liquidated Damages

a. Penalties Distinguished

Penalty clauses are designed to deter breaches by the prospect of punishment. Penalty clauses are void. Liquidated damages clauses are valid. Such clauses are designed to avoid or simplify litigation by liquidating the aggrieved party's damages in advance. A clause will be deemed a liquidated damages clause rather than a penalty if it is a reasonable, bona fide attempt to pre-estimate the economic injury that would flow from the breach.

b. Formulas Are Acceptable

Valid liquidated damages clauses are often expressed in formulas rather than in exact dollar amounts. Such an expression does not affect the validity of the clause.

c. Shotgun Clauses Are Dangerous

A clause providing that "$50,000 will be paid for breach of this contract" will be deemed a penalty because it does not proportion the damages to any particular kind of breach.

d. Can't Have It Both Ways

The courts will strike down a clause that attempts to fix damages in the event of breach while giving the aggrieved party the right to obtain judgment for additional actual damages that may be established. Such clauses do not involve a reasonable attempt definitively to pre-estimate the loss.

e. Specific Performance Not Excluded

A valid liquidated damages clause does not give a party an option to pay liquidated damages or perform. Therefore, the presence of such a clause does not preclude a decree for specific performance. The aggrieved party, however, cannot normally have both remedies, but if specific performance is decreed, such actual damages as may have been sustained between the time of the breach and the time of the decree are also recoverable.

f. Additional Agreed Damages—Attorney's Fees

The award of damages does not ordinarily include reimbursement of the successful party's attorney's fees.

7. Limitations on Damages

The U.C.C. and the common law permit the parties to limit damages, "as by limiting the buyer's remedies to return of the goods and repayment of the price or to repair and replacement of non-conforming goods or parts." U.C.C. § 2–719(1)(a). The Code further provides that: "Consequential damages may be limited or excluded unless the limitation or exclusion is unconscionable. Limitation of consequential damages for injury to the person in the case of consumer goods is prima facie unconscionable but limitation of damages where the loss is commercial is not." U.C.C. § 2–719(3).

8. **Failure of Essential Purpose**
"Where circumstances cause an exclusive or limited remedy to fail of its essential purpose, remedy may be had as provided in this act." U.C.C. § 2–719(2). This rule is statutory and does not exist at common law. It is far less broad than an initial reading might convey. The issue is not the conscionability of a limitation clause. Rather, the issue is the purpose of the limitation clause.

9. **Punitive Damages**
According to the majority view, punitive damages are not available in a contract action unless the breach involves an independent tort.

10. **Mental Distress**
The law does not compensate for mental distress caused by a contractual breach in most contractual contexts. In a few non-commercial cases; e.g., breach of contract for funeral arrangements, such compensation has been allowed.

11. **Nominal Damages**
Every breach of contract creates a cause of action. If the aggrieved party suffers no economic harm or cannot prove such harm with sufficient certainty, nominal damages, e.g., six cents, are recoverable.

B. **RESTITUTION**
1. **Goal of Restitution**
The basic goal of actions at law or in equity for restitution is to place the aggrieved party in the same economic position that existed prior to entering into the contract. This is accomplished by requiring restoration to the plaintiff what defendant has received from the plaintiff. Such restoration will not fully recapture the status quo ante if the plaintiff has incurred expenses in reliance upon the contract which have not benefited the defendant. A modern, but unorthodox, trend permits recovery of such expenditures in a restitution action.

2. **When Is Restitution Available?**
Restitution is available in six principal kinds of contractual situations.
   a. Restitution is available as a remedy for total breach; that is, where the breach is material and the aggrieved party has cancelled. Notice of cancellation must be given if the other party has not ceased performance or repudiated, or if the aggrieved party fails to offer return of returnable property in accordance with the rules stated in 3 below.

   b. The contract is avoided for incapacity, duress, misrepresentation, and the like.

c.   The agreement is not a contract because of indefiniteness, lack of an agent's authority, or the like.

d.   The agreement is unenforceable because of the Statute of Frauds or illegality.

e.   The agreement is discharged because of impracticability or frustration.

f.   A defaulting plaintiff seeks recovery for part performance.

3. The Plaintiff Must Offer to Return Property

A party who seeks restitution must first offer to return any property received pursuant to the contract. The offer may be conditioned on the other party's restitution of what that party has received. Exceptions and qualifications of this rule are discussed below. Exceptions:

a.   Equitable Action
     Specific restitution may be decreed in an equitable action despite the plaintiff's failure to offer to make restitution. The decree in equity can be conditioned upon the plaintiff's restoration.

b.   Worthlessness
     If the property received was worthless or became worthless because of its defects, failure to offer its return will not defeat the plaintiff's action.

c.   Consumption or Loss of Possession
     If services have been received, they, of course, cannot be returned. If part of goods received have been consumed or disposed of, return is not possible. Consequently, the requirement of an offer to return is dispensed with. Instead, the value of the services or goods will be offset from the plaintiff's recovery.

d.   Divisibility
     If the contract is divisible into several agreed exchanges and the grievance does not relate to all of them, the plaintiff need not offer to return those things received pursuant to a divisible portion about which plaintiff has no grievance.

4. Defendant's Refusal to Accept an Offered Return

If a defendant improperly refuses an offer of return, the plaintiff may assert a lien on the goods and may sell them. The price will be debited against the restitution claim.

5. Measure of Recovery

"Unjust enrichment," the principal philosophical underpinning of the restitution remedy, does not provide the measure of recovery. The plaintiff receives the reasonable value of services rendered, goods delivered, or property conveyed, less the reasonable value of any counter-performance received, irrespective of any enrichment and irrespective of the contract rate.

6. No Restitution After Complete Performance
Restitution is not available if a debt has been created.

7. Election of Remedies
In the absence of statute, a plaintiff cannot recover both restitution and damages. Under the U.C.C., recovery may be had under both headings.

8. Specific Restitution
    a.   In General

The typical restitution action at law for the reasonable value of one's performance is a "quasi-contractual" action. In equity, through various devices, such as a decree cancelling a deed, or the imposition of a constructive trust, specific restitution of property transferred or wrongfully acquired may be compelled. Specific restitution will be ordered where the legal remedy is inadequate.

    b.   Inadequacy of the Legal Remedy

The remedy at law is deemed inadequate where property is transferred in exchange for the promise of something other than a sum certain and the exchange will not be forthcoming and also where the contract breacher has acquired money or property in violation of a relationship of trust and confidence.

C. EQUITABLE ENFORCEMENT
1. Inadequacy of the Legal Remedy
Equity will enforce a contract by decreeing specific performance or by a restraining order only if the legal remedy of damages or restitution is inadequate.

    a.   Uniqueness

Equity will order specific performance to a contract purchaser if the subject matter of a contract of sale is unique. The legal remedy is inadequate because the disappointed purchaser cannot replace the subject matter on the market. Land is always deemed unique as are heirlooms, works of art, and other one-of-a-kind objects, as well as patents, copyrights, closely held stock, and other intangibles not readily available on the market.

    b.   Affirmative Rule of Mutuality

If a purchaser could have obtained a decree of specific performance in the event of the seller's breach because the purchaser's legal remedy would have been inadequate, the seller can obtain a decree of specific performance in the event of the purchaser's breach.

c.   Conjectural Damages
The legal remedy is inadequate if damages are conjectural and restitution does not carry out the ends of the contract.

2.   **Defenses to Specific Performance**
a.   Validity of the Contract and Value
Equity will not enforce a contract that is invalid. Moreover, it requires that the contract be for value. Nominal consideration will not suffice, and a contract under seal without consideration will not suffice.

b.   Exception
An option contract for a nominal (unbargained-for) consideration or under seal (in those jurisdictions where the seal is still viable) will be specifically enforced provided that it looks to further performances for a fair exchange.

c.   Certainty of the Contract
Equity requires that the parties' performances be described in the contract with greater precision than is the case in an action at law. Because the penalty for non-compliance with a decree is punishment for contempt, the parties must know what to do with reasonable certainty.

d.   Impossibility
Equity will not order a defendant to render a performance that is impossible even where impossibility will not excuse the breaching party in an action for damages.

3.   **Equitable Discretion**
Specific performance is never a matter of pure entitlement. The court has wide powers of discretion in determining whether or not to grant the remedy. The factors to determine when the discretion will be exercised against enforcement are reducible to certain doctrines, such as "difficulty of supervision," discussed below.

a.   Difficulty of Supervision
Equity, in its discretion, will refuse to order specific performance of contracts where supervision of performance by the court will be unduly burdensome.

b.   Personal Service Contract
Employment contracts are not specifically enforced against the employee. Such decrees would reek of involuntary servitude and possibly would run afoul of the Constitution. At times, however, an employee may be

enjoined against working for another, resulting in indirect enforcement (see below). Enforcement against an employer is normally denied because of the difficulty of supervision, or because of the adequacy of the legal remedy, but arbitration awards of reinstatement have been enforced.

c.   Undue Risk
If performance of the contract would impose an undue risk that the counter-performance will not be received, specific performance will be denied.

d.   Unconscionability
Under the doctrine of unconscionability, equity has refused to enforce contracts that are valid at law. Inadequacy of consideration coupled with any sharp practice, non-disclosure, overreaching, abuse of confidential relationship, etc., will result in a refusal of specific performance even where the inequitable conduct would not enable the party to avoid the contract.

e.   Unclean Hands
Specific performance will be denied if the plaintiff is guilty of any inequitable conduct with respect to the transaction, even if in concert with the defendant so that no unconscionability exists.

f.   Laches
Even if the statute of limitations has not run, specific performance will be denied if the plaintiff's failure promptly to pursue the remedy prejudices the defendant as by causing the defendant to change position or where the plaintiff has remained inactive until the subject matter has risen in value.

g.   Balancing Hardships
Specific performance will be denied where the hardship to the defendant or to the public will be greatly in excess of any benefit to the plaintiff.

4.   Specific Performance With an Abatement
When a vendor's title to real property is encumbered so that there is an inability to convey the interest contracted to be conveyed, the vendee may obtain a decree of specific performance with an abatement in price. In essence, this decree involves specific performance with an offset for damages for a partial breach. In rare cases, specific performance would be refused if only a radically different kind of estate can be conveyed from that contracted for.

5. Relationship Between Specific Performance and Damages

a. Specific Performance Plus Damages
A decree for specific performance is often accompanied by an award of damages. Often, this will be an award of damages for delay in performing, say, a contract to convey real property. In other cases, it may be an award of damages for partial breach of, say, an output contract.

b. Specific Performance and Liquidated Damages
The presence of a liquidated damages clause does not preclude an award of specific performance.

c. Effect of Denial of Specific Performance
If specific performance is denied because of the adequacy of the legal remedy or because of the exercise of equitable discretion, the plaintiff may thereafter commence an action for damages or restitution at law. The denial of specific performance on equitable grounds does not deprive the plaintiff of any legal remedy. Under modern practice, in many jurisdictions, a plaintiff may join an equitable action with a law action in one suit. In such a suit, if the equitable remedy is denied, the legal remedy may be granted.

6. Restraining Orders
Specific relief, of a sort, is often obtained by a restraining order. While these are most often sought in personal service contracts, they are not limited to such contracts.

a. Employment Contracts With Affirmative and Negative Duties
Where an employee promises to work exclusively for an employer for a given period, although equity will not compel the employee to work, it will enjoin the employee from working for another if the employer can show irreparable harm from breach of the express or implied negative covenant not to work for another.

b. Trade Secrets
A covenant not to divulge trade secrets will be enforced by injunction. Even in the absence of such a covenant, a duty not to divulge will be implied and enforced by injunction.

c. Covenants Not to Compete
An agreement not to compete, unconnected with another transaction, is void. An ancillary covenant connected with the sale of a business, an employment contract, a lease, and certain other transactions may be valid, if reasonable. If unreasonable, the orthodox view was that the entire covenant fell. The modern cases allow partial enforcement, limiting the injunction to a reasonable time and area.

(1) Ancillary to Sale of Business
Reasonableness is judged by whether the duration and territorial area of the restraint is in excess of the area in which the seller enjoyed good will or of the period of time the good will can reasonably be expected to continue.

(2) Ancillary to Employment
Covenants of this kind are tested by stricter criteria. Equity will enforce such a covenant to the extent necessary to prevent an employee's use of trade secrets or confidential customer lists. In rare cases such covenants will also be enforced where the employee's services are "special, unique and extraordinary." An injunction will be limited to the area and time necessary to protect the employer's interests.

VIII. AVOIDANCE OR REFORMATION FOR MISCONDUCT OR MISTAKE

A. DURESS
1. In General
Any wrongful act or threat that is the inducing cause of a contract constitutes duress and is grounds for avoiding the contract so formed. Where the coercion involves economic pressure, as in a. (3), (4), (5) below, rather than a threat of personal injury or the like, however, duress is usually not present unless the party coerced can show that there was no reasonable alternative but to assent.

a. What Constitutes Wrongful Conduct?
(1) Violence or Threats of Violence

(2) Wrongful Imprisonment or Threat of Imprisonment

(3) Wrongful Seizure or Withholding of Property, Including the Abuse of Liens or Attachments

(4) The Abuse of Legal Rights or the Threat Thereof

(5) Breach or Threat to Breach a Contract

b. Coercion by a Third Party
If the wrongful pressure is applied by a third person, the transaction can be avoided if the other contracting party knows of the coercion, or does not give value. If the other party gives value without notice of the wrongful conduct, the coerced party cannot avoid the contract.

2.   Voidable or Void?

We have been presupposing a valid transaction and its possible avoidance. The general run of duress cases involve voidable transactions. There is one situation where duress renders a transaction void. A transaction is void if it is in no sense the consensual act of the party. A contract signed because a shotgun is pointed at one's head is consented to if one has a general idea of what one is signing. The contract is voidable. If one does not have any idea of the contents of the writing, one is in no sense consenting. The document is void. These cases are rare; perhaps non-existent.

B.   UNDUE INFLUENCE

The gist of undue influence is unfair *persuasion* rather than coercion. Persuasion is unfair in two classes of cases. First, where a person uses a position of *trust and confidence* to convince the other to enter into a transaction that is not in the best interests of the persuaded party. Second, it is also unfair where a person uses a *position of dominance* to influence a transaction against the best interests of the subservient party. The foremost indicator of undue influence is an unnatural transaction resulting in the enrichment of one of the parties at the expense of the other.

C.   MISREPRESENTATION

If a misrepresentation constitutes an actionable tort, avoidance is allowed, but all of the elements of tortious misrepresentation are not required for avoidance.

1.   Scienter is Not a Requirement

A misrepresentation is an assertion that is not in accord with existing facts. Avoidance may be based on a negligent or even an innocent misrepresentation. However, an *intentional* misrepresentation *need not be material,* while an *unintentional* misrepresentation *must be material.* A representation is material if (a) it would influence the conduct of a reasonable person; or (b) the person using the words knows that it would likely influence the conduct of the other party.

2.   Deception

The party must have been deceived. If the party did not believe the representation, it cannot later be used as a basis for avoidance.

3.   Reliance

The party must have relied upon the representation in the sense that the party regarded the representation as an important fact and that it influenced the decision to enter into the transaction.

4.   Justification

The old idea that a party could not avoid a contract for fraud unless there was a "right to rely" has largely been superseded by the idea that avoidance will be allowed even "to the simple and credulous." The law is in flux on the question, but if the representation is purely factual (as opposed to a misrepresentation of fact and opinion or fact and intention), the modern law regards reliance as justified in almost every case. A party is justified in relying even if negligent in investigating or not investigating the facts.

5. Injury Not Usually a Requisite
Even if a party gets something as valuable as, or more valuable than, the performance promised, the party may avoid the contract. The reason is that the party's autonomy has been tinkered with when presented with untrue information that prevents the exercise of good judgment. A major exception is that most cases hold that where a purchaser of land misrepresents the purpose for which the purchase is made, avoidance is not permitted unless the seller owns adjacent land, the value of which will decrease because of the intended use.

6. The Misrepresentation Must Be of Fact and Not Opinion or Law
A party is not justified in relying on a statement merely of opinion. Nonetheless, many statements of opinion also imply factual assertions. "It's uncomfortably hot and muggy today," expresses an opinion but does imply certain facts about the temperature and humidity. An assertion of law is sometimes a statement of fact; e.g., "Iowa has adopted the U.C.C.," but more usually is a statement of opinion, as when the person making an assertion prognosticates how the Iowa courts will solve a "battle of the forms" case. Although one may not rely on what is merely an opinion, one may rely on the implied facts contained in an opinion if it is reasonable to do so. The following are categories of cases in which such reasonableness is likely to exist. In each case it is assumed that the other elements of avoidance (deception, reliance and justification) exist.

a. The representer is or claims to be an expert.

b. The representer has superior access to the facts upon which the opinion is based.

c. There is a relationship of trust and confidence between the parties.

d. The opinion intentionally varies radically from reality.

e. The representation is of the law of another jurisdiction.

7. Promissory Fraud and Untrue Statements of Intention
The making of a promise without an intention to carry it out is a misrepresentation of fact, as is a statement of intention when one has no intention to carry it out.

8. **Non–Disclosure**

We start with a general rule that there is no duty to disclose facts that would tend to discourage the other party from entering into a proposed deal. This general rule is being eroded by a group of exceptions.

Exceptions:

a.   Statutory disclosure rules, such as S.E.C., Truth–in–Lending, etc.

b.   Concealment (positive action to hide) is the equivalent of a misrepresentation.

c.   Where partial disclosure is misleading.

d.   Where changing circumstances cause an assertion to no longer be true or if the representer discovers that a representation made innocently is incorrect.

e.   Where one party becomes aware that the other is operating under a mistake as to a vital fact.

f.   Where there is a confidential relationship.

g.   In cases of suretyship, marine insurance, partnership, or joint venture.

h.   Where specific performance is sought.

9. **Misrepresentation by a Third Party**

If a party, prior to contracting, has received false or otherwise incorrect information from a third person who is not an agent of the other party, the deceived party cannot avoid a contract induced by that information unless the other party learned of the misrepresentation prior to contracting. This is a variant of the bona fide purchaser for value principle.

10. **Cure of a Misrepresentation**

If, after a misrepresentation is made, the facts are brought into line with the representation before the deceived party has avoided the contract, the contract is no longer voidable.

11. **Merger Clauses**

Despite a merger clause or a "there are no representations" clause, parol evidence is admissible to show that a misrepresentation was made. An "as is" clause excludes warranties, but does not exclude evidence of representations.

12. Election of Remedies

If the misrepresentation and ensuing deception, reliance and injury constitute a tort, the deceived party must elect between either a tort action or the exercise of the power of avoidance followed by a restitutionary action. Under the U.C.C. both remedies are available but items of recovery cannot be duplicated.

13. Restoration of Status Quo Ante

Where restitution is sought at law in a quasi-contractual action, the plaintiff must, before suing, offer to restore any tangible benefits received under the contract, but not if what has been received has perished because of its defects, is worthless, or consists of money that may be offset. However, in an equitable action no prior offer to restore is required, but the equitable decree can be conditioned upon such restoration. An equity action is available if something other than, or in addition to, a money judgment is sought; e.g., cancellation of a deed.

14. Fraud-in-the-Factum

Where a party signs a document that is radically different from that which was represented and the circumstances are such that a reasonable person similarly situated would have signed it, the document is void.

D. MISTAKE
1. Perspective

Certain kinds of mistakes may prevent the formation of contracts. These include misunderstandings (see p. 203 infra) and mistakes in transmission. (See p. 112 infra). Here, however, the discussion centers on mistake as a ground for *avoiding* a transaction.

2. Mistake of Fact Versus Mistake in Judgment

For avoidance, the mistake must relate to a basic assumption as to a *vital existing fact*. Risks as to *changing facts* are governed by the rules of *impracticability* and *frustration*. Risks of mistakes in judgment such as to the profitability of a stock purchase, or as to the number of labor hours required to complete a task, are quintessential contractual risks from which the court will not relieve a party.

3. Mutual Mistake

Where the parties are mistaken about a basic assumption upon which they base their bargain, the transaction can be avoided if, because of the mistake, a quite different exchange of values occurs from the contemplated exchange of values, provided, however, the risk is not otherwise allocated by agreement of the parties, or by the court because such other allocation is reasonable.

4. Mistake Versus Uncertainty

Where the parties are uncertain or consciously ignorant of a vital fact there is no right of avoidance.

5. Mutual Mistake as to Injuries

The orthodox view is that a release of a personal injury claim can be avoided if there are unknown injuries but not if there are unforeseen consequences of known injuries. Diagnosis is distinguished from prognosis. Some jurisdictions also allow avoidance if there is a vital mistake as to the nature and effect of known injuries.

6. Mutual Mistake as to Acreage

a. Avoidance

If the number of acres contracted to be conveyed or actually conveyed are discovered to be materially different from what the parties believed, the aggrieved party may avoid the contract or conveyance. Avoidance is permitted whether the sale is on a per acre basis or in gross.

b. Restitution

If the contract or conveyance is on a per acre basis, the purchaser may have restitution of the purchase price for any shortage of acres, and the seller has a restitution action for payment for additional acres. If the purchaser has not paid, an abatement in price rather than restitution is the appropriate remedy.

c. Perspective

These cases are treated under mistake, despite the fact that the vendor has made a misrepresentation of fact. The reasons are historical.

7. Unilateral Palpable Mistake

A mistake by one party of which the other is, or ought to be, aware is grounds for avoidance. Cases of this kind are sometimes treated, with the same result, as cases of fraudulent non-disclosure.

8. Unilateral Impalpable Mistake

Avoidance is allowed for unilateral mistake if (a) the mistake is computational, clerical or something of that sort, rather than a mistake in judgment; (b) enforcement of the contract would be oppressive, resulting in an unconscionably unequal exchange of values; and (c) avoidance would impose no substantial hardship on the other.

9. Mistake of Law

The orthodox view is that a mistake of law (except for mistake of the law of another jurisdiction) is not grounds for avoidance, but the modern trend and the Restatements take the position that relief will not be denied merely because the mistake is one of law. Mistake of law is not in all respects treated as mistake of fact. If the mistake relates to something other than the legal consequences of their words or conduct, the mistake, if vital, may be grounds for avoidance. Generally, a person is bound by the legal consequences of his or her acts such as making an offer, an acceptance, a waiver, etc., whether or not the person knows the legal consequences.

10. Mistake in Performance
Recovery may be had for payments, overpayments, deliveries of returnable goods, and conveyances of excessive land made in the mistaken belief that the performance was owed under a contract with another, even if the mistake is negligent and unilateral.

    a.   Exception
        If the party who mistakenly pays has a moral obligation to do so, restitution is not allowed.

    b.   Perspective
        The rule stated for mistake in performance refers to money, returnable goods and land and makes no reference to services. Services rendered by mistake cannot be returned. Consequently, there is no duty to pay for such services unless the receiver had a reasonable opportunity to reject them.

11. Defenses to Avoidance or Recovery for Mistake
    a.   Change of Position
        A contract cannot be avoided, or the value of a performance recovered, for mistake, if the other party has detrimentally changed position in reliance upon the contract.

    b.   Affirmance of the Transaction After Discovery of the Mistake
    c.   Failure to Avoid the Contract With Reasonable Promptness After Discovery of the Mistake

E. REFORMATION FOR MISTAKE, MISREPRESENTATION OR DURESS
1. Reformation for Mistake
Reformation of a writing for mistake is available if three requisites are met. (1) There must have been an agreement in writing. (2) There must have been a prior agreement to put the agreement in writing. (3) There is a variance between the prior agreement and the writing caused by mistake.

    a.   The Prior Agreement
        The prior agreement may have been oral or written. An indefinite or tentative agreement suffices. If by error, rather than by modification, clauses earlier agreed upon are misstated or omitted, the writing may be reformed.

    b.   The Agreement to Reduce to Writing
        Reformation is not available if the parties mutually intended to omit or misstate the term. Reformation is available on grounds of

misrepresentation, if one party, without the consent of the other, intentionally omits a term that has been agreed upon.

c.   The Variance
Frequently, the variance is an arithmetical error. Sometimes, it is a misdescription of the subject matter, as a typist's error in a metes and bounds description of real property. At times, the parties mistake the legal effect of their writing. Reformation is available in each of these circumstances.

2.   Reformation for Misrepresentation
If one party misrepresents the content or legal effect of a writing to the other, the other may elect to avoid the contract or to have it reformed to express what was represented.

3.   Reformation for Duress
Cases of reformation for duress are few. The remedy requires (1) a binding contract preliminary to entering into a more formal contract; and (2) coercion into agreeing to a more formal contract that is at variance with the original agreement.

4.   Reformation and the Parol Evidence Rule
The parol evidence rule is inapplicable in an action for reformation. However, a decree for reformation must be based on "clear and convincing" evidence, a higher standard than is normally required in a civil suit.

5.   Defenses to Reformation
a.   Bona Fide Purchasers for Value
Reformation will not be granted if the effect of the decree would infringe on the rights of a bona fide purchaser for value or other third persons who have justifiably relied upon the document as written.

b.   Equitable Defenses
Reformation is an equitable action. Consequently, it is subject to equitable defenses such as unclean hands and laches. A decree for reformation may be withheld in the sound discretion of the court.

c.   The Effect of Negligence
Negligence is no bar to reformation. It is important to note, however, that reformation is not available if one party carelessly believes that a writing will contain a particular provision. Unless this belief was shared or induced by the other, no proper case of reformation is made out. This is not because of negligence. Rather, it is because the writing is not at variance with the agreement.

F.   UNCONSCIONABILITY
1.   Unconscionability in Equity
For centuries, equity has refused to grant specific performance of contracts that were unconscionably obtained or unconscionable in content. Such decisions do not necessarily invalidate contracts but often leave the parties to their legal remedies.

2.   Unconscionability at Law
Since enactment of U.C.C. § 2–302, courts in sales cases and in non-sales cases have exercised the power to strike down or limit contracts or contract clauses on grounds of unconscionability. Prior to enactment of the U.C.C., courts sometimes reached similar results by indirection, particularly by spurious interpretation.

3.   What Constitutes Unconscionability
A U.C.C. comment indicates that there are two kinds of unconscionability. First, "unfair surprise," termed by some as "procedural" unconscionability. Second, "oppression," termed by some as "substantive" unconscionability.

   a.   Unfair Surprise (Procedural Unconscionability)
   A burdensome clause that does not come to the attention of a party adhering to a contract will be struck down if a reasonable person would not expect to find it in the contract and the reason it was not noticed was its burial in small print, or the inability of the adhering party to comprehend the language.

   b.   Oppression (Substantive Unconscionability)
   Provisions of a contract that are assented to but are grossly one-sided may be invalidated or modified by the court. A contract that suffers from total overall imbalance, that is, one that is grossly one-sided, may be invalidated.

   c.   The Hybrid—Surprise and Oppression
   Although analytically the surprise and oppression cases can be distinguished, in general, where unconscionability has been found, the facts contain a mixture of lack of knowledgeable assent and a clause or contract that unduly benefits the party who has drafted the contract.

4.   Judge Versus Jury
Unconscionability is a question of law for the court, not for the trier of fact. The court must allow evidence of the commercial setting and purpose of a provision prior to ruling on the question. Consequently, it is almost always impossible to read a contract and decide that it, or any part of it, is unconscionable. Extrinsic evidence is necessary prior to deciding.

5. The Irrelevance of Hindsight

Unconscionability must be judged by looking at the circumstances existing at the time of contracting without reference to future events. Supervening oppressiveness is governed by the doctrine of impracticability.

6. Consumer Protection

In the great majority of cases in which unconscionability has been found, the party protected by the finding has been a consumer. Generally, businessmen and business organizations are expected to protect themselves. There have been a few cases protecting a small business against a corporate giant.

7. Termination Clauses and Sales of Goods

Under § 2–309(1) of the U.C.C., a contract for the sale of goods that is indefinite in duration is not terminable except on reasonable notice. The Code's focus is on retail franchise and wholesale distributorships which envisage a continuing, often exclusive, relationship. But other relational contracts are also included; e.g., a requirements contract of indefinite duration. U.C.C. § 2–309(3) goes on to provide that an agreement dispensing with a reasonable period of notice is invalid "if its operation would be unconscionable."

8. Limitation on Consequential Damages—Personal Injuries

Although the Code permits limitations on damages and permits the exclusion of consequential damages, it indicates that the exclusion is subject to the rule of conscionability. "Limitation of consequential damages for injury to the person in the case of consumer goods is prima facie unconscionable but limitation of damages where the loss is commercial is not." U.C.C. § 2–719(3). It is, of course, possible to have a finding of unconscionability in the case of commercial losses based on the general doctrine of unconscionability. This would be most unusual, however.

G. "DUTY" TO READ
1. Perspective

The material discussed here is repetitious of rules stated elsewhere. A general discussion here might help crystallize the effect of not reading a document to which one assents.

2. In General

Assent to a document that purports to be a contract or other consensual transaction implies assent to the terms contained therein.

3.   Exceptions

a.   If the Document or Particular Provision Is Not Legible

b.   If the Provision Is Placed in Such a Way That It Is Not Likely to Come to the Attention of the Other Party

c.   Fraud

(1)   Fraud in the Execution

Where one party materially misrepresents the contents of a writing, the modern cases permit the defrauded party, despite a failure to read, to avoid the contract if the party was deceived and relied upon the representation. Alternatively, the contract may be reformed to conform to the representation.

(2)   Fraud-in-the-Factum

A contract is void where the misrepresentation goes not only to the content of the document but also to the nature of the document and the document is radically different from the kind represented and it was not unreasonable for the party to sign it.

d.   Mistake

(1)   Unilateral Mistake

If only one party assents to a document under the mistaken belief that it contains, or does not contain, certain provisions, this party is generally bound by the document. In two situations, however, relief may be granted.

(a)   Palpable Mistake

If the other party is, or ought to be, aware of the mistaken belief, the mistaken party may avoid the contract or have it reformed to conform to this belief.

(b)   Impalpable Mistake

If the other party has no reason to know of the mistake, the mistaken party cannot have reformation but may, however, avoid the contract if enforcement would result in an unconscionably unequal exchange of values, and avoidance would impose no substantial hardship on the other.

(2)   Mutual Mistake

If both parties share the same mistake as to the contents of a writing, it will be reformed to conform to their belief.

e.   Unconscionability

For analytical purposes two kinds of unconscionability are distinguished: unfair surprise and oppression. The second category is unrelated to "duty" to read because even if an oppressive clause is read and comprehended it can be voided by a court. The first category goes to the heart of this topic. Modern cases scrutinize burdensome, unexpected clauses that have not been read by, or explained to, a party adhering to a form contract. Sometimes such clauses are held to be void.

H. AFFIRMANCE OR RATIFICATION
1. Discussion
Affirmance and ratification are equivalent terms. Upon discovering a misrepresentation or mistake and on escaping duress or undue influence, a party has choices. One of these choices is to continue to accept the obligations of the contract. A manifestation of intent to continue with the transaction is an affirmance. No consideration is required for an affirmance. After affirmance, the power of avoidance and the right to seek reformation are lost.

2. Affirmance by Conduct
a. Exercise of Dominion
After a party's power to choose between affirmance and avoidance ripens, the continued exercise of dominion over property received under the contract or the continued acceptance of benefits under the contract affirms the contract.

b. Delay
An affirmance occurs if a party fails within a reasonable time to avoid the contract after the power to do so has ripened. What is a reasonable time is normally a question of fact. Three factors dominate the determination of reasonableness of time to avoid: (1) reliance by the other; (2) speculative benefit gained by stalling; and (3) fault.

3. The Party Avoiding Must Offer to Return Property Received
This requisite and its exceptions are discussed in connection with the remedy of restitution.

IX. THIRD PARTY BENEFICIARIES

A. TYPES OF BENEFICIARIES
1. In General
A party not in privity, other than an intended beneficiary, may not recover on a contract. Only a promisee is in privity.

2. Intended Beneficiaries
A third person to whom a promisee intended the benefits of a promisor's promise to run is an intended beneficiary. There is a wide variety of tests to determine who is an intended beneficiary. The most commonly used tests are: (1) to whom is the performance to run (if it is to run directly to the third person, this person is an intended beneficiary); and (2) whether the promisor reasonably understood that the promisee intended to benefit the beneficiary;

that is, whether the beneficiary was an ultimate intended beneficiary of the promisor's performance.

3. Incidental Beneficiary

A party who receives benefits from a promisor's performance but who was not intended to be a beneficiary, and therefore has no rights, is an incidental beneficiary.

4. Creditor Beneficiary

If a promisee extracts from the promisor a promise to render a performance to a third party because the promisee is indebted to the third party, the third party is a creditor beneficiary.

5. Donee Beneficiary

If the promisee's purpose in extracting the promise is to confer a gift upon the third party, the third party is a donee beneficiary. The distinction between donee and creditor beneficiaries is not ordinarily important on the issue of intent to benefit but may be important on other issues, such as when rights vest (see below).

6. Promises of Indemnity

The promise of an indemnitor against liability or an indemnitor against loss does not ordinarily give rise to a third party beneficiary situation because the intent to benefit is deemed to run to the promisee. An exception appears to have been made in the case of municipal contracts.

7. The Municipality Cases

Municipal contracts that create enforceable rights in third persons are of three types. These are: (1) where a contractor agrees to perform a duty that the municipality owes to individual members of the public and the breach of which would create tort liability against the municipality; (2) where the contractor promises the governmental body to *compensate* members of the public for injuries done them despite the absence of a governmental duty; and (3) where the governmental body enters into a contract to gain advantages for individual members of the public.

8. The Surety Bond Cases

Laborers, suppliers, and subcontractors are not third party beneficiaries of a performance bond because the purpose of this type of bond is to assure payment of damages to an owner in the event of a contractor's non-performance. They are generally held to be third party beneficiaries of a payment bond. While the motive of a promisee in procuring a payment bond is self-protection, the intent is also to benefit the laborers, suppliers, and subcontractors. It is presumed that these third parties are not intended beneficiaries of a joint performance-payment bond because the bond might be dissipated in paying third party beneficiaries without paying the promisee.

B.   PROMISOR'S DEFENSES
1.   In General
In the absence of agreement to the contrary, the promisor can assert against the beneficiary any defense the promisor has against the promisee.

2.   Exceptions
a.   Where the parties agree that the beneficiary will have enforceable rights despite any defense that the promisor might be able to assert against the promisee.

b.   Where the rights of the beneficiary have vested, the rights may not be varied by subsequent arrangement between the promisor and the promisee.

3.   When Rights Vest

a.   Omnipotence of the Contract
The parties may provide as they wish with respect to vesting. For example, the contract may validly provide that rights of third parties are always divestable or that they vest immediately.

b.   Creditor Beneficiaries
The rights of a creditor beneficiary vest, at the latest, when the beneficiary brings an action to enforce the contract or otherwise materially changes position in reliance on it. The tendency today is to hold that the rights vest as soon as the beneficiary learns of the promise and assents to it.

c.   Donee Beneficiaries
According to the original Restatement, the rights of a donee beneficiary vest immediately upon making the contract, but the Restatement, Second, and much case law has indicated that the same rule that applies to creditor beneficiaries should be applied to donees.

d.   Perspective
Vesting has a very limited role. It does not give the beneficiary the equivalent of a fee simple absolute in the promise. It only insulates the beneficiary from a curtailment of rights by mutual agreement of the promisor and promisee. It does not insulate the beneficiary from defenses such as failure of constructive condition.

4.   Counterclaim
The promisor can effectively raise against the beneficiary a counterclaim that the promisor has against the promisee only if it is in the nature of a recoupment; that is, if it arises out of the same transaction upon which the promisor is being sued. The recoupment may be used only as a subtraction from the beneficiary's claim and not for affirmative relief.

5.   Promisee's Defense Against the Beneficiary

Suppose the promisor, *A*, makes the promise to *B* for the benefit of *C*, a supposed creditor of *B*.   Afterwards, *A* discovers that *C* is not a creditor because *B* has a valid defense against *C*.   The availability of this defense to *A* depends upon the interpretation of the contract.   If the promisor promises to pay irrespective of any such defense, it cannot be raised.   If *A* promises merely to perform to the extent *B* is obligated, the defense may be raised.   If the promise is to pay a specific debt, it is generally held that the promise is to pay irrespective of such a defense.

C.   CUMULATIVE RIGHTS OF THE BENEFICIARY
1.   Creditor Beneficiary

A creditor beneficiary has rights against both the promisor and the promisee. Judgment may be had against both but only one satisfaction may be obtained.

2.   Novation Contrasted

If a creditor beneficiary releases the *promisee* in exchange for the promisor's assumption of the obligation, the substituted contract between promisor and beneficiary is called a novation.   No novation occurs in a normal third party beneficiary contract because the beneficiary does not impliedly release the debtor when the beneficiary assents to, or even attempts to enforce, the promisor's assumption.

3.   Donee Beneficiary

A donee beneficiary has rights against the promisor, but has no rights against the promisee, unless, after the rights have vested, the promisee has received a consideration to discharge the promisor.   The beneficiary's remedial rights are limited to the value of the consideration.

D.   RIGHTS OF THE PROMISEE AGAINST THE PROMISOR
1.   In General

In addition to liability to the beneficiary, the promisor is under an obligation to the promisee for performance of the contract.

2.   Discussion

It should not be forgotten that the promisor's contract is with the promisee. In the case of a donee beneficiary contract, the promisee usually suffers no damage by a promisor's breach and restitution may not be a satisfactory remedy.   In such a case the legal remedy may be inadequate and, if so, the promisee's action for specific performance will be entertained.   In a creditor beneficiary contract, breach by the promisor can cause substantial harm to the promisee.   If such damages occur, they are recoverable.

X. ASSIGNMENT AND DELEGATION

A. ASSIGNMENT OF RIGHTS
1. What Is an Assignment?
An assignment is a manifestation of intent by the owner of a right to the assignee to effectuate its present transfer.

2. Perspective
An assignment's closest relative is a sale of goods or a conveyance of land. It is an executed transaction. Consequently, words of promise do not create an assignment. An order communicated to the debtor alone is not an assignment.

3. U.C.C. Coverage
Although, in its simplest form, an assignment is an outright transfer, frequently an assignment is made as a security device. It is similar to a mortgage of real property rather than the conveyance of a fee simple. Although Article 9 of the U.C.C. focuses primarily upon security devices, it governs the assignment of "accounts" whether the assignment is an outright transfer or the creation of a security device. An account is "any right to payment for goods sold or leased or for services rendered not evidenced by an instrument or chattel paper whether or not it has been earned by performance." U.C.C. § 9–105(1)(g).

4. U.C.C. Exclusions
Although Article 9 of the U.C.C. governs assignments of accounts regardless of the purpose of the assignment, specific exceptions are enumerated in the Code. These include:

(a) Wage assignments;

(b) Assignments of accounts in connection with the sale of a business from which they arose;

(c) An assignment of rights under a contract coupled with the delegation of the assignor's duties to the assignee;

(d) Rights to receive rents from a lease of real property.

Where the transaction is not governed by Article 9, the common law rules apply, or, in some instances, other legislation. For example, most states have statutes regulating or outlawing wage assignments. Article 2 of the Code has several provisions that govern the assignment of rights in contracts for the sale of goods.

5. **Deviants From the Norm**
There are three types of assignments that deviate from the norm and create problems which do not exist in the case of an ordinary assignment.

    a. **Gratuitous Assignment**
        The fact that the assignor makes a gift of a right against the obligor is not a defense. An assignment, as an executed transaction, requires no consideration. But, as between the assignor and the assignee, the gift must be complete; otherwise the assignee's rights can be terminated by the death of the assignor, by a subsequent assignment of the same right or by a notice of revocation communicated to the assignee or to the obligor. Since a right cannot be physically delivered, the gift can be completed by other substitute delivery methods such as: the assignee receives payment, the right assigned is evidenced by a symbolic writing and the writing is delivered to the assignee, or the doctrine of promissory estoppel applies. An assignment given for a pre-existing debt is for "value" and is not deemed to be gratuitous.

    b. **Voidable Assignment**
        An assignment may also be voidable by the assignor because of infancy, insanity, fraud, duress, etc. The same rules that apply for avoiding a contract apply.

    c. **Assignment of Future Rights**
        An assignment of a future right is the assignment of a right to arise under a contract which has not yet been made. The generally accepted common law rule is that an assignment for value of a future right is an equitable assignment. At common law, such rights were generally considered to be superior to those of the assignor but inferior to those of a subsequent assignee of the same right for value without notice and to the rights of a subsequent attaching creditor of the assignor who is without notice of the claim of the assignee provided the attachment occurs before the right comes into being. Under the Uniform Commercial Code, generally speaking, if the assignee of future rights complies with the perfection requirements of the Code, the assignee will prevail. (U.C.C. §§ 9–204 and 9–402).

6. **Formalities**
In the absence of statute, an assignment may be oral. Under Article 9, a writing is required unless the assignee is in possession of the collateral involved. Possession of an account is not possible; consequently, if the assignment of the account is governed by Article 9, a writing is required. If there is no writing, the assignment is not enforceable against anyone. There is similar provision in Article 8 that relates to investment securities. (U.C.C. § 8–319.) An assignment or promise of assignment of rights that is not governed by Article 8 or 9 is not enforceable unless it is in writing, provided

the remedy sought is in the amount or value of $5,000 or more. (U.C.C. § 1–206.)

7. **Attachment of Security Interests in Accounts**
"Attachment" relates to the relative rights of the assignor and assignee. Once the rights of an assignee attach, the assignee's rights are superior to those of the assignor. Unless there is an agreement to the contrary, the rights of the assignee attach as soon as (1) there is an agreement that it attach; (2) value has been given; and (3) the account in which the assignee has rights is identified. It is important to remember that if Article 9 governs, the assignment must be in writing for the assignee's rights to attach.

8. **Perfection of Security Interests in Accounts**
"Perfection" relates to the rights of the assignee against third parties. Perfection cannot occur until the assignment attaches. Perfection, under Article 9, generally occurs when the assignee takes possession of the collateral, but in the case of accounts, since possession is not possible, filing of a notice (financing statement) of assignment in a public record office is the normal method of perfection. Filing is not required to perfect a security interest in an account where the assignment (either by itself or in conjunction with others) does not constitute a significant part of the accounts of the assignor. In this case, the rights of the assignee are perfected on attachment.

9. **Priorities Under the Code**
Under the U.C.C., an assignee who has perfected a security interest in an account has priority over a party whose rights are subsequently perfected, including lien creditors, secured creditors and a trustee of the assignor's bankrupt estate. A subsequent secured creditor, and a subsequent lien creditor, will prevail over an assignee who does not have a perfected interest. (U.C.C. § 9–301). A lien creditor is an unsecured creditor who has acquired a lien by attachment, levy or the like and includes a trustee of the assignor's estate in bankruptcy.

10. **Priorities in Non–Code Cases**
   a. Assignee Versus Attaching Creditor
       At common law, the priority between an assignee and a creditor who had obtained an attachment on the right assigned is governed by the rule: "prior in time, prior in right." Consequently, priority depended on the relative time of the attachment and of the assignment. However, the assignee may be estopped from asserting this priority. For example, it is often held that the assignee loses priority if the *obligor* has not received notice of the assignment in sufficient time to call the assignment to the attention of the court in the attachment proceedings. The more modern view deprives the assignee of priority only if the assignee fails to give notice of assignment prior to payment by the obligor to the attaching creditor.

b.   Successive Assignees
At common law, there are three competing rules to determine priority among successive assignees of the same claim:

(1)   New York Rule
Prior in time is prior in right.

(2)   English View
The first assignee to notify the obligor prevails provided this assignee gives value and has no notice of any prior assignment.

(3)   Four Horsemen Rule (Rule of the Restatements and the Prevailing Rule)
Prior in time is prior in right unless a subsequent assignee who pays value in good faith (1) obtains payment from the obligor; or (2) recovers judgment from; or (3) enters into a substituted contract with the obligor; or (4) receives delivery of an instrument that incorporates the debt.

c.   Latent Equities
An assignment to a bona fide assignee for value without notice destroys any latent equities third persons may have in the right. The older view was to the contrary.

11. Floating Lien
U.C.C. § 9–205 expressly validates a floating lien on a shifting stock of goods or accounts.

12. Non–Assignable Rights
A right is assignable except where the assignment would: (1) materially change the duty of the other party; (2) materially vary the burden or risk of the obligor; (3) impair materially the other party's chance of obtaining return performance; or (4) be contrary to public policy.

13. Contractual Prohibition of an Assignment
a.   Common Law Rule
At common law, a provision in a contract prohibiting an assignment of rights was generally sustained as valid under the general principle of freedom of contract, although several courts struck down such provisions as illegal restraints on alienation. If, however, the court was able to find that the provision was not drafted with sufficient clarity to accomplish the purpose of voiding the assignment, the anti-assignment clause was treated as a promise not to assign. An assignment would breach the promise and give the obligor an action for breach, but the assignment was valid. Because damages for breach of the provision are ordinarily nominal, the anti-assignment clause was frequently of no practical value.

b.   The U.C.C. Rule
Under U.C.C. Article 9 an anti-assignment clause is ineffective to prohibit
the assignment of an "account." Also Article 2 permits the assignment of
the right to damages for total breach or of a right arising from the
assignor's total due performance, despite a clause purporting to prevent
assignment.

c.   Interpretation Under Article 2
Article 2 of the Code—and the Restatement, Second, agrees—provides that
general language purporting to prohibit "assignment of the contract,"
should be construed as barring only the delegation of duties, unless the
circumstances indicate the contrary.

14. Option Contracts

Option contracts are offers but are also contracts. While offers are not
assignable, option contracts generally are. The offeree's rights in an option
contract are assignable provided the rights are otherwise assignable and the
duties otherwise delegable and any promise expected to be made by the offeree
has been made.

15. Defenses of the Obligor Against the Assignor

The obligor may assert against the assignee any defense which could have
been asserted against the assignor. The maxim is that the assignee stands in
the shoes of the assignor.

16. Vesting

As an exception to the rule stated immediately above, when the rights of the
assignee have vested they may not be discharged or curtailed by a subsequent
agreement or other voluntary transaction between the obligor and assignor.
Vesting occurs when the assignee notifies the obligor of the assignment.
Under Article 9 of the U.C.C., however, even after notice to the obligor, the
assignor and obligor have a limited right to curtail the rights of the assignee.
If the assigned right to payment has not yet been earned by performance, the
assignor and obligor may, in good faith and in accordance with reasonable
commercial standards, modify or substitute for the contract. When this occurs
the assignee has rights under the new agreement.

17. Counterclaims

To what extent may an obligor raise a claim against the assignor as a
counterclaim against an assignee? Under Article 9 of the U.C.C., this is made
to depend, in part, whether or not the counterclaim stems from the same
transaction.

a.   Same Transaction (Recoupment)
If the obligor's counterclaim arises out of the same contract from which
the assignee's rights stem, the obligor may raise the counterclaim by way

of defense. This defense, known as recoupment, cannot be used for affirmative relief against the assignee but only by way of subtraction.

b.   **Different Transaction (Set-off)**
If the obligor's counterclaim arose from a different transaction with the assignor, this counterclaim may be raised against the assignee only if it accrues before the obligor receives notice of the assignment. This defense, known as set-off, cannot be used for affirmative relief against the assignee but only by way of subtraction.

18. Waiver of Defenses or Counterclaims
Under Article 9 of the U.C.C., waiver of defense clauses are valid provided the assignee takes the assignment in good faith, for value, and without notice of the claim or defense, except that such a clause cannot effectively prohibit the raising of a real defense. (§ 9–206). Real defenses are: voidability for infancy; voidness for total incapacity, illegality or fraud in the factum; and discharge in insolvency proceedings. The U.C.C. provision validating waiver of defense clauses subordinates the rule to "any statute or decision which establishes a different rule for buyers or lessees of consumer goods. . . ." Many states have invalidated such clauses in consumer protection legislation, as has the F.T.C. The rule validating waiver of defense clauses continues to be viable only in non-consumer transactions.

19. Rights of the Assignee Against the Assignor
a.   **Express Warranties or Disclaimers of Implied Warranties**
Within broad limits, the assignee and assignor may agree as they wish as to warranties. Thus, the assignor will be held to any express warranty made. A warranty disclaimer is similarly upheld where the parties agree to the disclaimer.

b.   **Implied Warranties**
In the absence of an express agreement to the contrary, an assignor warrants that:

(1)   the assignor will do nothing to defeat or impair the value of the assignment;

(2)   the right exists and is subject to no defenses or limitations not stated or apparent; and that

(3)   any document delivered is genuine and what it purports to be.

B.   DELEGATION OF DUTIES
1.   What Is a Delegation?
A delegation occurs when an obligor (delegant) appoints another person (delegate) to render a performance that the obligor owes to a third person.

2. Liability of the Delegant

A delegant cannot obtain freedom from liability by delegating duties. This is perhaps the only immutable rule in the law of contracts. There is no way an obligor can be freed from liability other than by consent of the obligee or the decree of a bankruptcy court.

3. Liability of the Delegate

The delegate becomes liable to the third party only by making a promise that is deemed to be a promise that is for the benefit of the third person.

4. Non–Delegable Duties

a. What Duties Are Non–Delegable?

The test is whether performance by the obligor or under the obligor's personal supervision is required by the contract. Such a requirement may be expressed in the contract. If it is not, such a requirement will be implied: (a) where the contract is predicated on the unique skills of the obligor; and (b) where the contract is predicated on the trust and confidence that the obligee has placed in the obligor.

b. Delegation in Sales Contracts

In general, the delegation rules of the U.C.C. are the same as the common law. It will be recalled that, under the U.C.C., a general clause prohibiting assignment of the contract has the effect of prohibiting the delegation of duties. Also, under the Code, unless the language or circumstances point to a contrary intention, an assignment in general terms is treated as doing three things: assigning the rights, delegating the duties and creating an assumption of duties. The U.C.C. also authorizes the obligee to demand assurances from the delegate whenever the other party assigns rights and delegates duties to a third person.

c. Effect of Improper Delegation

An attempted delegation of a non-delegable duty is ineffective. It is also a breach. If persisted in, the breach is material.

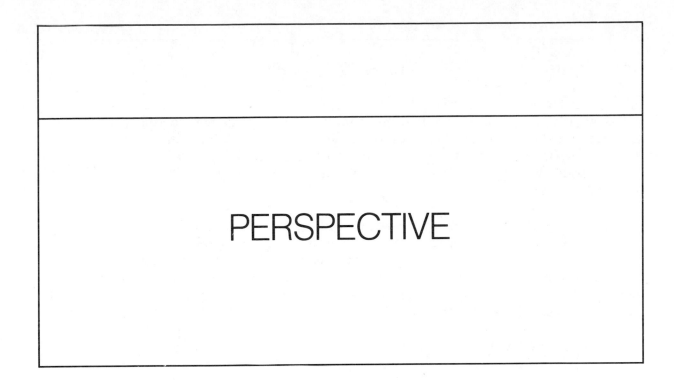

PERSPECTIVE

APPROACH TO CONTRACTS

Contracts is a very difficult course. At the same time it is a very important course. Not only is it the foundation for many other courses in the curriculum (for example, Sales, Mortgages, Suretyship) but it is also well suited to train students "to think like lawyers."

The course in Contracts is made up of a large number of individual problems that appear to be unrelated. However, they are related in the sense that it is easy (more so than in most courses) to put a large number of problems into a short fact pattern. Thus the function of this Outline is not only to state the general principles of Contract Law but to structure those principles in an orderly fashion.

You should be prepared to accept that in some areas there are a number of views. When this is so you will be required to state all of the views and the relative merits of each one. (More later.) Although Contracts is basically a common-law course there are a number of instances where the common law has been changed by statute. Here again it is important to know why the common law was changed and what the statute says. The most significant statute in this area is the Uniform Commercial Code.

HOW TO STUDY

Most schools use a case method of instruction. It goes without saying that the cases should be carefully briefed and analyzed. If you do not do this you will not be prepared for the intensive class discussion. The important thing is that you prepare critically. Question everything you read, including rules of law. Compare cases carefully. Remember that a change in one fact may change the result previously reached.

The most important tool that a lawyer needs is the ability to analyze. This ability will vary from person to person but to some extent it can be acquired. This means, as indicated above, that you should carefully analyze each assigned case with a passion. Get a clear understanding of the essential facts. To do this you should use your own words in the brief rather than the language of court. Try to state the precise issue in the case. Do not state a broad issue such as, "Was there a contract". Find the general principle. How was it applied to the facts? Is the decision sound? Can you make a good contrary argument? Remember, the party on the losing side thought there was a good case for a contrary decision.

Although preparation is important, what happens in class is much more important. Review the material prior to going to class. Get sufficient rest so that you are eager and alert. Then take the best set of class notes that is possible. How well you do this will depend on your professor and his method of instruction. The most important thing you can do is to organize your notes as soon after class as possible. This Outline should help you do that. If you are still troubled after reading this Outline you may wish to turn to a text such as the Calamari & Perillo Hornbook (West). Don't go to bed until you have mastered the lecture. It is most important to put the material in outline form and as has been suggested this Outline will help you do that. Continuously review your outline! Do not wait until exam time to learn it.

Notice *all* of the features of this book that are listed in the "Publisher's Preface" and use all of them.

EXAMINATION

If you have faithfully done what is stated above you should be well prepared for the exam. This does not necessarily mean that you will get a good grade. One reason is that law school is highly competitive and grades are relative. Another is that you may have a bad day and still a third is that you may not do a good job of analysis on one or more questions.

There is, however, an exam technique. One part of it may be termed mechanical. Bring a working watch. Budget your time. Do not spend it all on the first question. Follow all instructions carefully. Write legibly, otherwise your paper may not be read carefully. Use complete sentences and write grammatically.

These preliminaries aside, your first important job is to master the facts. Many students do poorly because they misread or misunderstood the facts. Read the facts carefully several times. As you do jot down the issues you see. To do this well you must get the overall picture. If the facts are complicated use a diagram. (Do not supply facts but you are free to indicate that important facts may be missing.) You must also look at each word in the question carefully. Do not lightly assume that any word is superfluous. Do not repeat the facts but as indicated below work them into your answer where they are relevant. Also notice the precise question that is asked.

When you have listed all of the problems try to put them in logical order. For example the question of whether a contract was formed should precede any discussion of breach of the contract.

Let us assume that the first problem in the question relates to the existence of an offer. Identify the problem and then state the general principle involved. For example, would a reasonable person the position of the plaintiff conclude that a promise (offer) has been made? Now the facts that relate to this issue must be analyzed. Some of the facts may lead to an affirmative answer, others to a negative one. Both sides should be explored and then you should reach a conclusion. Your conclusion is not nearly as important as your analysis.

If you conclude that there was not an offer, then as a matter of logic you could conclude that no further discussion of any other problems is required. Discretion in this instance is more important than logic. You must go on to discuss all of the other issues. You should go on to say, "Assuming that there was an offer the next question is one of acceptance."

The important thing is to raise each issue, and state the general principle that applies, then apply that principle to the facts showing how the facts fit the principle. If there is more than one view apply all of the views to the facts. If there is a relevant statute discuss it and apply it to the facts. Cover all of the possibilities. If your professor has stressed policy considerations it would be a good idea to bring them into the discussion. If you concluded that certain facts are "red herrings" it is also a good idea to state briefly why you so concluded. As a matter of fact your answer should reflect your mental operations. Do not bury an issue because you are unsure of the answer. After all this is done your ultimate conclusion should be stated. When you have finished your answer reread it so as to avoid inadvertent mistakes.

I

MUTUAL ASSENT—OFFER AND ACCEPTANCE

Analysis

A. Mutual Assent
   1. Nature of Mutual Assent
   2. Objective Theory of Contracts
     a. Discussion
     b. Law and Fact
   3. Must the Parties Intend to Be Bound or Intend Legal Consequences?
     a. Discussion
   4. Intention That the Agreement Be Reduced to One Formalized Writing
B. Offer
   1. Meaning of Offer
   2. Meaning of Promise
   3. Offers Distinguished From Statements That Are Not Offers
     a. Expressions of Opinions and Words of Reassurance
     b. Offers Distinguished From Statements of Intention, etc.
     c. Offers Distinguished From Inquiries or Invitations
     d. Offers Distinguished From Ads, Catalogues and Circular Letters

    e. Offers Distinguished From Price Quotations
    f. The Offer at Auction
    g. Offer v. Preliminary Negotiations
   4. Distinction Between Unilateral and Bilateral Contracts
    a. Basis of Distinction
    b. Acceptance of Offer Looking to a Bilateral Contract
    c. Acceptance of Offer Looking to a Unilateral
     Contract
    d. Ambiguous Offer
    e. U.C.C. and Restatement, Second
  C. Acceptance
   1. General Requirements
    a. Introduction
    b. Acceptance by Authorized Party
    c. Knowledge of the Offer and Intent to Accept
    d. Necessity for Communication in a Bilateral Contract
    e. Necessity for Notice of Performance in a Unilateral
     Contract
    f. Acceptance of an Offer Looking to a Series of
     Contracts
   2. Acceptance of a Bilateral Contract
    a. Acceptance by Silence
    b. Acceptance by Conduct
    c. When Is an Acceptance Effective?
    d. Offeror's Power to Negate Mailbox Rule
    e. When Offeree Sends Both Acceptance and
     Rejection
    f. Risk of Mistake in Transmission by an Intermediary
  D. Termination of Revocable Offers
   1. Introduction
    a. Lapse of Time
    b. Death or Lack of Capacity
    c. Revocation
    d. Death or Destruction
    e. Supervening Illegality
    f. Rejection or Counter–Offer by Offeree
  E. Option Contracts—Irrevocable Offers
   1. Introduction
   2. What Makes an Offer Irrevocable?
   3. By Statute
   4. The Nature of an Option Contract—Irrevocable Offer
   5. Termination of Irrevocable Offers
   6. When Is the Acceptance of an Irrevocable Offer
    Effective?
  F. U.C.C. § 2–206
   1. U.C.C. § 2–206
    a. Introduction
    b. Subdivision 1(a) of U.C.C. § 2–206
    c. Subdivision 1(b)
   2. The Restatement, Second

G. Certainty
  1. Common Law
     a. Introduction
     b. What Are Material Terms?
     c. When Is a Material Term Reasonably Certain?
     d. Types of Indefiniteness
     e. Uniform Commercial Code

A. MUTUAL ASSENT

1. NATURE OF MUTUAL ASSENT
Mutual Assent is ordinarily arrived at by a process of offer and acceptance.

Exception: *At times, mutual assent exists even though it is impossible to identify the process of offer and acceptance.*

Examples: (1) *A* makes an offer to sell *B* 1000 Mason Green Jars (quarts) for $1000, specifying all necessary terms. *B*, in turn, manifests an intent to accept the offer. Mutual assent has arisen through a process of offer and acceptance.

(2) While *A* and *B* are together, *C* suggests the term of an agreement for them and they simultaneously agree to these terms. Although it is impossible to identify the offer and acceptance, mutual assent exists.

2. OBJECTIVE THEORY OF CONTRACTS
With certain exceptions discussed later, whether there is mutual assent is determined under the objective theory of contracts rather than under a subjective approach.

a. Discussion
The objective theory of contracts states that mutual assent should be determined solely from objective manifestations of assent—what the party does and says rather than what the party subjectively intends or believes or assumes. Another portion of the credo of the objectivists is that objective manifestations of intent should be viewed from the vantage point of a reasonable person in the position of the other party. The phrase "in the position of the other party" means that the other party is charged not only with the knowledge of a reasonable person but also with what this party knows or should know because of superior knowledge. There are other approaches, both objective and subjective, which will be discussed below. In the meantime, the approach outlined above will be employed as an acceptable tentative test. The objective theory is designed to protect the reasonable expectations of the parties.

b. Law and Fact
What a reasonable person in the position of *B* will understand will ordinarily be a question of fact. But, if a reasonable person can reach only one reasonable understanding, the question is one of law. If the question is one of law, it will be decided by the trial judge and it is subject to appellate review. If the question is one of fact, it will be decided by the triers of fact (often a jury) and that determination is

ordinarily not subject to appeal because appellate courts ordinarily review only questions of law.

Examples: (1) *A*, in a newspaper's "joke column", promises to pay $1000 to anyone who provides *A* with Western Union's telephone number. *B* complies. Since *B*, as a reasonable person, should conclude that *A* was not serious, as a matter of law there was no offer and hence no contract.

(2) *A* makes an "offer" to sell certain property to *B* at fixed terms. *A* is jesting, but appears serious. Because *B*, as a reasonable person, would believe that *A* was serious, it must be concluded as a matter of law that *A* made an offer.

(3) Assume the facts in (2) above, except that while a reasonable person would conclude that *A* made an offer, *B*, by virtue of previous dealings between the parties, knew or should have known that *A* was joking. There would be no offer because of *B*'s special knowledge. Whether *B* knows or should know will often be a question of fact.

3. MUST THE PARTIES INTEND TO BE BOUND OR INTEND LEGAL CONSEQUENCES?

a. Discussion

It is well settled that parties need not manifest an intent to be bound or consciously consider legal consequences that might arise upon breach. This is a sound rule because the parties at the time of contracting rarely consider these matters, much less discuss them. However, if from their statements and conduct, or the surrounding circumstances, it appears that the parties did not intend to be bound, or did not intend legal consequences, there is no contract.

Examples: (1) *A* and *B* are two ignorant persons who are unaware that society offers a remedy for the enforcement of an agreement. They agree to exchange a horse for a cow. The agreement is enforceable; their ignorance of legal sanctions does not prevent the formation of a contract. In other words, their ignorance of legal sanctions does not raise any factual presumption that they did not intend legal obligations. This result is consistent with the rule that a mistake as to a rule of law does not necessarily deprive an agreement of legal effect.

(2) *A* and *B* enter into an agreement regulating their commercial relations, but further agree that their agreement is to create no legal obligations. Under the majority rule, the

agreement will not be enforced because the parties do not intend legal obligations. There are, however, cases holding that where the parties have *acted under the agreement* and it is unfair not to enforce the agreement, it should be enforced. Most of these cases have involved pension and employee death benefit plans and bonuses. The theory of these minority cases is promissory estoppel. (See pp. 176–181 infra.) There may also be the possibility of quasi-contractual recovery.

(3) *A* invites *B* to dinner. *B* accepts the invitation and arrives at *A*'s house at the appointed time, and *A* is not there. *B* would not have a cause of action because it is a reasonable factual presumption that the parties intended that a social, rather than legal, obligation should result. But the result would be different if the parties affirmatively indicated that they intended legal consequences.

(4) Husband and wife, while living together amicably, make an agreement as to the wife's allowance. There is no contract, because there is a reasonable factual presumption that the parties did not intend legal consequences but rather a working arrangement. This reasonable factual presumption would be overcome if the parties manifested a contrary intention. However, this type of agreement would raise questions of public policy. If the parties were separated so that they were not living "in amity," the separation agreement would be binding.

4. INTENTION THAT THE AGREEMENT BE REDUCED TO ONE FORMALIZED WRITING

If the parties agree that they are not to be bound unless and until they sign a formal agreement, they will not be bound until that time. If they intend the future writing to be merely a convenient memorial of their prior agreement, they are bound whether or not such a writing is executed.

Discussion: During the process of negotiations, parties often manifest an intention that when an agreement is reached it will be reduced to writing. When they so indicate, there are two possibilities. One is that they want the writing as evidence of their prior agreement: that is, as a convenient memorial. If this is so, it is clear that there was a contract from the time they agreed. In this situation, a refusal to execute the writing constitutes a breach of contract. But if they did not intend to be bound unless and until the writing is executed, there is no contract until that time. It is difficult to decide which intention the parties had. There are many factors to be considered in making this determination. Very often the question is one of fact.

B. OFFER

1. MEANING OF OFFER
An offer, with minor exceptions, is a promise to do or refrain from doing some specified thing in the future. For a promise to be an offer, it must justify the other party, as a reasonable person in the setting the promise was made, to conclude that his or her assent is invited and will consummate the process of offer and acceptance. It is possible to have an offer without a promise in the case of an exchange through barter, and in the case of a reverse unilateral contract. An offer empowers the offeree to create a contract by making an acceptance.

2. MEANING OF PROMISE
A promise is a manifestation of intent that gives an assurance that a thing will be done or will not be done.

Examples: (1) *A* says to *B*, "I will sell you my black horse for $1000." *B* says, "I accept." Even though *A* does not use the word "promise," *A* has made an offer because the language is promissory. In context, the language amounts to a promise: it justifies *B* as a reasonable person, to conclude that *A* has invited an acceptance and that this acceptance will conclude the deal.

(2) *A* says to *B*, "My car which is in your possession is yours if you pay me $1000." If *B* pays the $1000, there is an acceptance of the offer and a completed exchange without any promise being made. The exchange is arrived at through barter.

(3) *A,* a house owner, pays $200 to an insurance company asking for the company's promise to pay *A* $50,000 if *A*'s house is destroyed by fire. *A* is the offeror but has made no promise. Rather, *A* has requested a promise from *B*. When *B* makes the promise there is a reverse unilateral contract. The contract is reverse because *A,* the offeror, has not made any promise. The only promise is by the offeree. The contract arises when *B* makes the promise. The occurrence of the fire is a condition precedent to the insurance company's obligation to pay and not part of the offer and acceptance process.

3. OFFERS DISTINGUISHED FROM STATEMENTS THAT ARE NOT OFFERS
a. Expressions of Opinions and Words of Reassurance
Expressions of opinion and words of reassurance are not promises and, therefore, not offers.

Discussion: This distinction is crucial in the doctor-patient relationship, because the courts recognize that a doctor may make an express promise to cure or to obtain a specific result or to use a particular treatment. The difficult question to be resolved by the reasonable person test is whether the doctor has made such a promise or has merely stated an opinion or given a therapeutic reassurance. The distinction is also important in cases not involving doctors. The possibility of an implied promise is discussed in example (4).

Examples: (1) Doctor says to patient, "Don't worry you'll be back to work in three or four days." As a matter of law, there is no promise. A reasonable patient would conclude that this is an expression of opinion or words of reassurance.

(2) Doctor says, "Electroshock treatments are 100% safe," or "I promise to perform a Caesarean section," or "I guarantee that you will have a perfect hand." A reasonable person could conclude that a promise was being made. It is a question of fact if these expressions are promises.

(3) *B,* a tenant farmer, was behind in his rent. He told *A,* his landlord, about his problems, and *A* suggested that he should get more cattle. *B* replied, "If I stock up too heavy in the pasture and there be a short spell, I will be up against it and that is the reason I am waiting for you." *A* told *B,* "Never mind the water, John. I will see that there will be plenty of water, John, because it never failed in Minnesota yet." *A*'s statement was not a promise, it was nothing more than an opinion or a prophecy.

(4) Patient (*P*) came to doctor (*D*) for treatment. *D* makes no express promise, but *D,* in treating *P,* does not use requisite skill. Does *P* have a cause of action based upon a theory of breach of an implied promise to exercise requisite skill, or does *P* have a cause of action based upon a theory of malpractice (negligence), or are both theories available to *P*? In the doctor-patient relationship the answer appears to be that *P* is limited to an action in malpractice (negligence), except in those exceptional cases where (example (2)) the doctor makes an express promise. It does not follow that the same rule applies in other professional relationships. This problem begins to scratch the surface of the possibility that a set of facts may give rise to both a tort claim and a claim in contract.

b.   Offers Distinguished From Statements of Intention, etc.
A mere statement of intention or of hopes and desires does not constitute an offer. The same is generally true of an estimate.

Examples: (1) *A* says to *B*, "I am going to sell my car for $500." This is not an offer but a statement of intention.

(2) *A* asks *B*, for an estimate on certain work to be done. *B* estimates the work can be done for $5000. *B*'s statement is not a promise and therefore is not an offer.

c.   Offers Distinguished From Inquiries or Invitations
A mere inquiry or an invitation to the other party to make an offer does not constitute an offer.

Examples: (1) *A* writes to *B* saying, "Will you sell me your property on Rockledge Drive for $50,000?" This is not an offer but an inquiry. *A* is not making a promise but is simply seeking information.

(2) In reply to inquiry from *B* as to whether *A* would sell certain property for $6000, *A* answered "it would not be possible for me to sell it unless I was to receive $16,000 cash." *A* was only saying "make me an offer". *A* was therefore inviting an offer from *B* rather than making an offer (promise).

d.   Offers Distinguished From Ads, Catalogues and Circular Letters
Advertisements for the sale of goods, catalogues and circular letters are not ordinarily considered to be offers because they do not contain express language of promise and do not spell out the quantity term.

Examples: (1) *A* advertised a sewing machine for sale specifying the make, model and price. The ad is not an offer because there is no language of promise or commitment to any definable persons or for any definable quantity.

(2) A newspaper advertisement stated: "1 Black Lapin Stole, Beautiful, Worth $139.50 . . . $1 First Come First Served." This is an offer because there is language of commitment to an identifiable person ("First Come First Served"), and it states a quantity (one). "One" is also a quantity per person. If the ad had said "10 stoles" instead of "1", it is not clear whether it would be held to be an offer because, although it states a quantity, it does not state a quantity per person.

(3) *A* sends a catalogue to its customers listing the types of items to be sold and the price. The catalogue is not an offer because there is no language of promise and no quantity is stated.

(4) *A* wrote to *B*, "I have 18,000 bu. of millet seed of which I am mailing you a sample. I want $2.25 per cwt. for this seed." *The letter indicated that it was being sent to other potential buyers.* This is a circular letter. There is a fixed quantity, but the general language used is not deemed to be language of commitment. *B*, as a reasonable person, should conclude that *A* was not manifesting an intent to make offers to all of the individuals to whom the letter was sent. It should not be lightly assumed that *A* was manifesting an intent to make offers to all of the individuals to whom the letter was sent because this would expose *A* to multiple acceptances and therefore multiple breaches of contract.

(5) *X*, a supermarket, had a large display of bottled soda on its shelf with a sign stating that the price was six cans for $3. The older view is that this is not an offer, because there is no language of commitment and no quantity stated or at least no quantity per person. Some modern cases hold that it is an offer because there is an implied language of promise to sell the goods on display. These courts do not consider the question of quantity per person. These cases are not concerned with the niceties of the law of contracts. They are more concerned with allowing recovery under a warranty theory in a products liability case in which a bottle placed in the customer's shopping cart explodes, causing injury to the customer.

e. **Offers Distinguished From Price Quotations**
A price quotation is usually a statement of intention to sell at a given unit price. Under this definition the quantity term is not specified, and there is no offer. Even if a quantity term is stated in a communication addressed to an individual, and the word "quote" is used in this communication, it is commonly understood to mean that an offer is invited. But this is not a hard and fast rule; the word "quote" in context may mean "offer." Conversely, the word "offer" may mean "quote".

Examples: (1) *S* writes to *B*, "We quote you Hungarian flour $5.40 per barrel, car lots only. We would suggest your using wire to order as prices are rapidly advancing that they may be beyond reach before a letter would reach us." This is not an offer because even if it is assumed that the word "quote" means "offer" there is still no statement of quantity.

(2) *P* asked for *D*'s price on 1000 gross of Mason Green Jars (quarts). *D* answered, stating a price and other detailed

terms and using the word "quote" but also stating that the reply was "for immediate acceptance." *D*'s answer is an offer, despite the use of the word "quote." The court gave three reasons: (a) It came in response to an inquiry that obviously sought an offer; (b) *D*'s communication contained detailed terms and by implication the quantity of 1000 gross inquired about by *P;* (c) There was the use of the words "for immediate acceptance."

(3) *S* sends a letter to *B* saying, "We quote you two cars Hungarian flour at $5.40 per barrel." Williston indicates that this is an offer but the Restatement, Second, indicates that it should be considered an offer only if the communication contains detailed terms. It is also important to observe that here the alleged offer did not come in response to an inquiry seeking an offer as in example (2). There is no clear answer.

f.   The Offer at Auction
In the case of an auction "with reserve," an offer is made by each bidder, and the auctioneer is free not to accept. In an auction "without reserve," the auctioneer may withdraw the goods only until the first bid is made, provided it is made within a reasonable time. Thereafter, the auctioneer must sell to the highest bidder. However, in either case, a bidder is free to withdraw a bid before the fall of the hammer. A bid terminates all prior bids, but a bidder's retraction does not revive any prior bids. An auction is deemed to be "with reserve" unless it is stated to be "without reserve."

g.   Offer v. Preliminary Negotiations
The term "preliminary negotiations" covers any communication prior to an operative offer. Under this definition, the types of communications already discussed that were not offers amount to preliminary negotiations.

4.   DISTINCTION BETWEEN UNILATERAL AND BILATERAL CONTRACTS
a.   Basis of Distinction
An offer looking to a bilateral contract looks to a promise on the part of the offeree. An offer looking to a unilateral contract looks to an acceptance by performance.

b.   Acceptance of Offer Looking to a Bilateral Contract
An offer looking to a bilateral contract may be accepted by an express promise or an implied promise. In addition, an offer may designate an act that will serve as a promise; e.g., "Blink your eyes three times." According to the First Restatement, even if no promise is made, there is an acceptance if the offeree actually performs the act he was requested to

promise to perform. The performance must be completed while the offer is still open and the requisite notice of performance to the offeror given.

c. Acceptance of an Offer Looking to a Unilateral Contract
An offer looking to a unilateral contract may be accepted only by performance. A promise to perform does not amount to an acceptance.

d. Ambiguous Offer
At times an offer may be worded so that it is not clear whether it looks to a promise or a performance. In such a case, the orthodox view assumed that the offer looks to a bilateral contract.

e. U.C.C. and Restatement, Second
These authorities have changed the common law rules stated above and will be discussed later in this chapter.

Examples: (1) *A* says to *B*, "If you walk across Brooklyn Bridge, I will pay you $10." *A* has made an offer looking to a unilateral contract. *B* must accept by walking. *B* cannot accept by making a promise.

(2) *A* says to *B*, "If you promise to walk across Brooklyn Bridge, I will pay you $10." *A* has made an offer looking to a bilateral contract. If *B* makes the promise, there is an acceptance. There would also be an acceptance if *B* started to walk in *A*'s presence for in this situation *B*'s promise could be inferred. If *B* walked, but not in *A*'s presence, there would be no acceptance except possibly under the Restatement rule stated in 4.b. above.

(3) *A* says to *B*, "If you will paint my house, I promise to pay you $1000." The offer is ambiguous. Therefore, under the view of the first Restatement, it is presumed to be an offer looking to a bilateral contract. The more modern approach is considered at pp. 128–131 infra.

(4) *A*, a house owner, pays $1,000 to an insurance carrier asking for the company's promise to pay $100,000 if the house is destroyed by fire. The insurance company agrees. *A* has made an offer looking to a reverse unilateral contract. This is a situation where the offeror does not make a promise. The only promise is made by the offeree.

(5) *A*, a house owner, promises to pay $1000 to an insurance carrier asking for the company's promise to pay $100,000 if *A*'s house is destroyed by fire. *B* makes the promise, and the

house is destroyed by fire. When *B* makes the promise, there is a bilateral contract. The destruction of the house by fire is a condition precedent to the company's promise to pay $100,000.

C. ACCEPTANCE

1. GENERAL REQUIREMENTS

a. Introduction

An offer creates a power of acceptance in the offeree. The exercise of this power creates the set of legal relations called a contract. The acceptance of the offer terminates the power of revocation that the offeror ordinarily has.

b. Acceptance by Authorized Party

An offer may be accepted only by the person or persons to whom it is made.

The offeror is master of the offer and thus controls who has a power of acceptance. Since the power of acceptance is personal to the offeree, it follows that the offeree may not transfer the power of acceptance to another. To whom an offer is made is determined under the reasonable person test. In most cases the offeree is also the promisee but this is not necessarily so.

Examples: (1) *A* makes a revocable offer to *B*. *C* may not accept even though *B* makes an assignment of rights to *C*.

(2) *A* makes an offer jointly to *B* and *C*. *B* or *C* alone may not accept.

(3) *A* individually is doing business under the trade name of "Acme Supply Company" and *B* sends an order (offer) to "Acme Supply Company". *C* who buys out *A*, including the name, fills the order. The question to be answered is whether a reasonable person would conclude that *B* manifested an intention to make the offer to "Acme Supply Company" irrespective of who owned it. If so, *C* may accept. *C* may not accept if a reasonable person would conclude *B*'s manifested intention was to make an offer to Acme only so long as *A* was the proprietor. This could be a question of fact. If the offer is not made to *C*, there may still be a quasi-contractual recovery.

(4) *A* makes a promise to pay *B* $10 if *C* walks across Brooklyn Bridge. *B* is the promisee, and *C* is the offeree. For *B* to receive the money, *C* must walk Brooklyn Bridge.

Exceptions:

1) Options
    If *A* makes an irrevocable offer (option contract) to *B*, *B* may assign the rights to *C* consistent with the rules governing assignments.

2) Undisclosed Principal
    If the offeror has indicated a refusal to deal with a given person, an offeree who obtains an offer as an undisclosed agent for that person may not accept the offer.

c. **Knowledge of the Offer and Intent to Accept**
    The offeree must know of the offer and intend to accept.

    1) Knowledge of the Offer
        The rule that the offeree must know of the offer is always applied to a unilateral contract. In the case of an offer looking to a bilateral contract, this rule may come into conflict with the objective theory of contracts. In such a situation, the objective theory prevails. The principle that an offeree must know of the offer gives rise to the rule that identical cross offers do not create a contract. There is some conflict as to when knowledge of the offer must exist.

        Examples: (1) *A* writes to *B*, "If you walk across Brooklyn Bridge, I promise to pay you $10." Unless *B* knew of the offer, *B* would not recover even if *B* did the act called for. Note that this is an offer to a unilateral contract. Walking across the bridge is not objectively referrable to knowledge of the offer. There is a small minority view, but only in the case of reward offers, permitting recovery despite ignorance of the reward offer. The minority view at times has been applied to statutory rewards.

        (2) *A* sends an offer looking to a bilateral contract to *B* by mail. When *B* receives the letter, without opening it and without suspecting that it is an offer, *B* decides to confuse *A* by sending a letter which states, "I accept." *B* does not know of the existence of the offer, and so it could be held that there is no contract. But under the objective theory of contracts, there is an acceptance because *A*, as a reasonable person, could conclude that *B* accepted. The objective theory prevails, and there is a

contract. As stated above, this problem cannot arise in the case of an offer looking to a unilateral contract.

(3) *A* sends an offer through the mail to *B* offering to sell a certain item at a certain price. *B*, in ignorance of this offer, mails an offer to buy the same item at the same price. Because neither party knows of the offer of the other, there is no acceptance. This is a situation involving identical cross offers. The Restatement, Second, attempts a partial subversion of this rule when it asserts that two offerors could assent in advance to cross offers and suggests that such assent may be inferred when both parties think a contract has been made.

(4) *A* offers a reward of $100 to anyone who finds and returns a lost watch. *B* finds the watch, learns of the reward and returns it to *A*. The traditional rule is that *B* may not recover because *B* did not know of the offer at the start of performance. In other words, knowledge must exist when the offeree starts to perform. The more modern view is that it is sufficient that the offeree completes performance with knowledge of the offer.

2) Intent to Accept

In the case of an offer looking to a unilateral contract, the offeree must intend to accept. There are some other questions that are answered in the examples below. In the case of an offer looking to a bilateral contract, it is again possible to have a contract without an intent to accept because of the objective theory of contracts.

Examples: (1) *A* makes an offer to *B* looking to a bilateral contract. *B*, not intending to accept, carelessly mails an acceptance. There is a contract under the objective theory of contracts even though *B* did not intend to accept.

(2) *A* says to *B*, "I will pay you $10 if you walk across Brooklyn Bridge." *B* walks. It is clear that *B*'s walking is ambiguous on the issue of intent to accept. *B* may have walked to gain the $10 or to get exercise or from a combination of these two motives. To solve this problem, the traditional view is that *B* may testify that the walking was done with the intent to accept and, if believed, *B* will prevail. This will be true even if the trier of fact concludes that *B* performed for many reasons so long as one of them was to obtain the $10. A more modern view is that *B* may not testify to subjective

intention. Under this view, intent to accept is presumed in the absence of words or conduct to the contrary. Since the attempt to accept is merely assumed, if the offeree manifests an intent not to accept before the *offeror* performs, a disclaimer is effective and renders the promise of the offeror inoperative from the beginning.

(3) *A* makes an offer for information leading to the apprehension and conviction of a certain criminal. *B*, a friend of the criminal, is intimidated into giving vital information when interrogated by the police. *B* cannot collect the reward, because the acceptance is not intentional or voluntary.

d. Necessity for Communication in a Bilateral Contract
To create a bilateral contract, the offeree's promise must be communicated to the offeror.

1) Theory
   The offeree as a reasonable person should understand that the offeror expects to know that the offeree has made the requested return promise so that the offeror's conduct may be guided accordingly.

   Exception: Since the offeror is the master of the offer, the offeror may dispense with the need for communication.

   Examples: (1) *A* makes an offer to *B*. *B* tells *C,* a friend, that "I accept." There is no contract. If *C* were *A*'s agent, the result would be different.

                   (2) *A*, an agent for *B* Corp., presents *C* with a document that states the terms of a bilateral arrangement but adds that a contract will arise when approved by an executive officer of *B*. *C* signs the document. *B* Corp. has not made an offer, because *B* did not commit itself to anything. Its document stated that approval by an executive officer would be *B*'s commitment. Although *B* did not make an offer, *C* does when *C* signs the document. *C*'s offer includes the term relating to approval by an executive officer. This offer is accepted by *B* when the offer is approved by an executive officer even though acceptance is not communicated. The theory is that the language used in the offer dispenses with the necessity of communication.

e. Necessity for Notice of Performance in a Unilateral Contract

1) Introduction

A unilateral contract arises upon performance. Must notice of performance be given to the offeror by the offeree? There are three views.

2) Views

(a) If the offeree has reason to know that the offeror has no adequate means of learning of performance with reasonable promptness and certitude, the duty of the offeror is discharged. This is so unless the offeree exercises reasonable diligence to notify the offeror, or the offeror otherwise learns of performance within a reasonable time or the offeror expressly or by implication indicates that notice is not necessary.

(b) Same as (a) above except that, if notice is required, no contract is consummated until notice of performance has been sent.

(c) Notice is not required unless requested by the offeror.

3) Discussion of View (a)

The rule, supported by both Restatements, is designed to balance two factors. The offeror may wish to know that the act has been performed to avoid making a contract with another with respect to the same subject matter. On the other hand, if the offeror is in a position to learn of performance, notice should not be required. It is an exceptional case in which the offeror does not have the means of finding out what happened. Therefore, the offeror has a duty of inquiry, unless inquiry is not feasible.

Examples: (1) *A* makes an offer looking to a unilateral contract on November 1. The act called for is performed on November 2. A revocation takes place on November 3 and notice of performance is sent on November 4. According to the rule stated above, the revocation would not be effective because the acceptance had already taken place. Assuming that notice is required under the rule stated, the requisite is satisfied because the offeree has exercised reasonable diligence to give timely notice to the offeror. Under view (b) the revocation would be effective, unless the offer is irrevocable. There is no problem under view (c) because the offer did not specify that notice be given.

(2) Assume the same facts as above, except that notice of performance was not timely given. Under rule (a) the

contract that arose when there was performance is discharged by the failure to give notice. Stated another way, giving notice is a condition precedent to *A* 's obligation to perform. Under rule (b) there is no contract. Again there is no problem under rule (c).

(3) *G,* a guarantor, makes an offer to *C,* who lives in a foreign country, that if *C* delivers certain merchandise to *G*'s brother *P,* he, *G,* will pay if *P* does not. According to the Restatements, *C* is obliged to give notice of performance, otherwise *G* 's duty will be discharged.

f. Acceptance of an Offer Looking to a Series of Contracts

Generally, offers look either to a single bilateral or a single unilateral contract. But an offer may instead look to the formation of a number (series) of contracts, unilateral or bilateral. In this situation, the offer continues after the first contract is formed, so that the possibility of other contracts being formed exists. However, as to the future, the offer is as revocable as any other offer. Care must be taken to distinguish an offer looking to a series of acceptances from an offer looking to one acceptance with a series of performances. This distinction is a question of the intention of the parties and is often one of fact.

Examples: (1) *A,* on January 1, writes to *B,* "in consideration of your advancing money from time to time over the next twelve calendar months up to $5000, to *X,* at *X* 's request, at your option, I hereby undertake to make good any losses you may sustain in consequence." *B* lends $1000 to *X* on February 1, and another $1000 on March 1. *A* then revokes the offer. *B* makes an additional loan of $1000 on March 15. *A* 's offer looked to a series of unilateral contracts. The advance made on February 1 gave rise to a unilateral contract. The advance made on March 1 gave rise to a second unilateral contract. The offer continued into the future, but was terminated by revocation. Thus, the third acceptance on March 15 was preceded by a revocation and therefore ineffective. If this is a case where notice of performance is required, one notice would probably suffice.

(2) *A* offers *B* stated quantities of certain goods as *B* may order from time to time during the next year at fixed prices. *A* has made an offer looking to a series of bilateral contracts. The series is bilateral because each time *B* places an order *B* impliedly promises to pay.

(3) *A* offers to sell *B* 6000 tons of a specified type of coal, deliveries to be made in equal monthly installments during the months of May, June, July and August. The offer looks to one bilateral contract which will arise if and when *B* accepts. However, there will be a series of performances under the contract.

2.   ACCEPTANCE OF A BILATERAL CONTRACT
a.   Acceptance by Silence
Silence ordinarily does not give rise to an acceptance of an offer or a counter offer.

Exceptions:

(1)   The rule does not apply where:

(a) the offeror has given the offeree reason to believe that silence will act as an acceptance and the offeree intends by silence to accept; (see illustration 1)

(b) the parties have mutually agreed that silence will operate as assent;

(c) there is a course of dealing whereby silence has come to mean assent;

(d) someone takes offered services with a reasonable opportunity to reject them, and it is reasonable for the person to understand that the services are offered with expectation of payment.

Theory: The question is whether silence may amount to a promise. The issue to be resolved is whether the relationship of the parties and the fact pattern justifies the offeror's expectation of reply. In other words, when silence would be deceptive, there is a duty to speak.

Examples: (1) *A* makes an unsolicited offer to *B* by mail in which *A* states, "If I do not hear from you by next Tuesday, I shall assume you accept." *B* is silent. *B* has no duty to reply and does not remain silent at his peril, but it is agreed that *B* can accept by communicating an acceptance. Under the Restatement view, if *B* remains silent intending to accept, there is a contract. Because of the ambiguity, *B* may testify on *B*'s subjective intention to accept. This then creates a question of fact.

(2) *A* says to *B*, "I offer to sell you my black horse for $200." *B* replies, "If you don't hear from me by next Tuesday, you may assume that I accept." *A* agrees. By virtue of the agreement of both parties, *B* has a duty to speak. B's silence will constitute an acceptance.

(3) *A* wires *B* requesting that certain goods be sent on approval. *B* sends the merchandise. *A* fails to return the goods within a reasonable time. *A*'s acceptance is implied.

(4) *A*, the offeror, on a number of occasions has sent unsolicited goods to *B* who has always paid for the goods without protest. *A* makes an additional shipment of similar goods, and *B* retains the goods for an unreasonable period of time without notifying *A* that this time the goods are not wanted. *A*, as a reasonable person, could conclude that the offer was accepted because of *B*'s retention of the goods in the light of the prior course of dealing. The question may be one of fact. In this case, evidence of subjective intention is not admissible.

(5) *A*, through a salesman, has frequently solicited orders from *B*, the contract to arise when approved by *A* at *A*'s home office. *A* has always shipped the goods to *B* without prior notification and has billed for them after shipment. *A*'s salesman solicits and receives another order from *B*. *A* remains silent for a period of time. The issue is whether the offeror (*B*) would reasonably conclude that *A*'s silence indicated assent. Again, the question may be one of fact, and again evidence of subjective intention is inadmissible.

(6) *I*'s agent seeks to sell *A* insurance. *A* fills out the application and gives it to the agent together with a premium. It is clear that *I* must approve the application before there is a binding agreement. According to one view, acceptance may be implied from the retention of the premium and failure to reject within a reasonable time.

(7) *B*, the owner of property, sees *A*, a stranger, cutting *B*'s lawn and does nothing to stop *A*. *B* is liable because there is an opportunity to reject the services and, as a reasonable person, should understand that *A* expects to be compensated.

(8) Assume the same facts as in example (7), above, except that the grass is being cut by *S*, *B*'s son. Although *B* has an opportunity to reject the services, a reasonable person

could conclude that *S* did not expect to be compensated. When the services are rendered within the family relationship there is no reason to conclude that compensation is expected. There is a presumption that the services are rendered without expectation of compensation. The presumption may be rebutted. A family relationship can arise through blood, marriage, or by living together as a family, or a combination of the above.

b. Acceptance by Conduct
1) Discussion

Just as an offer may be accepted by silence, it may also be accepted by conduct. In addition, an acceptance may arise as a result of an act of dominion. An act of dominion is one's exercise of power over property as if one were the owner. If wrongful, the act of dominion results in the tort of conversion. But if the act of dominion constitutes an acceptance, it is not wrongful and there is not a conversion. This occurs when the offeree's act of dominion is referable to a power of acceptance granted by the offeror. In other words, in exercising dominion, the offeree is deemed to manifest an intent to accept. If the exercise of dominion is wrongful, as where the offeree takes the goods stating that the offer is rejected, the offeror has the option of proceeding upon a contract or tort theory because the offeree will be estopped, if the offeror wishes, from asserting that the conduct was tortious. U.C.C. § 2–606(1)(c).

Examples: (1) *A*, passing a market, picks up an apple from a box marked "30 cents ea." and holds it up so that the clerk sees it and nods assent. *A* has made an offer by conduct, and the clerk has accepted in the same way. A promise that arises by conduct is often referred to as an implied-in-fact contract.

(2) *A* sends a book to *B* saying, "If you wish to buy this book send me $6.50 within one week after receipt hereof, otherwise notify me, and I will forward postage for return." *B*, without replying, makes a gift of it to his wife. *B*'s act is an act of dominion referable to the offer. *B* has accepted the offer.

(3) The facts being otherwise as stated above, *B* writes to *A* stating that he has taken the book but that it is worth only $5.00 and that *B* will pay no more. Here the act of dominion is wrongful, because it is not referable to the offer made by *A* in the light of the letter sent by *B*. That letter shows that *B* does not intend to accept the

offered price.   Nonetheless, the offeror may sue either upon a theory of contract or conversion.   A fictitious contract is created by preventing *B* from testifying that *B*'s own conduct is wrongful when it could be referable to a lawful intent.   But *A* may not sue upon a contract theory if the offered terms are manifestly unreasonable. The measure of damages will be different depending upon the theory (contract or tort) selected.

(4) *S* (seller) sends a freezer unit on approval to *B*.   *B* used the freezer unit to operate an air conditioner.   *B* denies any intention to accept and claims the exercise of dominion was wrongful.   Thus *S* has the option of suing in tort or contract.   Note that in cases where persons claim their own conduct is wrongful, the motive usually is to escape contract prices that are allegedly more than the value of the goods.

2) Statutory Exceptions
In order to discourage the unsolicited sending of goods to unwary customers, several states have enacted legislation making it unlawful to offer merchandise for sale by the unsolicited sending of goods. These statutes generally also provide that a person who receives such goods has a complete defense to an action by the offeror.   The Postal Reorganization Act of 1970 provides that one who receives "unordered merchandise" by mail may treat the transaction as a gift.

c. When Is an Acceptance Effective?
1) Introduction
We have previously seen that ordinarily an acceptance in a bilateral contract must be communicated.   Is the acceptance effective when it is put out of the possession of the offeree or when it is received?

2) Prescribed Method of Acceptance
If the offeror prescribes an exclusive method of acceptance, a contract does not arise if the offeree uses another means of acceptance even if it comes to the attention of the offeror.   In this event the defective acceptance is treated as an offer.   The courts are reluctant to find that an exclusive means of acceptance has been prescribed.

Examples: (1) *A* offers to sell his land to *B* on certain terms.   The offer also states, "You must accept this, if at all, in person, in my office at ten o'clock tomorrow."   *B* sends a messenger who is on time and "accepts" the offer.   The words "if at all" make it clear that "in person" is prescribed as an exclusive method of acceptance.   Thus the attempted acceptance by the messenger is ineffective. This defective acceptance is treated as an offer that *A* may in turn accept.

(2) *A* makes an offer to *B* stating, "This offer shall be accepted by signing in the appropriate place and returning to me." According to some cases (probably a majority) signing and returning is not prescribed. Courts are reluctant to find that an exclusive means of acceptance has been prescribed. If there is not a prescribed method of acceptance, the rules stated in 3 below will apply.

3) Parties at a Distance
   a) Use of Authorized Means of Acceptance (Mailbox Rule)
   An acceptance by an authorized means is effective when the offeree has surrendered possession of the acceptance. The original Restatement states that in the absence of contrary indication, the offeror authorizes the means of communication authorized in transmitting the offer, and any other means customary at the time and place received.

   b) Unauthorized Means of Acceptance
   If an unauthorized means of acceptance is used, or an authorized means is carelessly used (improper addressing, insufficient postage, etc.), the acceptance will be effective upon receipt, provided the offer is still open upon its receipt.

   c) U.C.C. and Restatement Second
   Under the U.C.C. and the Restatement, Second, the means of acceptance need not be authorized but need only be "reasonable." The concept of reasonability is intended to be flexible and to enlarge upon the concept of "authorized." Under the Restatement, Second, even if an unreasonable means is used, it nevertheless will be effective when dispatched provided it is seasonably dispatched and provided it is received within the time a seasonably dispatched acceptance sent in a reasonable manner would normally have arrived. The Restatement, Second, has a similar rule where an authorized means is carelessly used. It states that the acceptance is effective when sent provided that it is seasonably dispatched and provided that it is received within the time a seasonably dispatched properly stamped and addressed acceptance would normally have arrived. The U.C.C. (§ 1–201(38)) has a similar rule with respect to carelessness. But it does not state any rule to cover a situation where an unreasonable means of acceptance is used.

Examples: (1) *A* makes an offer to *B* by telegram on Monday, stating that the offer lapses on Wednesday at noon. *B* mails an acceptance on Tuesday which *A* receives on Wednesday morning. *A* telephones a revocation on Tuesday afternoon. Assuming that the letter is an unauthorized (unreasonable) medium of acceptance, the revocation is ineffective because the acceptance was received within the time that a seasonably dispatched acceptance normally would have arrived. Under this rule, one must compare the actual acceptance with a hypothetical acceptance. The question is, did the unauthorized acceptance arrive before the authorized acceptance would have arrived? If the actual acceptance arrives before the hypothetical acceptance would have, the revocation is ineffective. Here the actual acceptance is received on Wednesday morning. The hypothetical acceptance would have been mailed on Wednesday noon. This acceptance would have been received later than Wednesday morning. Therefore, the revocation is ineffective.

d.   Offeror's Power to Negate Mailbox Rule

An offeror may negate the mailbox rule by providing in the offer that the acceptance will be effective only when and if received.

Examples: (1) *A* made an offer to *B*. *A* added; "Telegraph me 'yes' or 'no'. If I do not hear from you by the 20th, I shall conclude 'no'." *B* immediately telegraphed an "acceptance" which was never received by *A*. There is no contract because the language, "If I do not hear from you," etc. negates the mailbox rule.

(2) *D* sent an offer to *B* by mail. The last sentence of the offer read: "As soon as acceptance is received we shall send amongst the farmers and secure the first lots." *B* promptly sent a letter of acceptance which was lost and never received. The language does not negate the mailbox rule because it can be interpreted to mean that the offeror will act promptly once the acceptance is received, rather than that the acceptance is contingent on receipt. Therefore, there is a contract.

e.   When Offeree Sends Both Acceptance and Rejection
The rule that an acceptance is effective when sent is troublesome when the offeree sends both an acceptance and a rejection. A rejection, as we shall see, is effective when received.

1)   When a Rejection Is Sent First
An acceptance dispatched after a rejection has been sent is not effective until received and then only if received prior to the rejection.

> ***Examples:*** (1) Rejection sent, acceptance sent, rejection received, acceptance received. There is no contract and the acceptance is regarded as a counter-offer.
>
> (2) Rejection sent, acceptance sent, acceptance received, rejection received. There is a contract.

2)   When an Acceptance Is Sent First

> ***Example:*** Acceptance sent, rejection sent, rejection received, acceptance received. There is authority, including the Restatement, that a contract is formed. Otherwise the offeree could speculate at the offeror's expense by seeing how the market went. However, if the offeror relies on the rejection before receiving the acceptance, the offeree will be estopped from enforcing the agreement. Under the Restatement view, the overtaking rejection may be looked upon as an offer to rescind the contract or a repudiation.

3)   Lost or Delayed Acceptance
The majority rule is that the mailbox rule also applies to a lost or delayed acceptance. But according to the Restatement, Second, the offeror will not be guilty of a breach of contract unless the offeror receives notice from the offeree that the contract has been formed.

> ***Example:*** *A* offers to buy cattle for *B* from a third party on the understanding that if *B* telegraphs "yes", *A* will notify *B* of the amount of money needed, and *B* will supply the money. *B*'s "yes" telegram is duly dispatched but does not arrive within a reasonable time. According to the Restatement, Second, the contract formed by the dispatch of the telegram is discharged. The theory is that a condition of receipt of the acceptance should normally be implied where notice of acceptance is essential to enable the offeror to perform.

4)   Withdrawal of Acceptance
     If the offeree sends an acceptance that is effective when sent and is
     able to retrieve the acceptance in conformity with postal regulations,
     it is generally agreed that the withdrawal is ineffective.   There is a
     contract.   It may be, as a practical matter, that the acceptance will
     not come to the attention of the offeror.

5)   Parties in the Presence of One Another
     When the parties are in the presence of each other an acceptance is
     inoperative unless the offeror hears it or was at fault in not hearing
     it.   Even if the offeror is at fault in not hearing, there is still no
     contract if the offeree knows or has reason to know the offeror has
     not heard.

f.   **Risk of Mistake in Transmission by an Intermediary**
     1)   Introduction
          This topic involves a species of mistake that does not involve a
          mistake of a party or an agent, but rather a mistake by an
          independent contractor, such as a telegraph company.   It does not
          relate to a message that is not received, but to one that is received
          but is incorrectly transmitted.

          *The message as transmitted is operative unless the other party knows or
          has reason to know of the mistake.*

          Examples: (1) *A* deposits a message to *B* with the telegraph
                         company stating an offer to sell a horse, Beauty, for
                         $110.   When the message is transmitted, it states $100.
                         B accepts.   There is a contract based on the $100 figure.

                         (2) *A* makes an offer to sell the horse for $100.   *B*'s
                         reply is "no," but is transmitted as "yes."   There is a
                         contract.

                         (3) Assume the same facts as (1) above, except that the
                         message transmitted contained the price of $1.   There is
                         no contract, if by virtue of the magnitude of the
                         discrepancy, *B* knew or should have known of the
                         mistake.

     2)   Minority View
          This view holds that there is no contract, because the telegraph
          company is an independent contractor and the general rule is that
          one who hires an independent contractor is not liable for the
          negligence of the contractor.

3) Liability of the Intermediary

Once it is determined which of the two innocent parties must suffer a loss, it is clear that the injured party has a cause of action against the telegraph company. The sender of the telegram that is erroneously transmitted has an action for breach of contract. The other party, if damaged, has a tort action. However, the contract remedy may prove to be unsatisfactory because telegraph companies by agreement usually limit their liability. These limitations of liability have generally been upheld by federal regulation.

D. TERMINATION OF REVOCABLE OFFERS

1. INTRODUCTION

To ripen into a contract, a revocable offer must be accepted before the power of acceptance created by the offeror is terminated. It may be terminated in a number of ways.

a. Lapse of Time

An offer is terminated after the lapse of time specified in the offer or, if no time is specified, after a reasonable time has elapsed.

1) Time Specified in the Offer

A sends a letter to *B,* dated January 29, which states "Will give you eight days to accept or reject." *B* receives the offer on February 2 and on February 8 sends a letter of acceptance which is received on February 9. By its terms, the offer lapses after eight days, but the question is whether the eight days should be measured from January 29 or February 2. The generally accepted notion is that, in the absence of countervailing indications, the eight days should be measured from the day the offer is received. Hence, on the facts, the acceptance is timely. If the offer were delayed in the course of the post, the question becomes whether the eight days would be measured from the date it was received or when it should have been received. If the offeree knows, or has reason to know, of the delay, eight days should be measured from the date it should have been received. This is so even if the delay is due to the fault of the offeror.

2) Time not Specified in Offer

If the duration of the power of acceptance is not stated, it is deemed to be open for a reasonable time.

What is a reasonable time is ordinarily a question of fact depending upon the circumstances of the case including whether the transaction is speculative or not and the manifest purpose of the offeror. The

Restatement, Second, adds to these considerations the question of whether or not the offeree is acting in good faith.

a) Face to Face Offer
Where the offer is made in a face to face conversation, or in any other situation where there are direct negotiations, the offer is deemed, in the absence of a manifestation to the contrary, to be open only when the parties are conversing.

3) Termination Upon the Happening of a Particular Event
The offeror may stipulate in his offer that the power of acceptance shall terminate upon the happening of a certain event. If the event happens before the acceptance, the power of acceptance lapses even though the offeree does not know that the event has occurred.

4) Effect of Late Acceptance
If an offer lapses before an acceptance becomes effective, it would seem to follow that the late acceptance is an offer which in turn can be accepted only by a communicated acceptance. But this is only one of three views. A second view is that the offeror may treat the late acceptance as an acceptance by waiving the lateness without communicating this fact to the offeree at any particular time or perhaps "without limitation of time." Under an intermediate view, if the acceptance is late but sent in what could plausibly be argued to be a reasonable time, the original offeror has a duty to reply within a reasonable time. Otherwise, there is a contract. The theory is that the late acceptance is an offer that is accepted by silence. There is a duty to speak because it is not clear to the offeree that the original acceptance is late.

b. Death or Lack of Capacity
1) Death of Offeror
If the offeror dies between the making of the offer and the acceptance, the offer is terminated even if the offeree was unaware of the offeror's death. A minority view states that the death terminates the offer only if the offeree is aware of it.

> ***Examples:*** (1) *A* makes an offer to *B* looking to a bilateral contract. Before *B* accepts, *A* dies. *B* is not aware of *A*'s death. Under the majority view, *A*'s death terminates the offer. Under the minority view, there is a contract if *B* accepts in otherwise timely fashion.
>
> (2) *A* makes an offer to *B* looking to a bilateral contract. *B* accepts, *A* dies. The rule stated does not apply, because the death occurred after the acceptance. The

issue now is whether there is impossibility of performance of an existing contract. This topic is discussed below.

2)   Incapacity of Offeror
   a)   Adjudication of Incapacity
      Where there is an adjudication of mental illness or defect and, as a result, the property of the mental defective is placed under guardianship, any unaccepted offer previously made by the mental defective is terminated. This is so even though the offeree is unaware of what has transpired. There is a minority view to the contrary. Courts have generally applied the same rule in the case of an appointment of a guardian because of physical incapacity.

   b)   No Adjudication of Incapacity
      If there is no adjudication of incompetency, supervening mental incapacity terminates the offer if the offeree is or should be aware of the incapacity. What constitutes mental incapacity is discussed below.

3)   Death or Incapacity of the Offeree
      The supervening death or adjudication of incapacity of the offeree will prevent the offeree's representative from accepting the offer.

c.   **Revocation**
   1)   Direct Revocation
      If an offer has not been accepted, it may be terminated by a communicated revocation. Under the majority view, a revocation is effective when received. By statute, in some states, it is effective on dispatch. A written communication is received when the writing comes into the possession of the person addressed or of a person authorized to receive it, or when it is deposited in some place authorized by the person addressed as the place for this or similar communications to be deposited.

      Example: A mails an offer to B. B deposits an acceptance in the mailbox at 2:00 P.M. At 1:00 P.M. the same day, A deposits a letter of revocation which is received the next morning. Under the mailbox rule, the acceptance is effective at 2:00 P.M. Under the majority view, the revocation is effective when received. Therefore, there is a contract. Under the statutes mentioned, there is no contract because the revocation is effective when dispatched.

2)   Equal Publicity
     When an offer is made to a number of persons whose identity is
     unknown to the offeror, as for example a reward offer in a
     newspaper, the offer may be revoked by giving the revocation
     publicity equal to that given to the offer. Normally, this is
     accomplished by using the same medium for the revocation as was
     used for the offer. But even here, if the offeror knows of the identity
     of persons who are taking action on the offer, the revocation must be
     communicated to them.

3)   Indirect Revocation
     *Indirect revocation occurs when the offeree acquires reliable information
     that the offeror has engaged in conduct which would indicate to a
     reasonable person that the offeror no longer wishes to make the offer.*

     a)   Reliable Information
          Information is reliable if it is both objectively and subjectively
          reliable. Objectively reliable means that the information must be
          true. Subjectively reliable means that the information must come
          from a reliable source. If the source is not reliable, it may be
          ignored: if it is reliable inquiry should be made into its validity.

          Examples: (1) *D* is the owner of real property. *D* makes an
                          offer to sell the property to *P*. Later, while the
                          offer to *P* was still open, *D* contracted to sell the
                          same property to *A*. After *P* had received reliable
                          information of *D*'s contract with *A*, *P* attempted to
                          accept. The doctrine of indirect revocation applies,
                          because there was reliable information and conduct
                          (the contract of sale) which would indicate to *P*, as a
                          reasonable person, that *D* no longer wished to make
                          the offer. *D* would not wish to be under an
                          obligation to sell the same property twice when only
                          one sale could be made.

                          (2) Assume the same facts as above, except that *P*
                          hears that *D* has made an offer to sell the same
                          property to *A*. Would a reasonable person in *P*'s
                          position conclude that the offeror no longer wished
                          to keep open the offer to *P*? It could be argued that
                          P should conclude that *D* did not wish exposure to
                          double liability, but it could also be concluded that
                          because *D* did not bother to communicate a
                          revocation, *D* is willing to run the risk of making
                          two offers. The second view seems preferable. If
                          the second offeree learned of the first offer before

accepting, it is even clearer that the doctrine of indirect revocation would not apply.

b) **Limitations on the Doctrine**
The original Restatement limited the doctrine of indirect revocation to cases involving the sale of land and specific chattels. The Restatement, Second, removes these limitations.

c) **Special Problems Relating to Revocation of a Unilateral Offer**
The traditional, but obsolete, rule is that the offer to a unilateral contract may be revoked at any time up until the moment of complete performance because complete performance is required to accept the offer. This is an unfair approach. A second view is that a bilateral contract is formed with the beginning of performance. The modern and prevailing view is that once the offeree starts to perform, or tenders performance, the offer becomes irrevocable. Under this view, the offeree who has commenced or tendered performance is not obligated to complete the performance, but is not entitled to claim the offeror's promised performance without completing performance within the time allowable. If the offeror repudiates after the beginning of performance, the offeree has a contractual cause of action because the failure to complete performance is excused.

Examples: (1) *A* says to *B*, "If you paint my house according to the specifications set forth, I'll pay you $5000." When *B* is half finished, *A* says, "I have changed my mind." Under the first view, this is an effective revocation. Under the second view, the beginning of performance creates a bilateral contract and there is no longer any possibility of revocation. Under the third view, the offer became irrevocable when *B* began to perform. *A* may not revoke. Nonetheless, under the second and third views, *B* should quit painting because of the doctrine of mitigation of damages.

(2) *A* makes an offer to *B* looking to a unilateral contract. *B* starts to perform and *A* dies. Under the first view, the offer is terminated. Under the second view, there is a bilateral contract. Under the third view, the offer is irrevocable and not terminated.

d) Additional Problems Under Third View
(1) Preparation v. Performance
Under the third view, the offer becomes irrevocable only if the offeree has actually started to perform or has tendered part performance. Mere preparation is not enough. This distinction also applies to the second view.

(2) Promissory Estoppel
Preparation for performance by an offeree may create a right to relief under the doctrine of promissory estoppel.

d. Death or Destruction
Death or destruction of a person or thing essential for the performance of the offered contract terminates the offer if it occurs before acceptance.

e. Supervening Illegality
If between the time of the making of the offer and the acceptance, a change of law or regulation renders the proposed contract illegal, the offer is terminated.

f. Rejection or Counter Offer by Offeree
1) Common Law
An offeree's power of acceptance is terminated by a rejection or a counter offer, unless the offeror or the offeree manifests a contrary intention.

Discussion: A rejection is a statement by the offeree declining to accept the offer. A counter offer is a response to an offer that adds qualifications or conditions. A counter offer acts as a rejection even if the qualification or condition relates to a trivial matter ("ribbon matching" or "mirror image" rule). A counter offer may in turn be accepted. A rejection is effective when it is received.

Examples: (1) *A* makes an offer to *B*. *B* accepts but adds: "Prompt acknowledgement must be made of receipt of this letter." Under the mirror image rule, this is a counter offer because the alleged acceptance states a qualification or condition. Therefore it operates as a rejection.

(2) *A* makes an offer to *B*. *B* replies, "for the present, I reject your offer, but I am keeping it under advisement." Although the language is language of rejection, it does not terminate the offer because the offeree manifests a contrary intention by using the words "keeping it under advisement."

a) Counter Offer Distinguished From Other Communications
A counter offer must be distinguished from a counter inquiry, a comment upon the terms, a request for the modification of an offer, a request for a modification of the contract, a grumbling assent, an acceptance plus a separate offer, and a future acceptance. If an acceptance contains a term that is not expressly stated in the offer, but is implied therein, there is an acceptance and not a counter offer.

Examples: (1) *A* makes an offer to *B* to sell an object to *B* for $100.

(a) *B* says "I'll pay $80." This is a counter offer that terminates the offer. A later attempted acceptance is ineffective.

(b) *B* replies: "Will you take $80?" This is a counter inquiry and does not terminate the offer.

(c) *B* replies: "Your price is too high." This is considered to be a comment upon the terms.

(d) *B* replies: "Send lowest cash price." This is a request for a modification of the offer.

(e) *B* replies: "I accept, but I would appreciate it if you give me the benefit of a 5% discount." This is an acceptance. The 5% clause is not a qualification or condition. It merely requests or suggests the addition of this term and is a request for modification of the contract.

(f) *B* says "Send me the object but I wish you would give us a better price." This has been described as a "grumbling assent."

(2) *A* offers to sell specified hardware to *B* on stated terms. *B* replies, "I accept your offer; ship in accordance therewith. Please send me also one No. 5 hand saw at your list price." There is a contract. *B* has made a separate offer, not a counter offer.

(3) *G*, a general contractor, is about to bid on a project. *G* receives a bid (offer) from *S*, a subcontractor. *G* accepts the offer on the condition that *G*'s bid is successful. *S*, either expressly or

impliedly, agrees to the condition. The parties are not presently bound. But once the future event (the award of the general contract to *G*) occurs, neither party is free to withdraw. There is no further necessity for any additional manifestation of intention. But it may be necessary for the offeror to give the offeree notice that the event has occurred. This situation is referred to as a future acceptance.

(4) *A* makes a written offer to *B* to sell Blackacre. *B* replies: "I accept your offer, if you can convey me a good title." Because good title is already implicit in the offer, there is an acceptance and not a counter offer.

2) U.C.C. Section 2–207
  a) Introduction
  This section is designed to negate the "mirror image" rule in cases involving the sale of goods. It is also designed to change the "last shot" principle of the common law. The first two subdivisions relate to the mirror image rule and the third relates to the "last shot" principle.

  b) The Framework of the Statute
  Whether or not there is a contract by virtue of the communication of the parties is determined under the provisions of subdivision 1. If it is decided that there is a contract, then subdivision 2 determines the terms of the contract. If there is no contract by virtue of the communications of the parties, then subdivision 3 determines whether there is a contract formed by the conduct of the parties and the terms of such a contract.

  c) Subdivision 1
  This subdivision provides that, even though the alleged acceptance contains "additional" or "different" terms (so that at common law there would be a counter offer), there is an acceptance provided (1) the alleged acceptance amounts to a "definite and seasonable expression of acceptance" and (2) the acceptance "is not expressly made conditional on assent to the additional or different terms."

    (1) Definite Expression of Acceptance
    What constitutes a definite expression of acceptance under the Code is not precisely clear. It is clear that the alleged acceptance must purport to be an acceptance. It is also clear that the existence of an additional or a different term does not prevent the communication from being an

acceptance. But according to the majority of cases, if the acceptance diverges significantly from the offer as to a dickered term, there is not a definite expression of acceptance. Dickered terms certainly include the description of the goods, price, quantity and delivery terms.

Examples: (1) *A* makes an offer to buy a drum of emulsion from *B*. *B* immediately sends an acknowledgement and an invoice repeating the dickered terms but negating implied warranties. There is a definite and seasonable expression of acceptance. Warranties are not generally considered to be dickered terms. (But if the parties "haggle" over a warranty or any other term, it is a dickered term.)

(2) *A* makes an offer to sell *B* 10 drums of emulsion. *B* sends a communication purporting to accept 5 drums. According to one view, there is not a definite and seasonable expression of acceptance. Quantity, above all other terms, is likely to be deemed a dickered term.

(2)   Not Conditional on Assent
According to the vast majority of the cases, the statutory words—"unless acceptance is expressly made conditional on assent to the additional or different terms"—are to be taken literally.

Examples: (1) *A* makes an offer to *B*. *B* sends what appears to be an acceptance but adds, "This acceptance is expressly made conditional on assent to the new terms contained herein." Here the acceptance is conditional on assent to the additional terms.

(2) *A* makes an offer to buy a certain item from *B*. *B* sends an acknowledgment and invoice that repeats the dickered terms of the offer and adds: "All goods sold without warranties express or implied. Seller's liability hereunder shall be limited to the replacement of any goods that materially differ from the seller's sample." The acceptance is not expressly made conditional on assent to the additional or different terms,

because the words used are not conditional upon the express assent of *A* to the additional terms.

(3) Structure Reemphasized

Once it is decided that there "is a definite and seasonable expression of acceptance," and that the acceptance is not "expressly made conditional on assent to the additional or different terms," there is a contract by virtue of the communications of the parties. One then proceeds to Subdivision 2 to ascertain whether the additional or different terms incorporated into the acceptance become part of the contract.

d) Subdivision 2

(1) Introduction

In this subdivision the statute makes a distinction between merchants and non-merchants. One must also consider the meaning of the words "additional" and "different" terms.

(2) Additional Terms—Non-merchants

If either of the parties is *not* a merchant, the statute states that "additional terms are to be construed as proposals for addition to the contract." This means that the additional term or terms stated in the acceptance do not become part of the contract unless accepted by the offeror.

Examples: *A*, a non-merchant, makes an offer to *B*, a merchant. *B* accepts under the provision of subdivision 1, but includes an arbitration clause in the acceptance (additional term). Because one of the parties is not a merchant, the part of the subdivision 2 quoted above applies. Under this provision, the arbitration clause does not become part of the contract unless *A* assents to it. *A* has not assented. The term does not become part of the contract. The silence of *A* is not normally considered to be an acceptance.

(3) Additional Terms—Merchants

If both parties are merchants, additional terms become part of the contract unless: (a) the offer expressly limits acceptance to its terms or; (b) they materially alter it or; (c) notification of objection to them has already been given or is given within a reasonable time after notice of them is received.

Example: *A*, a merchant, makes an offer to *B*, a merchant. *B* in his acceptance includes, as an additional term, an arbitration clause. On the facts the only issue is whether the arbitration clause is a material alteration. According to the majority view, it is. Therefore, this term does not become part of the contract. What is or is not a material alteration is often a question of fact.

(4) Different Terms

(a) What Is a Different Term

A different term is one that contradicts a term of the offer. An additional term is one that introduces a new term. There is some question as to whether a term in the acceptance that contradicts an implied term in the offer should be considered to be "additional" or "different".

Examples: *A* makes an offer to *B* to buy a certain item and insists that the sale include a warranty of fitness for purpose. *B* accepts the offer, but states that there is to be no warranty of fitness for purpose. The term in the acceptance negating a warranty of fitness is a different term.

(b) Rules for Different Terms

Essentially there are two views relating to the effect of a different term. (1) Comment 3 to U.C.C. § 2–207 indicates that different terms should be treated as additional terms. Prof. Summers concludes that, as a practical matter, this means that different terms do not become part of the agreement unless accepted by the offeror. This is certainly true in the case of a non-merchant. As between merchants, he argues that a different term would automatically be ejected under the provisions of 2(c) because notification of objection to the different term would already have been given. In any event, his conclusion (as opposed to his reasoning) is in accord with a number of cases that ignore this comment and conclude that different terms do not become part of the agreement unless in turn accepted by the offeror. This approach is clearly in accord with the plain meaning of the statute (as opposed to the comment). (2) Prof. White concludes that different terms cancel each other out. The canceled term is to be replaced by any gap-filler that is available under the Code.

e)   Subdivision 3

This subdivision relates to acceptance by conduct in a case where the communications of the parties do not result in a contract. The rule announced changes the "last shot" principle of the common law. If the communications of the parties do not produce a contract, but the conduct of the parties recognizes the existence of a contract, there is a contract. The terms of the contract are those upon which the writings of the parties agree "together with any supplementary terms incorporated under any other provisions of this act."

Examples: B (Buyer) makes an offer to S that includes a warranty of merchantability. S's reply is expressly conditioned on B's assent to a no-warranty provision. There is no contract by virtue of the communications of the parties, because S expressly conditioned acceptance upon B's assent to the no-warranty clause. Therefore, S has made a counter offer whether we apply the common law approach or U.C.C. § 2–207.

Suppose, thereafter, B does not reply and S sends the goods. B takes and uses them; that is, B exercises dominion over them. The goods are defective, and B sues for breach of warranty of merchantability. At common law, under "the last shot principle," S's sending of the goods was looked upon as a performance of the counter offer. B, in turn, accepted by the exercise of dominion over the goods, thereby (intentionally or unintentionally) accepting S's offer, including the no-warranty provision. Under Subdivision 3 of the U.C.C., there is a contract but on a different theory. The terms of the contract are those upon which the parties agree "plus any supplementary terms incorporated under any other provision of this Act." The Act referred to is the entire Uniform Commercial Code other than Section 2–207 itself. Thus, the question is, does the Code contain a provision creating warranties of merchantability? It does. Thus, a warranty of merchantability based upon the provisions of the Code would be included in the contract.

If B had expressly conditioned acceptance upon an arbitration clause, the analysis would be the same, except that the arbitration clause would not be in the contract, because the U.C.C. does not have a provision relating to arbitration clauses.

f) Confirmation
(1) Language of Statute
U.C.C. § 2–207(1) also governs confirmations. It provides that "A written confirmation which is sent within a reasonable time operates as an acceptance even though it states terms additional to or different from those agreed upon." It appears strange that a written confirmation may operate as an acceptance, because a confirmation confirms a contract that has already been formed.

(2) Application of Rule
This provision seems to apply in only two situations. a) Where an agreement has been reached either orally or by informal correspondence, and one or both of the parties later send formal acknowledgments or memoranda and additional terms are introduced in the memoranda. If there is no conflict between the additional terms, the rules previously stated with respect to additional terms in acceptance apply. b) Where there are additional terms in memoranda that conflict, the conflicting terms do not become part of the contract. The contract consists of the terms originally agreed upon, terms on which the confirmations agree, and terms supplied by the Act including U.C.C. § 2–207(2). The last phrase includes terms that come into the contract by virtue of a) immediately above, and additional or different terms that become part of the contract under the rules stated in U.C.C. § 2–207(2).

Examples: (1) X and Y exchange correspondence and enter into a contract containing terms "A, B and C." X sent a written confirmation listing terms "A, B, C, and D." "D" is an additional term. Whether "D" becomes part of the contract depends upon the rules for additional terms stated above.

(2) In Example (1) assume that both parties send memos. X's memo lists terms "A, B, C, and D." And Y's memo sets forth terms, "A, B, C" and specifically states "not D." Since "D" and "not D" are conflicting terms, neither term becomes part of the contract.

(3) In Example (1) assume that X's memo mentions terms "A and B" but does not mention term "C." Y should be able to show the

existence of term "C" even though it is not in the memorandum. The problem involves the parol evidence rule. (See below.)

g) Restatement, Second
U.C.C. § 2–207 applies only to contracts for the sale of goods, unless a court decides to apply it to other contracts by analogy. The Restatement, Second, has borrowed the rule of the U.C.C. and applied it to other contracts. However, at this point it is clear that the mirror image rule is still the common law rule.

E. OPTION CONTRACTS—IRREVOCABLE OFFERS

1. INTRODUCTION
The topic is *irrevocable offers rather than revocable* offers discussed above. The terms "irrevocable offers" and "option contracts" are, generally speaking, interchangeable.

2. WHAT MAKES AN OFFER IRREVOCABLE?
An offer can be made irrevocable a) by consideration; b) by statute; c) under the prevailing rule relating to the revocation of offers to unilateral contracts; d) under the doctrine of promissory estoppel (to be discussed later); and e) in some jurisdictions by virtue of a sealed instrument.

Examples: (1) *A* makes an offer to sell specific property to *B* and states that the offer is open for 10 days. At common law, this is a revocable offer.

(2) In example (1), *A* states that the offer is irrevocable for 10 days. At common law, this is still a revocable offer.

(3) In example (1), *A* states to *B* that the offer is irrevocable for 10 days provided that *B* pays $10 for this privilege. *B* pays $10. The offer is irrevocable because *B* has given consideration to make the offer irrevocable.

(4) *A* says to *B*, "If you paint my flat, I promise to pay you $1000." *B* starts to perform. *A* attempts to revoke the offer. Under the prevailing view, discussed above, relating to the termination of an offer looking to a unilateral contract, when *B* starts to perform, the offer becomes irrevocable. Therefore the offer is not terminated by the revocation.

3. BY STATUTE

U.C.C. § 2–205 empowers an offeror to create an irrevocable offer without consideration. The requisites are: (a) a signed writing; (b) language assuring that the offer will be held open; (c) the offeror must be a merchant; (d) the period of irrevocability may not exceed three months, but the option may be renewed; and (e) if the language of irrevocability appears on the offeree's form it must be separately signed by the offeror. There are other local statutes with similar provisions that are not limited to offers for the sale of goods. (E.g., Michigan and New York.)

Example: *A*, a merchant, makes an offer to sell goods to *B*, stating in a signed writing that this is a "firm" (irrevocable) offer for 10 days. Under the U.C.C., this is an irrevocable offer. If no time is stated in the offer, it is irrevocable for a reasonable time.

4. THE NATURE OF AN OPTION CONTRACT—IRREVOCABLE OFFER

An option contract is not only a contract; it is also an offer. The contract that exists is the binding promise that makes the offer irrevocable for a period of time. Thus, the offeree has the option of accepting or not accepting the offer during that period of time.

Example: *A* makes an offer to sell specific real property to *B* for $50,000 and states that the offer is open for 10 days, provided *B* pays $10 for this privilege. *B* pays $10. As we have seen, there is an option contract that makes the offer irrevocable for 10 days. *B* has the option of buying or not buying the property. Acceptance of the underlying offer (relating to the sale and purchase of real property) is, except as indicated below, governed by the rules of acceptance set forth above. The option contract may be unilateral or bilateral and the same is true of the underlying contract.

5. TERMINATION OF IRREVOCABLE OFFERS

Irrevocable offers are terminated by:

(a) *lapse of time;*

(b) *death or destruction of a person or thing essential for the performance of the offered contract;*

(c) *supervening legal prohibition.*

Irrevocable offers are not terminated by:

(a) *revocation;*

(b) *death or supervening incapacity of the offeror or offeree;*

(c) *rejection (modern view).*

Examples: (1) *A* makes an offer to sell specific real property to *B* for $50,000 and states that the offer is open for 10 days, provided that *B* pays $10 for this privilege. *B* pays $10. *B* attempts to accept the underlying offer after the offer has lapsed. Although the offer was made irrevocable by the payment of $10, the attempted acceptance is too late. The offer terminated by lapse of time.

(2) In example (1) if *A* dies after *B* paid the $10, the offer would still be irrevocable and *A*'s death would not terminate the offer. If *B* accepted, the issue would be impossibility of performance (discussed below).

(3) In example (1) above, *B* rejects the offer but later, within the ten day period, attempts to accept. *A* relies on the rejection and sells to another party. The offer is irrevocable. Under the older view, the irrevocable offer would be terminated. Under the more modern view, it would not. There would be a contract, except that *B* would be estopped from asserting the existence of the contract, because *A* justifiably relied upon the rejection.

6.   WHEN IS THE ACCEPTANCE OF AN IRREVOCABLE OFFER EFFECTIVE?

We have already seen that the acceptance of a revocable offer may be effective, under the "mailbox rule," when it is sent. But in the case of an irrevocable offer, the weight of authority is that the acceptance is effective when received by the offeror. The "mailbox" rule is often justified upon the theory that it protects the offeree against revocation. When dealing with an irrevocable offer, the offeree does not require the protection of this rule.

F.   U.C.C. SECTION 2–206

1.   U.C.C. § 2–206

a.   Introduction

This section deemphasizes the common law distinction between a unilateral and bilateral contract (Subdivision 1, (a) and (b)). It also, as we have seen, makes changes in the mailbox rule. In addition, it changes the rule that is referred to as "the unilateral contract trick" (subdivision 1(b)). It also changes the rules relating to the effect of part performance.

b. Subdivision 1(a) of U.C.C. § 2–206

1) Unilateral–Bilateral

At common law, except in unusual cases, the offer looked to either a bilateral or unilateral contract. If the offer was ambiguous as to the manner of acceptance, it was presumed that the offer invited a promise. The U.C.C. has substituted for this common law presumption the notion that in the vast majority of the cases the offer is indifferent as to the manner of acceptance. This means that normally the offer may be accepted by an act or promise or by beginning performance. But this is not so if it is clear from the language or the circumstances that the offeror insists upon a particular manner of acceptance.

Examples: (1) *A* makes an offer requesting that *B* deliver certain goods to *A* at a stated price. At common law this would be deemed to be an offer looking to a unilateral contract. Under the Code the offer may be accepted by performance, by a promise or by beginning performance. The offer is indifferent.

(2) *B* makes an offer to *S* stating, "*S* shall mail to *B* a signed duplicate hereof." The offer is not indifferent. It clearly calls for a promise. Although signing is an act, it is not a performance. The signature creates a promise.

2) Mailbox Rule

This common law rule states that where an offer looks to a bilateral contract the acceptance is effective when sent (e.g., by letter), if it is sent in an authorized manner. Under the Code, the acceptance is effective when sent, provided it is sent "by any manner reasonable in the circumstances." The concept of reasonableness is intended to be more flexible than the previously prevailing concept of an "authorized" means of transmission.

c. Subdivision 1(b)

1) Order to Buy Goods for Prompt or Current Shipment

This subdivision provides that "an order or other offer to buy goods for prompt or current shipment shall be construed as inviting acceptance either by a prompt promise to ship or by the prompt or current shipment of conforming or nonconforming goods." This provision exemplifies the provision of subdivision 1(a) that ordinarily the acceptance may be made by performance or by promise. If the acceptance is by performance, failure to give notice is a ground for rejection only if there is a material delay in shipment or if loss ensues. The Restatement, Second, has a different rule but it would not be relevant in a sale of goods situation.

2)   The Unilateral Contract Trick—Subdivision 1(b)
      At common law, if *A* ordered goods from *B* and *B* sent non-conforming goods, the sending of the non-conforming goods was looked upon as a counter offer which *A* would accept by the acceptance and retention of the goods.   Under this provision of the Code, the sending of the non-conforming goods creates a contract and simultaneously a breach.   However, there is no contract if "the seller seasonably notifies the buyer that the shipment is offered only as an accommodation to the buyer."

3)   Subdivision 2
      There are four propositions to be made with respect to this subdivision.   a) The first question is whether the beginning of performance is a reasonable mode of acceptance.   b) The second question is whether the beginning of performance unambiguously expresses the offeree's intent to contract.   This means it must be determined whether or not the offeree intends to contract by beginning performance.   Ordinarily performance is begun with the intent of completing, but there may be situations in which the offeree does not intend to be bound when starting to perform.   If the offeree within a reasonable time after beginning performance notifies the offeror of an absence of intention to be bound, there is no acceptance. c) If the first two questions are answered affirmatively, the beginning of performance binds the offeree, but the offeror is not bound unless notice of beginning performance is given within a reasonable time.   A U.C.C. comment states that such notice must be given in every case. This is logical because, under the U.C.C., notice completes the contract.   However, if timely notice is not given, the offeror may elect to say that there is or is not a contract.   d) Whether the offeror may revoke after the offeree has begun performance is determined by the common law rules relating to the revocation of an offer looking to a unilateral contract.

2.   **THE RESTATEMENT, SECOND**
     The Restatement, Second, follows the rules of the Code with two important exceptions.

     a.   The Restatement, Second, has a different version of the effect of notice of the beginning of performance.   It says that the beginning of performance constitutes an acceptance so that both parties are bound at this point by a bilateral contract.   However, reasonable notice of beginning performance is required in most cases, because it is unlikely that the offeror would know of the beginning of performance.   It adds, however, that notice is not required when it is dispensed with or the offeror has otherwise learned of the beginning of performance.   When notice is required, it acts as a condition precedent to the offeror's duty to perform and, if not given, the offeror is discharged. Although the offeror may elect to be discharged, the offeror has a right to continue with the contract. This is similar to the U.C.C. rule above.

b. Under the Restatement, Second, the topic of revocation is irrelevant because, under the rule stated in a. above, there is a bilateral contract at the beginning of the performance.

G. CERTAINTY

1. COMMON LAW
a. Introduction
The offer must be so definite as to its material terms or require such definite terms in the acceptance that the performances to be rendered by each party are reasonably certain.

> *Comment:* Even though the parties have gone through a process of offer and acceptance, resulting in mutual assent, the contract is void if the content of their agreement is unduly uncertain. Indefiniteness as to an immaterial term is not fatal. However, it is true that the more terms that are indefinite the less likely it is that the parties intend to contract. However, uncertainty and lack of contractual intent are analytically distinct concepts.

b. What Are Material Terms?
Material terms include subject matter, price, payment terms, quantity, quality, duration and the work to be done. Given the infinite variety of contracts, it is obvious that no precise definition can be formulated.

c. When Is a Material Term Reasonably Certain?
What is reasonably certain depends upon subject matter, the purposes and relationship of the parties, and the circumstances under which the agreement was made. A term need not be set forth with the utmost specificity. It is enough that the agreement is sufficiently explicit so that the court can determine the respective obligations of the parties.

d. Types of Indefiniteness
Indefiniteness problems arise in three categories: a) where the parties have purported to agree upon a material term but have left it indefinite (not reasonably certain); b) where the parties are silent as to a material term; and c) where the parties have agreed to agree on a material term.

1)   Where the Parties Have Purported to Agree on a Material Term But
     Have Left It Indefinite
     Where this occurs, at common law there is no room for implication or
     gap-fillers (see below) and, therefore, the agreement is void. However,
     indefiniteness may be cured by the subsequent conduct of the parties
     or by a subsequent agreement of the parties.

Examples: (1) *A* makes an offer to sell from 1 to 10 copies of a
specified book at a certain price and adds: "State the
number in your acceptance." *B* replies, "I'll take five."
Although the offer, standing alone, does not state a
precise quantity, the contract itself is definite. It is the
contract and not the offer that must be definite.

(2) *A* says to *B*, "If you work for me for one year as a
foreman of my plant I promise to pay you a fair share of
the profits." A majority of the cases would say that the
agreement is unduly uncertain and would limit *B* to a
quasi-contractual recovery.

(3) *A* promises to make a tailor made suit for *B* for $200,
and the material is not specified. *A* commences to make
the suit with cotton cloth and *B* acquiesces. The
agreement is too vague and indefinite to be enforced, but
the conduct of the parties cured the indefiniteness so
that *A* is entitled to $200 rather than a quasi-contractual
recovery as in example # 2.

(4) *A* promises to pay *B* "well and enough" upon
retirement. When *B* retired, *A* promised to pay *B* $20
per week. *B* agreed. The initial indefiniteness was
cured by the subsequent agreement of the parties.

(5) In a construction contract involving $1,000,000, an
item involving $9,300 was left open. This was held to be
an immaterial term.

(6) *P* agreed to sell and did sell his real property to *D*
for a fixed sum that was paid. In addition *D* promised
to build "a first class theatre" on the site sold. *P*, as *D*
knew, desired the theatre to enhance the value of *P*'s
other properties in the area. *D* sold the property to a
third party without having built the theatre. *P* sued for
damages. *D* argued indefiniteness. The court,
expounding the more modern view, said that the
agreement was sufficiently definite and made the

following points: a) The law leans against destruction because of uncertainty. b) This is especially true where, as here, there has been performance under the contract. c) Evidence of subjective intention was properly admitted and helped to resolve the meaning of the words. d) Since the purpose of *P* was to enhance the value of *P*'s other property, that purpose could be served by the erection of any theatre that fit the definition of a first class theatre. e) Less certainty is required in an action for damages than where specific performance is sought.

2) **Where the Parties Are Silent as to a Material Term**
If the parties are silent as to a material term, or discuss it but do not purport to agree upon it, there is the possibility that the term may be implied from the surrounding circumstances or supplied by a court using a gap-filler. A gap-filler is a term supplied by the court because it thinks that the parties would have agreed upon this term if it had been brought to their attention, or because it is a term "which comports with community standards of fairness."

Examples: (1) *A* hires a plumber to do certain work. No price is set. The gap-filler supplied is that a reasonable price is to be paid or, according to some courts, that the plumber is to be paid what the plumber usually receives for the work.

(2) In a case involving the sale of goods where no price is set, it is assumed that the parties contracted on the basis of a reasonable price. This rule has been continued by the U.C.C.

(3) If no time is stated for the delivery of goods or for the completion of a building contract, a reasonable time is assumed.

(4) If the parties are silent as to the kind or quantity of goods or the specifications in a building contract, no gap-filler is supplied because no objective standard can ordinarily be found in such cases.

(5) *A* and *B* agree that *A* will work for *B* for $5,200 per year. The majority view is that this is a hiring at will. The minority view is that this is a binding contract for one year. Under the majority view, until recently, when an employment agreement did not expressly state a duration term, it was assumed that there was only a

hiring at will. But in recent years, this assumption has become only a rebuttable presumption. The courts are now willing to examine all of the facts and circumstances to see if a duration period can be implied. A corollary of the hiring at will doctrine is that such an agreement may be terminated for good cause, for no cause or even for an immoral cause. There is, however, a growing list of exceptions. These include a discharge that is against public policy (e.g., an employee is discharged for filing a Worker's Compensation claim), and an abusive discharge (e.g., where a female employee is discharged for resisting the advances of a foreman). According to a few courts, a dismissal that is in violation of an implied covenant of good faith and fair dealing is wrongful (e.g., where an employee is discharged to prevent a pension from vesting) and where the doctrine of promissory estoppel would apply (e.g., where the employee left existing employment in reliance on the defendant's promise of employment). Wrongful discharge is sometimes treated as a tort.

(6) In the case of a promise of *permanent employment*, the majority of courts have held that, in the absence of a contrary intention, the hiring is at will because the duration term is too vague. Under the minority view, the employee is entitled to work at least until retirement age, so long as the employee is able to do the work properly, and the employer continues in the business in which the employee was hired. Even under the majority view, if a consideration over and above the employee's services is given, some courts have indicated that the hiring will not be considered to be at will.

(7) In the case of a promise of "lifetime employment," there are again two views. Some cases hold that such a promise amounts to a hiring at will, but others take the position that the term should be taken literally.

(8) In most non-employment cases, where no duration is specified in the agreement, the court will imply that the contract will last for a reasonable time. But some courts still conclude that the arrangement is at will especially where there is no way to determine what is a reasonable time.

3) Where the Parties Agree to Agree

a) Traditional Rule

The traditional common law rule is that an agreement to agree as to a material term does not result in a binding contract. It is not a case where the parties are silent. Therefore, because the parties have manifested an intention to fill the gap themselves, the gap-filler mechanism may not be used. But an agreement to agree must be distinguished from a case where the parties have agreed to use reasonable efforts to reach an agreement. In such cases there is a duty to negotiate in good faith.

b) Modern View

Some of the more modern cases (even without relying on the U.C.C. and the Restatement, Second, to be discussed below), have recognized that an agreement to agree serves a valuable commercial purpose and that the traditional rule may operate unfairly where the party uses the rule to defeat an agreement that the parties intended to be binding. Some courts have allowed a gap-filler where there is an agreement to agree. Other courts have held that there is a duty to negotiate in good faith even though there is no such provision in the agreement. The U.C.C. and the Restatement, Second, are generally in accord with these modern approaches to the question of an agreement to agree. (See below.)

Examples: (1) *A* agrees to sell and *B* agrees to buy 1000 gidgets. All of the material items are agreed upon except that the parties agree to agree on the price at a later date. Under the traditional view, the agreement to agree as to a material term would result in fatal indefiniteness. Under the more modern common law, a court could use a reasonable price as a gap-filler. Under the U.C.C., the price would be a reasonable price at the time of delivery. But, if the parties did not intend to be bound unless agreement were reached on price, there still would be no contract. (U.C.C. § 2–305).

(2) *A* and *B* negotiate an oral agreement which they intend to be binding, but are aware that they have not reached an agreement on price. They later reaffirm their agreement and agree that they shall make every effort to reach an agreement on price. Before any further negotiations take place, *A*, because of a change in market conditions, refuses to negotiate the price. *A* has breached a duty to

negotiate in good faith. This problem does not involve an agreement to agree.

(3) There is an option in an existing lease that permits the tenant to extend the lease under specified terms "at a rental fee to be agreed upon at the time of the exercise of the option." Under the traditional view, the agreement to agree as to a material term prevents the exercise of the option. Under the more modern view, the option could be exercised and the rental would be a reasonable rent at the time of the renewal. The court would be using a gap-filler in the case of an agreement to agree.

(4) P entered into an agreement with D whereby P obtained an option to buy a piece of real property for the sum of $23,500 "on payments and terms to be negotiated provided the same is exercised by June 1." On May 15, P sought to exercise the option. P offered to pay $5,300 and to assume two mortgages in the combined amount of $18,200. D changed his mind about selling and refused to negotiate. This is not a case, as in Example 2, where the parties agreed to make every effort to reach an agreement. Under the traditional common law rule, the agreement would be too vague and indefinite. The court, however, held that the parties were obliged to negotiate in good faith and that D's refusal amounted to a breach. The court decreed specific performance on the proposal set forth by P because the proposal would satisfy a reasonable person.

e. Uniform Commercial Code
1) Introduction
    The provisions of the U.C.C. relating to indefiniteness are of two types. There are provisions relating to specific problems. And there is also a very important general provision. Section 2–305 is an example of a provision relating to a specific problem. It relates to an open price term and has already been mentioned. These specific provisions all assume that there has been no contrary agreement.

    a) Specific Provisions
        (1) Place of Delivery
             If the place of delivery is not stated, it is the seller's place of business or if he has none, his residence. In the case of

identified goods, if the parties know that the goods are elsewhere, that location is the place of delivery.

(2) Time for Shipment or Delivery
If the time for shipment or delivery is not specified, it is deemed to be a reasonable time.

(3) Time for Payment
If the time for payment is not specified, payment is due at the time and place where the buyer is to receive the goods.

(4) Failure to Specify Assortment

> *Example:* *S* agrees to sell and *B* agrees to buy 5,000 gallons of W Brand Motor Oil, SAE 10–70. This term designates seven weights of oil. The price for each weight is definite. Before any weight specifications were submitted, *B* repudiated the agreement. At common law about one half of the cases held that the agreement was too vague and indefinite to be enforced unless the assortment was specified prior to repudiation. Under U.C.C. § 2–311, there is a contract. The buyer is bound to specify, and the seller is bound to permit the buyer to specify. The specifications are to be made in "good faith and within limits set by commercial reasonableness." When the party who has the duty fails to specify, the other may proceed in any reasonable manner, such as by making the specification and treating the breach as total.

b) General Provision
Even if one or more terms are left open, a contract for sale of goods does not fail for indefiniteness if the parties have intended to make a contract and there is a reasonably certain basis for giving an appropriate remedy. (U.C.C. § 2–204).

> *Discussion:* The test is not certainty as to what the parties were to do nor as to the exact amount of damages due to the plaintiff. Rather commercial standards on the issue of indefiniteness are to be applied. This provision is designed to prevent, if at all possible, a contracting party, who is dissatisfied with his bargain, from taking refuge in the doctrine of indefiniteness to renounce an agreement. This

section relates to all three categories of cases discussed above. Thus, a gap-filler could be used even though the parties purported to agree upon the term in question or made an agreement to agree with respect to it. But the section goes beyond gap-fillers and permits a court to use any reasonably certain basis for giving an appropriate remedy. Whether the parties intended to contract is normally a question of fact. Whether there is a reasonably certain basis for giving an appropriate remedy is a question of law. The Restatement, Second, is generally in accord with the U.C.C.

Example: *A* agrees to sell, and *B* to buy gidgets, "the quantity to be agreed upon from time to time." Under the traditional common law rule, the agreement to agree as to quantity would be fatally indefinite. At common law and under the Code, the fact that price, duration, etc. are missing is not necessarily fatal because gap-fillers can be used. Under the U.C.C., an agreement to agree is not necessarily fatal. The first question under U.C.C. § 2–204(3) is whether the parties intended to contract. The Code provides no clear guide to answering this question of fact, but one of the comments to the Code states that the more terms the parties do not cover the less likely it is that they intend to be bound. The second question is whether there is a reasonably certain basis for giving an appropriate remedy. Where, as here, the quantity term is not covered, it would be an unusual case where it can be found that there is a reasonably certain basis for giving an appropriate remedy.

REVIEW QUESTIONS

1. T or F *A* owned a $15 set of harness which was stolen from him. While in a state of wrath and in a boastful and blustering manner, *A* in the presence of a crowd, including *P*, promised to pay $100 to the one who recovered the harness. *P* recovers the harness and sues for the reward. *P*, in fact, believed that *A* was serious, but a reasonable person in *P*'s position would conclude otherwise. *P* may not recover.

2. T or F *P* was in the business of manufacturing automobile parts. *P*'s customers were major auto manufacturers. *P* wished to sell to other buyers such as Midas Muffler but believed that this would displease

the auto manufacturers. To achieve secrecy, *P* set up a subsidiary to distribute its products. *P* and *E*, a trusted employee, signed a document which stated that *E* had bought the business of the subsidiary for $5,000. It was orally agreed between the parties that, despite the agreement, *E* was acting as an agent of *P*. *E* sues on the written agreement. *E* may not recover.

3. T or F   When Mrs. Stewart conceived at the age of 37, after two previous stillbirths, she was convinced that she could not have a normal delivery. Consequently, when she and her husband consulted with *D*, a doctor, they demanded that a Caesarian section be performed. *D* agreed. *D*'s medical opinion was that a Caesarian would not be necessary, and so *D* later refused to perform a Caesarian when Mrs. Stewart had labor pains. The baby died. Mrs. Stewart does not have a cause of action for breach of contract against *D*.

4. T or F   The Chicago Tribune, a daily newspaper, publishes a booklet called "General Advertising Rates," which lists its charges for advertisements, and another booklet called "The Chicago Tribune Advertising Guide" which indicates that the Tribune will refuse advertising which is dishonest, indecent or illegal. *P*, a labor union, tendered to the Tribune an advertisement urging readers not to patronize a certain department store because of its policy of featuring imported clothing made by low wage foreign labor. It was conceded that the tendered advertisement was not dishonest, indecent or illegal. The union also tendered sufficient funds to pay for the advertisements in accordance with the "General Advertising Rates." The Tribune refused to print the advertisement. *P* has a cause of action for breach of contract against the Tribune.

5. T or F   *D* caused circulars to be distributed to dealers throughout the country announcing that an auction would be conducted without reserve of the famous Smith collection of antiques. *P* flew from California to New York, the announced site of the auction. On arrival *P* discovered that the auction had been cancelled because of a recession in the antiques market. *P* does not have an action for breach of contract against *D*.

6. T or F   *P* asked *D* whether *D* would consider selling certain property. *D* stated that, if *P* made an offer, *D* would consider it. *P* named a sum and *D* refused. *P* then stated, "Will you accept $49,000?" *D* answered "I will not sell it for less than $56,000." *P* said, "I accept." There was a contract.

7. T or F   *A* offered a $10 reward to anyone who finds and returns *A*'s lost watch. *B* never learned of the reward offer but returned the watch knowing it belonged to *A* because of engraved material on the back.

B may not recover for the sole reason that *B* was legally bound to return the watch.

8. T or F   In problem 7, assume that *B* knew of the offer before *B* found and returned the watch and that *B* had no legal duty to return the watch. Assume further that, when *B* returned the watch, *B* did not mention the reward. *B* offers testimony that *B* intended to accept and did not say anything about the reward because of embarrassment. As a matter of law, *B* may not recover the reward.

9. T or F   *A*, a newspaper, requests *B* to discontinue publication of a rival newspaper, and offers to pay $10 per week as long as *B* abstains from such publication. One must conclude that *A* had made an offer looking to a series of contracts.

10. T or F   *A*, the owner of an unimproved piece of realty, spent the summer in Europe. When *A* returned there was a beautiful house where the empty lot had been. As *A* was about to enter, *B* informed *A* that *B* had caused the structure to be built and that, if *A* used the house, *A* would be contractually obligated to pay for it. *B* is correct.

11. T or F   *A* was seriously injured in an accident. *B*, a doctor, came upon the scene and treated *A* while *A* was unconscious. *B* is entitled to a contractual recovery from *A*.

12. T or F   *A* invited a number of brokers to submit proposals for fire and theft insurance. Later, upon *A*'s request, *B*, one of the brokers, revised the bid several times. *A* then awarded the contract to another. *B* sues to recover the cost incurred in preparing the bid and its various revisions. *B* may recover.

13. T or F   Under a claim of right made in error but in good faith, *A* digs a well on *B*'s unused land and takes water therefrom which has no market value and no value to *B*, doing no injury to the value of the land. *B* notifies *A* that *B* will charge $50 a day for every day on which *A* takes water from the land. If *A* takes water, *A* is bound to pay $50 per day.

14. T or F   *A* sends an offer by mail to *B*, who promptly sends what amounts to a counter-offer the next day. This letter is lost. The following day, *B* at 2:00 P.M. sends a letter of acceptance which was also lost. On the same day *A* sent a telegram of revocation at 1:00 P.M. which was received by *B* at 5:00 P.M. Under the majority view there is a contract.

15. T or F *A* sent to *B* an offer to sell certain realty stating all material terms and added, "this offer is not subject to revocation for thirty days." *B* immediately rejected the offer, and *A* then stated that *A* withdrew the offer. At this point the offer had been effectively terminated.

16. T or F *A* sends a telegraphic offer to sell oil at a fixed price which at the time is subject to rapid fluctuations in price. The offer is received near the close of business hours, and a telegraphic acceptance is sent the next day after the offeree has learned of a sharp price rise. There is a contract.

17. T or F *D* offered a reward of $200 for information leading to the conviction of the person who set a specific fire. Three years and two months later, the culprit was convicted as a result of information supplied by *P* three months before the trial. *P* may not recover because the offer has lapsed.

18. T or F *A* makes an offer to *B* saying that it is to remain open for two weeks but is to end at once if *A*'s factory is destroyed by fire. If the factory burns down two days later and *B* accepts the next day, not knowing that the factory burned down, there is a contract.

19. T or F *A* in a telephone conversation makes an offer to *B* to which *B* did not reply. After the conversation ends, *B* sends a letter of acceptance. There is no contract.

20. T or F *A* made an offer to *B* looking to a series of unilateral contracts. Under the terms of the offer, *B* was to make deliveries to *A*. After *B* made the first delivery, *A* was adjudicated an incompetent and a guardian of *A*'s property was appointed. *B* had no knowledge of this fact and continued to make deliveries. Under the majority view, *B* may recover contractually for all deliveries.

21. T or F *A*, a newspaper, publishes an offer of prizes to persons who procure the largest number of subscriptions as evidenced by cash or checks received by a specified time. *B* completes and mails an entry blank giving *B*'s name and address, which is received by *A*. Thereafter during the contest, *A* publishes a notice that personal checks will not be counted. *B* does not see the notice. Assume that the offer continued to be revocable. *B* is bound by the notice.

22. T or F *A* makes an offer to *B* to sell Blackacre for $10,000. *B*, at *A*'s request, pays *A* $100 to keep the offer open for one week. Two days later, *B* tells *A* that *B* will purchase but at a price of $8,500. *A* declines. The next day *B* manifests an intent to buy at the original price and tenders $10,000.   Under the modern view, there is a contract.

23. T or F   A makes a written and signed offer to sell goods to B which states, "This offer is for one week."   The letter was dated and sent on Jan. 2.   It was received on Jan. 3.   B sent a letter of acceptance on Jan. 9.   This letter was received on Jan. 12.   There is a contract.

24. T or F   A, a manufacturer, agrees to sell to B, a retailer, 5,000 gidgets (goods).   A stated the price which varied according to the size of the gidgets.   B accepted.   Before anything else happened, A "withdrew the offer."   There is no contract.

25. T or F   A and B enter into an employment arrangement for a period of one year.   They agree that the salary to be paid should be determined by them "in a cooperative effort" at the end of each month.   There is no contract.

26. Essay   Case owned a tractor located in the woods near Oswego, New York. On February 16, 1975, Thompson called Case about buying the tractor. Case said: "I will sell the tractor to you, or to anybody else for that matter, for $450.   Upon an agreement, you may take possession of the tractor."   On March 1, Thompson picked up the tractor and brought it home and so informed Case on March 15, 1976.   On March 1, Peterson, who had learned of the offer from Thompson, sent in a notice of acceptance.

    (a) Discuss the rights of the parties.

    (b) Would the result be different if Case had not said, "Upon an agreement, you may make take possession of the tractor."

    (c) What would be the result if instead of picking up the tractor on March 1, Thompson had sent a letter stating: "This letter is sent to confirm that I am purchasing the tractor of which we spoke on the terms indicated.   Naturally I expect that an arbitration clause is part of our deal?"

27. Essay   Prior to February 20 the plaintiff and defendant had engaged in conferences and negotiations respecting the purchase by the plaintiff of all of the property and assets of the defendant, Anchor, whose president, Conroy, owned 93% of the Anchor stock.

On February 20 plaintiff wrote a letter setting forth a detailed agreement, numbered 1 through 20, giving the plaintiff a 60 day option to purchase Anchor's business and assets.   There was a space on this letter for the signature of the defendant. The defendant did not sign but instead sent its own letter signed by Conroy on February 28 which read as follows:

"We are unwilling to enter into a formal option with your company as proposed in your letter of February 20. We would be willing to sell the assets of our company to you for $4,025,000 in accordance with paragraphs 3, 5, 6, 7, 8, 9, 11, 13, 14 and 17 of your letter of February 20, if such an offer were made today without the reservations elsewhere contained in that letter, and subject to the exceptions noted below. You may consider this as a letter of intent authorizing you to make the survey you deem necessary to make your offer a firm and binding one; and we assure you of our full cooperation in making it. We suggest that it be completed as quickly as possible.

You are assured that should you make a firm offer within 50 days from this date, we will enter into a contract with you on the basis of the terms of the above numbered paragraphs of your letter of February 20 with the following exceptions:

(a) That suitable assurances are given for the retention of lower level executive personnel;

(b) That mutually satisfactory arrangements are made for the continued employment of Charles L. Conroy.

Plaintiff spent large sums of money in making the survey in question and on April 1, wrote to the defendant saying that the plaintiff had decided to proceed in the acquisition of Anchor's assets. This letter in addition read in part as follows: "Please consider this our formal offer, therefore, to enter into agreement in accordance with our previous correspondence. You have already indicated that this offer will be accepted by you. We trust that you will have your General Counsel contact our General Counsel in order that the formal agreement between us can be prepared promptly."

Was there a contract between the parties at this point? Discuss all of the contract problems involved.

*

II

CONSIDERATION and ITS EQUIVALENTS

Analysis

A. Introduction
B. Consideration
    1. Elements of Consideration
        a. The Promisee Must Suffer Legal Detriment
        b. Detriment Must Induce the Promise
        c. The Promise Must Induce the Detriment
    2. Motive and Past Consideration
    3. Adequacy
    4. Sham and Nominal Consideration
    5. Invalid Claims
    6. The Pre-existing Duty Rule
        a. Introduction
        b. Duties Imposed by Law
        c. Modification in a Two Party Case
        d. The Three Party Cases
        e. Agreement to Accept Part Payment in Satisfaction
           of a Debt
    7. Accord and Satisfaction
        a. Liquidated and Unliquidated Claims
        b. Definition
        c. Problems Presented

8. *U.C.C. Inroads on Pre-existing Duty Rule and Foakes v. Beer*
   a. *U.C.C. § 2–209(1)*
   b. *U.C.C. §§ 2–209(2) and (3)*
   c. *U.C.C. § 2–209(2)*
   d. *Subdivision 4*
   e. *Subdivision 5*
   f. *Duress*
   g. *U.C.C. § 1–207*
   h. *U.C.C. § 1–107*
   i. *U.C.C. § 3–408*
9. *Bilateral Contracts*
10. *Mutuality of Obligation*
    a. *Introduction*
    b. *Unilateral Contracts*
    c. *Voidable and Unenforceable Promises*
    d. *Illusory Promises*
    e. *Right to Terminate a Contract by Virtue of a Provision Contained Therein*
    f. *Conditional Promises*
    g. *Aleatory Promises*
    h. *Consideration Supplied by Implied Promise*
    i. *Agreements Allowing a Party to Supply a Material Term*
    j. *A Void Contract Is Not Necessarily a Nullity*
11. *Requirements and Output Contracts*
    a. *Introduction*
    b. *Validity of Requirement Contracts*
    c. *U.C.C. § 2–306*
    d. *How Much Is a Requirements Buyer Entitled to Demand?*
    e. *May a Requirements Buyer Diminish or Terminate Requirements?*
    f. *Does a Requirements Buyer Have a Duty to Promote the Goods?*
12. *Must All of the Consideration Be Valid?*
13. *Conjunctive and Alternative Promises*
    a. *Conjunctive Promises*
    b. *Alternative Promises*
C. *Moral Obligation*
   1. *Introduction*
   2. *Exceptions*
      a. *Promises to Pay a Liquidated Debt*
      b. *Promises to Pay Fixed Amounts for Services Previously Requested*
      c. *Promises to Pay a Fixed Amount for Services Not Requested*
      d. *Promises to Pay Debts Discharged or Rendered Unenforceable by Operation of Law*
      e. *Promises to Perform a Voidable Duty*

        f. Statute of Frauds

        g. Miscellaneous Promises Supported by Antecedent Events

        h. To Whom the Promise Must Be Made

  D. Promissory Estoppel

     1. Introduction

     2. The First Restatement

     3. Restatement, Second

     4. The Roots of the Doctrine of Promissory Estoppel

     5. Present Approach to a Gift Promise

     6. Doctrine Not Limited to Gratuitous Promises

     7. Approach to a Problem

  E. Sealed Instrument

     1. Effect of a Seal

A. INTRODUCTION

This chapter relates to the type of promises the law should enforce. Under the doctrine of consideration, gratuitous promises are not enforced, but they may be enforced under the doctrine of promissory estoppel or under certain statutes. In addition, a moral obligation may make a promise enforceable but only in certain instances. Some jurisdictions still enforce a gratuitous promise made under seal.

B. CONSIDERATION

1. ELEMENTS OF CONSIDERATION
A promise which is not supported by consideration or its equivalent is not enforceable. For a promise to be supported by consideration, three elements must concur.

(a) *The promisee must suffer legal detriment—that is, do what the promisee is not legally obligated to do; or refrain from doing what the promisee is legally privileged to do.*

(b) *The detriment must induce the promise. The promisor must have made the promise in exchange, at least in part, for the detriment to be suffered by the promisee.*

(c) *The promise must induce the detriment. This means, as indicated above, that the promisee must know of the offer and intend to accept.*

a. The Promisee Must Suffer Legal Detriment
Although the rule is here stated in terms of legal detriment suffered by the promisee, the rule is often phrased in terms of either legal detriment to the promisee or legal benefit to the promisor. The result is invariably the same, because if the promisee suffers legal detriment, the promisor obtains a legal benefit. Despite the statement of the rule in terms of legal detriment suffered by the *promisee,* it is well established that it does not matter from whom or to whom the detriment moves so long as it is bargained for and given in exchange for the promise. In other words, someone other than the promisee may suffer the detriment.

b. Detriment Must Induce the Promise
This means that the promisor makes the promise in exchange for the conduct of the promisee. If the promisor manifests a gift making state of mind, rather than an offering state of mind, it is clear that the detriment does not induce the promise because there is no element of exchange. In other words, a promise to make a gift is not enforceable. But note that the promisor need only exchange the promise in part for the detriment. Exchange may coexist with other motives.

c.   The Promise Must Induce the Detriment

As stated above, this means that the offeree must know of the offer and intend to accept. In other words, the offeree is induced to act because of the offer.

Examples: (1) *A* says to *B*, "If you paint my house according to my specifications, I promise to pay you $2,000." *B* performs. *A* is the promisor and *B* is the promisee-offeree. The promisee, *B*, has suffered legal detriment by doing an act (painting) that *B* was not legally obligated to do. On the facts, it is a reasonable conclusion that *A*, the promisor, was exchanging the promise for the act of painting. It is also a reasonable conclusion that the promisee, *B*, painted with knowledge of the offer and an intent to accept. The arrangement here is unilateral. There is only one promise. In the case of a bilateral contract there are two promisors and additional problems are presented. These are discussed below.

(2) *A* writes to his sister-in-law, "If you will come down and see me, I promise you a place on my farm to raise your family." Although moving from one place to another is a detriment, the court held that *A* made a promise to make a gift. Moving was simply a condition of the gift. A promise to make a gift is not enforceable. In other words, the moving was not bargained for in exchange for the promise. The result undoubtedly would be different if *A* had asked his sister-in-law to work for him, because selfish benefit to the promisor is an indication of a contract making state of mind. Whether the detriment is bargained for is often a question of fact.

(3) Uncle made a promise to his nephew to pay $5,000 if the nephew refrained from drinking until he was twenty-one. Not drinking is a detriment and here, contrary to example 2, the court held that the detriment was bargained for. The cases are based on different findings on the issue of whether an exchange was intended. Again, we are dealing with a question of fact.

(4) Landlord (*L*) offered to extend *T*'s lease for an additional four years if *T* promised to make improvements that would cost approximately $10,000. *L* suggested that *T* retain an architect to check figures on the proposed improvements of the premises. *T* argued that the offer became irrevocable. *T*'s reasoning was that the consideration of hiring the architect made the offer irrevocable. The court sustained the

finding of fact made by the trial court that the hiring of the architect was not consideration, because it was merely suggested and not bargained for.

(5) *A* is moved by friendship to promise to sell his horse, worth $100, for $10 to *B*. Because the detriment to be surrendered ($10) need not be the sole or even the predominant inducement, the only issue is whether there was in fact an exchange. The Restatement, Second, states that the exchange element exists unless *B* knows or should know that the $10 introduced into the transaction by *A* is a pretense.

(6) *A* promises *B* to pay *B* $100 if *C* (*B*'s son) paints *A*'s house. *A* is the promisor, *B* is the promisee, and *C* is the offeree. Although the detriment comes from *C*, *B* may enforce *A*'s promise. The result would be the same if, under the offered terms, *C* was to paint *D*'s house.

2. MOTIVE AND PAST CONSIDERATION
Past consideration and motive are not consideration.

The term "past consideration" is itself a contradiction in terms. Consideration is essentially an exchange and parties cannot make an exchange involving something that has already occurred. A party's motive in making a promise is not related to the question of detriment. However, if there is detriment, the motive of the promisor in entering into the transaction is relevant, because it relates to the issue of exchange. In other words, ordinarily the motive of the promisor is to induce action on the part of the promisee and conversely the motive of the promisee is to gain what is offered by the promisor.

Examples: (1) *F* says to *S*, "in consideration of the fact that you have named your child after me, I promise to pay you $5,000." The promise did not induce the detriment, because *S* did not know of the offer or intend to accept when the child was named.

(2) *F* says to *S*, "in consideration of the fact that you are not as wealthy as your brothers, I promise to pay you $5,000." Although *F* has stated the motive for the promise, there is no detriment.

3. ADEQUACY
Any detriment, no matter how economically inadequate, will support a promise provided that the detriment is in fact bargained for.

Exceptions:

(1) A promise to exchange a specific amount of money or fungible goods for the same or a lesser amount of money or goods at the same time and place (e.g., "in consideration of $1.00 each to the other paid.") is not legally enforceable. Here the Court takes judicial notice of the value of the things exchanged and cannot indulge in the supposed normal presumption of equivalence between the detriment and the promise.

(2) Under the doctrine of unconscionability. (See below.)

Examples: (1) *A* promises to pay *B* $10,000 for the surrender of a piece of paper which is in fact worthless. (Result: there is detriment, and, as the facts are stated, the piece of paper is bargained for. *A*'s promise is enforceable.)

(2) *A*, a poor Spanish speaking person, promises to pay $1145 for a $348 appliance. (Result: despite the general rule, the contract is unconscionable.)

(3) A widow promised a bank to pay off her husband's note in exchange for the surrender of the note. Her husband died insolvent. The surrender of the worthless note constitutes detriment, but the question would remain whether this detriment was in fact bargained for. In addition, the economic inadequacy may be evidence of duress, over-reaching, undue influence, mistake, or indicate that the detriment was not in fact bargained for. The case might even be considered under the heading of "Invalid Claims" to be discussed below.

Comment: When equitable relief is sought, adequacy of the detriment may be considered.

4. SHAM AND NOMINAL CONSIDERATION

The basic question presented here is whether a pretense of consideration will suffice as consideration. The problem arises in two recurring fact patterns. The first involves an instrument that falsely recites that a consideration has been given. The second arises where the parties, having learned that a gratuitous promise is unenforceable, attempt to make the promise enforceable by cloaking it in the form of a bargain. The different views are set forth in connection with the illustrations below.

Examples: (1) A writing contains the phrase, "in consideration of $100 in hand paid, I promise to sell you my horse." The $100 was not in fact paid. Because the alleged consideration is a "sham" (a pretense), the promise is not supported by consideration. The parol evidence rule does not exclude this evidence.

(2) A writing contains a false provision that $10 is given as consideration for an option (irrevocable offer). Under the majority view, there is no consideration to make the offer irrevocable. But in the case of an option contract, there are two additional views. These views hold that there is consideration to support the option contract, either (1) upon a theory that the parties are estopped from contradicting the writing, or (2) upon the theory that the recital gives rise to an implied promise to pay. The Restatement, Second, synthesizes these two views stating that "an offer is binding as an option contract if it is in writing and signed by the offeror, recites a purported consideration for the making of the offer, and proposes an exchange on fair terms within a reasonable time." These three views also apply with respect to a sham recital of consideration in the case of an offer of guaranty. In the case of a guaranty, the Restatement, Second, does not mention the "exchange on fair terms," etc.

(3) *A* wishes to make a binding contract to convey certain property worth $10,000 to his son, *B,* one year later. *A* intends a gift, but being aware of the doctrine of consideration, drafts an instrument in which *A* promises to convey in return for *B*'s promise to pay $10. *B* knows or should know that the $10 is merely a token. There are two views. The Restatement, Second, takes the position that the promise should not be enforced because the alleged consideration is not truly bargained for. It argues that to hold otherwise destroys the doctrine of consideration. The contrary view is supported by the original Restatement. It argues that there ought to be a way of making a gratuitous promise binding especially in a jurisdiction where this cannot be done through the mechanism of a seal.

5. INVALID CLAIMS

Discussion: A promise to surrender a valid claim constitutes detriment and, if bargained for, constitutes consideration. But there are a number of views as to whether the surrender of or a forbearance to assert an invalid claim is detriment.
(1) The earliest view is that the surrender of an invalid claim does not constitute detriment. This view has generally been abandoned. (2) The surrender of an invalid claim serves as a detriment if the claimant has asserted it in good faith, and a reasonable person would believe that the claim is well founded. (3) Still other courts have held that the only requirement is good faith. (4) The Restatement, Second, takes the position that either good faith or objective uncertainty as to the validity of a claim is sufficient. These rules do not apply in a quit-claim type case. It should be noted that we are discussing only whether the

surrender of an invalid claim constitutes detriment. Under most of the views stated above it can. But even if it does, in many cases one still must confront the question of what is bargained for. For example, does the promisor bargain for the surrender of a worthless piece of paper or the surrender of an invalid claim?

Examples: (1) *D* guaranteed in writing an obligation of a third party to *P*. The guaranty was not enforceable under the existing law. *D* promised *P* that *D* would pay the amount stated in the writing if *P* returned the written document of guaranty. The return of the paper is detriment, and the court held that this is what *D* bargained for. But the court could have as easily discussed the case under the heading of invalid claims. In that event the rules stated above would apply.

(2) *H,* a married man, died insolvent and was liable to *P* on a note. *P* agreed to return the note in exchange for *H*'s widow's promise to pay *H*'s obligation. Under the great majority of cases the return of the note, even though it is an uncollectible claim, constitutes detriment. The next question would be what did the widow bargain for? (See discussion of this case at p. 151 above.) Another interesting question is whether the case can be considered as involving an invalid claim. This approach can be taken only if the claim can be treated as invalid simply because it is worthless.

(3) *A,* an insurance company, requests *B,* who has been injured, to execute a release in exchange for $200 because it wishes to close its file. *B* was not asserting any claim and in fact believes that no valid claim exists. The execution of the release constitutes consideration. This is because *A* sought the release for its own purposes and with knowledge that the claim was invalid. This is similar to a situation involving a quit-claim deed. *A* is bargaining for a piece of paper.

6. THE PRE-EXISTING DUTY RULE
a. Introduction
The pre-existing duty rule states that if parties do what they are legally obligated to do, or refrain from doing what they are not legally privileged to do, they have not incurred detriment, because performing a legal obligation is not detriment. No legal right is surrendered. This rule has been much criticized, and as a result, exceptions exist which are illogical or tenuous at best. The criticism is based upon the notion that it is unreasonable for the law to prevent competent parties from modifying their legal obligations, absent duress, even if there is no consideration for the modification.

b. Duties Imposed by Law

The pre-existing duty rule applies not only to a duty that exists under a contract but also to a duty that is not contractual in nature; that is, a duty imposed by law. This includes not only official duties but also duties imposed on a person as a member of the public or as a member of a family.

Example: A sheriff is not entitled to a reward offered for the capture of a criminal if the capture is within the general scope of the sheriff's duties. But if the sheriff does more than the law requires, detriment has been incurred.

c. Modification in a Two Party Case

Discussion: The vast majority of the cases follow the pre-existing duty rule when parties modify an agreement, but some jurisdictions do not apply the pre-existing duty rule on a wide variety of theories. 1) A party suffers a legal detriment by giving up the right to breach the contract. This is incorrect because there is no such right. 2) The Wisconsin rule instead employs the fiction that the original consideration is imported into the new agreement. 3) Still other cases have looked upon the modification as an attempt to mitigate damages. But, for our purposes, these erroneous theories may be ignored. The vast majority of jurisdictions continue to follow the pre-existing duty rule. But limited exceptions have been introduced even in these jurisdictions. The rule and the exceptions can best be explained by a series of illustrations.

Examples: (1) In August, B hires A at $900 per week for a one year term to commence in November. In October, the parties modify the agreement so that the salary is to be $1000 per week. B's promise to pay the additional $100 per week is not enforceable, because A has suffered no detriment. A is merely doing what A is legally obligated to do. If A assumed even a light additional duty, and this detriment was bargained for, there would be consideration for the modification.

(2) In example 1, if the parties rescinded their original agreement in early October, and entered into a new agreement for $1000 in late October there would not be any pre-existing duty problem because the original agreement had been rescinded. This rescission is supported by consideration on both sides, and it terminated all duties under the initial agreement. Thus, when the late October agreement was

entered into, there could be no question of pre-existing duty. Note that in this case there are three separate and distinct agreements.

(3) Assuming the facts in example 2 except that the rescission and the agreement to pay $1000 are simultaneous so that there are only two agreements. In this case it should be concluded that the pre-existing duty rule is violated, because the parties clearly intend that the rescission be contingent on the new contract, which in turn is contingent on the rescission. Some courts have reached an opposite conclusion. The Restatement, Second, rejects these cases.

(4) *A* agrees to do excavation work for *B* for a stated price. When solid rock is unexpectedly encountered, *A* notifies *B*. They agree that *A* will complete the job, and *B* will pay double the contract price, which is reasonable in relation to the work to be done. *A* does not have the defense of impossibility of performance and therefore has a legal duty to continue performance. Thus, in completing the work, *A* is only doing what the contract requires, and *B* is not obligated to pay the agreed additional sum. This is the traditional rule. A more modern view is that the modification will be upheld even if it is without consideration if the modification is made after unforeseen difficulties. The Restatement, Second, upholds the modification "if the modification is fair and equitable in view of the circumstances not anticipated when the contract was made." This rule is also applied to example 3 above.

d. The Three Party Cases
Again the situation and the competing views can best be explained by means of two illustrations.

Examples: (1) *A,* a jockey, enters into a bilateral contract with *B,* the owner of a horse, to ride in a race for $1,000. *C,* an outsider, who does not have the right to performance under the contract, owns the dam of *B*'s horse and would receive a prize if *B*'s horse wins. *C* promises to pay a bonus of $500 to *A* if *B*'s horse wins. The horse wins. According to the traditional rule, *A* may not recover the $500 because *A* was only performing an obligation owed under the contract with *B*. A second and untenable view would enforce *C*'s promise if the arrangement between *A* and *C* is bilateral but not if it is unilateral. A third view, adopted by both Restatements, is that *C*'s promise is enforceable whether or not the arrangement with *A* is unilateral or bilateral. One of the reasons given for this view is that there is less likelihood of duress in the three party cases than in the two party cases.

(2) *A* and *B* enter into a binding bilateral contract. In time, they decide to rescind the agreement as they have a right to do. *C,* who has an interest in seeing the contract performed, promises to pay X dollars to *A* and *B* if the agreement is not rescinded. Because *A* and *B* have a right to rescind their agreement, their refraining from rescinding constitutes detriment for *C*'s promise even under the traditional view.

e. **Agreement to Accept Part Payment in Satisfaction of a Debt**

Discussion: Part payment by a debtor of an amount here and now indisputably due is not detriment to support a *promise* by the creditor to discharge the entire amount. The same is true even if there is a purported *discharge.* For example, if the creditor released the debtor in exchange for the part payment, there is no detriment and no discharge. This is another application of the pre-existing duty rule because the debtor, in making the part payment, is only paying part of what is legally owed. This rule is sometimes referred to as the rule of *Foakes v. Beer.* The rule has been rejected by a small minority of jurisdictions. The majority of jurisdictions follow it, but some jurisdictions do make exceptions. The rule does not apply if in addition to the part payment, there is a detriment that is in fact bargained for.

Examples: (1) A lease calls for the payment of $1,250 per quarter. The lessor subsequently agreed to accept and accepted $875 per quarter. An action brought by the lessor to recover $375 per quarter would be successful since the lessee in paying $875 was only performing part of the legal obligation. But there are a number of jurisdictions holding that, when a person is entitled to money payable in installments, as for example under a lease, acceptance of a lesser sum in full payment discharges the debtor as to that installment despite the absence of detriment. In this illustration, if the lessee received in each case a receipt marked "payment in full" there could be a completed gift if one assumes a donative intent. There are even cases holding that part payment is sufficient if unforeseen hardships make full payment more onerous than anticipated. This would occur if there was an economic depression.

(2) *D* owes *C* $5,000 here and now indisputably due. *C* agrees to take $2,500 in full payment if *D* agrees to give *C* security for the debt in the amount of $1,000. Because the giving of security is something *D* was not legally obligated to do, *C*'s promise is enforceable.

(3) *D* owes *C* $5,000 here and now indisputably due. *D* is insolvent, and *C* agrees to accept $2,500 in full payment. *C*'s promise is not enforceable. The result would be different if the debtor refrains from bankruptcy on insolvency proceedings at the request of the creditor or if there is a composition among creditors.

(4) *D* owes *C* $5,000 here and now indisputably due. *C* agrees to take $1,000 plus a horse, hawk or robe. The giving of "a horse, hawk or robe" is obviously detriment but the question is whether it is bargained for. If it is merely a token, it is not consideration according to the Restatement, Second.

7. ACCORD AND SATISFACTION
a. Liquidated and Unliquidated Claims
The rule of *Foakes v. Beer* (discussed above) applies only to liquidated claims, that is, claims that are undisputed as to their existence and amount. Unliquidated claims are those about which there is a good faith dispute. The dispute could be as to liability, the amount due, or some other question, for example, the method of payment.

b. Definition
An accord is an offer to give or to accept a stipulated performance in the future in satisfaction or discharge of the obligor's existing duty plus an acceptance of that offer. The performance of this agreement is the satisfaction. If the agreement is not executed there may be an executory bilateral accord and different rules apply. (See p. 290 below.)

c. Problems Presented
When a question of accord and satisfaction is presented, the discussion should be divided into three parts. 1) Have the parties gone through a process of offer and acceptance? The rule relating to an offer of accord is that the offeror must make it clear that the offeror seeks a total discharge. If it is not made clear, any payment made and accepted will be treated as a part payment. 2) Has the accord reached been carried out (satisfaction)? 3) Is there consideration? There are many problems and many views, and so the emphasis for the most part will be on the majority view. The problem can best be explained through a number of illustrations. The illustrations used here involve the use of *Foakes v. Beer*

in a check cashing situation. How the rules of accord and satisfaction apply in a different fact pattern is discussed below.

Examples: (1) D (debtor) owes C (creditor) $100 here and now indisputably due (liquidated). D sends a check for $50 marked "payment in full," and C cashes it. (a) By the use of the words "payment in full," according to the majority view, D has made it clear that D seeks a total discharge, but the actual language used is only one of the factors to be considered. (b) Most cases hold that the cashing of the check constitutes an acceptance on the part of C. (Many cases hold that the retention of the check for an unreasonable period of time amounts to an acceptance.) The cashing of the check operates not only as acceptance; it also amounts to performance. (c) But, on the facts, the accord and satisfaction is not supported by consideration, because there is no consideration to support C's promise to take (or his actual taking of) a lesser sum. Thus, C is entitled to recover the additional $50.

(2) Assume the same facts as in example 1 except that there is a good faith dispute. C tells D that C is entitled to $100 and D tells C that C is only entitled to $50. D sends a check for $75 marked "payment in full" and C cashes it. The issues of offer, acceptance and performance are the same as in example 1. Here, however, it is clear that there is consideration to support the accord and satisfaction, because of the existence of the good faith dispute and a settlement which involved the surrender of detriment by both parties. Here, C's claim is unliquidated.

(3) Assume the same facts as in example 2 except that D admits to owing $50 and sends a check in that amount. C cashes it. As above, there is offer, acceptance, and performance. But there is some division on the question of consideration. The majority of the courts have held that since the claim is unliquidated, there is consideration to support the accord and satisfaction. The minority view disagrees arguing that D is only doing what D is legally obligated to do. The Restatement, Second, states that the issue is whether D is contractually bound by the admission. If D is contractually bound by the admission, D is only doing what D is legally obligated to do.

(4) Assume the facts in example 3 except that C, before cashing the check, strikes out the words "payment in full"

written on the check or notifies the debtor that the check is accepted only in part payment. At common law, the creditor's action is of no avail for in cashing the check in violation of the conditions upon which it was tendered the creditor is held to assent to its terms (imputed assent). This is analogous to cases where an offeree exercises dominion over unordered goods. (See p. 107 above.) However, if the U.C.C. governs, C may cash the check and reserve rights. Whether and when such a reservation is effective is discussed at p. 161 infra.

(5) P and D enter into an agreement that specifies the work to be done by P, and D promises to pay $6,000. P does the work, and there is a dispute as to whether the work was done properly. The parties settle the controversy at a figure of $5,000. The case is like example 2 except that the accord and satisfaction (offer and acceptance) arose prior to the cashing of the check. Thus, in this case, the cashing of the check relates only to the performance of the agreement.

(6) P owned a quantity of apples and requested D to obtain a purchaser. D did so and collected the price. P claims that the service rendered by D was gratuitous. D claims there was an agreement to pay a 10% commission. After collecting from the buyer, D sent a check for the proceeds less 10%. C cashes it. This is like example 3, and under the majority view, the expected holding is that there is a binding accord and satisfaction. But the cases are different because in example 3 the relationship was debtor-creditor whereas here the relationship is principal and agent, a fiduciary relationship. The importance of this distinction can be stated in two ways. A debtor who pays with the debtor's money may attach the condition that the check is sent in full payment, but an agent who is accounting for money belonging to the principal may not lawfully impose such a condition. In addition, to allow a fiduciary to proceed in this way is a "flagrant abuse of the opportunities and powers of a fiduciary position."

(7) D, in exchange for P's promise to do certain work, promised P among other things that P would receive ⅓ of the receipts from the products of D's dairy. This contract was entered into on October 4, 1904. Prior to this arrangement, P had been working for D on a daily (per diem) basis and, as of March 1, 1905, there was concededly due to P on this per diem arrangement the sum of $17.15. Soon after March 1, 1905, P received $17.15 from D and signed

and delivered a receipt stating that $17.15 was received "in full payment of all accounts and demands to date." *P* brought an action under the second arrangement for the period between October 7, 1904 and March 1, 1905. The court assumed that the situation was similar to example 3 above but concluded that a holding of accord and satisfaction was inappropriate. It held there was no accord and satisfaction because payment of a liquidated obligation is not consideration to support the surrender of a second claim that is wholly distinct. But if the disputed claim is closely related to the undisputed claim, payment of the amount admittedly due on the undisputed claim can be consideration for the surrender of the two claims in the absence of unfair pressure or economic coercion.

8. U.C.C. INROADS ON PRE-EXISTING DUTY RULE AND FOAKES V. BEER

a. U.C.C. § 2–209(1)

Under subdivision (1) "An agreement to modify a contract within this article needs no consideration to be binding."

b. U.C.C. §§ 2–209(2) and (3)

The statute says that, for the modification to be effective, it must be in writing in two situations. It must be in writing if the agreement as modified is required to be in writing under the Statute of Frauds. (Discussed later.) The second situation in which a writing is required is under subdivision (2) which is discussed immediately below.

c. U.C.C. § 2–209(2)

This section provides, "A signed writing which excludes modification or rescission except by a signed writing cannot be otherwise modified or rescinded, but except as between merchants such a requirement on a form supplied by the merchant must be separately signed by the other party." This subdivision relates to a signed contract that contains a provision that it cannot be modified or rescinded except by a signed writing. Such a provision (contrary to the common law) will be honored if set forth in a signed writing. (But see d. below.) The clause that starts with the words "except as between merchants" involves a situation where a merchant sends a form that contains the provision discussed above. In such a case, a non-merchant who signs the form at the bottom is not bound by this provision unless, in addition, the non-merchant signs the provision in question. If the case involves two merchants, this clause is not applicable.

d. Subdivision 4

This subdivision provides, "Although an attempt at modification or rescission does not satisfy the requirements of subdivision 2 . . . it can operate as a waiver." In other words even though the modification is not in a signed writing it can still operate as a waiver. The normal rule with respect to a waiver is that a waiver is retractable unless there is an estoppel—justifiable reliance on the promise made in the modification (See subdivision 5 immediately below.)

e. Subdivision 5

This subdivision states: "A party who has made a waiver" affecting an executory portion of the contract may retract the waiver by reasonable notification received by the other party that strict performance will be required of any term waived, unless the retraction would be unjust in view of a material change of position in reliance on the waiver." In other words, despite performance under the modification agreement, a party, as to the unperformed part, may reinstate the original agreement unless doing so would be unjust in view of a material change of position by the other party as a result of reliance on the modification.

Example: S and B, both merchants, entered into a signed contract for the purchase and sale of goods over a two-year period. There was a provision excluding modification except by a signed writing. The agreement also contained a provision that merchandise could not be returned for credit unless returned within 5 days of receipt. After one year the parties orally agreed to drop the 5 day limitation; thereafter B returned articles after 5 days of receipt and received credit. The contract still has 6 months to go, and S wishes to reinstate the 5 day limitation as to the future. As to the 6 months that the parties operated under the modification agreement, S is estopped from insisting upon the 5 day limit on returns. As to the remaining 6 months, S may insist upon the 5 day return period unless for some reason, not readily apparent on the facts, there was a material change of position on the part of B that would make it unjust not to enforce the modification agreement as to the future.

f. Duress (see pp. 330–333 below)

g. U.C.C. § 1–207

We have already seen that, as a common law proposition, cashing a full payment check in settlement of an unliquidated claim is deemed acceptance of an offer of accord despite the creditor's protest to the contrary. The creditor's deeds speak louder than words. Thus, there is a binding accord and satisfaction. On this point U.C.C. § 1–207 provides: "A party who with explicit reservation of rights performs or promises to perform or assents to performance in a manner demanded or offered by such other party does not prejudice the rights reserved. Such words as 'without prejudice,' 'under protest' or the like are sufficient." There is serious doubt as to whether this section was intended to apply to the accord and satisfaction puzzle. However, there are a number of jurisdictions which have concluded that the section does apply in the area of accord and satisfaction. Clearly, under this assumption, the common law rule mentioned above is changed. These jurisdictions reason that this section is designed to increase and not to diminish the common law rights of the creditor. But what nexus with the Code is needed to make U.C.C. § 1–207 applicable to the particular case? There are two views. (1) That the section applies by virtue of the use of a check (Article 3 nexus). (2) That the section applies only where the underlying transaction is covered by the Code, for example where the underlying transaction involves a contract for the sale of goods (Article 2 nexus). Note that proposed revisions of Article 3 of the U.C.C. seek to restore the common law rule.

Examples: (1) *D* (debtor) indisputably owes *C* (creditor) $100 here and now. *D* sends a check for $50 marked "payment in full" and *C* cashes it with a notation that it was accepted "under protest." Under the majority common law view (discussed above), there is no accord and satisfaction because there is no consideration and *C* may recover the remaining $50. If U.C.C. § 1–207 applies, the fact that *C* reserved rights does not change this result, because the section is designed to increase and not to diminish the rights of *C*.

   (2) There is a good faith reasonable dispute between *C* and *D*. *C* claims $100, and *D* claims that only $50 is owed. *D* sends a check for $50, marked "payment in full" which *C* cashes. Before cashing the check, *C* reserves rights to the remaining $50. At common law, according to the majority view, there is a binding accord and satisfaction despite the attempted reservation of rights. If U.C.C. § 1–207 applies to this problem, the result is changed, and *C* may sue for $50. But *D* may litigate what amount is owed unless *D* is contractually bound by the earlier admission that $50 was due.

h. U.C.C. § 1–107

The pre-existing duty concept led to the rule that a release of a duty is ordinarily ineffectual without consideration. U.C.C. § 1–107 provides, however, that "any claim of right arising out of an alleged breach can be discharged in whole or in part by a written waiver or renunciation signed and delivered by the aggrieved party." Under this section, a release that is written, signed, and delivered will be effective to discharge an alleged breach in whole or in part even though the release is not supported by consideration. The section applies to all transactions that are covered by the U.C.C.

i. U.C.C. § 3–408

This section deals with negotiable instruments (commercial paper). It provides that no consideration is necessary for an instrument given in payment of or as security for payment of an antecedent obligation of any kind.

9. BILATERAL CONTRACTS

A promise in a bilateral contract is consideration for the counterpromise only if the performance that is promised would be consideration.

> ***Example:*** *B* says to *A,* "if you promise to pay me the $50 that you owe me, I promise to give you a hat worth $10." *A* promises. *B*'s promise is not supported by consideration because (1) the mere utterance of *A*'s promise does not constitute legal detriment and (2) the act called for (payment of a debt here and now due) is not detrimental because *A* is only doing what *A* is legally obligated to do.

10. MUTUALITY OF OBLIGATION

a. Introduction

The doctrine of mutuality of obligation is commonly expressed in the phrase that in a bilateral contract "both parties must be bound or neither is bound." But this phrase is an over-generalization. The doctrine is not mutuality of *obligation;* rather it is mutuality of *consideration.* In essence, this means if one party to a bilateral contract has not suffered detriment, neither party is required to perform. The point is that if *B*'s promised performance is not consideration, *B* may not enforce *A*'s promise. Conversely, *A* may not enforce *B*'s promise even though *A* has suffered detriment because ordinarily this would not be fair.

> ***Example:*** *B* here and now owes *A* a liquidated debt of $1,000. *A* promises not to collect the debt for six months, and *B* promises to pay the debt without interest at the end of six months. Under the approach we took earlier, we would conclude that *A*'s promise would not be enforceable because *B* is doing only what *B* is legally obligated to do, but that *B*'s promise would be enforceable because *A,* in forbearing, is suffering a detriment which acts as consideration to support *B*'s promise. However, under the rule of mutuality of consideration, *A* may not enforce *B*'s promise because for a bilateral arrangement to be valid both parties must have parted with consideration. Otherwise, the contract is void— neither is bound.

b. Unilateral Contracts

Under the traditional view relating to a unilateral contract, it is clear that there is no mutuality of obligation because at no point is the offeree bound to perform. In a typical unilateral contract when the offeree performs, and the performance is detrimental, mutuality of consideration exists. But in a unilateral arrangement it is immaterial if the offeror is promising only what he or she is legally obligated to do.

> *Example:* A owes B $100. A promises to pay B the $100 if B paints A's fence. B performs. B could sue on the original claim or on the unilateral contract, but there would be only one recovery. The fact that A is promising to do only what A is legally obligated to do is not important because B has suffered detriment. The fact that A did not suffer detriment is immaterial because the doctrine of mutuality of consideration does not apply to unilateral contracts.

c. Voidable and Unenforceable Promises

Fraud, duress, mistake and lack of capacity generally result in a *voidable* contract. A promise is *unenforceable* when its enforcement is subject to the defense of the Statute of Frauds or the statute of limitations. Because the real issue is mutuality of consideration, it is well settled that a voidable or unenforceable promise is consideration. Thus, there is no problem in these situations with mutuality of consideration. The reason why a voidable or unenforceable promise is held to be consideration for a counterpromise is that if it were otherwise the arrangement would be void and the policy of the law in making a contract voidable or unenforceable would be subverted. In the case of a voidable contract the party who has a right to avoid it may instead ratify it.

> *Example:* A, an infant, enters into a contract with B, an adult. A has a power to avoid the contract because of infancy. A's promise, even though voidable, is consideration for B's promise and there is no mutuality problem. As stated above, if A's promise were not deemed to be consideration, the agreement would be void and the policy of the law in classifying an infant's promise as voidable would be subverted.

d. Illusory Promises

A bilateral contract is void if there is no mutuality of consideration. This will occur, for example, if the promise made by one or both parties is illusory. An illusory promise is an expression cloaked in promissory terms but which upon closer examination, reveals that the promisor has made no commitment. The modern decisional tendency is against finding a promise to be illusory and in general against defeating contracts on the technical grounds of lack of mutuality. One method of circumventing the illusory promise problem is by interpolating into an agreement that otherwise seems illusory the requirements of good faith and reasonableness. Consequently, the nature of the performance is not left to the whim and caprice of the promisor.

Example: *A* makes a promise "to spend such time as he personally sees fit in developing a business." Under the older view, this promise would be deemed illusory. Under the modern approach, a court would hold that *A* must exercise good faith in determining the time to be spent.

e. Right to Terminate a Contract by Virtue of a Provision Contained Therein

The new approaches towards the illusory promise problem are also being applied where the contract contains a provision permitting one or both parties to terminate. Such contracts are generally treated as involving alternative performances. In such a case, the rule is that in order to have consideration each alternative must be detrimental (see p. 171 below). U.C.C. § 2–309(3) speaks on the problem and states "Termination of a contract by one party except on the happening of an agreed event requires that reasonable notification be received by the other party and an agreement dispensing with notification is invalid if its operation would be unconscionable." (If the term is unconscionable, it should be stricken and a reasonable time substituted.)

Examples: (1) *A* and *B* enter into a bilateral contract whereby *A* agrees to provide services for one year, and *B* promises to pay a stipulated wage. In addition, *B* retains the power to terminate the agreement upon giving 30 days notice. *B* has made alternative promises, having agreed either to pay the wages for one year or for 30 days. Because both alternatives are detrimental and the exchange element appears to be satisfied there is no consideration problem. If U.C.C. § 2–309(2) were applicable, there might be a question of unconscionability. But the section is not applicable because the case does not involve a sale of goods.

(2) In example 1, above, if *B* reserved the right to terminate simply by giving notice at any time, the older cases have held that giving notice at any time is not detrimental. This is because *B*'s performance is at *B*'s unfettered discretion and therefore one of *B*'s alternative performances does not constitute consideration. But later decisions lean to the view that each alternative is detrimental because even the act of giving notice is detrimental. The question that would remain is whether notice is a bargained-for alternative, but this question seems to have been ignored in an effort to make the agreement enforceable. Under the U.C.C., which is not applicable, reasonable notice would ordinarily be required.

(3) In example 1, above, if *B* reserved the right to terminate the agreement without notice at any time, the older cases agree that the promise is illusory. According to the U.C.C., which is not applicable, the issue is unconscionability. Some of the modern cases, irrespective of the U.C.C., have placed the case on a different footing by a process of interpretation. These cases have ignored the words "at any time" and interpolated words requiring notice of termination within a reasonable time after formation of the contract. Once this is done, the consideration problem disappears.

(4) In example 1, above, assume *B* reserved the right to terminate at any time, and nothing is said with respect to notice. Some courts have interpreted the language as requiring notice, and others have reached the opposite conclusion. Once this problem of interpretation is resolved, the fact pattern fits either example 2 or 3 above. The U.C.C., which is not applicable, states specifically that in this case reasonable notice is required. Thus, under the modern view, one can usually conclude that a promise is not rendered insufficient as consideration by reason of a power of termination reserved by the promisor.

f. Conditional Promises

The question here is whether a promise is made illusory by a condition attached to it. If the happening of the condition is outside the control of the party who makes the promise, the promise is not illusory. This is also true if the condition relates to an event that is outside of the promisor's unfettered discretion. At times, an illusory promise problem is avoided by treating the express language of condition attached to the promise as implied language of promise.

Examples: (1) *A* promises to pay $500 "if I feel like it." The promise is illusory.

(2) *A* promises to perform "if war does not break out." The promise is not illusory because the condition is not within the control of the promisor.

(3) *A* promises to buy real property if *A* is able to obtain a mortgage loan. The promise seems illusory because *A* has not expressly promised to seek a loan. But it is routinely held that the buyer has impliedly promised to use best efforts to bring about the condition. Thus the conditional promise is not illusory.

g. Aleatory Promises

An aleatory promise is one conditional on the happening of a fortuitous event or an event supposed by the parties to be fortuitous. An aleatory promise is not illusory, because the condition is based upon an event that is wholly or partially outside of the control of either party.

Examples: (1) In consideration of a payment of $100, A makes a promise to repay $10,000 "if I recover my gold mine." The promise is aleatory because it is conditional on a fortuitous event and is not illusory.

(2) F has two sons, A and B. A says to B, "You know how eccentric our father is. Let us agree that no matter what his Will contains, we will divide whatever he leaves to either of us equally." B agrees. F left all of his assets to A. Although B suffered no actual detriment, B may enforce A's promise because A bargained against the possibility that B would be favored. Because the parties believed that the event was fortuitous, the promise is binding even if the will in favor of A had already been drawn.

h. Consideration Supplied by Implied Promise

Here we are talking about resolving an illusory promise problem not by implying a promise from language of condition (see above), but rather by inferring a promise from the entire fact pattern. Sometimes the promise inferred is called an implied promise. At other times it is referred to as a constructive promise (see below). But whichever conclusion is reached, the result is the same.

Example: In an elaborate written instrument, D promised to give P an exclusive agency and P promised to pay ½ of the profits to D. P already had an organization in place that was adapted to carrying out the exclusive agency. P's promise would be illusory if P were not required to do anything to bring about profits. A promise on the part of P to use reasonable efforts was inferred. The rule is codified in U.C.C. § 2–306(2). It provides: "A lawful agreement by either the seller or the buyer for exclusive dealing in the kind of goods concerned imposes unless otherwise agreed an obligation by the seller to use best efforts to supply the goods and by the buyer to use best efforts to promote their sale."

i. Agreements Allowing a Party to Supply a Material Term

If a bilateral agreement permits a party to the contract to supply a material term, that party's promise, at earlier common law, was deemed to be illusory and the bilateral agreement void under the mutuality doctrine. Modern cases have reached a different conclusion where a party is given the right to alter or modify a material term of the contract upon the theory that the right to modify the term must be exercised in good faith. The U.C.C., with its insistence on good faith, is clearly on the side of the modern cases. (See Indefiniteness topic above.)

j. **A Void Contract Is Not Necessarily a Nullity**
Although a void contract is ordinarily a nullity, this is not necessarily true where there has been performance under it. If there is performance under a void bilateral contract, the case should be treated as if an offer looking to a unilateral contract were made to the party who performed. Two requirements are essential before this doctrine can be applied. 1) All of the requisites of the law of offer and acceptance must be fulfilled, including the requirement that the promise requested must have been given. 2) The act performed by the party seeking to enforce the contract must be detrimental. This approach has been referred to as "forging a good unilateral contract out of a bad bilateral contract," or "forging a series of good unilateral contracts out of a bad bilateral contract."

Examples: (1) *D* was under an undisputed obligation to pay *P* a liquidated debt. The parties entered into an agreement whereby *P* agreed to forbear from suing on the obligation for six months, and *D* promised to pay the debt at the end of six months without interest. *P* did forbear for six months and then brought an action, not on the debt but upon *D*'s promise to pay the debt. It is clear that the agreement was void for want of mutuality of consideration. But it is equally clear that the performance permits the use of the doctrine of forging a good unilateral contract out of a bad bilateral contract.

(2) In a case involving the sale of goods, if the parties fail to agree on the quality of the goods but the seller sends a particular quality which the buyer accepts, it can be said that a good unilateral contract has been forged out of a bad bilateral contract.

(3) *D* agreed to appoint *P* as exclusive agent within a certain territory in exchange for *P*'s promise to develop a market for *D*'s products. *P* was to be paid a commission for each sale made. No duration was stated. The court concluded the arrangement was indefinite and therefore void. When, however, *P* performed under the agreement, *P* was entitled to be paid a commission for all sales *P* made, thus forging a series of good unilateral contracts out of a bad bilateral contract. The more recent cases would conclude that a valid

bilateral contract existed at the outset. The arrangement would last for a reasonable time.

11. REQUIREMENTS AND OUTPUT CONTRACTS
a. Introduction
This topic involves cases where the quantity term is measured by the requirements of the buyer (requirements contract) or the output of the seller (output contract). Because the rules relating to output and requirements contracts are basically the same, as a matter of convenience, emphasis will be on the topic of requirements contracts.

b. Validity of Requirements Contracts
At one time, requirements contracts were not enforced. They were deemed illusory because the buyer could refrain from having requirements. Later, they were generally upheld upon the theory that consideration could be found in the surrender of the buyer's privilege of buying elsewhere. But there was a minority view that refused to enforce the agreement when the buyer was entering into a new business or was a middleman. Under U.C.C. § 2–306 it is clear that requirements and output contracts are valid.

c. U.C.C. § 2–306
"A term which measures the quantity by the output of the seller or the requirements of the buyer means such actual output or requirements as may occur in good faith except that no quantity unreasonably disproportionate to any stated estimate or in the absence of a stated estimate to any normal or otherwise comparable prior output or requirements may be tendered or demanded."

d. How Much Is a Requirements Buyer Entitled to Demand?
At common law there were two views. (1) The buyer was entitled to his actual good faith requirements. (2) The buyer was entitled to his normal requirements. At common law, an estimate by the buyer had no effect except if made in bad faith in which event it operated as a maximum to the seller's liability. Under the Code, the buyer is entitled to good faith requirements. But two limitations are placed on the rule of good faith. (1) If there is a stated estimate the buyer is not entitled to any quantity unreasonably disproportionate to the estimate. (2) If there is no estimate or maximum or minimum stated in the contract, the buyer may demand only "any normal or otherwise comparable prior requirements." In essence, this means that a buyer cannot demand an amount disproportionate to the quantity reasonably foreseeable at the time of contracting.

e.   May a Requirements Buyer Diminish or Terminate Requirements?
Essentially the question here is whether a requirements buyer may go out of business and have no requirements or change the method of doing business so that the requirements are fewer. Under the U.C.C., the buyer may go out of business or change business methods if this is done in good faith. This is so even if the reductions are disproportionately less than normal prior requirements or stated estimates. There is some conflict as to whether a buyer acts in good faith if the shutdown is to curtail losses. Comment 2 seems to indicate that the buyer is not free to do so, but some cases indicate that the buyer may do so if the losses are "more than trivial."

f.   Does a Requirements Buyer Have a Duty to Promote the Goods?
U.C.C. § 2–306(2) states that, in an exclusive dealing contract, the buyer has the obligation "to use the best efforts to promote" the sale of the goods. A requirements contract is ordinarily an exclusive dealing contract. Is the requirements buyer obliged to promote the sale of goods? Obviously the question arises only if the goods are purchased for resale. But Comment 5 suggests that this duty exists only if the buyer is an agent with an "exclusive territory."

12.   MUST ALL OF THE CONSIDERATION BE VALID?
All of the consideration need not be valid.

Example: Uncle promises nephew, "In consideration of your past good conduct and in consideration of your promise to refrain from smoking until one year has passed, I will pay you $500." The fact that part of the recited consideration is past, does not prevent the valid part from serving as consideration.

13.   CONJUNCTIVE AND ALTERNATIVE PROMISES
a.   Conjunctive Promises
If one of the conjunctive promises is consideration it is sufficient to support a counter-promise.

> ***Example:*** *A* says to *B*, "I promise to give you my black horse if you pay me the liquidated sum of $50 you owe me and paint my fence." Although in paying the debt *B* is only performing a legal obligation, in painting the fence *B* is suffering detriment. Therefore, *B* is supplying consideration for *A* 's counter promise. For *B* to recover, *B* must paint and pay the debt. Even though the payment is not consideration, it is still a condition that must be performed if *B* is to recover on *A* 's promise.

b. Alternative Promises

1) Where the Choice of Alternatives Is in the Promisor
We have already seen that where the choice of alternatives is in the promisor, the rule is that each alternative promise must be detrimental. The Restatement, Second, says that the rule does not apply if there is a substantial possibility that events may eliminate the alternative which is not detrimental before the promisor makes a choice.

> *Example:* *A* promises to paint for *B*. In exchange, *B* promises to do masonry work for *A*, or to pay *A* the liquidated debt of $500 that *B* owes *A*. *B* has made alternative promises. Because one of the alternative promises is not detrimental (paying the debt), *B*'s promises are not consideration for *A*'s promises. Therefore under the mutuality doctrine, there is no valid contract.

2) Where the Choice of Alternatives Is in the Promisee
If the choice of alternatives is in the promisee, the alternative promises supply consideration if any one of the alternatives is detrimental.

> *Example:* *A* promises to paint for *B*, and *B* promises to do masonry work or to pay a liquidated debt. The choice of alternatives is in *A*, the promisee. Because *A* is free to choose to have *B* perform the masonry work, no consideration problem is presented.

C. MORAL OBLIGATION

1. INTRODUCTION
Subject to several exceptions, a promise made in recognition of a prior moral or legal obligation is not enforceable.

> ***Discussion:*** This section discusses promises that are enforceable despite the absence of consideration or detrimental reliance. The discussion centers on promises made because the promisor is under an antecedent moral or legal obligation to the promisee. The promise relates to the performance of the antecedent legal or moral obligation. The rule is logical because the promise is based solely upon past consideration and there is no detriment given in exchange to support the promise. There are a number of exceptions to this rule. For the most part the exceptions are explained not by logic but by history.

2. EXCEPTIONS

a. Promises to Pay a Liquidated Debt

At early common law, a promise to pay an existing debt was enforceable despite the fact that the consideration for the promise was past. There are two views as to whether this exception continues. a) The promise is enforceable provided it is co-extensive with the pre-existing liquidated debt. b) The promise is not enforceable. The problem is academic if suit may still be brought on the original claim. The effect that the promise would have on the statute of limitations is discussed below.

Example: C lends D $1,000 which is to be repaid by D on January 2, 1985. D fails to repay but again promises to repay on March 1, 1989. There is no consideration to support the promise of March 1. However, the promise is enforceable under the majority rule, but it is not under the minority rule. See also U.C.C. § 3–408 which provides that if a promise to pay a pre-existing debt is made in an instrument (such as a note or a check) governed by Article 3 of the Code, the promise is enforceable despite the lack of consideration.

b. Promises to Pay Fixed Amounts for Services Previously Requested

A *requests* B to perform services for A. B performs. There was no agreed upon price prior to performance. It is clear that A is liable for the reasonable value of the services rendered. If A makes a promise (offer) to pay a fixed amount in discharge of the obligation, it should be equally clear that such promise should not be enforced unless it is accepted by B. In addition, without B's acceptance there is no consideration for A's promise. Nevertheless, for reasons rooted in history, it is generally held that the promise is enforceable without new consideration and without mutual assent. Under a minority view the promise is enforced only to the extent that it is not disproportionate to the value of the services. However, if the services were rendered without expectation of payment, most cases hold that the promise is not enforceable.

c. Promises to Pay a Fixed Amount for Services Not Requested

1) Where Promisee Is Entitled to a Quasi–Contractual Recovery
If B performs services for A without A having requested them, B is entitled to a quasi-contractual recovery in limited situations. In this type of case if A subsequently promises to pay a fixed amount, the rules stated above with respect to services requested apply.

2) Where Promisee Is Not Entitled to a Quasi–Contractual Recovery
Under the majority rule, where the promisee is not entitled to quasi-contractual relief, a promise to pay a fixed amount is not enforceable. There is a contrary minority view which has been adopted by the

Restatement, Second. The Restatement, Second, states that the promise is enforceable "to the extent necessary to prevent injustice." There will be no recovery, even under the minority view, if the benefit was conferred as a gift or if the promisor is not unjustly enriched. Recovery is limited to the extent of the benefit received by the promisor. The Restatement section dwells upon promises to pay for benefits received in emergencies or in a business setting and promises made to rectify mistakes. In some states by statute, the minority view has been extended to cover promises to compensate for injury to the promisee. See Cal.C.C. § 1606 and N.Y.G.O.L. § 5–1105. Under these statutes, a promise to pay an additional sum for benefits conferred under a contract would also be enforceable if required formalities are complied with.

Example: D's adult son, S, falls ill while he is away from home. Without any request from D, B takes care of S. Later, D promised to reimburse B for the expenses of S's care. Under the majority view, it is clear that D's promise is not enforceable. Nor is it enforceable under the minority view, because D did not receive any economic benefit. However, B could recover under the statutes mentioned above. New York requires that the promise be made in writing.

d. Promises to Pay Debts Discharged or Rendered Unenforceable by Operation of Law
If a claim is discharged or rendered unenforceable by operation of law, a subsequent promise to pay that obligation is enforceable despite the absence of consideration.

1) Discharge in Bankruptcy
   Until recently, a promise to pay a debt discharged in bankruptcy was enforceable despite the absence of consideration for the promise. The recent federal Bankruptcy Act has made it impossible to make a binding reaffirmation agreement in the case of a debt discharged or to be discharged in bankruptcy, except those made in the bankruptcy proceeding itself. The statute does not apply to debts discharged under the prior law.

2) Statute of Limitations
   A promise to pay all or part of any antecedent contractual or quasi-contractual obligation for the payment of money, whether liquidated or not, causes the commencement of the running of the statute of limitations anew.

Discussion: An acknowledgment of the obligation is treated as an implied promise to pay unless there is an indication of a contrary intention. In most states the promise or acknowledgment must be in writing. A voluntary part payment of principal or interest or the giving of a collateral may have the same effect as an acknowledgment and be treated as the equivalent of a writing. The action is limited by the terms of the new promise. A promise not to plead the statute of limitations generally has the same effect as a promise to pay the debt. But in most jurisdictions, if the promise is made in the original contract or before maturity of the debt, it is void as contrary to public policy.

Examples: (1) *A* lends *B* $1,000 on January 2, 1979, the money to be repaid on January 2, 1980. No payment is made. On January 2, 1983, *B* promises to pay. Assume a six year statute of limitations. The six year statute of limitations would start running anew on January 2, 1983, so that the debt would be barred in 1989. If instead, in 1987, after the statute had run, *B* promised to pay, the statute would start to run again so that the statute would expire in 1993.

(2) *D* owes *C* $10,000, but the debt is barred by the statute of limitations. *D* acknowledges the debt and that it should be paid but adds, "I will never pay it." Although there is an acknowledgment of the debt and this is normally sufficient, the quoted language manifests a contrary intention and therefore the promise that normally would be implied from an acknowledgment does not arise.

(3) *D* owes *C* $10,000, but the debt is barred by the statute of limitations. *D* promises to pay "when I am able." Because *C* is limited by the promise, *C* may not bring an action until *D* is able to pay.

e. Promises to Perform a Voidable Duty

A promise to perform a voidable duty is enforceable despite the absence of consideration as long as the new promise does not suffer from an infirmity that would in turn make it voidable.

Discussion: A party whose promise is voidable may either avoid the contract or ratify it. An effective ratification terminates the right to avoid the contract. The rule stated above does not generally apply to void contracts.

Examples: (1) *A* is induced by fraud to promise to pay $1,000 in return for certain property. As a result, the promise is voidable. Upon discovering the fraud, *A* again promises to pay $1,000. The promise is enforceable without consideration because in the case of a voidable contract the party who has a right to avoid the contract may also elect to continue it. The result would be different if *A* did not know of the fraud at the time *A* elected to ratify the agreement.

(2) *I*, an infant, enters into a contract that is voidable because of infancy. Before reaching majority, *I* again promises to perform the contract. The promise to ratify the agreement is voidable, because *I* is still an infant. *I* can still avoid the promise.

f. Statute of Frauds

A contract within the Statute of Frauds not evidenced by a writing is unenforceable, but a sufficient memorandum made at any time makes the original contract enforceable. If a party who has the defense of the Statute of Frauds subsequently promises to perform, but the promise does not satisfy the Statute of Frauds, two problems arise. One problem relates to consideration, and the other involves the Statute of Frauds. Most cases hold that consideration is not a problem and make an analogy to e. above. As to the Statute of Frauds, it is generally held that the subsequent oral promise is not enforceable because to enforce it would defeat the policy of the Statute. However, a written promise has at times been enforced even though it is in a writing that does not state the terms sufficiently to satisfy the Statute of Frauds.

Example: In a jurisdiction that includes a promise to pay a commission to a real estate broker within the Statute of Frauds, *A*, a real estate agent, without any written agreement, procures *P*, a purchaser for *B*'s land. *P* enters into a signed written contract of sale with *B*. In that instrument, *B* promises to pay *A* $1,000 (the usual commission) for services rendered. Despite the consideration problem and the Statute of Frauds problem there are cases holding that the promise is enforceable, even if the writing does not state the terms sufficiently to satisfy the Statute of Frauds.

g. Miscellaneous Promises Supported by Antecedent Events

These include (a) a subsequent promise of a surety or endorser who has been discharged on technical grounds; (b) a promise to repay sums collected by the force of an erroneous but valid judgment; (c) a promise to pay for benefits received under an illegal bargain where the illegality does not involve moral turpitude.

h. To Whom the Promise Must Be Made
Under the majority view, a new promise to pay an antecedent obligation, to be enforceable, must be made to an obligee or the obligee's agent.

D. PROMISSORY ESTOPPEL

1. INTRODUCTION
We saw in the discussion of consideration that a donative promise is not supported by consideration even though the promisee relied upon it. To rectify the injustice in contract law caused by cases that rigidly applied this approach, the First Restatement gave birth to the doctrine of promissory estoppel as a separate and specific doctrine. The Restatement, Second, made significant changes in the formulation of the doctrine.

2. THE FIRST RESTATEMENT
Restatement, First, § 90 provides "A promise which the promisor reasonably expects to induce action or forbearance of a definite and substantial character on the part of the promisee and which does induce such action or forbearance is binding if injustice can be avoided only by the enforcement of the promise." In this statement a number of elements required by the doctrine may be identified. (1) A promise is required. Thus, a statement of intention would not be sufficient. (2) The promise must be one that the promisor should reasonably expect will lead the promisee to act or forbear. The same thought could be expressed by saying that the promisee must justifiably rely upon the promise. (3) The reliance must be of a substantial character and must be injurious rather than detrimental in the consideration sense. (4) The reliance must be of a kind that the promisor could definitely have expected; that is, foreseen. (5) The promise will not be enforced unless injustice can be avoided only by the enforcement of the promise. (6) Although not stated, the notion is that the promise will be enforced as made or not at all. This means that the choice is between a full contractual recovery or no recovery at all.

Examples: (1) *A* gave his granddaughter a promissory note indicating that it was for the purpose of freeing her from the necessity of working. It was clear that he was not requesting that she cease work in exchange for the note. There was no consideration, because *A* made a gift promise. He did not bargain for anything. The court applied the doctrine of "estoppel in pais," but really was creating a new doctrine of promissory estoppel. Estoppel in pais had been based upon a misrepresentation of fact, not upon a breach of a promise. (See below.)

(2) *A* makes a gratuitous promise to give *B* $5,000 with which to buy a car. According to Williston, *B* may enforce the promise if *B* buys the car but not if *B* spends the money for a different

purpose. In the latter situation Williston says that the reliance is not foreseeable. Corbin also identifies the question as one of foreseeability, and states the approach should follow that taken in the law of negligence.

3. RESTATEMENT, SECOND

The Restatement, Second, has made four important changes in the formulation of the doctrine. (a) It has excised the words "of definite and substantial character" in the text of the section. However, one of the comments makes it clear that the definite and substantial nature of the reliance are still factors to be considered. (b) It added a new sentence permitting flexibility of remedy. Thus, the promise need not be enforced as made but may be enforced to the extent of reasonable reliance. (c) It also provides for the contingency of reliance by a third party on a promise and reliance by a promisee that inures to the benefit of a third party beneficiary. (d) It contains a provision that a charitable subscription or a marriage settlement is binding without proof that the promise induced action or forbearance. (See p. 178 below.)

4. THE ROOTS OF THE DOCTRINE OF PROMISSORY ESTOPPEL

The roots of the doctrine of promissory estoppel can be found in a number of cases that enforced a promise because of injurious reliance despite there being no consideration for the promise. In these cases the courts did not use the term promissory estoppel but either stretched the doctrine of consideration or formulated narrow specialized doctrines. The cases for the most part involved family promises, promises to make gifts of land, gratuitous agencies and bailments, charitable subscriptions and marriage settlements.

Examples: (1) *U,* Uncle, promised *P,* nephew, that if *P* would take a trip to Europe he would reimburse his expenses. The nephew made the trip. It was concluded that *U*'s promise was supported by consideration. It is true that *P* suffered detriment, but it is not likely that the detriment was bargained for in exchange for the promise.

(2) *A* promises to make a gift of land to *B,* his son-in-law. *B,* with knowledge and assent of *A,* takes possession of the land and makes improvements. *B* is entitled to specific performance or other equitable remedies. The modern basis of the action is promissory estoppel.

(3) *A,* a carter, agreed with *B* to transport a keg of brandy free of charge. The keg of brandy was damaged by the carter's negligence. An action lies for the breach of the implied promise by *A* to use due care. Although there is in reality no consideration for *A*'s promise as it was gratuitous, *B* relied on the promise and suffered injury. If *A* had refused to take possession

of the keg, the result would be different. The distinction made was between misfeasance and nonfeasance. In other words if the gratuitous bailee (promisor) takes possession of the goods and fails to carry out the implied promise to use requisite care, liability has been found to exist. If, however, the promisor fails to take possession, traditionally there is no liability on the gratuitous promise because there is only nonfeasance.

(4) *A* told *B*, an agent of the life insurance company with which she had a policy on her husband's life, that she did not have money to pay a particular premium. *B* assured *A* that the payment would be taken care of. In reliance on *B*'s promise, *A* did not obtain a loan to pay the premium. The insurance policy lapsed and the husband died. The doctrine of promissory estoppel was applied to this gratuitous agency situation. Notice that in this situation nonfeasance is involved. Nevertheless, the promise is enforced. The older cases, based upon the distinction between misfeasance and nonfeasance, refused to enforce such a promise. If *B* attempted to take care of the payment and did it negligently, this would have amounted to misfeasance. (See example 3 above.)

(5) *A* promises to pay *B*, a college, $50,000 in four annual installments in connection with *B*'s general fund raising campaign. Two annual installments are paid before *A* dies. There is no consideration to support *A*'s promise, because *A* did not bargain for anything. Nor is *B* able to show that there was injurious reliance on *A*'s promise. But *A*'s promise has been enforced under a wide variety of erroneous theories including promissory estoppel. The Restatement, Second (see above), recognizing the theoretical problem, states that public policy requires a charitable subscription to be enforced despite the absence of consideration or injurious reliance (promissory estoppel).

(6) *A* and *B* are engaged to be married. In contemplation of the marriage, *B*'s Father (*F*) and *A* enter into a formal agreement in which *F* promises to make certain payments to *A* "in consideration of the marriage." The marriage occurs. If *A*, in marrying, is doing something that he is not legally obligated to do, there is consideration if it is assumed that *F* is bargaining for the marriage rather than promising a conditional gift. If *A* is legally bound to marry *B*, then his only theory is promissory estoppel. If the engaged couple would have married even though *F* had not made his promise, *A* would not be able to show injurious reliance. Because of the public policy in favor of marriage settlements the Restatement, Second, provides that such

promises are enforceable "without proof that the promise induced action or forbearance."

5. PRESENT APPROACH TO A GIFT PROMISE
Initially the courts used promissory estoppel as a substitute for consideration mostly in cases of gift promises, for the most part in the types of cases listed in 4 above. It is fair to say that there is now a trend toward using promissory estoppel in just about any gift promise case where all of the necessary elements are present. This trend has been given much impetus by the two Restatements.

6. DOCTRINE NOT LIMITED TO GRATUITOUS PROMISES
Initially there was some authority that promissory estoppel should be limited to gratuitous promises and should not be applied to bargain transactions. However, the trend today is in the other direction. Thus, the doctrine has been used (1) to make an offer irrevocable; (2) to enforce a promise that is part of an otherwise unenforceable or defective contract; and (3) to enforce a promise made during the course of preliminary negotiations.

Examples: (1) *A,* a subcontractor, submits a bid (offer) to *B,* a general contractor, who uses the bid in calculating *B*'s bid on a construction project. *A* attempts to withdraw the offer prior to acceptance by *B.* Under the traditional rules of offer and acceptance, the revocation would be effective. But under the doctrine of promissory estoppel, the offer is irrevocable, because of *B*'s reliance on *A*'s offer. It is irrevocable until *B* learns that it has been awarded the contract and has a reasonable opportunity to notify *A* that *A*'s offer has been accepted. (*B* cannot reopen the bargaining with *A* and claim a continuing power to accept the original offer.) It is unusual to invoke promissory estoppel in the context of an offer to a bilateral contract. Ordinarily, the offeree of an offer looking to a bilateral contract is not justified in relying on the offer. Normally the offeree need only accept it prior to relying.

(2) *B* sent a letter to *S* stating that *B* would buy poultry raised by *S* at prevailing ceiling prices so long as ceilings should be established by law. Upon receiving the letter *S* purchased and began raising 7,000 chicks for future delivery. At this point, *B* attempted to withdraw the offer. Under the Restatement, Second, and some decisions, the offer is made irrevocable under the doctrine of promissory estoppel even though the acts performed are merely acts of preparation. Applying the notion of flexibility of remedy mentioned above, damages might be limited to reliance damages.

(3) *A* has been employed by *B* for 40 years. In consideration of *A*'s previous service, *B* promises to pay *A* $200 per month when *A* retires. In reliance on the promise *A* retires and forbears to work elsewhere for several years, and *B* pays the pension for a time and then repudiates. Because past consideration is not consideration, the parties have entered into a void bilateral contract. The promise, however, is enforceable under the doctrine of promissory estoppel because of *A*'s injurious reliance on the promise. *A* quit in reliance on the pension instead of continuing to work or seeking other employment.

(4) *P* owned a lot and desired to construct a commercial building thereon. *P* entered into an agreement with *D* under which *D* was to obtain a loan in the sum of $70,000 in favor of *P* from a third party or provide it himself. *D* in turn was to be paid $5,000 plus 5% of the rent of tenants procured by *D*. After the agreement was signed, *D* assured *P* that the money would be available and urged *P* to demolish the buildings presently on the site. *P* complied. The loan arrangement was held to be too vague and indefinite to be enforceable, but the doctrine of promissory estoppel was applied because of *P*'s injurious reliance. Damages were limited to a reliance measure.

(5) *A* was the lessee of an apartment house under a 99 year lease given by *B* for a rent of $10,000 per year. Because of war conditions, many of the apartments became vacant. To enable *A* to stay in business, *B* agreed to reduce the rent to $5,000. The reduced rent was paid for five years. When the war was over and the apartments were finally fully rented, *B* demanded that the full rent called for by the lease be paid, including the balance for the five years during the war. Under the traditional rule, the modification was void for lack of consideration. But it was enforced for the five year period because of injurious reliance by *A*. As to the future, *B* was allowed to reinstate the full rent. There was injurious reliance because *A* lost a large amount of money by staying in business and should not be punished further.

(6) *A* was assured by *B* that if *A* took certain steps and raised $18,000 worth of capital, *B* would grant *A* a supermarket franchise. In compliance with the recommendation of *B*, *A* sold a bakery, purchased a grocery to gain experience and resold it, acquired an option on land for building a franchised outlet and moved nearer to where the franchise was to be. *A* raised the necessary capital by borrowing from a close relative. At first, *B* approved this plan, but later withdrew approval of this method of financing and demanded that *A* procure from the relative a

statement that the advance was a gift. *A* refused and sued. At the time of the rupture the parties had not come to any agreement as to size, cost, design, layout or the terms of the lease. The agreement was not only too vague and indefinite to be enforced, but the parties did not intend to be bound until a later date so that up to the point of the rupture there had been nothing but preliminary negotiations. Nevertheless, under the theory of promissory estoppel, *A* was permitted to recover the amounts expended in reliance upon the negotiations.

7. APPROACH TO A PROBLEM

In the logical order, before turning to the doctrine of promissory estoppel one should determine whether conventional consideration exists. If there is consideration, the applicability of the doctrine will ordinarily be an academic question. But if there is no consideration or if its existence is doubtful under some or all views, the promissory estoppel approach should be considered. The question then is, does the fact pattern present all of the elements required for the doctrine of promissory estoppel? The only remaining question, and this varies from jurisdiction to jurisdiction, is does that jurisdiction accept promissory estoppel as a substitute for consideration in the particular case? As we have seen, the tendency is to employ it in any case to which it applies because the doctrine is "an attempt by the court to keep remedies abreast of increased moral consciousness of honesty and fair representations in all business dealings. . . ."

SEALED INSTRUMENT

1. EFFECT OF A SEAL

At common law any promise contained in a delivered sealed instrument was held to be enforceable despite the absence of consideration. The rule still holds true in some jurisdictions. However, many states have enacted statutes that either abolish the binding effect of a seal or provide that a seal raises a presumption of consideration. The presumption is rebuttable, but the burden of proof on the issue of the absence of consideration is on the promisor. The U.C.C. eliminates the effect of a seal in sales transactions.

REVIEW QUESTIONS

1. T or F   The putative father of an illegitimate child promised the mother that if she named the child Wallace if it were a boy or include the name Wallace if it were a girl, he would pay $100 per week for the support of the child until the child reached the age of 21. The child was so named. The mother has no cause of action.

2. T or F   *D* promised *P* that if *P* delivered specified merchandise to *D*'s brother, *D* would pay for items previously delivered and for items to be delivered. *P* performed. *P* is entitled to enforce *D*'s promises.

3. T or F   *D* was the legal guardian of *P*, a 12 year old boy. *P* left the home of *D* and went to live with a relative. *D* promised *P* that if *P* would return and live with him, *D* would not charge *P* board and would send him to school without charge. *P* returned. *P* is entitled to enforce *D*'s promise.

4. T or F   *P* and *D* entered into a contract whereby *P* was to do certain work and *D* was to pay $8,000. The first payment of $5,000 was to be made by the assignment of a bond and mortgage held by *D*. *P* performed, and when *D* offered to assign the bond and mortgage, *P* refused to take it unless *D* guaranteed payment. *D* was not obligated to do so. *D* then executed the assignment with a guaranty of payment. The guaranty is not supported by consideration.

5. T or F   Plaintiffs were sailors on *D*'s vessel and agreed to work for a certain sum for a particular voyage. Midway through the voyage, the plaintiffs demanded an increase in wages and *D* promised to pay an additional $X. Under the majority view, *D*'s promise is not supported by consideration.

6. T or F   *P* and *D* entered into a contract for the sale and delivery (in installments) of 4,000 wooden display stands at a price of 65 cents each. After 2,000 stands had been delivered and paid for, *P* truthfully told *D* that "due to increased costs" *P* would have to charge 75 cents for each stand delivered in the future. *D* acquiesced. *P* is entitled to 75 cents for each stand delivered in the future.

7. T or F   *P* entered into a contract with *D* to paint a shopping center. The contract provided that the agreement could not be modified except by a signed written agreement. There was an oral modification agreement supported by consideration. The oral modification agreement is not binding.

8. T or F   *A* promises to work for *B* for one year in return for *B*'s promise to pay *A* a fair share of the profits. *A* performs. *A* is not entitled to a contractual recovery.

9. T or F   *P* and *D* entered into an agreement by the terms of which *D* was to sell and *P* was to buy 1,500,000 gallons of a specified grade of oil, shipments to be made equally in February, March and April. The agreement also provided as follows: "Seller may cancel any unshipped portion of this order on five days notice." *D* has suffered detriment.

10. T or F   *S* and *B* entered into an agreement by the terms of which *S* agreed to sell and *B* agreed to buy 12 carloads of Ko–Hi flasks at a stipulated price. There was a clause in the agreement which read as follows: "It is agreed that Buyer may have the privilege of increasing quantity by an additional 13 carloads during the period covered by the agreement." *B* is entitled to receive the additional 13 carloads.

11. T or F   *A* asked *B*, a builder, to build a stable. *B* agreed to do the job. The parties did not discuss price. *B* did a fine job and upon seeing the stable for the first time, *A* promised *B* $10,000. The reasonable value of the work was $7,200. Before *B* assented to this figure, *A* withdrew the promise. *B* is not entitled to recover $10,000.

12. T or F   Father (*F*) promised to give his daughter (*D*) $17,000 for the purpose of enabling her to purchase a house. In reliance on the promise, *D* entered into an option contract for the purchase of the property and expended $2,000 of her own money for this purpose. *F* declines to furnish the $17,000 promised. *D* is entitled to recover at least $2,000 from *F*.

13. T or F   *P* was away from home on an extended trip and had parked a car in his driveway. *P* heard a weather forecast predicting an early and heavy frost. Fearing for the wellbeing of the car, *P* telephoned *D*, a neighbor, who agreed to take *P*'s car to a service station that very day to have anti-freeze placed in the cooling system. *D* failed to do anything, and the predicted frost severely damaged *P*'s car. Under the traditional view, *P* does not have a cause of action against *D*.

14. Essay   *A* and *B* were boyhood chums in Poland. At one point *B* had saved *A*'s life and as a result *B* had suffered a permanent injury to his leg. *A* came to the United States and prospered. *B* remained in Poland and informed *A* that he was having troubles with the authorities. *A* then sent the following letter to *B:* "In view of our success and our friendship and your previous kindnesses to me, I am willing to send you enough money to come to the United States and when you get here I will be glad to give you permanent employment in my business." *B* answered that he was delighted. *A* sent the money. *B* sold his farm in Poland and came to the United States. *A* gave *B* a job as a truck driver. One day, during a vodka drinking contest, they had an argument and *A* fired *B*. Does *B* have any claim against *A?*

*

III

LEGAL CAPACITY

Analysis

A. Infants
    1. Who Is an Infant
    2. Is an Infant's Promise Void or Voidable?
    3. Avoidance or Ratification
        a. Avoidance
        b. Ratification
    4. Restitution After Disaffirmance
        a. Infant as Defendant
        b. Infant as Plaintiff
    5. Necessaries
    6. Infant's Liability for Benefits Received
    7. Ignorance of Law and Fact
    8. Torts Connected With Contracts
        a. Infant's Torts Stemming From Contracts
        b. Effect of Misrepresentation of Age
        c. Torts and Agency Relationships
B. The Mentally Infirm
    1. Is Promise of a Mentally Infirm Person Void or Voidable?
    2. Test of Mental Infirmity
    3. Requirement of Restitution
    4. Avoidance and Ratification

5.   Liability for Necessaries
6.   Intoxicated Persons and Drug Users
7.   Exploitation of Alcoholics and Weak Minded Persons

A. INFANTS

1.   WHO IS AN INFANT?

At common law a person remained an infant until the age of twenty-one. By legislation enacted mostly in the 1970's, the age of majority is now eighteen in almost all jurisdictions. To be more accurate, persons remain infants until the first moment of the day preceding their 21st or 18th birthdays depending upon the law of a particular jurisdiction. Infancy continues despite emancipation by parents and despite marriage.

2.   IS AN INFANT'S PROMISE VOID OR VOIDABLE?

An infant's promise is voidable rather than void. Not only is a contract voidable, but also executed transactions, such as sales, conveyances or releases. The power of avoidance resides only in the infant or infant's guardian; in the event of death, the infant's heirs, administrators or executors have the power of avoidance. The power does not reside in the adult party. However, the infant may not disaffirm certain contracts because of public policy or a statute so provides or because the infant has done or promised to do something which the law would compel even in the absence of a contract; e.g., to support an illegitimate child. After an infant has exercised the power to avoid the contract, the transaction is treated for many purposes as if it were void from the beginning. Thus, by disaffirming a conveyance, the infant may reclaim real property from a subsequent purchaser who purchased in good faith without notice of the fact that an infant had preceded the vendor in the chain of title. As to sale of goods, however, the Uniform Commercial Code provides that a subsequent bona fide purchaser for value obtains goods free from an infant's power of disaffirmance.

3.   AVOIDANCE OR RATIFICATION

a.   Avoidance

The exercise of the power of avoidance is often called disaffirmance. The effective surrender of this power is known as ratification. An infant may disaffirm a contract at any time prior to ratification. The entire contract must be avoided. Disaffirmance may effectively be made during infancy and once made is irrevocable. In the case of real property, however, the majority rule is that the infant's conveyance may be avoided only after majority.

b.   Ratification

An effective ratification cannot take place prior to the attainment of majority. Any purported ratification prior to that time suffers from the same infirmity as the contract itself. After majority, the infant may ratify in three ways. 1) The first is express ratification. As to contracts not yet performed by the former infant, a mere acknowledgement of the contract is not enough and nothing less than a promise will suffice. The authorities agree that if the contract is fully executed, an acknowledgement or other words consistent with an intention to stand on the contract is sufficient to constitute ratification. 2) The second is ratification by conduct. Retention and enjoyment of property received for more than a reasonable time after attaining majority will ordinarily amount to ratification. Receipt of performance from the other party after attaining majority will also be normally considered to be ratification by the infant. On the other hand, part payment or other performance by the infant, without more, will not ordinarily be deemed a ratification. 3) The third is failure to make a timely disaffirmance. The rule is that an infant may disaffirm contracts until a reasonable time after reaching majority. What is a reasonable time is often a question of fact dependent upon such circumstances as whether or not there has been any performance by either or both parties, the nature of the transaction and the extent to which the other party has been prejudiced by any extensive delay in disaffirming. Ordinarily, however, if the infant has obtained no benefits under the contract, as will usually be the case where the adult has not performed, there is no reason to bar the infant from disaffirming at any time up until the statute of limitations has run. Where it has been performed by the adult or both parties, it would ordinarily be inequitable to permit the infant to retain the benefits of the contract for a long period of time and then disaffirm. Under the majority view, the rules stated above apply to conveyances of real property, but many cases hold that in the absence of estoppel, the former infant has the right to avoid a conveyance until the statute of limitations has run.

4. RESTITUTION AFTER DISAFFIRMANCE
a. Infant as Defendant
Upon disaffirming, the infant is liable for the return (or the value) of any tangible benefits received and retained. This rule is subject to one extension. If the infant has exchanged or sold the property, and the proceeds of the exchange or sale can be traced, the infant will be liable to the extent of the traceable assets.

b. Infant as Plaintiff
If upon disaffirmance the infant sues for the return of the consideration, under the modern view recovery will be allowed, but minus the value of the use and depreciation of any property obtained from the defendant. The maxim is that infancy may be raised as a shield and not a sword. The more traditional rule was that the infant need only return what consideration the infant retains and need not account for its use and depreciation.

5. NECESSARIES
It is well settled that an infant is liable for the reasonable value of necessaries furnished. This liability is quasi-contractual rather than contractual. The concept of "necessaries" is relative to the infant's status in

life. Thus, it is a fruitless quest to analyze the cases to determine, for example, whether an automobile is a necessary. Food, shelter, clothing and medical services are generally considered to be necessaries but the kind of food, etc. is another question. Education is also a necessary but to what level is again another question. Business and employment expenses have received variable treatment. If an infant borrows money for the purpose of purchasing necessaries and so uses it, the infant is liable to the lender. The liability of the infant also depends upon whether or not the infant has an existing supply of necessaries, or parents or guardians who are able and willing to supply the infant with the necessities of life. In addition, it must appear that the goods or services were supplied on the credit of the infant and not of the parent, guardian or a third person. Thus, the liability, although quasi-contractual, requires that there be a contract with the infant.

6. INFANT'S LIABILITY FOR BENEFITS RECEIVED

Many jurisdictions now require that an infant who seeks to disaffirm a contract and obtain restitution must return or account for benefits received under the contract. If, however, the infant is a defendant and sets up a defense of infancy, the infant is liable only for necessaries or the value of tangible consideration still retained. Several recent cases have taken the position that it is immaterial whether the infant is the plaintiff or defendant, holding that if the infant has received benefits, whether necessaries or not, the infant is liable in an action for restitution for their value.

7. IGNORANCE OF LAW AND FACT

A ratification is ineffective if the former infant is unaware of the facts upon which his or her liability depends. There is a split of authority as to whether the infant must know that the law gives a power of avoidance. The majority view applies the maxim that everyone is presumed to know the law and that lack of knowledge of the law is immaterial.

8. TORTS CONNECTED WITH CONTRACTS

Very often tort liability is intimately connected with a contractual relation. Although infants are not generally liable on contracts, they are liable for torts. At least three kinds of problems arise from the interplay of tort and contract liability in cases involving infants.

a. Infant's Torts Stemming From Contracts

The other party to a contractual relation may not sue the infant for tort if the tort is in essence a breach of contract. An illustration of this rule is an action on a bailment where it is possible to frame a cause of action sounding in negligence or in contract. A tort or contract action will be dismissed. The infant, however, would be liable for conversion of a chattel because this type of wrong is deemed to be independent of the contract.

b. **Effect of Misrepresentation of Age**
The majority view is that infants may exercise the power of avoidance
even if they misrepresented their ages. The minority view is that infants
who misrepresented their ages and who wish to disaffirm must place the
adult parties in status quo ante. The question remains whether the
infants are liable in tort for willful misrepresentation of age. Again,
there is a split of authority. The division stems from the rule that a tort
action will not be allowed against an infant if in essence it involves the
enforcement of a contract. The question is whether the tort action is
sufficiently independent of the contract. The infant's fraudulent
misrepresentations of age or other material fact will permit the other
party to avoid the contract on grounds of fraud.

c. **Torts and Agency Relationships**
According to the majority view, an infant may also avoid liability for the
torts of the infant's agents, at least in so far as the tort liability stems
from the doctrine of *respondeat superior*.

B. THE MENTALLY INFIRM

1. **IS PROMISE OF A MENTALLY INFIRM PERSON VOID OR VOIDABLE?**
The overwhelming weight of modern authority is that promises of the mentally
infirm are voidable. However, in many jurisdictions the promise is deemed
void if the person so afflicted has been adjudicated an incompetent and a
guardian of property has been appointed prior to the incompetent's entering
into the transaction.

2. **TEST OF MENTAL INFIRMITY**
Under the traditional rule, it must be established that the person with a
mental infirmity did not understand the nature and consequences of the
transaction. Under a subsidiary test, the transaction would be voidable if the
person in question was rational except for "insane delusions" as to the
particular transaction. The more modern view, espoused by the Restatement,
Second, adopts in addition to the cognitive test "of ability to understand," the
position that the contract is voidable if the party "by reason of mental illness
or defect . . . is unable to act in a reasonable manner in relation to the
transaction and the other party has reason to know of this condition." These
rules apply to insane persons, and to other mental infirmities, such as senility,
mental retardation, delirium deriving from physical injuries, intoxication (see p.
191 below) and the side effects of medication.

3. **REQUIREMENT OF RESTITUTION**
In the case of an unadjudicated incompetent, contracts that are executory or
based upon grossly inadequate consideration are voidable. But if the
transaction is executed, and the other party took no advantage of the
incompetent, and had no reason to know of the infirmity, it is not voidable

unless the incompetent can place the other party in status quo ante. If the incompetency would be obvious to a reasonable person, there is no obligation upon the incompetent to make restitution if the consideration has been consumed or dissipated. Under a minority view, the appearance of sanity is immaterial and only the consideration still in the incompetent's possession need be restored.

4. AVOIDANCE AND RATIFICATION

As in the case of an infant's contracts, there is no power of avoidance in the competent party. The power of avoidance and ratification is reserved to the incompetent or a duly appointed guardian and the incompetent's heirs or personal representative after death. If a guardian is appointed, the power is vested in the guardian. The incompetent may ratify the contract after capacity is restored. As in the case of infants' contracts, ratification can be effected by conduct or words and, once ratified, the contract may not be avoided. After ratification, the former incompetent may have an action for damages if exploitation of the incompetent amounted to actionable fraud.

5. LIABILITY FOR NECESSARIES

As in the case of an infant, a mental incompetent is liable in a quasi-contractual action for necessaries. Roughly the same classes of goods and services considered necessaries for infants are necessaries for incompetents.

6. INTOXICATED PERSONS AND DRUG USERS

When a person is so far intoxicated or under the influence of narcotics that the person does not understand the nature and consequences of the transaction, the afflicted person may avoid the transaction under circumstances similar to those available to other classes of the mentally infirm. Under the rule laid down in the Restatement, Second, contracts made by an intoxicated party are voidable only if the other party has reason to know that the intoxicated party is unable to act in a reasonable manner in relation to the transaction or lacks understanding of it. Where the other party is aware of the intoxication, the rules alluded to in the next paragraph also come into play.

7. EXPLOITATION OF ALCOHOLICS AND WEAK MINDED PERSONS

Mental infirmity, feebleness of intellect or intoxication may exist to a lesser degree than required by law for avoidance of a contract. The cases frequently reveal exploitation of such people. The fact patterns usually involve subtle forms of duress, fraud, undue influence, or overreaching. Some degree of infirmity, coupled with the unfairness of the bargain, will often result in a finding of fraud, undue influence, overreaching, or even mental incapacity. The recent enlargement of the doctrine of unconscionability offers another, more forthright, approach to cases of this kind.

REVIEW QUESTIONS

1. T or F   *A*, a minor, sold a painting for $100. On reaching the age of majority, *A* received a book on French art. While perusing the book, *A* noticed that the painting was now worth $15,000. In an action to recover the painting brought promptly thereafter, *A* will succeed upon accounting for the $100 received.

2. T or F   *A*, a minor, sought to purchase a $500 stereo unit. The vendor would not give *A* credit, but promised to put the unit aside if the youth would make periodic payments towards the purchase price. After having paid $300, *A* reached majority, and told the vendor that payment would soon be made. A week after this meeting, *A* disaffirmed the contract and brought suit to recover the payments that had been made. *A* will succeed.

3. T or F   On March 1, Icarus went to a Rolls Royce dealer and bought a Silver Cloud with cash. The deal went smoothly and was fair. Icarus immediately attempted flight and the car was destroyed. Icarus' executor brought suit to recover the purchase price. The executor will recover.

4. Essay   Janice, a 17 year old high school senior in N.Y., has been accepted by Berkeley. Ace Airlines offers a discount flight for persons under 18 for $150, one-half of the adult fare. To attend the school, Janice, who has no money, misrepresents her age in order to obtain credit from the airline which is available only to adults. Naturally, the credit was for full fare. Upon arrival in San Francisco, Janice's grandfather gave her $200, as he had previously promised, to reimburse her for the cost of the flight. She then disaffirmed the contract with the airline and the airline brought suit. What result? Discuss.

IV

PROPER FORM (WRITING) AND INTERPRETATION

Analysis

A. Parol Evidence Rule
    1. The Nature and Meaning of the Rule
        a. What Type of Evidence May Be Excluded by the Parol Evidence Rule?
        b. Theory of the Rule
    2. How to Determine Finality
    3. How to Determine Completeness
        a. Four Corners Rule
        b. The Collateral Contract Rule
        c. Williston's Rules
        d. Corbin's View
        e. The U.C.C. Approach (U.C.C. § 2–202)
    4. Approach of Trial Judge
    5. Separate Consideration
    6. Subsequent Agreement
    7. Is the Rule One of Substantive Law or Procedure?
    8. Is the Term Offered Consistent or Contradictory?
    9. Undercutting the Integration
B. Interpretation
    1. Introduction
    2. Varying Views
        a. Plain Meaning Rule—Ambiguity

      b. *Williston's Rules*
      c. *Corbin's Rules—Restatement, Second*
      d. *U.C.C. on Interpretation*
   3. *The Relationship Between Parol Evidence and Interpretation*
      a. *Plain Meaning Rule*
      b. *Williston's Rules*
      c. *Corbin's Rules—Restatement, Second*
      d. *U.C.C.*
   4. *Course of Dealing, Course of Performance and Usage of Trade*
      a. *Introduction*
      b. *Meaning of Course of Dealing and Course of Performance*
      c. *Usage of Trade*
      d. *For What Purposes May They Be Used?*
   5. *Other Rules of Interpretation*
C. *Statute of Frauds*
   1. *Introduction*
   2. *Major Classes of Cases Covered by Writing Requirements*
      a. *Suretyship Agreements*
      b. *Real Property*
      c. *Contracts Not to Be Performed Within a Year*
      d. *Contracts in Consideration of Marriage*
      e. *Contracts for the Sale of Goods*
   3. *Sufficiency of the Memorandum*
      a. *Introduction*
      b. *Contents of the Writing*
      c. *What Is a Signature?*
      d. *Who Is the Party to Be Charged?*
      e. *Parol Evidence and the Memorandum*
      f. *Consideration*
      g. *More Than One Writing*
   4. *Provisions of the U.C.C.*
      a. *Contents of the Memorandum*
      b. *Written Confirmation Between Merchants*
   5. *Auction Sales*
   6. *Agent's Authority*
   7. *Purpose of the Statute*
   8. *Effect of Non–compliance With the Statute of Frauds*
   9. *Part or Full Performance*
  10. *Estoppel*
      a. *Promissory Estoppel*
      b. *Estoppel in Pais*
  11. *Effect of Some Promises Being Within and Others Without the Statute of Frauds*
  12. *Oral Rescission or Modification of a Contract Within the Statute*
  13. *Relationship of Various Subdivisions*

A. PAROL EVIDENCE RULE

1. THE NATURE AND MEANING OF THE RULE

A total integration (a writing which the parties intend to be final and complete) may not be contradicted or supplemented. A partial integration (a writing which the parties intend to be final but not complete) may not be contradicted but may be supplemented by consistent additional terms.

a. What Type of Evidence May Be Excluded by the Parol Evidence Rule?

The rule excludes evidence of certain terms agreed upon prior to an integrated writing, whether the terms are written or oral. According to Williston and the great majority of cases, it also excludes a term agreed upon contemporaneously with the writing but only if the term is oral. In other words the rule does not exclude terms contained in a contemporaneous writing. In fact, under this view, the contemporaneous writing is deemed to be part of the integration.

b. Theory of the Rule

If the parties intend the writing to be final and complete, they intend to supersede their *prior* agreements. In addition, good public policy also requires that *contemporaneous* oral agreements should be covered by the rule because the writing deserves a preferred status against potential perjury.

2. HOW TO DETERMINE FINALITY

Any relevant evidence is admissible. The writing need not be signed and need not be in any particular form. The crucial requirement is that the parties have regarded the writing as the final embodiment of their agreement. The more complete and formal the instrument, the more likely it is that it is intended as an integration. Most writings that evidence a valid contract are final and therefore at least partial integrations. An illustration of a writing that is not considered to be final is a memorandum prepared by one party and not shown to the other party. Such a document is not final because the party who has not seen it cannot possibly consider it to be the final embodiment of the agreement. Another illustration of a non-final writing is a draft contract not assented to by one of the parties. The question of finality, although actually one of fact, is decided by the trial judge because the courts feel that unsophisticated jurors could be easily beguiled by an artful presentation and thus would not give the writing the protection it deserves.

3. HOW TO DETERMINE COMPLETENESS

Once it is determined that there is finality, the next question is whether there is completeness so that there is a total integration. This is a difficult problem because there is no unanimity on how this is to be determined. The six most widely accepted approaches are as follows.

a.   Four Corners Rule

If the instrument is complete on its face, the instrument is presumed to be a total integration. Whether it is complete on its face is determined by the trial judge solely by looking at the instrument. The rule is losing favor because it is impossible to tell whether an agreement is complete on its face simply by looking at the writing.

b.   The Collateral Contract Rule

Unfortunately, there are two versions of this rule. Under one version, if the term offered does not contradict the writing, it may be received in evidence. In effect, this means that the writing is only a partial integration. Under the other version, the important issue is whether the term offered relates to a subject matter that is dealt with in the writing. If the term offered is dealt with at all in the writing, there is a total integration. If the term offered relates to a subject matter that is not covered by the writing, the writing is treated as a partial integration. This rule is also losing favor.

c.   Williston's Rules

Professor Williston states three rules. (1) If the writing expressly states that it is a final expression of all the terms agreed upon and that it is a complete and exclusive statement of these terms—often referred to as a merger clause—this declaration conclusively establishes that the integration is total unless the document is obviously incomplete or the merger clause itself was included as a result of fraud or mistake, etc. However, even a merger clause does not prevent enforcement of a separate agreement supported by a separate consideration on both sides. The last statement is accepted under all versions of the rule. (2) In the absence of a merger clause, the determination is made by looking to the writing. Consistent additional terms may be proved if the writing is obviously incomplete on its face. In other words, in this situation there is a partial integration. Even if the writing appears to be complete, there will still be a partial integration when the writing expresses the undertaking of one party only, as in the case of deeds, bonds, bills and notes. (3) Where the writing appears to be a complete instrument expressing the rights and obligations of both parties, it is deemed a total integration unless the alleged additional terms were such as might naturally be made as a separate agreement by parties situated as were the parties to the written agreement, in which event there is a partial integration.

d.   Corbin's View

Professor Corbin is determined to search out the actual intention of the parties on this issue of total integration rather than some fictional or presumed intent. He states that all relevant evidence should be taken into account in making the determination. He would admit evidence of prior negotiations. He seems to indicate that the rule should not apply to contemporaneous agreements. He states that a merger clause is only one of the factors to be considered in determining whether there is a total integration. Under his view, a writing is ordinarily a partial integration.

e. The U.C.C. Approach (U.C.C. § 2–202)

1) U.C.C. § 2–202(b)

Clause b states the common law rule that a total integration may not be contradicted or supplemented, but it does not determine the existence of a total integration according to any of the rules previously discussed. Rather, the presumption is that a writing is a partial integration. This presumption is overcome if the parties actually intend the writing to be a total integration (Corbin), or if it is *certain* that parties similarly situated would have included the term in the writing, a variation of Williston's third rule. An example of an intent to have a total integration could be shown by a merger clause, and some courts have followed the traditional rule in cases that arise under the U.C.C. But the notion is gaining currency that a merger clause should not have any effect unless it is a dickered merger clause. If the clause is merely "boiler plate" it should have no effect. This section follows Williston's rule with respect to contemporaneous agreements, giving the same treatment to such agreements as is given to prior agreements.

2) U.C.C. § 2–202(a)

Under this clause, a course of dealing or a usage of trade may be used to supply a consistent additional term even though the writing is deemed to be a total integration under the rule stated in clause (b) above. Thus, under this rule there is at most a partial integration, and the only question to be decided is whether evidence of the course of dealing or usage of the trade contradicts the integration. This would seem to be in accord with Williston's rules because it would be natural for parties situated, as they were, not to include the course of dealing or usage of the trade. Under the Code what is the effect of a merger clause upon a usage of the trade or a course of dealing? The general answer is that a merger clause does not rule out this type of evidence unless specific reference is made to this type of evidence.

3) Confirmations

Under the common law, a confirmation often acts as a total integration if the other party makes no response to it prior to performance. It could be argued that this problem could arise under the Code only if there were "confirmatory memoranda"—the language of the statute. But it is generally agreed that it is possible to have a total integration based upon a single confirmatory memorandum. The rule to be applied is the rule stated in 1) above. Under this rule, a confirmation, unless it is objected to, is presumed to be a partial integration unless the parties intended it to be final and complete, or it is certain that parties similarly situated would have included the alleged term in the confirmation.

4) The Restatement, Second

The major premise of the Restatement, Second, is Corbin's rule that the actual intent of the parties should be sought in determining whether there is a total or a partial integration. It goes on to say that, even if this test leads to a determination of a total integration, consistent additional terms are still admissible (a) if the alleged agreement is made for a separate consideration or (b) if the offered agreement is not within the scope of the integration or (c) if the offered terms might naturally be omitted from the writing. In fact, the Restatement, Second, appears to say that it is impossible to have more than a partial integration.

4. APPROACH OF TRIAL JUDGE

There are a number of issues that arise under the rules stated above that would generally be treated as questions of fact (e.g., would it be natural to include a particular term in the writing?) However, under the parol evidence rule, these questions are generally decided by the trial judge as a question of law. If the judge decides that the parol evidence rule applies, the judge excludes the offered term not because it was not agreed upon but because it is legally immaterial. Conversely, if the judge decides that the parol evidence rule does not apply, the judge admits the term agreed upon into evidence but then leaves to the jury the issue of fact as to whether such a term was actually agreed upon.

5. SEPARATE CONSIDERATION

As previously mentioned, if the term offered into evidence has separate consideration on both sides, there is at most a partial integration. The question becomes solely whether the ancillary term contradicts the main agreement.

6. SUBSEQUENT AGREEMENT

The parol evidence rule never excludes subsequent agreements. By statute, it is possible to prohibit oral proof of a subsequent agreement by inserting a "no oral modification clause" into the contract. (See p. 160 above.)

7. IS THE RULE ONE OF SUBSTANTIVE LAW OR PROCEDURE?

Although the earlier cases said the parol evidence rule was a rule of evidence, the more modern cases look upon it as a rule of substantive law. In truth it has both a procedural and a substantive aspect. It is procedural because it excludes evidence; it is substantive because it helps to determine the terms of the contract. The main consequence of the classification as procedural or substantive relates to whether the parol evidence can be raised for the first time on appeal. A majority of the courts conclude that if the rule is one of substantive law, the parol evidence issue may be raised for the first time upon appeal despite the failure to object at trial.

8. IS THE TERM OFFERED CONSISTENT OR CONTRADICTORY?

There is little or no consistency on the question of how to determine whether an offered term is contradictory or consistent. There are cases that have found the offered term inconsistent in the following situations: (1) where it contradicts an express term of the contract; (2) where it contradicts a merger clause; (3) where it contradicts an inference that all of the seller's obligations were listed in the contract. For example, if a contract lists a number of obligations of the seller, and the buyer offers proof that the seller assumed an additional obligation, it has been held that the term contradicts the inference that all of the seller's obligations are listed. (4) Where it contradicts an implied in fact term. But an implied in law term that becomes part of the agreement may be contradicted. There is no clear distinction between an implied in fact and an implied in law term. The more modern cases, including those decided under the U.C.C., lean to the view that to be contradictory a term must contradict an express term of the integration.

Examples: (1) *L* (Landlord) and *T* (Tenant) signed a two year lease. Under the terms of the lease, the tenant agreed not to sell tobacco in any form but was permitted to sell soft drinks. At the trial *T* seeks to introduce into evidence an oral agreement made contemporaneously with the writing that in consideration of the promise not to sell tobacco, *L* promised an *exclusive* right to sell soft drinks on the premises, and *L* breached this promise. The court assumed that there was an integration, which is another way of saying that there was at least a partial integration. The issue was whether there was a *total* integration. There would undoubtedly be a total integration under the "four corners" rule. Under the collateral contract approach, it would depend on which version of the rule the court decided to apply. The court used Williston's approach and concluded that it would have been natural for parties similarly situated to have included this term in the writing. This means that there is a total integration. The term is excluded even if it is a consistent additional term. If Corbin's view were employed, the term would be admissible without deciding the issue of total integration because it was a *contemporaneous* agreement and according to Corbin a *contemporaneous* agreement is not excluded by the parol evidence rule. The U.C.C. does not apply because the case does not involve a sale of goods. As we have seen the Restatement, Second, does not take a position on contemporaneous agreements. In any event, under its rule there would undoubtedly be a partial integration, and the issue would be whether the term offered is a *contradictory* term or a *consistent* additional term. The term would most probably be looked upon as a consistent additional term because it does not contradict an express term of the writing. Therefore it would be admissible.

(2) *D.M.* and his wife conveyed a ranch to *D.M.*'s sister and her husband. The deed contained an option to repurchase. *D.M.* was adjudged a bankrupt. His trustee in bankruptcy and his wife seek to exercise the right to repurchase. The grantees assert that there was a prior oral agreement that the option to repurchase was personal to the grantors and could not be invoked by the trustee in bankruptcy. The case was decided under Williston's view. We will limit our discussion to that approach. The court assumes that there is an integration, and the first question is whether there is a total integration. Would it have been natural for parties situated as these parties were to have included this term in the deed? The court concluded that it was not, because a deed has limited space, expresses the rights and obligations of only one party, and the family relationship implies trust. Thus, there is only a partial integration and the issue is whether the term is contradictory. It was agreed that the term offered (option personal to grantors) contradicts an implied term of the writing—namely, free assignability. The implied term is implied in law rather than implied in fact and therefore could be contradicted.

(3) *A* and *B*, in a signed writing, agree to buy and sell a specific automobile. Contemporaneously, they orally agree that *B* may keep the automobile in *A*'s garage for one year in return for *A*'s promise to pay $15 per month for the year. The contemporaneous agreement is admissible because it is supported by a separate consideration on each side and it does not contradict the main agreement.

(4) *S* and *B* entered into a written agreement for the sale and purchase of a truck on September 6. On September 7, they orally agreed that *B* might try out the truck for a week and if it did not prove satisfactory *B* might return it and receive a refund. Because the agreement is subsequent to the writing, no parol evidence problem arises. The only issue is one of consideration for the oral modification. In most jurisdictions, as a common law proposition, *S*'s promise would not be enforceable because *B* suffered no detriment. The result is different under U.C.C. Section 2–209(1). (See p. 160 above.)

(5) The parties entered into an agreement whereby *P* agreed to sell and *D* agreed to buy 31,000 tons of phosphate during the next

calendar year. The contract specified a price per ton that was subject to an escalation clause. *D* took only part of the 31,000 tons. *D*'s defense was that there was a usage of the trade and course of dealing to the effect that "because of uncertain crop and weather conditions, farming practices, and government agricultural programs, express price and quantity terms in contracts for materials in the mixed fertilizer industry are merely projections to be adjusted according to market forces." Because the case involved a sale of goods, U.C.C. Section 2–202(a) applied. Under this subdivision a usage of trade and a course of dealing may be used to supply a consistent additional term even though the writing is deemed to be a total integration. The court decided that the usage of the trade and course of dealing were consistent additional terms. Obviously, a different result could have been reached. This proves again that it is difficult to determine whether a particular term is contradictory or consistent. The same case raised the question of the effect of a merger clause upon evidence of a usage of the trade and a course of dealing. It indicated that a merger clause should not rule out this type of evidence unless the clause makes specific reference to this type of evidence.

9. UNDERCUTTING THE INTEGRATION

Despite the existence of a merger clause, parol evidence is admissible to show that the agreement is void or voidable or to show grounds for granting or denying rescission or reformation. Under this rule, a party may show, for example, that the agreement was a sham, not intended to be operative, unconscionable, or illegal. In addition, it may be shown that there is duress, mistake, fraud, or a condition precedent to the formation of the contract. Many cases hold that fraud includes promissory fraud; where a promise is made by a party who has no intention of performing. Thus, to defeat the contract under the fraud exception it is permissible to introduce evidence that an oral promise was made with no intent to perform. The theory behind undercutting the integration is that the parol evidence rule should not be applied until it is decided that there is a contract. But a number of cases hold that such evidence is not admissible if the basis of the attack on the writing is a term that contradicts specific language in the writing. Although the rule discussed here is not explicitly found in the U.C.C., it is generally agreed that the courts will apply all aspects of this rule to U.C.C. cases.

Example: *P* and *D* agreed to transfer the stock of corporations that each owned to a new corporation. The new corporation agreed to issue its stock to *P* and *D*. *P* made the transfer of stock to the new corporation, but *D* refused to do so. *D*'s defense was that *P* and *D* orally agreed that the agreement was not to operate until an equity expansion fund of $672,000 was procured. The raising of the equity expansion fund was a condition precedent to the *formation* of the contract and therefore it was held that the term could be received in evidence to show that there was no contract until this event occurred. Some courts would admit the evidence only if it did not contradict explicit terms of the writing. Some courts allow the same kind of evidence even if the evidence shows a condition precedent to the *performance* of the contract.

B. INTERPRETATION

1. INTRODUCTION

Interpretation relates to the meaning of a communication. In interpretation there are two fundamental questions. (1) Whose meaning is to be given to the communication—in technical language, what standard of interpretation is to be used? (2) What evidence may be taken into account? Again, there is a wide variety of views (see 2 below). While interpretation relates to ascertaining the meaning of the parties, construction relates to the legal effect of the manifestations of intent. The distinction between interpretation and construction is not a clear one, and most courts do not appear to concern themselves with it. Nor do we.

2. VARYING VIEWS
a. Plain Meaning Rule—Ambiguity

The Plain Meaning Rule states that if a writing or the relevant term appears to have a plain meaning that meaning must be given effect without resort to *extrinsic* evidence of any kind. The opposite of plain meaning is ambiguity. Whether there is plain meaning or ambiguity is a question of law to be determined in the first instance by the trial judge by looking solely to the writing in question. Some of the modern cases are holding that the trial judge should consider extrinsic evidence before making this determination. If the trial judge finds the term is ambiguous, under the older view, extrinsic evidence could be received to resolve a latent ambiguity but not a patent ambiguity. But the more modern cases tend to hold that all types of extrinsic evidence are admissible in both situations. A patent ambiguity is one that is apparent. A latent ambiguity is one that is not apparent on its face: the ambiguity arises because of something in the outside world (e.g., the two ships "Peerless"). The term "extrinsic evidence" includes prior and contemporaneous negotiations, surrounding circumstances, subjective intent, what the parties said to each other about meaning, trade usage, course of performance and course of dealing.

b. Williston's Rules

1) Integration

As to integrated writings, Williston's standard of interpretation is the meaning that would be attached to the integration by a reasonably intelligent person acquainted with all operative usages and knowing all of the circumstances prior to and contemporaneous with the making of the integration. However, he excludes what the parties said to each other about meaning (e.g., "buy" was to mean "sell") and what the parties subjectively believed the writing meant at the time of agreement. But when these rules are applied and the result is ambiguity, then Williston's non-integration rules will be applied. (See 2 below.)

2) Non–Integration

Where there is no integration and no ambiguity, Williston's standard is the meaning that the party making the manifestation should reasonably expect the other party to give it—the standard of reasonable expectation—a test based primarily on the objective theory of contracts. (Compare the tentative working test set up under Mutual Assent, (p. 90 above), which set up the standard of reasonable understanding.) In the case of a non-integration, where there is no ambiguity, all extrinsic evidence is admissible except evidence of subjective intention. If there is an ambiguity, in the case of a non-integration, evidence of subjective intention is also admissible and, when it is introduced, Williston argues that the rules indicated in the example below apply.

Example: S agreed to sell, and B agreed to buy, certain cotton. Shipment was to be from Bombay on the ship, Peerless. It happened that there were two ships, Peerless. One was to sail from Bombay in October; the other in December. The evidence was to the effect that B meant the ship Peerless that sailed in October, and S meant the one that sailed in December. The possible results in this type of situation are as follows. (1) If both parties meant the same ship, Peerless, there is a contract based on that meaning. (2) If one party knew or had reason to know of the ambiguity, and the other did not know or did not have reason to know, there is a contract based upon the meaning of the party who was not at fault. (3) If both parties knew or should have known of the ambiguity or neither party knew or should have known of the ambiguity, there is no contract if they meant different ships, Peerless. Notice that this rule does not weigh fault—that is to say, it makes no difference whether one party knew and the other merely should have known.

c. Corbin's Rules—Restatement, Second

Under Corbin's view, *all* relevant extrinsic evidence is admissible on the issue of meaning, even if there is an integration and there is no ambiguity. Under this rule, most parties will introduce evidence of subjective intention. When this evidence is introduced, the problem is similar to the Peerless case discussed above. When Corbin's rules are applied in this situation the following results obtain. (1) If both parties mean the same ship, Peerless, there is a contract based on that meaning. (2) Where the meanings do not coincide, the meaning is the meaning of the party who is less at fault. Who is less at fault depends on what a party knows or should know. For example, if one party knows that there are two ships, Peerless, and the other party only should know of this fact, the meaning of the party who should know will prevail. Notice that Williston's rule is different on this point. (3) If both parties are equally at fault, there is no contract where, as here, one is dealing with a material term. If evidence of subjective intention at the time of contracting is not introduced, the parties may still assert the meaning they now attach to the term in question. When such evidence is introduced, the issue again becomes who is more responsible for the misunderstanding. Professor Corbin tempers his more liberal rules by stating that the trial judge must initially determine whether the asserted meaning is one to which the language, in the light of all of the evidence taken in context, is reasonably susceptible. If it is not, then the asserted meaning may not be attached to the language in question unless both parties mean the same thing. The Restatement, Second, is generally in accord with Corbin.

d. U.C.C. on Interpretation

U.C.C. Section 2–202 does not have a comprehensive rule in the area of interpretation, but it does reject the plain meaning rule and permits extrinsic evidence of meaning even if there is no ambiguity. Discussed below are its particular rules of interpretation in the area of usage of the trade, course of dealing and course of performance.

3. THE RELATIONSHIP BETWEEN PAROL EVIDENCE AND INTERPRETATION

At times it has been said that a total integration may not be contradicted, *varied* or supplemented. The word "varied" is often used in the context of interpretation. The notion is that just as the first phase (Part A) of the parol evidence rule prevents a party from introducing a term that contradicts an integration, so also the interpretation phase of the parol evidence does not permit a party to introduce evidence that varies the meaning of the language in the writing. Whether this last statement is true depends upon the court's choice of the competing rules of interpretation discussed above.

a.   Plain Meaning Rule

Under the Plain Meaning Rule, if it is determined that there is a plain meaning, no contradiction is permitted because extrinsic evidence of all types is excluded.

b.   Williston's Rules

Williston foresaw the possibility that the parol evidence rule could be undermined under the guise of interpretation. Therefore he structured a rule for an integration that does not permit the integration to be contradicted by evidence of what the parties said to one another about the meaning of language in the integration or by evidence of subjective intent.

c.   Corbin's Rules—Restatement, Second

Corbin's basic position is contrary as is the Restatement, Second. They take the position that the parol evidence rule (Part B) should have no effect on the question of interpretation—the meaning of language. Corbin states that, before extrinsic evidence can be excluded, the meaning of the writing must be ascertained, because one may not determine whether a writing is being contradicted or even supplemented until one knows what the writing means. Thus, all types of extrinsic evidence are admissible on the issue of meaning. The only limitation is that "the asserted meaning must be one to which the language of the writing read in context is reasonably susceptible in the light of the evidence introduced." The rules of the Restatement, Second, are basically the same.

d.   U.C.C.

We have already seen that the U.C.C. does not have a comprehensive rule in the area of interpretation but that it does reject the plain meaning rule. We also saw that there are provisions in the U.C.C. relating to interpretation in the area of usage of trade, a course of dealing, and a course of performance. These provisions will be discussed below in connection with our general discussion of these three topics.

4.   COURSE OF DEALING, COURSE OF PERFORMANCE AND USAGE OF TRADE
a.   Introduction

We have already mentioned course of dealing, trade usage, and course of performance in connection with our discussion of the parol evidence rule (Part A) and interpretation. Here, our main purpose is to define these terms and to determine when a trade usage exists, and assuming it exists, when the parties are bound by it. In addition, we shall discuss the effect of an established course of dealing, usage of the trade, or course of performance. This discussion may overlap to some extent our prior discussion of the parol evidence rule and interpretation.

b. Meaning of Course of Dealing and Course of Performance
A course of *dealing* is defined in the Code as "a sequence of previous conduct between the parties to a particular transaction which is fairly to be regarded as establishing a common basis of understanding for interpreting their expressions and other conduct." A course of *performance* relates to conduct after the agreement in question, according to the Code as "where the contract for sale involves repeated occasions for performance by either party with knowledge of the opportunity for objection to it by the other." A course of dealing and a course of performance can be established by the testimony of the parties.

c. Usage of Trade
The Code defines a usage of trade as "any practice or method of dealing having such regularity of observance in a place, vocation or trade as to justify an expectation that it will be observed with respect to the transaction in question." A trade usage is established by expert testimony. This concept and the two discussed above are not limited to cases involving sales of goods. At early common law, in order to establish a usage, including a trade usage, it had to be (1) legal, (2) notorious, (3) ancient or immemorial and continuous, (4) reasonable, (5) certain, (6) universal and obligatory. Under the Code, the trade usage need not be ancient or immemorial or universal or certain. Reasonableness is also eliminated and substituted is a requirement against "unconscionable contracts and clauses." Instead of being notorious the Code requires that the usage have regularity of observance . . . as to justify an expectation that it will be observed with respect to the transaction in question. Another question is, who is bound by an established usage? The general notion is that a person is bound by a usage of the trade if the person is aware of it or should be aware of it. Under the Code, a party engaged in a trade is bound by its usages whether or not the party knows of them.

d. For What Purposes May They Be Used?
1) Usage of Trade and Course of Dealing
At common law, and under the Code, the rule is that a trade usage and a course of dealing may be added to a writing as an additional term if the term is "not inconsistent" with the agreement. They may also be used on the issue of meaning. Under the modern common law, a usage of trade and a course of dealing may be shown to contradict the plain meaning of the language. Whether this rule has been changed under the U.C.C. will be discussed in connection with one of the problems below.

2) Course of Performance
A course of performance may be used to add a term, because it is subsequent to the writing and therefore it is not excluded under the parol evidence rule (Part A). Thus, if a course of performance is used

to add a term to the writing, the issue is modification or waiver. A course of performance may add a term or subtract one. But a course of performance is also relevant on the issue of meaning. At common law it could be used in aid of interpretation if a reasonable person could attach that meaning to the manifestation. Whether this rule has been changed under the U.C.C. will be discussed in connection with one of the problems below.

Examples: (1) *S* and *B* enter into a written contract for the sale and purchase of 1000 shingles. At trial, evidence was offered that two packs constitute 1000 shingles even though not containing that exact number. The court received this evidence on the issue of meaning and ruled that a jury could find that the parties intended the usage to take priority over the facially inconsistent express provision. Stated differently, does the express provision manifest an agreement to negate the trade usage? This approach represents the modern common law approach. The older approach was based on the plain meaning rule. Does the U.C.C. follow this modern common law approach? U.C.C. § 2–202 adopts this rule when it, in effect, states that a usage of the trade or a course of performance must be looked at in its commercial setting to ascertain if the parties wished the usage of the trade or course of performance to take priority over the language of the writing. This is a question of fact. However, under U.C.C. Section 1–205 an order of priority is established. It reads, "The express terms of an agreement and an applicable course of dealing or a usage of the trade shall be construed wherever reasonable as consistent with each other; but when such construction is unreasonable express terms control both course of dealing and usage of the trade and course of dealing controls usage of trade." There is a companion provision in U.C.C. § 2–208. Some courts have used this order of priority to exclude evidence if the term offered is facially inconsistent with an express provision. This result was never intended. It has been called a "false parol evidence approach."

(2) *M*, a manufacturer, sues *B*, an authorized agent, for electronic equipment supplied and delivered. By the terms of the writing, *B* had no right to return conforming goods and obtain credit. *B* now asserts that the parties continually ignored the agreement and that over a period of time 210 units were returned for credit.

Here we are dealing with a course of performance. U.C.C. § 2–202 indicates that the course of performance by the parties is the best indication of what the parties meant. This would appear to be so under U.C.C. § 2–202 even if the course of performance is carefully negated or is inconsistent with the writing. But, as above, some courts would exclude the course of performance by virtue of the provisions of U.C.C. §§ 1–205(4) and 2–208. The court should also consider the question of waiver and modification because a course of performance is subsequent to the integration.

5. OTHER RULES OF INTERPRETATION

There are many rules of interpretation that have not been mentioned. There is also much learning on the relation of these rules to standards of interpretation. In an outline of this size it is sufficient to mention only a few of these rules. These include: (1) specific terms are given greater weight than general terms; (2) separately negotiated terms are given greater weight than standardized terms; (3) if there is an inconsistency between typed and printed terms, a typed term prevails over a printed term; (4) in choosing among reasonable meanings the instrument should be construed against the party who drafted it; (5) it is the policy of the law to uphold contracts and courts prefer to construe them so that they are lawful and operative rather than unlawful and inoperative.

C.   STATUTE OF FRAUDS

1. INTRODUCTION

When oral promises became enforceable in England, perjury and subornation of perjury became commonplace. In 1677 Parliament enacted an Act for the Prevention of Fraud and Perjuries. While a writing requirement obviates perjury, it also promotes certainty by preventing faulty recollection. In addition, it promotes deliberation and seriousness. While these are desirable goals, carrying them out may frustrate honesty and fair dealing. The rule may prevent oral terms, actually agreed upon, from being received in evidence. The ability of the Statute to cause injustice has had a strong impact on judicial decisions. Thus, courts have given it a narrow construction and have developed devices "for taking the contract outside" the Statute.

2. MAJOR CLASSES OF CASES COVERED BY WRITING REQUIREMENTS

Writing requirements affect five major classes of cases: (1) a promise to answer for the debt, default or miscarriage of another, including the promise of an executor or administrator to answer for the obligations of the decedent out of the administrator's or executor's own pocket; (2) a contract to transfer an interest in real property or an actual transfer of real property; (3) a promise which by its terms is not to be performed within one year from the making thereof; (4) *a promise in consideration of marriage;* (5) *a contract for the sale of goods (U.C.C.).*

a.   Suretyship Agreements

In a suretyship case, three parties are normally involved: One party has made the promise and now pleads the Statute as a defense (*D*). The person to whom the promise is made who is ordinarily the creditor (*C*) and the person on whose behalf *D* makes the promise (*TP*—third party).

1)   **Cases Where There Is No Prior Obligation Owing From *TP* to *C* to Which *D*'s Promise Relates**
     In this type of case, the promise of D is original (not within this subdivision of the Statute so that it is not a defense) unless (1) there is a principal-surety relationship between TP and D to the knowledge of C, and (2) the promise is not joint, and (3) the main purpose rule does not apply.   If all of these elements are present, D's promise is collateral (the Statute of Frauds is a defense).

> *Discussion:*   A principal and suretyship relation exists between *TP* and *D* if both are liable to *C* for the same obligation, but as between the two (*TP* and *D*) the principal (*TP*) rather than *D* (the surety) should ultimately pay. Therefore, if *D* (surety) pays, *D* is entitled to reimbursement from *TP* (principal).

> *Examples:*   (1) *D* says to *C*, "Deliver these goods to *TP* and I will see that you are paid." *C* delivers the goods to *TP* but manifests an intent not to treat *TP* as his debtor, relying solely on the credit of *D*. The promise of *D* is original, because *TP* never became liable to *C*. Therefore, by definition, there is no suretyship relationship between *TP* and *D*.

> (2) When goods are being purchased from *C*, *D* promises to pay and *TP* orally guarantees *D*'s payment. *C* is informed that the goods are to be delivered to *D*. *C* delivers the goods to *D* who, in turn, according to a prior agreement, delivers them to *TP*. Credit is extended to both so that both *TP* and *D* are liable to *C*. There is a principal and suretyship relation between *TP* and *D*, and *C* knows that one party is the principal and the other is the surety. But *C* reasonably thinks *D* is the principal, therefore *D*'s promise is enforceable (original). *TP*'s promise is also enforceable because *TP* is in fact the principal.

(3) When goods are being purchased from *C, D* orally promises to act as surety for *TP. C* insists that they undertake a joint obligation and the parties agree. Although there is a principal-suretyship relationship between *TP* and *D,* to the knowledge of *C, D's* promise is original (not within the Statute) because of the joint nature of the promise. This rule does not apply where the obligation is joint and several or several.

(4) The Main Purpose Rule is discussed below.

2) **Cases Where There Is a Prior Obligation Owing From *TP* to *C* to which *D*'s Promise Relates**
Such a promise is collateral (the Statute is a defense).

Exceptions: (1) where there is a novation;

(2) where *D* 's promise is made to *TP;*

(3) where the Main Purpose Rule applies.

Examples: (1) *TP* owes *C* $1,000. For a consideration, *D* orally promises to become a surety. *D's* promise is collateral. Therefore it is unenforceable.

(2) *TP* owes *C* $1,000. *D* says to *C,* "Release *TP* and I will pay." *C* releases *TP.* There is a novation, and therefore *D's* promise is enforceable.

(3) *TP* owes *C* $1,000. *TP* and *D* enter into a contract by the terms of which *D,* for a consideration, agrees to assume the obligation. Although there is not a novation, *D's* promise is enforceable because it is made to *TP* rather than to *C.* In addition *D* is the principal debtor.

(4) The Main Purpose Rule is discussed below.

3) **Main Purpose Rule**
Where the object of a promisor is a benefit which the promisor did not previously enjoy, and the benefit accrues immediately to the promisor, the promise is original (enforceable), whether or not TP was obligated at the time of the promise and even though the effect of the promise is to answer for the debt, default or miscarriage of another.

Examples: (1) *TP* owes *C* $1,000. *C* is about to levy an attachment on *TP's* factory. *D,* who is an unsecured creditor of *TP,* orally promises that if *C* forbears *D* will pay *TP*'s debt if *TP* does not. *D*'s promise is original because *D*'s main purpose is to secure *D*'s own economic advantage.

(2) *TP* is indebted to *C* and, as a result, *C* has a lien upon *TP*'s property. *D* orally promises to pay the debt if *TP* does not, provided that *C* discharges the lien of the mortgage. *C* discharges the lien of the mortgage. The Main Purpose Rule does not apply because there is no benefit to *D*, and under the rules previously stated *D*'s promise is not enforceable.

4) Promises of Indemnity

A contract of indemnity is a promise to hold a person harmless or to reimburse the person against loss irrespective of the liability of third persons. Contracts of indemnity do not fall within the Statute. So also, according to the majority view, a promise to indemnify against any loss suffered by one becoming a surety is one of indemnity and not of suretyship.

Examples: (1) *A* promises *B* that if *B* becomes liable as a result of the operation of a motor vehicle, *A* will pay any judgment obtained against *B*. *C* obtains a judgment against *B*. Since *C* is not a third party beneficiary of *A*'s promise to *B*, only *B* is liable to *C*, and therefore suretyship cannot exist. *B* is an indemnitor against liability, and the Statute does not apply.

(2) *A* promises *B* that, in the event that *B* is compelled to pay *C*, *A* will reimburse *B*. Because *C* is not a third party beneficiary of *A*'s promise made to *B*, only *B* is liable to *C* and suretyship cannot exist. *B* is an indemnitor against loss.

(3) *A* promises *B* that, in the event *B*'s car is damaged in a collision, *A* will reimburse *B* for the loss. *C* and *B* have a collision for which *C* is responsible. Here the possibility of suretyship exists, because *C* and *A* are both liable to *B* for the same loss. But *A*'s promise is considered one of indemnity, because *A*'s promise is made irrespective of whether *C* is liable or not.

(4) *A* promises *B* that in the event that *C*, *B*'s employee, steals money from *B*, *A* will reimburse *B*. Here *C* and *A* are liable to *B*, and the potential for suretyship exists. *A*'s promise is one of suretyship because *A*'s promise is

not made *irrespective* of *C*'s liability but because of *C*'s liability.

(5) *D* requests *P* to become a surety on *TP*'s obligation to *C,* and *D* orally promises *P* that if *P* is compelled to pay, *D* will reimburse *P.* This is a *four* party situation, and the majority of the cases have held that *D*'s promise made to a surety (*P*) is a promise of indemnity and therefore it is enforceable.

5) **Promise of the Del Credere Agent**
An oral promise of a del credere agent is enforceable (original). A del credere agent (*D*) is one who receives possession of goods for sale upon commission and who guarantees to his own principal (*C*) that those to whom he sells (*TPs*) will perform.

6) **Promise of Assignor**
The promise of an assignor to the assignee guaranteeing performance by the obligor is original (enforceable).

7) **Promise to Buy a Claim**
If *TP* owes *C* $100, and *C* assigns this right to payment to *D*, and *D* orally promises to pay a stated sum for the assignment, *D*'s promise is enforceable. *D*'s promise is a promise to buy a claim and not a promise to answer for the debt, default or miscarriage of another.

8) **Promise by Executor or Administrator**
The Statute applies only where executors or administrators promise to pay out of *their own* funds a debt of the deceased. Thus, this provision is merely a particular application of the Suretyship Statute of Frauds.

b. **Real Property**
A conveyance of land or of an estate in land or a promise to transfer an interest in land or a promise to pay for an interest in land are all required to be in writing.

1) **What Is a Contract for Sale of Land?**
This term covers any agreement that contains a promise to create or transfer an interest in land. It also applies to an option contract, but interests created by operation of law (equitable liens, constructive trusts) are not included. It does not cover an agreement by an agent or a broker to arrange a transfer on behalf of another. Some states cover this type of arrangement by a special provision.

2)   **What Is an Interest in Land?**
The law of real property determines what is an interest in land. Not only is a promise to transfer a legal estate covered, but also a promise to create or transfer a lease or assign a lease (an exception is made for a short term lease, typically those for one year or less), an easement or rent, and, according to the majority rule, a restriction on land. Also covered is an equitable interest in lands such as an assignment of a right to purchase land. Unlike an easement, a license is not within the Statute. A promise to give a mortgage or other lien as security is within the Statute. However, an assignment of a mortgage is not within the Statute. The mortgage is looked upon as a chose in action because it is connected with the debt it secures.

3)   **What Is Real Property?**
According to the Restatement, Second, real property comprises all tangible property other than goods. There are some difficult problems on what is land and what are goods but the U.C.C. clarifies the area very well. It provides that a contract for sale "of growing crops and other things attached to realty and capable of severance without material harm thereto . . . or of timber to be cut" is a sale of goods. It also provides that in the case of a "contract for the sale of minerals or the like (including oil and gas) or a structure or its materials to be removed from realty" the determination depends upon who is to sever the property to be sold. If the seller is to sever, it is a contract for the sale of goods. If the buyer is to sever, it is a contract of the sale of an interest in land.

4)   **Effect of Performance**
If the vendor of property conveys to the vendee, the vendee's oral promise to pay is enforceable. On the other hand, payment by the vendee in whole or in part does not make the promise of the vendor enforceable unless there is other conduct that is "unequivocally referable" to the agreement. This occurs in some jurisdictions where there is payment and either possession by the vendee or the making by the vendee of valuable improvements upon the land with the consent of the vendor. Even if the acts of part performance are insufficient to take a case out of the Statute, the promisor may, in a proper case, be estopped from asserting the defense. If the vendee fails to succeed in these approaches, a right of restitution exists.

c.   **Contracts Not to Be Performed Within a Year**
1)   **Bilateral Contracts**
The Statute applies only to a promise which by its terms does not admit of performance within one year from the making thereof. If by its terms performance is possible within one year, however unlikely or improbable

that may be, the promise is not within this section of the Statute of Frauds. The question is not how long performance is to run but, by its terms, can it be performed within one year from the making thereof.

Examples: (1) *A* makes an oral promise on June 1, 1990, to perform for one hour on July 1, 1991. The promise by its terms cannot be performed within one year from the making thereof. It is unenforceable unless in writing.

(2) *A* promises to work for *B* for two years. The promise is within this section of the Statute of Frauds. Therefore, it is unenforceable unless in writing.

(3) *A* promises to pay upon the completion of a dam. It is contemplated that the erection of the dam will take three years and it does. According to the majority view, the promise is not within this section because, by its terms, it can be performed within a year without breaching the contract. It is enforceable.

a)   Promises of Uncertain Duration
Promises of uncertain duration are not generally deemed to be within the one year provision. These include a promise conditional upon an uncertain event, and a promise of extended performance that may come to an end upon the happening of a condition that may occur within a year.

Examples: (1) *A* promises to pay *B* $10,000 when *A* sells Blackacre. The promise is not within the one year section of the Statute of Frauds because the act of selling can be performed within a year, and it is possible that the condition will occur within a year.

(2) *A* makes a promise to pay *B* $10,000 when *A* dies. The promise is not within this section of the Statute of Frauds because *A* may die within a year. In some states, by virtue of an additional statute, a promise that cannot be performed before the end of a lifetime is not enforceable. In some jurisdictions, a promise to leave a bequest by will is also subject to a statutory writing requirement.

(3) A promise of permanent employment is one of indefinite duration and is not within the one year section of the Statute of Frauds.

(4) *A* promises to supply *B* with goods for the duration of the war. *A*'s promise is not within the Statute, because the war may end within one year.

(5) *A* promises to pay for the support of a four-year old child until the child becomes 21. Since this promise, by its terms, is to last for 17 years (a definite term) it would seem that, under the general rule, the promise should be within the Statute. In other words it cannot be performed within one year from the making thereof. But the majority of the cases hold that because the purpose of the contract, (support), can be completely attained within a year by the death of the child, the case is not within the one year section of the Statute of Frauds. There are some contrary cases, particularly in the area of a promise not to compete.

b) Contracts for Alternative Performances
Where a party promises alternative performances, the promises are not within the one year section if any of the alternatives can be performed within one year form the time of the making thereof. It does not matter which party has the right to name the alternative.

Example: A promises *either* to work for *B* for two years *or* to deliver 20 bales of cotton within six months. Because one of the alternative promises of *A* may be performed within one year from the making thereof, the promises are not within the one year section of the Statute of Frauds.

c) Contracts With Options to Terminate or Renew
In the case of a fixed term contract where one or both parties has the option to terminate within a year, the majority view is that the Statute applies because termination is not performance. The minority view is to the contrary, on the theory that the rule with respect to alternative promises applies. The same two views exist in the case of a contract for less than one year where one or both parties has the right to extend or renew it.

Example: A promises to perform services for *B* for five years. The contract gives *A* or *B* the power to terminate within a year by giving thirty days' notice. Under the majority rule, *A*'s promise is within the Statute of Frauds. Under the minority rule, *A*'s promises are looked upon as alternative promises. *A* promises either to perform for one year or 30 days. Because one of the alternatives (30 days) can be performed within one year, *A*'s promise is not within the Statute of Frauds.

d) **Effect of Performance Under One Year Section**

Under the majority view, full performance by one party makes the promise of the other party enforceable. Some jurisdictions qualify this view by holding that performance must have actually taken place within one year from the making of the contract. A minority of jurisdictions, however, hold that the performance is ineffective to render the contract enforceable. These jurisdictions restrict the performing party to a quasi-contractual remedy. Part performance does not permit a party to enforce the contract, except possibly under the doctrines of divisibility and estoppel. A quasi-contractual recovery is available.

e) **How Is the Year Measured?**

It is generally accepted that if *A* contracts to work for *B* for one year, the work to begin more than one day after making the agreement, the contract is within the one year section. If the work is to begin the very next day, the contract is not within the Statute, on the theory that the law disregards fractions of a day. However, if when the employment begins, the parties restate their bargain and the restatement can be regarded as the making or remaking of the contract, the year begins to run from that time.

f) **Unilateral Contracts**

There is substantial authority to the effect that unilateral contracts do not fall within this subdivision of the Statute of Frauds, because, as we have seen, under the majority view full performance by one party takes the case out of the one year provision of the Statute of Frauds. But even in jurisdictions where this is not true, because a unilateral contract does not arise until there has been performance, it is not within the Statute of Frauds even if the offeree's performance is not completed within one year from the making of the offer.

Example: A says to B, "If you walk across Brooklyn Bridge two years from today, I promise to pay you $10." *A*'s promise is not within the one year section because the contract does not arise until *B* performs.

g) **Scope of One Year Section**
The one year section applies to all contracts no matter what their subject matter, except for a short term lease, even if the lease begins at a distant future date. It does not prevent specific performance of a land contract if the part-performance exception applies. According to the weight of authority, mutual promises to marry, if not performable within one year, are within the one year provision, although not within the consideration of marriage subdivision.

h) **Is a Promise or a Contract Within the One Year Section?**
It appears to be settled that where any of the promises on either side of a bilateral contract (except for alternative promises) cannot be fully performed within one year from the formation of the contract, all of the promises are within the one year section of the Statute of Frauds. This means that the contract is unenforceable by either party in the absence of a sufficient memorandum or performance, or the application of the doctrine of estoppel. (See 9 at p. 221 below.)

d. **Contracts in Consideration of Marriage**
The Statute applies to any agreement in consideration of marriage except mutual promises to marry. Thus, the Statute includes marriage settlements or pre-nuptial agreements even if the promise is made by a third party. If the marriage is not the consideration, as where a promise is made in contemplation of marriage, this subdivision of the Statute does not apply. The same is true if the marriage is merely an incident of the contract and not an end to be attained. The fact that a marriage has taken place is not sufficient to take the contract outside of the Statute. But additional performance may be sufficient to render the contract enforceable.

e. **Contracts for the Sale of Goods**
A contract for the sale of goods for a price of $500 or more is within the Statute (U.C.C. § 2–201).

Exceptions:

(1) A contract for the sale of goods to be manufactured is within the Statute unless "the goods are to be specially manufactured for the buyer and are not suitable for sale to others in the ordinary course of the seller's business and the seller, before notice of repudiation is received and under circumstances which reasonably indicate that the goods are for the buyer, has made either substantial beginning of their manufacture or commitments for their procurement." It is clear

that under this exception, the seller need not also be the manufacturer but may be a third party.

(2)   A contract is enforceable "if the party against whom enforcement is sought admits in his pleading, testimony or otherwise in court that a contract for sale was made, but the contract is not enforceable under this provision beyond the quantity of goods admitted."

(3)   The writing requirement is dispensed with as to those items which have been received and accepted.   Receipt means taking physical possession of the goods.   Acceptance relates to an intention to keep the goods.

(4)   The writing requirement is also dispensed with as to goods "for which payment has been made and accepted."   This seems to say that part payment should give rise only to partial enforcement.   This should be true if a just apportionment can be made; if not, part payment should make the entire contract enforceable.

1)   What Is Covered?
The section relates to "a contract to sell or sale of goods."   This covers both a present sale of goods and a contract to sell goods at a future time.   The word "goods" relates to tangible property in existence or to be manufactured.   It does not, for example, apply to contracts for work labor and service, real property, interests in land (see above), or assignments of choses in action including securities. (See below.)

2)   Other U.C.C. Provisions
Three other provisions in the Code are in effect Statutes of Frauds. 1) U.C.C. § 8–319 provides that contracts for the sale (assignment) of securities must be evidenced by a signed writing, or that certain other tests be met.   2) U.C.C. § 1–206 requires a writing signed by the party to be charged where there is an assignment of, or promise to assign, a general intangible, and the amount sought to be enforced exceeds $5,000.   General intangibles include patents, royalties and certain rights under executory bilateral contracts.   3) U.C.C. § 9–203 requires that a debtor sign a security agreement that contains a description of the collateral and the land, if any, involved.

3.   SUFFICIENCY OF THE MEMORANDUM
a.   Introduction
A writing can satisfy the Statute of Frauds even though it is not formal or integrated.   A note or memorandum will suffice.   The memorandum may be in any form.   It need not be made at the time the contract is entered into.   It need not be prepared with the purpose of satisfying the

Statute, except in the case of a contract in consideration of marriage, and need not be delivered. It need not be in existence at the time of suit. For the memorandum to be sufficient it must "amount to an acknowledgment by the party to be charged that he has assented to the contract that is asserted by the other party."

b.   Contents of the Writing

The writing, including a memorandum of the contract, should (1) indicate that a contract has been made or that the signer has made an offer; (2) state with reasonable certainty (a) the identity of the contracting parties, (b) the subject matter and (c) the essential terms in contrast to details or particulars; and by whom and to whom the promises are made; and (3) be signed by the party to be charged. Implied terms are deemed to be part of the memorandum.

c.   What Is a Signature?

A signature is any mark, written, stamped or engraved which is placed by a party anywhere on the writing with intent to assent to and adopt (authenticate) the writing as the party's own. For example, initials are sufficient. If the Statute says "subscribed," some courts have held that the writing must be signed at the end.

d.   Who Is the Party to Be Charged?

The party to be charged is the one against whom the claim is being made. Therefore, if A sends a signed written offer to B and B orally accepts, the contract is enforceable against A but not B. But if A is to perform first A may demand that B sign a sufficient memo and, if B does not, A need not perform. A memorandum is sufficient if signed by an authorized agent of the party to be charged. Further, the authority of the agent need not be expressed in writing, except under the real property provision where many jurisdictions require a writing.

e.   Parol Evidence and the Memorandum

1)   Offered by Plaintiff

The interaction of the parol evidence rule and the Statute of Frauds produces complicated problems. If a plaintiff seeks to introduce evidence of essential terms not contained in the memorandum, the evidence will be barred whether or not there is an integration. But consistent additional non-essential oral terms may be shown unless there is a total integration.

2)   Offered by Defendant

The defendant may show that the memorandum does not reflect the true agreement and, thus, defeat the claim, unless, of course the parol evidence rule excludes such evidence. If the writing is a total integration, the writing cannot be contradicted or supplemented in order to defeat the claim. If it is a partial integration, the writing may not be contradicted, but it may be supplemented and, if the supplemental term is an essential term, the claim will be defeated because the term is not contained in the writing.

3) Interpretation

Oral evidence is admissible in aid of interpretation unless it is excluded under the rules of interpretation set forth above. For the purposes of interpretation, Williston treats a memorandum under the Statute of Frauds as if it were an integration.

f. Consideration

If the consideration is a promise that is still executory it must be stated. In some states the consideration must be stated in the writing even though it has been performed.

g. More Than One Writing

Where the terms necessary to satisfy the Statute are in two or more documents and only one is signed by the party to be charged, is the Statute satisfied? The issues presented are the connection between the documents and assent to the unsigned document. If the unsigned document is physically attached to the signed document at the time it is signed, or if one of the documents by its terms expressly refers to the other, there is no problem. Even when this is not true, the better view is that the unsigned document is part of the memorandum if the documents by internal evidence refer to the same subject matter or transaction. In that event extrinsic evidence is admissible to help show the connection between the documents and the assent of the party to be charged.

4. PROVISIONS OF THE U.C.C.

a. Contents of the Memorandum

Under the U.C.C., there are only three requirements: The memorandum must (1) evidence a contract for the sale of goods; (2) it must be signed by the party to be charged; and (3) it must specify a quantity. Thus, the memorandum is sufficient even though it omits other essential terms agreed upon. However, the contract is enforceable only as to the quantity of goods specified in the writing.

b. Written Confirmation Between Merchants

If a merchant sends a signed memorandum to another merchant in confirmation of the agreement, and the memorandum is sufficient against the sender, it is also sufficient against the receiver. For this result to obtain, it must be received and the party receiving it must have reason to know its contents, and must fail to give written notice of objection to its contents within ten days after receipt. Such a written confirmation satisfies the Statute of Frauds, but does not conclusively prove the terms of the contract.

5. AUCTION SALES

If goods having a price of $500 or more, or real property are sold at auction, the Statute of Frauds must be satisfied. It is well established that the auctioneer is authorized to sign a memorandum on behalf of both parties for a limited period of time after the sale.

6. AGENT'S AUTHORITY

A memorandum is sufficient if signed by an authorized agent of the party to be charged. By the great weight of authority the agent's authority to sign need not be set forth in writing, but some statutes provide the opposite. Often, however, this requirement of a signed authorization is limited to the Real Property Statute of Frauds.

7. PURPOSE OF THE STATUTE

The purposes of the Statute are to prevent perjury and to promote certainty by protecting against faulty memory. In addition, the required formality of a writing promotes deliberation and seriousness and indicates a genuine act of volition.

8. EFFECT OF NON–COMPLIANCE WITH THE STATUTE OF FRAUDS

Under the majority view, failure to comply with the Statute renders the contract unenforceable rather than void. Under the majority view, the oral promises are valid but they may not be sued upon. Some consequences of this approach are: (1) the Statute must be raised as an affirmative defense; (2) the issue can be raised only by the parties to the contract and those in privity; (3) the unsubscribed promise constitutes consideration for a subscribed counter promise; (4) if one party has signed and the other has not, the contract can be enforced against the party who signed by the party who has not signed. Under the minority view the contract is void; no contract is formed. If there is performance and the Statute prevents enforcement, a quasi-contractual recovery will be allowed.

9. PART OR FULL PERFORMANCE

As we have seen, complete performance on both sides eliminates any Statute of Frauds problem. The effect of part performance varies under each subdivision of the Statute of Frauds. This matter has already been covered under the individual subdivisions except that it has not been mentioned that part performance has no effect under the Suretyship Statute of Frauds.

10. ESTOPPEL

a. Promissory Estoppel

A number of cases have allowed recovery where there was substantial reliance upon an unenforceable oral promise. The phrase that is often used is "unconscionable injury." According to the Restatement, Second, the application of this doctrine of estoppel depends upon a number of factors including, the adequacy of other remedies, the extent of the reliance, that is, whether it was substantial, reasonable and foreseeable, and the extent to which the evidence corroborates such reliance.

b. Estoppel in Pais

If a *representation* produces detrimental reliance an estoppel will be raised. For example, a party who represents to the other that a written memorandum of the contract has been signed will be estopped from raising the Statute of Frauds as a defense.

11. EFFECT OF SOME PROMISES BEING WITHIN AND OTHERS WITHOUT THE STATUTE OF FRAUDS

Where one or more of the promises in a contract are within the Statute and the others are not, no part of the contract is enforceable.

Exceptions:

(1) Where all of the promises which are within the Statute have been performed;

(2) Where the party who is to receive the performance under the only promise or promises within the Statute agrees to abandon that part of the performance;

(3) Where a promisor makes a promise of alternative performances, one of which is within the Statute and the other without, the promisee may enforce the promise which is without the Statute except in the case of the one year Statute where either promise may be enforced. (See p. 215 above.)

12. ORAL RESCISSION OR MODIFICATION OF A CONTRACT WITHIN THE STATUTE

a. Rescission

A written executory contract within the Statute of Frauds may be rescinded orally except in the case of a contract to rescind a transfer of property within the Real Property or U.C.C. Statutes of Frauds.

b. Modification

(a) If the new agreement is not within the Statute of Frauds, it is not only enforceable without a writing, but also serves to discharge the previous agreement.

(b) If the new agreement is within the Statute and is unenforceable because it is oral, the former written contract remains enforceable unless the new agreement is enforced under the doctrine of waiver or estoppel.

13. RELATIONSHIP OF VARIOUS SUBDIVISIONS

It should be obvious that a promise may contravene one of the subdivisions of the Statute of Frauds and not the others. If it contravenes even one subdivision, a writing is required unless the case is removed from the Statute under the doctrines of performance (full or part) or under an estoppel theory. For example, a promise that by its terms may be performed within one year from the making thereof may still violate the subdivision relating to sale of goods. However, where a land contract is specifically enforceable under the doctrine of part performance, the other clauses of the Statute do not prevent enforcement.

REVIEW QUESTIONS

1. T or F   P, seller, and D, buyer, entered into a detailed written agreement for the purchase and sale of 150,000 yards of fill. At the trial evidence was offered to the effect that D's obligation would be effective only if D obtained a contract with the City of Brockton. This evidence is inadmissible.

2. T or F   P was engaged in leasing equipment. It entered into an integrated written agreement with D which provided in part that "discount and payment periods will start from the date of receipt of equipment by the Lessee." The Lessee offered evidence that prior to signing the writing the parties had agreed that payments were to be deferred until D started to show a profit as a result of the use of the equipment. This evidence is not admissible.

3. T or F   Jobber (J) entered into a written agreement with supplier (S) by which S agreed to sell J its requirements of raw material for a stated consideration for an extended period. There was a merger clause in this agreement. At trial J sought to introduce evidence that S violated a contemporaneous oral agreement that S would sell 50 shares of its stock to J for an agreed price. J's evidence is inadmissible.

4. T or F   P and D entered into an oral agreement for services for one year to be rendered by P. The service was to commence as soon as P could sever P's employment with P's present employer. The contract is within the Statute of Frauds.

5. T or F   Twenty years ago the defendant railroad orally agreed with plaintiff that if plaintiff contributed to the installation of a switch and siding the defendant would maintain the switch and siding for the plaintiff's benefit for as long as the plaintiff needed it. Plaintiff made the agreed contribution and also built a saw mill adjacent to the siding. Although plaintiff still needs the switch and siding, defendant has torn it up. Plaintiff's action for breach will be defeated by the defense of Statute of Frauds.

6. T or F   *D,* a grocer, sold his stock of groceries and his good will to *P.* It was orally agreed that *D* would not re-enter the grocery business in a limited area for two years. *P* sues for breach of this oral promise. Since the promise runs for a fixed term of two years the promise is certainly within the Statute of Frauds.

7. T or F   *P* lived in California, and *D* operated a dealership in Hawaii. In early April, they agreed that *P* would act as general manager for *D* starting on May 1. The hiring was for one year. *P* then left his job in California and moved to Hawaii and leased an apartment in Hawaii. *P* worked for two months for *D* when he was terminated without just cause. *P* is not entitled to any recovery because the contract is within the one year section of the Statute of Frauds.

8. T or F   Five years ago, *D* promised *P* that *D* would leave *D*'s entire estate consisting of tangible personal property and securities to *P* if *P* would take care of *D* for the rest of *D*'s life. *D* died five years later having made no provision for *P.* *P* sues *D*'s representative. *D*'s representative has a defense under the one year section of the Statute of Frauds.

9. T or F   *P* and *D* railroad reached an oral agreement whereby for five years *P* would have the exclusive concession for advertising on *D*'s right of way, stations and cars. A written memorandum of agreement containing all of the terms was drawn by *D*'s staff and approved and signed by *D*'s president. The president later struck off the signature and filed the memorandum. In an action by *P, D* may successfully plead the defense of Statute of Frauds.

10. T or F   *D* wrote to *P* offering a franchise for two years on given terms. *P* accepted orally. In an action by *P* for breach, *D* may successfully plead the defense of Statute of Frauds.

11. T or F   *P* entered into a written contract for two years employment as a physician with defendant clinic. After six weeks the parties orally agreed that the agreement would be rescinded immediately. *P* soon thereafter, and before any change of position by *D,* changed her mind,

tendered her services which were refused, and brought suit to enforce the written contract. *P* may succeed since the second agreement was oral.

12. T or F Assume the same facts as in 11 except that the oral conversation resulted in an agreement that the employment would expire in two months. The oral modification is enforceable.

13. T or F Assume the same facts as in 11 except that the oral conversation resulted in an agreement that the employment term would be extended an additional six months. The oral modification is enforceable.

14. T or F The parties orally entered into a two year employment agreement. *D,* the employer, prepared two memoranda. One was signed and contained all of the terms except the duration. The other was unsigned and contained the duration term and referred by internal evidence to the same subject matter. Since all of terms necessary to the Statute of Frauds were not contained in a signed writing or writings the memoranda were not sufficient to satisfy the Statute of Frauds.

15. T or F *E,* the executor of *A*'s estate, in compromising a claim against the estate, orally promised to guaranty its payment. *E*'s promise is not enforceable under the Statute of Frauds.

16. T or F *X, a* salesman for *S,* visited *B,* a physician, at his office and attempted to sell him a sailboat. *B* said he would think about it for a week or two before deciding. *X* falsely reported to *S* that an oral agreement was reached and *S* sent a written confirmation of the alleged sale. *B,* in annoyance, ripped up the paper and threw it in the wastebasket. A month later, *S* tendered the boat. *B* refused to take delivery and *S* sues. *B* would have the defense of Statute of Frauds.

17. T or F *S* and *B* entered into an oral contract for the purchase and sale of specified quantities of oats to be delivered over a 16 month period. *S* sent *B* a written confirmation of an oral contract bearing number 6077. After several months *B* wrote *S,* stating: "We have no further need for oats, consequently we will accept no further deliveries under contract number 6077." *S* brought suit, and *B* pleads the U.C.C. and the one year provisions of the Statute of Frauds. *B* would not have the defense of Statute of Frauds.

18. T or F *A* and *B,* an engaged couple, orally agree that after the marriage they will live in *A*'s house. In exchange *B* agrees to pay $20,000 to *A.* This agreement is within the Statute of Frauds.

19. T or F   *A* and *B*, are engaged to be married. *F*, who is *A*'s father, orally promised *A* and *B* a new Jaguar automobile as a wedding gift. *F* subsequently repudiated his promise. *F*'s promise is not enforceable. (In answering do not take into account the doctrine of promissory estoppel.)

20. T or F   In an oral agreement *S* retained *X*, a licensed real estate broker, to procure a buyer who would pay $10,000 cash for Blackacre. *S* promised *X* a commission of 6%. *X* produced *B* who purchased Blackacre for $10,000. In an action by *X* against *S* for a commission, *S* pleads the real property Statute of Frauds. *S* has not set forth a meritorious defense.

21. T or F   *S*, the owner of Blackacre, orally authorized *A*, *S's* agent, to sell Blackacre for $10,000 and to sign any necessary papers. *A*, as agent, agreed to sell Blackacre to *B* for $10,000 in a writing signed by *A* but not by *S*. Under the Statute of Frauds, *A*'s authority need not be in writing.

22. T or F   *S* orally agreed to transfer Blackacre to *B*, and *B* orally agreed to pay the purchase price in six months. Pursuant to further terms of the agreement, *S* conveyed the property. At the end of six months *B* has not paid. The Statute of Frauds is a defense to *S*'s action for the price.

23. Essay   Engineering Company (*E*) agreed to do the inspection and testing needed during construction by Constructor Corp. (*C*) of a complex belt conveyor for an industrial plant. *C* estimated completion in fifteen months.

> During negotiations the parties had agreed that if overtime became necessary, it should be added on a time-and-a-half basis. Their written contract, however, merely called for *C* to pay *E* $90,000 in fifteen monthly installments. It recited that "this contract may be amended only in a signed writing."

> After three months, *C* having paid *E* $18,000 in three monthly installments, it became obvious that the conveyor would not be completed on time.

> *E* told *C* that it would be necessary to hire workers for more months than anticipated and for more than 40 hours a week. *E* asked that the contract be amended accordingly. *C* orally agreed to pay *E* $6,000 per month until the job was completed, plus time-and-a-half for all employee hours worked over forty hours per week.

E submitted bills on this basis for an additional 6 months, when the job was completed. *C* had not paid the bills on receipt, explaining it was short of cash. Upon completion *C* paid *E* $2,000, refusing to pay any additional amounts. *E* sues *C* for $6,000 for the additional 6 months work plus $15,000 for sums disbursed for overtime wages.

What are the rights of the parties?

*

V

CONDITIONS, PERFORMANCE AND BREACH

Analysis

A. Nature and Classification of Conditions
    1. Definition
    2. Classifications of Conditions
    3. Effect of Failure of Condition
    4. Distinguishing Promises From Conditions
B. Conditions and Promises as Related to Substantial
    Performance and Material Breach
    1. Failure of Condition and Breach of Promise
    2. Factors Used to Determine Materiality of Breach (May
        the Aggrieved Party Cancel?)
    3. Factors Used to Determine Substantial Performance
        (May the Defaulting Party Recover?)
    4. Effect of Delay
    5. The Satisfaction Cases
    6. Demand
C. Recovery Despite Material Breach or Failure to Perform
    Substantially
    1. Divisibility
    2. Independent Promises
    3. Independent Promises in Leases
    4. Independent Promises in Insurance

5. Quasi–Contractual Recovery
        6. Statutory Relief
    D. Excuse of Conditions
        1. Prevention
        2. Estoppel, Waiver and Election
            a. Equitable Estoppel (Estoppel in Pais)
            b. Waiver
        3. Excuse of Conditions Involving Forfeitures
            a. Discussion
        4. Excuse of Conditions Because of Impossibility
    E. Prospective Unwillingness and Inability to Perform:
        Repudiation
        1. Repudiation as a Breach Creating a Cause of Action
        2. Prospective Unwillingness and Inability as a Prospective
            Failure of Condition Creating a Defense
        3. Role of Good Faith
        4. Retraction of a Repudiation or Prospective Failure of
            Condition
        5. Urging Retraction
        6. Effect of Impossibility on a Prior Repudiation
        7. Constructive Repudiation Under The U.C.C. and
            Restatement Second
            a. Is the Common Law Displaced?
            b. What Are Adequate Assurances?
            c. The Restatement, Second
        8. Insolvency
            a. Insolvency Defined
            b. The Effect of a Buyer's Insolvency
            c. Effect of a Seller's Insolvency
        9. Repudiation of a Debt
       10. Repudiation and Right to Elect
    F. Performance of the Sales Contract
        1. Obligations of the Seller
            a. Perspective
            b. Qualification and Exceptions
        2. Obligations of the Buyer
            a. How Much Must Be Tendered?
            b. Form of Tender
            c. Buyer's Duty to Accept Goods
            d. Buyer's Duties With Respect to the Rejected
                Goods (U.C.C. §§ 2–602—2–604)
    G. Warranties in the Sales Contract
        1. Express Warranties (U.C.C. § 2–313)
            a. "Merely" Opinion
            b. Basis of the Bargain
        2. Implied Warranties
            a. Merchantability (U.C.C. § 2–314)
            b. Fitness for Particular Purpose (U.C.C. § 2–315)
            c. Free and Clear Title
            d. Infringement (U.C.C. § 2–313(3))

3. *Disclaimer of Warranties*
    a. *Disclaimer of Express Warranties*
    b. *Disclaimer of Implied Warranties*
    c. *Limitations Upon Remedies*

A. NATURE AND CLASSIFICATION OF CONDITIONS

1. DEFINITION

A condition is an act or event, other than a lapse of time, which, unless the condition is excused, (1) must occur before a duty to perform a promise in the agreement arises (condition precedent) or (2) which discharges a duty of performance that has already arisen (condition subsequent). A promise may be conditional or it may be unconditional (independent, absolute).

> ***Examples:*** (1) *A* promises to pay *B* $100 if a certain event occurs. *A*'s promise is conditional. *A*'s duty to perform the promise arises only if the event occurs.
>
> (2) *A* promises to pay *B* $100 on July 5. *A*'s duty to perform arises after a lapse of time. Because a lapse of time is the only event which must occur before *A* is obliged to pay, *A*'s promise is, by definition, unconditional.

2. CLASSIFICATIONS OF CONDITIONS

Conditions are classified in two ways. One classification is based on when the conditioning event is to occur in relation to the promise. Under this classification, conditions are labeled as precedent, concurrent, and subsequent. A condition precedent must be performed or occur before a duty to perform a promise arises. Performance of a concurrent condition must be tendered before the promise of the other party must be performed. Conditions subsequent are very rare. Such a condition discharges a duty of performance after it has already arisen. The second classification is based on whether the condition has been agreed upon and placed in the contract by the parties (express or implied in fact condition) or has been imposed by the court to meet the ends of justice (constructive condition). The various classes of conditions are illustrated after 4 (below).

3. EFFECT OF FAILURE OF CONDITION

Only a party who makes a *promise* and breaches it is liable for breach of contract. Failure of condition may result in the inability to enforce a promise made by the other party but it imposes no liability, unless the party protected by the condition has promised that the condition would occur.

4. DISTINGUISHING PROMISES FROM CONDITIONS

There is no conclusive or exclusive test to determine whether particular contractual language creates a condition or a promise. Indeed, express language of condition may also be implied language of promise. Similarly, express language of promise may be construed to create an implied in fact or constructive condition. Certain introductory words almost always create conditions. Among these are: "on condition that" the ship sails, "provided that" the ship sails, "if" the ship sails, "subject to" the ship's sailing. Certain words are almost always promissory: "I will" sail the ship, I "promise" to sail the ship, I "warrant" that the ship will sail. Some contract terms are ambiguous as to the intended legal effect. "The ship is to sail on or before February 4," may be interpreted as creating either a condition or a promise (or both). the normal processes of interpretation are used to determine the intent of the parties. *If this intent cannot be determined, the court will treat the words as creating a promise rather than a condition.*

Examples: (1) *S* agrees to sell and *B* agrees to buy a named book. *S* sues for the price without first tendering the book. In the absence of an agreement to the contrary, payment and delivery are constructive concurrent conditions. This means that, in order for *S* to put *B* in default, *S* must make conditional tender of performance or show that tender is excused. The same is true if *B* were to sue. Concurrent conditions occur primarily in contracts for the sale of goods and contracts for the conveyance of land.

(2) *I* insures *B* against loss by fire. *B*'s house is destroyed by fire and *B* has a claim against *I.* A provision in the insurance policy states: "No action shall be brought after the expiration of 12 months from the occurrence of any loss." *B* sues in the thirteenth month. *B*'s failure to bring suit within twelve months discharges *I*'s duty of performance that had already arisen. This is a true condition subsequent. True conditions subsequent are rare, but at times conditions which are, by definition, precedent are treated as subsequent because the language used is subsequent in form. The distinction is important primarily on the issue of burden of proof. The claimant has the burden on conditions precedent, the other party on conditions subsequent. At times a condition precedent is treated procedurally as a condition subsequent so that the burden of proof is placed upon the party with knowledge of the facts. (See the next illustration.)

(3) *D* promised to pay *P* 60 cents per gallon for oil. *D* also promised to pay an additional 25 cents per gallon with the proviso that this second promise would be void if a greater quantity of oil should arrive in whaling vessels at Nantucket and New Bedford between the first day of April and the first day of October both inclusive than had arrived at these places within the same period of time the previous year. This is clearly an express condition precedent. The note was not to be paid unless a smaller quantity of oil arrived this year than last. Nonetheless, this court held the parties to the *form* of the language, thrusting the burden on the defendant to prove that more oil had arrived this year. Some other cases reach the opposite conclusion, holding that substance should prevail over form.

(4) *A* offers to pay $10 if *B* walks (unilateral) across Brooklyn Bridge. *B* does not perform. *B*'s walking the bridge is an express condition precedent to *A*'s duty to pay. Thus, if *B* does not walk, *B* is not entitled to the $10. However, *B* is not liable to *A* because *B* has not made any promise.

(5) *B* promises to paint *A*'s house, and to complete the work by February 1. *A* promises to pay the agreed price on that day. Painting the house is a constructive condition to *A*'s promise to pay *B*. The condition is constructive because there is no language of condition in the contract, only language of promise. Thus, on the general notion that, unless otherwise agreed, the doing of the work should precede paying for it, the court constructs a condition that *B* must perform before *B* is entitled to be paid. Although express conditions must be strictly performed, constructive conditions require only substantial compliance.

(6) *B*, a subcontractor, promises to do certain painting work for *A*, a general contractor. *A* promises to pay *B* "when *A* is paid by the owner." *B* has completed the painting work. *A* refuses to pay *B* because of (a) some slight defects in the painting work and (b) because *A* has not been paid by the owner. As pointed out in problem (5) above, *B* must prove substantial performance of the constructive condition of painting. In addition, some cases have held that *B* is entitled to be paid only after the owner pays *A*, because the owner's payment is an express condition precedent to *A*'s duty to pay. Others have held that the "when clause" does not create a condition; therefore *B* is entitled to payment within a reasonable time after performance even if *A* has not been paid. Because a "when" clause is inherently ambiguous, extrinsic evidence is admissible to determine its intended legal effect. If no other persuasive evidence of intent exists, the court will generally follow trade usage; e.g., construction subcontractors rarely work for contingent fees, but real estate brokers usually work for contingent fees.

(7) *S* agrees to sell a paper mill to *B* who promises to pay the purchase price in paper. *S* impliedly promises to instruct *B* in the art of manufacturing paper. *S* fails to instruct. *S*'s promise to instruct *B* in the art of making paper is not a constructive condition but an implied-in-fact condition. An implied-in-fact condition is a true condition and must be strictly performed. Strict performance is the same rule that applies to express conditions. Clearly, the implied-in-fact condition must occur before *B* is required to pay. Implied-in-fact conditions are rare and ordinarily limited to situations involving cooperation.

(8) *S* and *B* enter into a contract for the sale and purchase of real property. The contract contains a clause that performance is "contingent upon *B* obtaining" a described mortgage loan. The phrase quoted is clearly language of express condition precedent but, in addition, *B* has impliedly promised to use reasonable efforts to obtain the described loan.

(9) A contract states "in the event of any breach by the seller, the buyer shall give seller written notice of such breach within 30 days." Buyer commences an action for breach without complying with this provision. The problem is whether the quoted language is language of promise or language of express condition. If it is language of express condition, the buyer's claim would be dismissed. If it is language of promise, the breach would only be immaterial and, under the rules stated immediately below, *B*'s action can proceed. Thus, when there is a question of whether particular words are language of express condition or language of promise, the court will presume that the words create a promise rather than an express condition. If the language is looked upon as language of promise, the result is fairer.

B. CONDITIONS AND PROMISES AS RELATED TO SUBSTANTIAL PERFORMANCE AND MATERIAL BREACH

Express conditions and implied-in-fact conditions must be fully performed but constructive conditions need only be substantially performed.

1. FAILURE OF CONDITION AND BREACH OF PROMISE

Discussion: The relationship of rules concerning failure of condition and the related question of breach of promise can be put into focus by the following illustration. *A*, in England, agrees to charter a vessel to *B*, in the United States, and *B* agrees to pay for the vessel when it arrives. The critical clause in the agreement states "the vessel to sail from England on or before February 4." The vessel in fact sails from England on February 5. There are three possible interpretations of the quoted language.

(1) The quoted language is only language of express condition. If so, *B* is free to cancel the deal because the express condition has not been literally performed. However, *B* may not sue *A*, because, if the language only creates a condition, *A* did not make a promise.

(2) If the quoted language is only language of promise so that, although *B* has promised to cause the vessel to sail on or before February 4, there is

no language of express condition, the case can be approached in two possible ways.

(a) If A sues B for refusing to accept the ship, the doctrine of constructive conditions is involved. There is no express condition, but the court constructs the condition that A must perform before B. Therefore, the issue is whether A has substantially performed the constructive condition.

(b) If B sues A, the issue is materiality of the breach. If the breach is material, B would be free to cancel and also sue for a total breach; but if the breach is immaterial B must perform and can only sue for a partial breach.

(3) If the quoted language were language of express condition as in (1) but also implied language of promise, B would be free not to proceed irrespective of whether the delay materially affected B's interests and could also sue for total breach of contract.

Comment: It is important to note that substantial performance and material breach are usually opposite sides of the same coin. If a party has substantially performed, any breach by this party can only be immaterial. Conversely if a party has committed a material breach, this party's performance cannot be substantial. Thus, the way in which the issue is stated is ordinarily not of great importance. However, there are instances where the two ways of framing the issue are not interchangeable. If one party is late in performing and substantial performance has not been rendered, a material breach has not necessarily occurred.

Examples: (1) A promises to restore B's antique automobile and to fix a flat spare tire. B, in exchange, promises to pay $8,500. A delivers the restored automobile but fails to fix the tire. When the car was delivered, A had substantially performed and therefore there was no material breach. A is entitled to $8,500, minus B's damages for A's failure to fix the tire.

(2) Vendor agreed to deliver title to a certain lot and to cinderize the streets in the subdivision in which the lot is located. Vendor tenders a conveyance of title but has not cinderized the streets. Vendee rejects the tender and refuses to pay. Vendor has not substantially performed. Cinderizing the streets is more important than changing the tire was in the previous illustration. Although Vendor has not substantially performed, it may be that Vendor is not yet guilty of material breach.

2. FACTORS USED TO DETERMINE MATERIALITY OF BREACH (MAY THE AGGRIEVED PARTY CANCEL?)

(a) To what extent, if any, the contract has been performed at the time of breach?

(b) The earlier the breach the more likely it will be regarded as material.

(c) A willful breach is more likely to be regarded as material.

(d) A quantitatively serious breach is more likely to be considered material.

(e) The degree of hardship on the breaching party.

(f) The extent to which the aggrieved party has or will receive a substantial benefit from the promised performance.

(g) The adequacy with which the aggrieved party may be compensated by damages for partial breach.

(h) The type of contract involved. For example, in a contract for the sale of goods, the "perfect tender" rule applies except in the case of installment delivery contracts. In construction contracts, and most other contracts, the doctrine of substantial performance is applied.

Example: Harrison, a dry-cleaner, entered into an agreement with Walker, whereby Harrison, as lessee, leased a sign for a three year term at $150 per month. At the expiration of the lease, Harrison was to receive title to the sign. During the term of the lease, Walker was obligated to maintain the sign. After the first month, someone splattered the sign with a tomato. Walker ignored many telephone demands by Harrison that it send someone to clean the sign. Angrily, Harrison telegraphed Walker that he was cancelling the contract. Walker sues for the rent. Judgment for Walker. The damage was easily curable. If Harrison had hired someone to clean the sign, he could have recovered this sum from Walker. Harrison had the substantial benefit of the sign and cancellation of the contract would result in a harsh forfeiture of Walker's performance.

3. FACTORS USED TO DETERMINE SUBSTANTIAL PERFORMANCE (MAY THE DEFAULTING PARTY RECOVER?)

(a) To what extent has the injured party obtained the benefits sought by contracting?

(b) To what extent may the injured party be adequately compensated in damages?

(c) To what extent has there been performance or preparation for performance?

(d) How great is the hardship if the breaching party is not permitted to recover?

(e) Was the breach willful?

(f) How certain can the court be that the party in breach would have completed performance?

Example: *A* agrees to build a house for *B*. One of the promises made in the contract is that Reading brand pipe will be installed. *A*'s plumbing subcontractor installs mostly Cohoes brand pipe, which, although just as good as Reading, is a breach by *A*. This breach was not discovered until after most of the plumbing is encased in plaster walls. *B* refuses to pay *A* the final payment. *B* has obtained the desired result: a house that generally conforms to his contract. *A*'s deviation was not willful. *A* may recover the agreed price minus *B*'s damages, if any. A contrary result would impose a harsh forfeiture.

4. EFFECT OF DELAY

If the contract makes "time of the essence," ordinarily any lateness will be considered a material breach. Otherwise, a reasonable delay will not be considered a material breach. In the case of contracts for the sale of goods, however, the U.C.C. makes time of the essence except in the case of installment contracts.

Examples: (1) *S* contracts to deliver a lathe to *B*'s plant on November 15. *S* tenders delivery on November 16. Under the "perfect tender" rule of the U.C.C. (see p. 253 infra), *B* may reject the goods and hold *S* liable for total breach.

(2) *A* agrees to build a building for *B* to be completed by June 30. On June 30 the work is incomplete and it appears that it will take an additional two weeks to complete. *B* purports to cancel the contract. Absent extraordinary circumstances known to *A* at the time of contracting that makes completion by June 30 essential, *A*'s delay is not a material breach. *B*'s purported cancellation is a wrongful repudiation. Note carefully that although *A*'s delay is not material, it is a breach and *A* is liable for delay damages.

(3) *A* agrees to convey Blackacre to *B* for $20,000 on June 30. The contract states that "time is of the essence." On June 30, *A* is unable to convey marketable title because of an ancient mortgage that is still of record. *A*'s lawyer informs *B* that a proceeding to clear the records had been started and a decree quieting title will likely issue in a day or two. *B* cancels. *B*'s cancellation is proper. The phrase "time is of the essence" indicates an intent that tender of performance by the date stated is an express condition precedent. Consequently, as in the case of other express conditions, the general rule is that strict compliance is required. However, there is a growing school of thought that indicates that "such stock phrases" do not necessarily have this effect. They are to be considered along with other circumstances in determining the effect of delay.

5. THE SATISFACTION CASES

If a *party* to a contract promises to pay for a performance "on the condition that I am personally satisfied," payment will not be required if the party in *good faith* is dissatisfied. However, if the performance is one that is a matter of mechanical fitness, utility, or marketability, the courts rewrite the contract to mean that if the performance is objectively satisfactory, it must be paid for. This is clearly a violation of the general rule that an express condition requires strict performance. However, in most jurisdictions where the personal satisfaction of a *third party* (e.g. an architect) is involved, the courts do not rewrite the contract.

Examples: (1) *A* agrees to rebuild a boiler in *B*'s factory and is to be paid "if the work is to the entire satisfaction of *B*." *A* does an excellent job but *B*, an honest but super-finicky eccentric, is not satisfied. If the jury finds that *B* is unreasonable, *B* must pay. Underlying reasons are (1) the thought that one ought not be a judge in one's own cause and (2) that an unconscionable forfeiture would otherwise occur. The result would be different if the person to be satisfied were an independent professional engineer rather than a contracting party.

(2) *A* agrees to paint a portrait of *B*'s daughter for $3,000, for which *B* need pay only if *B* is entirely satisfied with it. *A* paints a portrait that is critically acclaimed as a masterpiece. *B*, however, is not satisfied and rejects the portrait. *B* is not liable for the price. *B*'s judgment of the performance is a matter of taste and therefore the judgment is personal and subjective. Note that there is no element of unjust enrichment or forfeiture because if *B* rejects the portrait, *A* keeps it. Contrast the boiler in example (1) which, as a fixture, becomes the property of *B*, the factory owner. This is an important element in determining

whether to apply a subjective test of good faith or an objective test of reasonableness. Note also that although the standard is personal, the dissatisfaction must be genuine. If *B* manifests dissatisfaction with the bargain; for example, by stating that the price is too high, or by refusing to examine the portrait, *B* is liable. *B* is not dissatisfied with the performance but with the bargain.

6. DEMAND

If a promise is made to render a performance upon demand, demand is an express condition precedent. But it is generally held, by way of exception, that a debtor's promise to pay upon demand is enforceable without demand.

C. RECOVERY DESPITE MATERIAL BREACH OR FAILURE TO PERFORM SUBSTANTIALLY

A party who does not substantially perform is not entitled to a recovery, unless performance is excused or the case comes under one of the following exceptions.

1. DIVISIBILITY

A contract is divisible if the performances of each party are divided into two or more parts and the performance of each part by one party is the agreed exchange for a corresponding part by the other party. If a divisible portion is substantially performed, recovery may be had for that portion despite a material breach of the overall contract.

Examples: (1) *A* and *B* agree that *A* will be *B*'s secretary for one year at a salary of $400 per week. *A* works for a week and quits for no good reason. *A* is entitled to $400 because *A* has performed one part of a divisible contract. *B*, however, is entitled to counterclaim for damages. (Note also, that while most hirings are "at will," this illustration involves an employment contract for a specific term.)

(2) *T* agrees to transport 5 truckloads of widgets for *X* at $30 a mile. Four truckloads are duly delivered to destination, but the fifth is totally demolished half-way to destination. *T* sues for payment. *T* is entitled to payment for the four completed deliveries. Each has an apportioned calculable price and *independent value* to *X*. As to the fifth, *T* has no claim. The carriage of the goods half-way to destination has no value to *X*. Indeed *X* has an action against *T* for breach.

(3) A contractor agrees to make alterations for $3,075, payable as follows: $150 on signing the contract, $1,000 on delivery of

materials to the site, $1,500 on completion of rough carpentry and $425 on completion of the job. The first two payments are duly made. The contractor wrongfully repudiates upon completion of the rough carpentry and sues for $1,500 on a theory of divisibility. The contractor does not recover as the contract is not divisible. It can hardly be said that $150 was the agreed equivalent for signing the contract or that delivery of plaintiff's materials was worth $1,000 to defendant. Construction contracts are rarely divisible.

2. INDEPENDENT PROMISES

A promise is independent (unconditional) if it is unqualified or if nothing but a lapse of time is necessary to make the performance of the promise presently enforceable. The promisee may enforce an independent promise without rendering substantial performance of the promisee's part of the bargain.

Example: A promises to paint B's house and B promises to pay A $3,000 upon completion of the work. A, without justification, fails to start the job within a reasonable time. B may cancel and sue A for total breach. A's promise is, unconditional, because A must paint before B must pay, and there are no other express or implied conditions to A's duty of performance. Consequently, B may cancel and sue for total breach despite B's own nonperformance. B need only prove that he or she would have been ready, willing and able to pay had A performed.

Caveat: Relativity of the Definition. Although in the above example A's promise to paint is said to be unconditional by definition, the definition is relative to the facts given. In special circumstances such as destruction of the house before A has an opportunity to start performance (see p. 271 infra), or B's repudiation, conditions may be constructed to protect A in the light of the facts.

3. INDEPENDENT PROMISES IN LEASES

Under the traditional common law, the doctrine of constructive conditions did not apply to leases. Consequently, a tenant's duty to pay rent was treated as independent of the landlord's covenants to repair and to provide services. This rule has been abolished or eroded in most jurisdictions.

4. INDEPENDENT PROMISES IN INSURANCE

Absent a provision in an insurance policy that makes payment of the premium an express condition, the insurer's duty is not conditioned on payment of the premium. Consequently, if a casualty loss ensues, the insurer must pay although the premiums are in arrears. This rule does not prevent the insurer from inserting a clause permitting it to cancel a policy for non-payment.

Until the cancellation is effectuated, however, the insurer's promise remains independent of the payment of premiums.

5. QUASI–CONTRACTUAL RECOVERY

Although all jurisdictions recognize the availability of quasi-contractual relief where services are rendered under a contract that is defective for reasons such as indefiniteness, or non-compliance with writing requirements, or that fails because of impossibility of performance, there is disagreement with respect to giving relief to a party who has breached the contract. The orthodox and still prevailing view is that a party in default may not recover from the other party even though the breaching party has conferred benefits on the other party in excess of the damages caused by the breach. The modern trend, however, permits such recovery.

6. STATUTORY RELIEF

A number of statutes permit a defaulting party to recover. For example, legislation in most states requires that workers be paid at periodic intervals, and that accrued wages be paid when the employment relation ends, regardless of any contract condition to the contrary. The U.C.C. allows a defaulting buyer to obtain restitution to the extent the buyer's payments exceed the smaller of (a) $500 or (b) 20% of the purchase price. The buyer's claim for restitution is subject to an offset in the amount of the seller's actual damages and the value of benefits received by the buyer.

Example: (1) *B* contracts to purchase living room furniture from *S* for $2,100, paying $700 of the purchase price. *B* repudiates and sues for restitution of the down payment. *B* obtains restitution of $700 minus the lesser of $500 or 20% of the price ($420). Since $420 is less than $500, *B* obtains judgment for $700–420 that is, $280.

D. EXCUSE OF CONDITIONS

1. PREVENTION

A condition is excused by prevention, substantial hindrance or the failure to cooperate provided that the conduct is wrongful. Moreover, in every contract there is a constructive condition that one will not wrongfully prevent or substantially hinder the other party's performance.

Examples: (1) A nephew agreed to care for his granduncle for the rest of the granduncle's life. The granduncle promised his nephew that he would be paid by his estate. Later, the granduncle pointed a gun at his nephew and unjustifiably ordered him to leave. The nephew sues for damages and recovers. Although the nephew's performance under the contract was a constructive condition precedent to the granduncle's duty to pay, this condition was excused because the granduncle prevented its occurrence.

(2) Assume all the facts in example (1) except that the granduncle sues the nephew for breach of the nephew's promise to take care of him for life. Case dismissed. There is a constructive condition to the granduncle's rights that he not prevent his nephew from performing. Because this condition failed, he has no cause of action.

(3) *B* lists a house for sale with *A*, a real estate broker, agreeing to pay a commission "upon closing of title." *A* procures a purchaser who signs a contract of purchase. Later at the purchaser's request, *B* agrees to a mutual rescission of the contract. *A* sues *B* for the agreed commission. *A* recovers. *B*'s conduct actively prevents the condition that title close. Consequently, the condition is excused.

(4) Assume the same facts as in the previous example, except that no mutual rescission occurs. Instead the purchaser repudiates the contract. *B* retains the down payment but takes no action against the purchaser. *A* sues *B*, contending that *B* should have sued the purchaser for specific performance thereby bringing about the condition to *B*'s own duty to pay a commission to *A*. Action dismissed. Although there are times one must cooperate affirmatively to bring about a condition to one's own duty, heroics are not required. An action for specific performance involves expense, annoyance and risks.

(5) *S* agrees to sell Blackacre to *B* for $100,000 and *B* agrees to purchase, subject to *B*'s obtaining a mortgage loan of $75,000 at specified terms. *B* makes no effort to get financing. *S* sues *B* for breach. *S* recovers. Although a condition to *B*'s duty to purchase has not occurred, it is excused because *B* failed to cooperate by using reasonable efforts to obtain a mortgage loan. An affirmative duty of cooperation is implied, because the condition cannot occur without *B*'s cooperation. A duty of affirmative cooperation is implied when it accords with "justice, common sense and the probable intention of the parties."

(6) *S* agreed to sell to *B* 2,600 tons of widgets for $41 a ton. *S* failed to deliver and set up as a defense that widgets were in short supply and that *B* bought up the widgets from the suppliers from whom *S* planned to buy, driving up the market price. Judgment for *B*. Although there was substantial hindrance by *B*, there was no wrongful conduct by *B*. Sellers who agree to sell

goods they do not possess ("selling short") assume the risk of market forces, including the possibility that the buyer may be actively purchasing in the market.

(7) Assume the same facts as in the prior example except that *B* has bought up all the widgets available on the world market ("cornered the market"). *S* will be excused, because *B* has made it impossible for *S* to perform.

2. ESTOPPEL, WAIVER AND ELECTION
a. Equitable Estoppel (Estoppel *in Pais*)
Equitable estoppel has traditionally been held to exist where one party has misrepresented a fact and the other party has injuriously relied upon that misrepresentation. Today, an estoppel may be based upon even an innocent misrepresentation of fact or upon a promise.

b. Waiver
A waiver is an intentional relinquishment of a known right. The important thing to remember is that even though there is a waiver under this definition it may be without effect. Another thing to remember is that this discussion concerns waiver of condition and not the renunciation of a right to damages or the discharge of a contract, both of which are discussed in the section on discharge.

1) Waiver Before Failure of Condition
A waiver of a condition that constitutes a material part of an agreed exchange is ineffective in the absence of consideration, its equivalent, or an estoppel. A waiver of a condition that is not a material part of the agreed exchange is effective but it may be reinstated by notice prior to any material change of position by the other party. An effective waiver disables the party from cancelling but does not discharge the aggrieved party's right to damages.

Examples: (1) *A* agrees to paint *B*'s house, and *B* promises to pay $1,000. Immediately after the agreement *B* promises to pay the $1,000 even if *A* does not paint. The waiver of condition is ineffective; any other rule would completely subvert the doctrine of consideration. Thus what has occurred is a modification without consideration, its equivalent, or an estoppel. *B*'s promise is unenforceable.

(2) *A* agrees to build a structure for *B* before January 1. Time is made of the essence. Before January 1, *B* tells *A* that the performance will be accepted even if it is not complete until February 1. On January 30, *A* completes the performance and *B* refuses to pay. *A* sues.

Judgment for *A*. Although the condition that time is of the essence is material, it is not a material part of the agreed exchange. The waiver is effective even without an estoppel. The practical result is that the waiver is effective even if it can be shown that *A* could not have finished the building by January 1.

(3) Assume the facts given in example (2), except that the day after *B* had made the waiver and before any change of position by *A, B* communicated a retraction of the waiver. The condition that time is of the essence is reinstated.

2) **Who Can Waive**
Only the party for whose benefit the condition has been imposed can waive it.

Example: *S* and *B* agree to the sale by *S* to *B* of Blackacre, "subject to *B*'s obtaining financing" on specified terms. *B* fails to obtain the financing but decides to dip into savings to make the purchase. As the condition is clearly for *B*'s protection, *B* may waive it. *S* cannot.

Perspective—Waiver Before Contracting: At times one party will present a pre-printed form contract to the other for signature. After discussion, the party who is proposing the form may assure the other that a given term of the printed form will not be applied in this case. Many courts have treated the situation as involving waiver although obviously the real problem is the application of the parol evidence rule. Generally, if the words of assurance have induced the adhering party to sign, the court will rule that the propounding party is estopped from enforcing the term in question.

3) **Waiver After Failure of Condition**
A waiver after a failure of express or constructive condition is an election. An election may take place by conduct or by promise. No consideration is needed for an election and, according to the majority rule, an election once made cannot be withdrawn.

Examples: (1) *A* promises to charter a vessel from *B* on the condition that the vessel arrive on or before February 4. The vessel arrives on February 5. The express condition clearly has failed and *A* can elect to cancel the deal because *A* is entitled to literal performance. However, if *A* elects to continue, both parties are bound.

(2) *A* promises to build a house in exchange for *B*'s promise to pay. *A* falls so behind schedule that there is a material breach. There is a failure of a constructive condition which gives *B* the right to elect to continue the contract and sue for a partial breach or to terminate *B*'s obligations under the contract and sue for a total breach.

4) Repeated Waivers
If a party repeatedly waives a condition, the other party can reasonably expect that future waivers will be made unless the first party reinstates the condition by reasonable notice.

Example: A mortgagee had consistently waived the condition of timely payment by accepting late payments. Then without giving any notice, the mortgagee refused to accept a late payment and began a foreclosure action. Case dismissed. The mortgagor had reason to believe that late payments would be accepted. The mortgagee is estopped from insisting on its right to timely payment until it has given the mortgagor reasonable notice that the condition is reinstated.

3. EXCUSE OF CONDITIONS INVOLVING FORFEITURES
A condition may be excused if (1) it involves an extreme forfeiture, (2) its occurrence is not a material part of the agreed exchange and (3) if one of the foundations for equitable jurisdiction exists.

a. Discussion
If a case is an equity case in the sense that earlier in our history the case would have been brought in a separate court of equity, certain special rules and maxims apply, including the maxim that "equity abhors a forfeiture." Whenever a party seeks, and plausibly is entitled to, specific performance, specific restitution (except replevin), or an injunction, the case is an equity case even in a jurisdiction where law and equity are administered in the same court.

Example: Holiday Inns obtained a 4½ year option to purchase certain vacant land from Knight for $200,000. The consideration for the option was $10,000 paid on acquiring the option and four additional $10,000 payments payable on July 1 of each of the next four years. The option agreement provided that the dates of payments were of the essence. Two of the annual installments were duly made. The third, tendered on July 2, was rejected. Equity jurisdiction exists because each parcel of land is deemed unique. The failure of condition is slight, and the forfeiture is extreme. The plaintiff is not attempting to extend the option period, but only to obtain relief from forfeiture that would be caused by a late installment payment. The $30,000 already paid for the option would otherwise be forfeited because of the slight delay.

4. EXCUSE OF CONDITIONS BECAUSE OF IMPOSSIBILITY
Impossibility excuses a condition if the condition excused is not a material part of the agreed exchange and if a forfeiture would otherwise occur.

Example: A agrees to erect a building for *B*. *B* promises to pay on the condition *A* produce the certificate of a named architect. After *A* performs the work, the named architect dies. *A* is entitled to enforce *B's* promise to pay, because the condition is excused. The result would be otherwise if the architect died prior to the contractor's commencement of performance.

E. PROSPECTIVE UNWILLINGNESS AND INABILITY TO PERFORM: REPUDIATION

1. REPUDIATION AS A BREACH CREATING A CAUSE OF ACTION
A repudiation is a promisor's unjustified statement *positively* indicating that he or she will not or cannot substantially perform, or the promisor's *voluntary act* that renders the promisor's substantial performance impossible or apparently impossible. A repudiation is a total breach whether or not performance is due now or in the future. The only exception is the case of a unilateral obligation not yet due (see p. 252 infra). To establish a cause of action, the aggrieved party must prove (1) the contract, (2) the breach by repudiation, and (3) that he or she would have been ready, willing and able to perform but for the repudiation.

2. PROSPECTIVE UNWILLINGNESS AND INABILITY AS A PROSPECTIVE FAILURE OF CONDITION CREATING A DEFENSE
If a party repudiates the obligations of the contract or appears unwilling or unable to perform, under the doctrine of prospective failure of condition, the other party may, depending on the circumstances, (1) continue performance; (2) suspend or withhold performance; (3) change position or declare that the contract is cancelled. If the prospective unwillingness is a repudiation as defined above, the other party has no right to elect to waive the breach but must cease performance except in the rare case where continuation of performance will minimize damages. In cases not involving a repudiation, which of the responses is permissible depends on the facts of the case. "The question must resolve itself into one of degree and probability."

Examples: (1) *S* agrees to sell and *B* agrees to buy a specific car, delivery to be made on June 1. On April 25, *S* tells *B* that *S* will not perform. Result: *S* has repudiated. Therefore *B* may, first, sue now for anticipatory breach or sue after June 1 for actual breach, and, second, change position or otherwise indicate that the contract is at an end. Thus, *B* may elect any of the responses indicated above, except that *B* cannot continue performance or make plans based upon obtaining the car on June 1.

(2) *S,* instead of telling *B* that the car will not be delivered, sells the car to *X.* *B* has precisely the same rights as in the preceding illustration because *S*'s conduct amounts to a repudiation.

(3) *A* agrees with *B* to sing the lead part in an opera for two months. Prior to opening night, *A* becomes ill and her physician expresses the opinion that she will not be able to sing for two weeks. Although her illness excuses the prospective non-performance, the prospective inability to perform is serious, and *B* may respond by hiring a substitute and declaring the contract at an end. *B* may not recover in any suit for breach.

(4) A serious shortage of steel exists because of wartime conditions. A general contractor asks the steel subcontractor whether it will be able to get sufficient steel to perform. The subcontractor states that it is unable to give a positive promise that it will be able to perform. It has not repudiated because it has not positively stated it will not perform but has indicated prospective inability. Although the general contractor cannot sue, it would be justified in changing position by contracting with a steel subcontractor who can assure it of performance. If the U.C.C. were applicable, the first subcontractor would be liable for breach because it failed to give adequate assurances (see U.C.C. § 2–609 p. 250 infra). However, because wartime conditions were impeding the procurement of steel, it may have the defense of impossibility of performance.

(5) *S* contracted to sell certain real property to *B.* Closing was set for December 15. On November 30, *B* wrote to *S* that there were certain defects in title, and *B* was therefore cancelling the contract and demanding the return of the down payment. *B* did not specify what defects had been discovered. The defects were curable within a reasonable time after December 15. *B* sues for restitution, and *S* counterclaims for damages to the extent these exceed the down payment. Judgment for *S.* Although *B*'s title search showed that *S* was prospectively unable to perform, it did not conclusively establish inability. Consequently, *B*'s cancellation

was an overreaction and, therefore, a repudiation. While *B* would be justified in withholding any payments due before or at the closing date, *B* was not free to cancel absent a finding that title was incurable. Unless (a) title is incurable or (b) the seller repudiates, the buyer may place the seller in default only by (c) tendering the buyer's own performance coupled with a demand for a conveyance of marketable title within a reasonable time followed by failure of the seller to tender such a conveyance. *In short, tender, demand and breach.* The seller also recovers on the counterclaim. To place a buyer in breach, the seller must normally show the seller's own tender and demand as well as breach by the buyer. Here, however, tender is excused by the buyer's repudiation. The seller need only show the buyer's repudiation and that the seller would have been ready, willing and able to perform within a reasonable time but for the repudiation.

3. ROLE OF GOOD FAITH
A promisor's good faith but unjustified cancellation of the contract is a repudiation.

Example: See example involving the tomato-streaked dry cleaning sign on p. 237 supra.

4. RETRACTION OF A REPUDIATION OR PROSPECTIVE FAILURE OF CONDITION
A repudiation may be retracted, and a prospective unwillingness or inability to perform can be cured unless the aggrieved party has cancelled or materially changed position or otherwise indicated that the contract is at an end.

Example: *S* contracts to deliver steel to *B* in 10 monthly installments, commencing June 1. On May 1, *S* repudiates the contract. On May 5, threatened by a law suit and advised by counsel of the probability of an adverse judgment, *S* notifies *B* that the steel deliveries will be made as scheduled. The withdrawal of the repudiation effectively reinstates the duties of the contract. The result would be different if *B* had contracted elsewhere for steel to replace the steel expected under *S*'s contract: in this case *B* could hold *S* liable for total breach of contract.

5. URGING RETRACTION
The aggrieved party may urge the repudiator to retract without prejudice to the aggrieved party's rights.

Example: *S* contracts to deliver steel to *B*, deliveries to commence on June 1. *S* repudiates on May 1. *B* immediately begins to negotiate with *C* for steel to replace the steel expected under *B*'s contract with *S*.

At the same time *B* urges *S* to retract. On May 6, *B* enters into a replacement contract with *C.* Later that day, *B* receives a retraction from *S.* The retraction is ineffective. By urging *S* to retract, *B* did not lose the right to change position.

6.   EFFECT OF IMPOSSIBILITY ON A PRIOR REPUDIATION
Subsequent impossibility will discharge an anticipatory breach and partial impossibility will limit damages for the breach.

Examples: (1) *A* and *B* enter into a contract whereby *B* hires *A* for a one year term commencing June 1. On May 11, *B* repudiates. On May 25, *A* dies. *A*'s estate sues *B* for breach. *A*'s estate fails to establish a cause of action. Although *B* was guilty of committing an anticipatory breach, *A*'s estate cannot establish that *A* would have been ready, willing and able to perform but for the repudiation.

(2) Assume the same facts as in example (1) except that *A*'s death occurs on June 30. *A*'s estate establishes a cause of action, but under the better view, recovery is limited to damages for a thirty-day period. The view is better because it fully takes into account all facts known at the time of trial. The other view is that *A*'s rights vest at the time of the repudiation.

7.   CONSTRUCTIVE REPUDIATION UNDER THE U.C.C. AND RESTATEMENT SECOND
Under § 2–609 of the U.C.C., if a party has reasonable grounds for insecurity, that is, reasonably fears that the other party is unable to or unwilling to perform, that party may demand adequate assurance of performance and also has the right to suspend performance until such assurance is received. Failure to give adequate assurance within a reasonable time, not exceeding 30 days, operates as a repudiation.

a.   Is the Common Law Displaced?
Whether the right to demand adequate assurance displaces other rights (e.g., to change position) or is simply an additional right is not yet clear.

b.   What Are Adequate Assurances?
The adequacy of an assurance varies greatly with the commercial context. Words of assurance from a reputable party may suffice, but where the prospective inability is grave even a reputable buyer may be required to furnish a financial statement or produce a bank letter of credit.

c.   The Restatement, Second
The Restatement, Second, follows the lead of the U.C.C. and permits the insecure party to demand adequate assurances and suspend performance

until such assurances are received. If assurances are not furnished within a reasonable time, the demanding party may treat the failure to provide them as a repudiation. Under the Restatement, Second, the right to demand assurances replaces other permissible reactions to prospective inability or unwillingness, except the permissible responses to a repudiation or insolvency. Thus, except in the case of a repudiation (see above) or insolvency (see below), the insecure party can cancel or change position *only at its peril.* If the other party tenders or demands timely performance, the insecure party will be in breach if it is no longer able or willing to perform. Thus, the Restatement, Second, would disagree with example 3 on page 248 supra. The courts have not yet accepted the Restatement position.

8. INSOLVENCY
a. Insolvency Defined

A particular form of prospective inability is insolvency, at least in cases where a party's solvency is relevant. The insolvency of an employee, for example, may be irrelevant to performance of the employment contract. The U.C.C. § 1–201(23) enumerates three kinds of situations that constitute insolvency:

(1) cessation of payment of debts in the regular course of business;

(2) inability to pay one's debts as they mature;

(3) insolvency within the meaning of the Federal Bankruptcy Act. Subject to complex qualifications (11 U.S.C. § 100(26)), this occurs when one's debts are greater than one's assets.

b. The Effect of a Buyer's Insolvency

When a seller discovers that a buyer is insolvent, the seller may take the following steps:

(1) Refuse delivery except for cash, including payment for all goods previously delivered under the same contract;

(2) Stop delivery of goods in transit;

(3) Reclaim goods delivered on credit to a party while insolvent, provided that demand for their reclamation is made within ten days of receipt by the buyer.

(4) Reclaim goods delivered on credit to a party while insolvent irrespective of the ten day period, if the buyer has made a misrepresentation of solvency to the particular seller in writing within three months before delivery.

c.   Effect of a Seller's Insolvency
The buyer who has paid in whole or in part for goods identified to the contract may recover the goods if the seller became insolvent within ten days after receipt of the first installment of their price. The buyer's rights may be subordinate, however, to the rights of secured creditors and of the trustee in bankruptcy.

9.   REPUDIATION OF A DEBT
The doctrine of anticipatory breach was greeted with skepticism in this country. It was early held that the doctrine of anticipatory repudiation cannot be used to accelerate a debt. This early exception remains entrenched in our law. The exception is usually stated to be that no action lies for repudiation of a unilateral obligation to pay a sum of money at a fixed time or times.

Examples: (1) Plaintiff purchases a disability insurance policy that promises to pay $500 a week for life in the event of permanent total disability. Plaintiff, after duly paying premiums, becomes permanently and totally disabled. The insurer refuses to pay. Plaintiff sues for total breach, claiming the present value of all payments due. The action for total breach fails. Plaintiff is entitled only to the payments due at the time of judgment.

(2) Defendant promises to pay $500 a month for ten years to plaintiff in exchange for a parcel of land to be conveyed at the end of that period. After making six payments, defendant repudiates. Plaintiff may sue immediately for total breach. The case falls outside the exceptional category of repudiation of a debt. There are interdependent obligations: defendant's duty to pay and plaintiff's duty to convey.

10.   REPUDIATION AND RIGHT TO ELECT
As a general rule, the aggrieved party may elect to continue the obligations of the contract despite a material breach. However, where there is a repudiation, anticipatory or otherwise, the aggrieved party cannot elect to continue the contract. There is no right to recover damages that could have been avoided by ceasing performance or preparation for performance. Under the U.C.C. this principle is relaxed to a slight extent. The aggrieved party may urge retraction and "may for a commercially reasonable time await performance by the repudiating party."

Example: *A* contracts with *B*, a municipality, to construct a bridge. Prior to performance, *B* repudiates. *A* angrily insists that it has a contractual right to build the bridge, builds it and sues for the price. Although *A* recovers under the doctrine of anticipatory breach, *A* failed to mitigate damages. *A* does not recover the price but only the profit that would have been made under the contract; that is, contract price minus cost of performance.

F. PERFORMANCE OF THE SALES CONTRACT

1. OBLIGATIONS OF THE SELLER
The seller must tender goods conforming in every respect to the contract. If tender is not perfect, unless otherwise agreed, the buyer may reject the whole, accept the whole or accept any commercial unit or units and reject the rest.

a. Perspective
The perfect tender rule is so undermined by exceptions and qualifications that it may be misleading. Nevertheless, if none of the qualifications or exceptions applies, a buyer can tell a seller's delivery agent to "take them away, there is a defect" or, after delivery (but before acceptance), tell the seller, "pick them up, there is one short-weighted box."

b. Qualification and Exceptions
1) "Unless Otherwise Agreed"
The *express terms* of the contract may restrict the perfect tender rule, for example, it may provide that the seller's obligations are limited to replacement of defective items. A *trade usage* that constitutes an implicit term of the contract may be inconsistent with the perfect tender rule. For example, a trade usage may limit the buyer's remedy to a price adjustment for certain kinds of defects.

2) Cure (U.C.C. § 2–508(1))
   a) Within the Contract Time
   If a non-conforming tender is made and the time for performance has not yet expired, the seller may seasonably notify the buyer of the seller's intention to cure and may then within the contract time make a conforming delivery.

   Example: B contracts to purchase a new Aston–Martin automobile from S. On tender of delivery, B notices some small dents and scratches that were made in the course of shipment from the factory to S. S offers to repair and the time for delivery has not expired. S has the right to cure by repair. The result would likely be different if the transmission had been defective and required replacement because such a serious defect may be symptomatic that other major defects will occur.

b)   A Further Reasonable Time (U.C.C. § 2–508(2))
     Where the buyer rejects a non-conforming tender which *the seller
     had reasonable grounds to believe would be acceptable* with or
     without a money allowance the seller may, if it seasonably
     notifies the buyer, have a further reasonable time to substitute a
     conforming tender.   There are two kinds of situations where the
     seller may have reasonable grounds to believe that the buyer will
     accept a non-conforming tender.

     (i)   The Seller Knows of Non–Conformity.
           A seller may know of the non-conformity and still be
           reasonable in tendering the goods.   The contract between a
           buyer and a dealer calls for hearing aid model A–660.   The
           manufacturer delivers to the dealer model A–665 which it
           describes as an improved version of model A–660.   The
           dealer is reasonable in tendering A–665 to the buyer.   Again
           by virtue of a trade usage or prior course of dealing, a seller
           can reasonably believe the buyer will accept, say, Cohoes
           instead of Reading pipe, or will accept short-weight shipments
           (with a price allowance).   In each of these instances, if the
           buyer rejects, the seller has additional time to make a
           conforming tender.

     (ii) The Seller Does Not Know of the Non–Conformity.
           Goods are often shipped in sealed containers.   Distributors
           buy and resell to retailers without opening the containers.
           Retailers also deliver factory sealed containers to consumers.
           Absent a history of non-conforming goods in the same kind
           of containers from the same source or other special
           information, it is reasonable for the seller to believe that the
           goods are acceptable.   If, upon inspection, the goods are
           properly rejected, the seller has a reasonable additional time
           to cure.

           Example: S contracted to sell to B a tankerload of oil,
                      testing out at .5% sulphur or less.   S then
                      purchased a tankerload that was on the high seas
                      from T who gave S a certificate from a refiner
                      that the cargo of oil had a .5% sulphur content.
                      When it was tendered on February 14, B's
                      inspection revealed that the sulphur content was
                      .9%.   S offered to cure by delivering the cargo of
                      another ship arriving on February 28.   B refused.
                      (Among its reasons was a 25% drop in the
                      market price of crude oil between the time of
                      contracting and February 14).   It was held that

B's refusal was a wrongful repudiation. *S*, relying in good faith on the certificate, had reason to believe that the tender would be acceptable and therefore had a further reasonable time to cure.

3) Acceptance (U.C.C. § 2–606)
    Once goods have been accepted, rejection is no longer possible, although revocation of acceptance may be an available alternative.

    a) Express Acceptance
        If, after a reasonable opportunity to inspect the goods, the buyer signifies to the seller that the goods are conforming or that they will be kept despite their non-conformity, the buyer has accepted. A buyer who signs a seller's form stating the goods have been inspected and are conforming has not accepted under this rule unless there genuinely was a reasonable opportunity to make more than a cursory inspection.

    b) Failure to Make an Effective Rejection
        Failure to reject does not operate as an acceptance until the buyer has had a reasonable time to inspect the goods. To make an effective rejection, the buyer must seasonably notify the seller of the rejection. After a rejection is properly communicated, it is to be remembered that the seller often has the right to cure. Consequently, the Code provides in § 2–605 that when goods are rejected the buyer must state all defects that are discoverable by reasonable inspection. To justify a rejection or a claim of breach, the buyer cannot rely on any discoverable unstated defect that the seller could have cured.

        Between merchants, a more drastic rule prevails. When a seller requests in writing a full and final statement of all defects on which the buyer proposes to rely as grounds for rejection, the buyer cannot rely upon unstated defects (even if the defects could be cured) that reasonably could have been discovered.

    c) "Acts Inconsistent With the Seller's Ownership"
        According to U.C.C. § 2–606(1)(b), acceptance takes place if the buyer does "any act inconsistent with the seller's ownership." This provision is not to be read literally, because the right to inspect often includes the right to use. For example, a vehicle inspection requires that the vehicle be driven. However, the use of the vehicle after the defects are known may be inconsistent with the seller's ownership. Use after a rejection is certainly wrongful. (U.C.C. § 2–602(2)(a)). When the acceptance is by

wrongful conduct, there is an acceptance only if the seller opts to treat it as an acceptance.

4) Revocation of Acceptance (U.C.C. § 2–608)
The buyer may revoke acceptance of a lot or commercial unit whose non-conformity substantially impairs its value to the buyer provided (a) the goods were accepted on the reasonable assumption that the seller would cure and has not been seasonably cured or (b) acceptance was reasonably induced by the difficulty of discovery or by the seller's assurances.

a) "Substantially Impairs the Value to the Buyer"
Revocation of acceptance is grounded on material breach rather than on perfect tender. (See p. 237 supra on the question of what breaches are material). Materiality of the breach under the U.C.C. is based on a personal standard ("value to the buyer") of the effect of the non-conformity upon the particular buyer.

b) Time Limitation
Revocation must take place "within a reasonable time after the buyer discovers or should have discovered the ground for it and before any substantial change in the condition of the goods which is not caused by their own defects." Notification is required.

Example: B purchases a new station wagon and accepts delivery. During the next 12 months it was returned to the dealer for repair on 30 occasions. New piston rings, a new carburetor, and a new fuel pump were installed. The vehicle continued to break down and consumed oil heavily. Revocation of acceptance is permitted. The value of the vehicle was seriously impaired. The seller's repair attempts were continued assurances of cure, justifying retention and use of the vehicle for 11 months.

c) Effect
After a valid revocation, the buyer has the same rights and duties with respect to the goods in question as if the goods had been rejected. (See p. 259 infra.)

5) Installment Contracts (U.C.C. § 2–612)
a) Presumption Against (U.C.C. § 2–307)
Unless otherwise agreed, all goods called for by the contract are to be tendered in one lot. An agreement to the contrary can be inferred from circumstances as where the buyer's known storage space cannot accommodate the full quantity or the seller's known

capability of hauling is insufficient. Despite the presumption against installment deliveries, if the contract either explicitly or implicitly requires or authorizes delivery in separate lots, it is subject to the rules of installment contracts despite a contractual agreement to convert each delivery into a separate contract. Such a term of the contract is void.

b) Effect

The perfect tender rule does not apply to installment contracts. Where a non-conformity with respect to one or more installments *substantially impairs* the value of the whole contract the buyer is justified in rejecting the delivery in question and cancelling the whole contract. However if the non-conformity of an installment substantially impairs the value only of the installment, the buyer must accept the installment if it can be cured and the seller gives adequate assurance of its cure. If the seller cannot or does not assure its cure the buyer may reject the installment.

Example: B contracted to buy 20 carloads of plywood from S. Nine percent of the first carload consisted of non-conforming sheets of plywood. B cancelled the contract. S sued. B is liable for breach. As Professor Quinn points out: "It's tough to reject any single installment under an installment contract, and even tougher to get rid of the rest of the whole contract." A substantial impairment of the value of the installment of this contract does not substantially impair the value of the entire contract. Moreover, it is doubtful whether B could have rejected the first carload. Even if its value is substantially impaired, S is entitled to attempt a cure. One method of cure would have been a price allowance for the non-conforming nine percent of the plywood.

6) Improper Shipment (U.C.C. § 2–504)

In a shipment contract the seller is obligated to make a reasonable contract with a carrier for transportation and give prompt notice of shipment to the buyer. These obligations are not subject to a perfect tender rule. A buyer may reject because of breach of these obligations only "if material delay or loss ensues".

2. OBLIGATIONS OF THE BUYER

Absent an agreement to the contrary, receipt of the goods and tender of payment are concurrent conditions. U.C.C. § 2–511(1). Thus, even in a shipment contract where the seller delivers the goods by placing them on board a carrier, payment is not due until the goods are received at their destination. U.C.C. § 2–310(a).

a. **How Much Must Be Tendered?**
Unless credit has been extended the buyer must tender the entire amount.

b. **Form of Tender**
Under Federal legislation a seller may insist on "legal tender" (greenbacks). Under the U.C.C., however, "Tender of payment is sufficient when made by any means or in any manner current in the ordinary course of business unless the seller demands payment in legal tender and gives any extension of time reasonably necessary to procure it." (U.C.C. § 2–511(2)).

c. **Buyer's Duty to Accept Goods**
Failure to accept conforming goods or wrongful revocation of acceptance constitutes a breach.

1) Perspective
"Accept" is here used in its technical sense, discussed at p. 255 supra. Remember, the mere fact that a buyer pays for and takes possession of goods does not mean that they have been accepted.

2) Right of Inspection (U.C.C. §§ 2–512, 2–513)
Unless otherwise agreed, the buyer's duty to accept and pay for a tender of goods is subject to the buyer's right to inspect them at any reasonable time and in any reasonable manner. When the seller is required or authorized to send the goods to the buyer, the inspection may occur after arrival and for a reasonable time after receipt of possession.

a) Exception
Unless otherwise agreed, the buyer has no right to inspect prior to payment if the contract provides that delivery is C.O.D. or payment is to be against documents of title. Even in these cases, however, the buyer has the right to inspect before acceptance.

b) Place and Method of Inspection
If the parties agree upon a place or method of inspection, it is presumed to be exclusive. If inspection as stipulated becomes impossible or if there has been no agreement on these matters, then the buyer may inspect at any reasonable time and place and in any reasonable manner. However, if the parties clearly meant for the inspection to be carried out as agreed, and it is not done so, the rights and obligations of the parties would be discharged.

d. Buyer's Duties With Respect to the Rejected Goods (U.C.C. §§ 2–602—2–604)
If the buyer properly rejects (or revokes acceptance of) goods the buyer must refrain from any acts of ownership over the goods, and hold them with reasonable care at the seller's disposition for a time sufficient to permit a seller to remove them.

1) Extra Duties of Merchant Buyer
   After rejection, the merchant buyer is under a further duty to follow any reasonable instruction of the seller with respect to the goods. This is contingent on the seller providing indemnity for expenses upon demand by the merchant buyer, and on the seller having no agent. If no instructions are given and if there is no local agent of the seller, the merchant buyer must make reasonable efforts to sell perishables or other goods that are likely speedily to decline in value.

2) The Seller is Silent
   Aside from the rule with respect to perishables and the like, the buyer who receives no instructions within a reasonable time after rejection has no duty to sell or return the goods, but merchant and non-merchant buyers alike have the option to sell, return or store rejected goods without thereby tortiously "accepting" the goods.

G. WARRANTIES IN THE SALES CONTRACT

1. EXPRESS WARRANTIES (U.C.C. § 2–313)
An express warranty is a description, affirmation of fact, or promise with respect to the quality or future performance of goods that becomes part of the basis of the bargain. The affirmation may be in words or by sample or model. An affirmation merely of the value of the goods or merely of the seller's opinion of the goods is not a warranty.

a. "Merely" Opinion
If a seller of a used car describes it as being in "A–1 condition," is this merely the expression of an opinion or is it an affirmation of fact? This kind of case has divided the courts for over a century. Is the seller honestly expressing an opinion? If not, whether or not there is a warranty, there is a fraudulent misrepresentation, for which the identical remedies are available. (U.C.C. § 2–721). If the speaker is an expert speaking to a non-expert, the expression is not "merely" opinion. There is a large grey borderland between fact and opinion.

b. Basis of the Bargain
The affirmation or promise must be part of the basis of the bargain. It need not be the inducing cause of the buyer's purchase. If the buyer did

in fact rely, a warranty is created. Additionally, if the statement is one that would naturally induce a purchase, a warranty exists. This second standard is objective: a buyer can enforce a document entitled "limited warranty" that accompanied a good even if the buyer neither read it nor was aware of its existence. A statement of fact or promise made after a contract of sale may also be an express warranty effective as a modification without consideration under U.C.C. § 2–209. How can a subsequent statement be part of the basis of a bargain? It would seem to qualify as such if it in part induced the buyer to use the good in a particular way or it induced the buyer not to request a rescission of the contract.

2. IMPLIED WARRANTIES
a. Merchantability (U.C.C. § 2–314)
If the seller is a merchant with respect to the kind of goods in question, unless effectively disclaimed, there is an implied warranty that the goods be such as "pass in the trade under the contract description" and "are fit for the ordinary purposes for which such goods are used."

Discussion: Perfection is not required. If goods of a certain description are acceptable in the trade despite 3% or less of the lot being rotten, the warranty is not breached by rotten goods within this range. In many cases where the warranty of merchantability is raised, personal injury or physical injury to property has occurred and tort thinking about strict product liability dominates. The following examples are limited to purely economic losses.

Examples: (1) *B* purchased a used car from *S,* a dealer in used cars. While *B* was driving the car home, the transmission fell out. This was repaired, and soon thereafter the brakes failed. *B* returned the car and revoked acceptance of it. *B*'s revocation of acceptance was proper because the car was not merchantable. *S* is a merchant. A car with a defective transmission and brakes is not fit for the *ordinary* purpose— driving—for which a car is used.

(2) *B* purchased floor tiles from *S,* a merchant. Shortly after installation, the tiles began to yellow. *B* sues for damages. *B* recovers. The tiles are unmerchantable. A tile which discolors shortly after installation is not of fair average quality.

b. Fitness for Particular Purpose (U.C.C. § 2–315)
If the seller has reason to know that the buyer wants the goods for a particular purpose and knows that the buyer is relying on the seller's skill and

judgment, unless effectively disclaimed, there is an implied warranty that the goods shall be fit for that purpose.

Example: B, a sawmill operator, went to S, a Mobil dealer, and asked for oil that would be suitable for use in the sawmill's hydraulic system. When asked by S to describe the system, B accurately described it. S checked with Mobil and suggested Ambex 810, which B used for two and one half years, at which time B discovered not only that Ambex 810 was unsuitable for the hydraulic system, but was also the cause of frequent breakdowns and production losses. S is liable for general and consequential damages for breach of warranty of fitness for a particular purpose. B relied on the Mobil organization in selecting the appropriate oil. Mobil was aware that inappropriate oil would lead to the breakdown of a sawmill.

Comment: In the illustration above the buyer expressly discussed the particular purpose with the seller, but all that is required is that the seller have reason to know the buyer's purpose and reason to believe that the buyer is relying on the seller's judgment and skill. Note that even a non-merchant may make this warranty.

c. **Free and Clear Title**
Unless effectively disclaimed, a seller impliedly warrants that the title conveyed is good and its transfer is rightful and that the goods are free from any security interest or lien of which the buyer was unaware at the time of contracting.

Comment: This warranty applies whether or not the seller is a merchant.

d. **Infringement (U.C.C. § 2–313(3))**
A merchant who regularly deals in the kind of goods in question warrants, unless effectively disclaimed, that no patent or trademark is being infringed, but if the buyer furnishes the specifications, the buyer must hold the seller harmless against any third party claim of infringement arising out of the use of the specifications.

3. **DISCLAIMER OF WARRANTIES**
a. **Disclaimer of Express Warranties**
It is lawful for a contract to provide that no express warranties are given. Problems arise primarily in two situations. In the first, suppose that a written contract provided that there are no express warranties, but elsewhere in the writing affirmations of fact or promises are made that

constitute express warranties as defined in U.C.C. § 2–313. A rule of construction is provided in U.C.C. § 2–316(1) which mandates that whenever possible the two contractual provisions be construed as consistent with each other. If consistency cannot be attained, the disclaimer is inoperative. (If both the express warranty and the disclaimer are oral the same rule prevails.) In the second situation, the written contract disclaims express warranties, but an express warranty has been made by statements in an advertisement or orally by an authorized agent of the seller. The substantive rule is again the same, but the practical question is whether the parol evidence rule will bar evidence extrinsic to the contract. This, of course, depends on whether a court deems the writing to be the final and complete expression of the parties' intent. See p. 195 supra. Even if it so finds, remember that some warranties may constitute misrepresentations and be admitted on that theory in a tort or restitution action.

b. Disclaimer of Implied Warranties

All implied warranties (except free and clear title) can be disclaimed if the buyer is warned by language such as, "as is," "with all its faults," or similar phrases. Implied warranties are also eradicated as to discoverable defects if the buyer had an opportunity fully to examine the goods. Implied warranties can also be excluded or modified by course of dealing or course of performance or usage of the trade. If the disclaimer is by contractual language other than phrases such as, "as is," certain distinctions are made.

1) Merchantability

The warranty of merchantability is difficult to exclude. If the exclusion is in writing, the language of exclusion *must use the word "merchantability"* and must be conspicuous. Conspicuousness is often achieved by highlighting the exclusions by heavier print or contrasting color. The essence of the conspicuousness requirement is to avoid surprise. Consequently, even if an inconspicuous clause is used, it is effective if the buyer is aware of it.

2) Fitness

The implied warranty of fitness for a particular purpose can be excluded *only in writing* and only if the exclusion is conspicuous. The word "fitness" need not be used. (Do not lose sight of the fact that there is no implied warranty of fitness in most sales.)

Example: A contract conspicuously states: "THERE ARE NO WARRANTIES WHICH EXTEND BEYOND THE DESCRIPTION ON THE FACE HEREOF." The implied warranty of fitness is effectively disclaimed. Evidence of *extrinsic* express warranties are likely barred by the parol evidence rule but the implied warranty of merchantability is not disclaimed because the word "merchantability" is not used.

3) Free and Clear Title
The implied warranty of free and clear title can be excluded or modified only by specific language or circumstances which give the buyer reason to know that the seller does not claim title or is only purporting to sell such right as the seller has. Thus, in addition to unusual cases where the seller reveals special circumstances casting doubt on the seller's own title, there is no implied warranty of title at a sheriff's or other forced sale, or at a sale by an executor.

c. **Limitations Upon Remedies**
Even if there is no disclaimer, remedies for breach of warranty may be limited pursuant to the provisions of U.C.C. §§ 2–718 and 2–719. (See p. 311 infra.)

REVIEW QUESTIONS

U called N, his nephew, and stated, "If you promise to take care of me for the rest of my life, and if you carry out the promise, you shall have free room and board in my house and $25,000 on my death." N made the promise and commenced performance. Shortly thereafter, U evicted N without cause.

1. T or F Since an express condition to U's promise was not fulfilled, N may not recover damages against U but is entitled to the reasonable value of his services.

2. T or F If before N started to perform, U had told N that he was withdrawing from the deal, U would be under no liability because, in effect, he would merely be revoking an offer.

Brush, a portrait painter, agreed to paint a picture of Handsome, promising to complete it before June 20, Handsome's birthday. In exchange, Handsome promised to pay $5,000 on completion "on condition Handsome was satisfied it captured Handsome's essence."

3. T or F The satisfaction clause is so subjective that Handsome's promise is illusory.

4. T or F Assume that on June 1 the painting had not been started and Handsome heard accurate information from a reliable source that Brush had left for Europe to teach summer courses. Handsome,

under the doctrine of indirect revocation, would be free to retain a substitute painter without liability.

X Corp. entered into a contract to construct a 10 mile length of Z Railroad's line. One mile of it was to be tunnelled through a mountain. The price was to be $10,000,000. At the completion of each mile Z was to pay X $1,000,000.

5. T or F   If X repudiates after completing 3 miles, X is entitled to a contractual recovery of $3,000,000 minus any damages suffered by Z.

6. T or F   If the contract had not called for installment payments and if there is no custom for such payments, X would not be entitled to any payment until it had completed the work.

Insured had a disability policy that provided for payment of $500 per week in any period during which insured was totally disabled.

7. T or F   If insured sustained a total permanent disability which the insurer refused to recognize, refusing to make any payments, the insured could not sue for total breach.

8. T or F   The policy is a divisible contract.

A, an architect, contracted on February 1 with Z to prepare plans for the construction of a building. A agreed to start work on the plans by June 1. On May 1, A suffered a stroke. When Z inquired, A referred Z to A's doctors who predicted that A would be disabled from working for at least 10 months. Thereafter, on May 15, Z contracted with B for preparation of the plans. A's doctors were, however, wrong in their prognosis and on June 1, A was ready, willing and able to perform.

9. T or F   In an action by A against Z, Z has the defense of prospective inability to perform.

10. T or F   In an action by B against Z (assuming Z refused to honor the contract with B), Z has the defense of impossibility of performance by virtue of Z's prior contract with A.

B contracted in a subscribed writing to purchase a house and lot from S. Title was to be conveyed free of any encumbrance on June 1. A title search made on March 1 revealed that a mortgage existed as a lien upon the property.

11. T or F B may cancel on grounds of prospective inability to perform.

12. T or F B may sue S for anticipatory breach.

13. T or F   *B* writes *S* on March 1 saying, "I will take title despite the mortgage." On March 3, *B* writes *S* saying, "I have reconsidered. I will not take title unless the mortgage lien is removed." *B* is not obligated to take title encumbered by the mortgage.

B contracted in a subscribed writing on February 1 to purchase a house and lot from *S*. Title was to be conveyed on June 1 of the same year. The contract recited: "Time is of the essence." It further recited valid and sufficient reasons why time should be of the essence.

14. T or F   Tender of marketable title by *S* on June 1 is an express condition to *B*'s duty to pay the price.

15. T or F   Tender of marketable title by *S* on June 1 is a constructive condition to *B*'s duty to pay the price.

16. T or F   Failure by *S* to tender marketable title on June 1 is a failure of condition but not a breach of contract.

17. T or F   Failure by *S* to tender marketable title on June 1 is a breach of contract but not a failure of condition.

18. Essay   Constructor, Inc. entered into a contract with Housing Authority to be the general contractor for a housing project. The contract provided that the facility would be completed "no later than July 16" of the following year. Constructor then entered into a contract with *X* whereby *X* would do the masonry work. Constructor's contract with *X* also provided for a completion date of July 16. *X*'s work was delayed partly because of weather conditions. When it seemed clear that *X* could not complete on time, Constructor brought in another contractor, *Y*, to do part of the masonry work. *Y* began paying its masons above the union scale with the result that many of *X*'s employees went to work for *Y*. In early July, Constructor fired the carpentry sub-contractor, and to some extent this slowed *X*'s progress. Similar delays had occured earlier. As of August 2, *X* had completed only 65% of the work that still was allocated to *X*. On that day, Constructor notified *X* that *X*'s contract was cancelled.

The contract provided that delays caused by delays of other sub-contractors should be credited to *X*, but only if a written claim was made within 48 hours from the beginning of such a delay. No such written claim was ever made. *X*, however, offers evidence that a representative of Constructor had stated on a number of occasions that *X* would be credited with delays caused by other subcontractors.

What are the rights of the parties? Explain.

*

VI

DEFENSES

Analysis

A. *Impracticability*
    1. *Impracticability Is Not Necessarily a Defense*
    2. *When Impracticability Is a Defense*
        a. *Three Part Test*
    3. *Temporary and Partial Impracticability*
    4. *Temporary and Partial Impracticability Under the U.C.C.*
        a. *Temporary Impracticability Under the U.C.C.*
        b. *Partial Impracticability Under the U.C.C.*
    5. *Impracticability of Means of Delivery or Payment*
        a. *Delivery*
        b. *Payment Before Delivery*
        c. *Payment After Delivery*
    6. *Impracticability and Conditions*
        a. *Perspective*
B. *Frustration*
    1. *What Constitutes Frustration*
        a. *Impracticability Compared*
        b. *Elements*
        c. *Perspective*
        d. *Restitution After Discharge for Impracticability or Frustration*

C. Risk of Casualty Losses
    1. Real Property
    2. Leases
    3. Sale of Goods
        a. Effect of Risk of Loss
        b. "Shipment" Versus "Destination" Contracts—Use of
            Common Carriers
        c. Distinguishing "Shipment" From "Destination"
            Contracts
        d. Delivery by Seller's Own Truck or on Seller's
            Premises
        e. Goods Held by a Bailee
        f. The Effect of Seller's Breach on Risk of Loss
        g. The Effect of the Buyer's Breach on Risk of Loss
    4. Risk of Loss and Impracticability
    5. Two Special Situations: Sale on Approval and Sale or
        Return
        a. Sale on Approval
        b. Sale or Return
    6. The Omnipotence of the Contract
D. Illegality
    1. What Is an Illegal Bargain?
        a. Generally
        b. Bribery Cases
        c. Licensing Cases
        d. Depositaries
        e. Knowledge of Illegal Purpose
    2. Effect of Illegal Bargain
        a. Illegal Executory Agreements
        b. Illegal Bargains Executed in Whole or in Part
        c. Change of Law
        d. Change of Facts
E. Discharge of Contractual Duties
    1. Mutual Rescission
        a. Rescission Requires a Mutual Agreement
        b. Distinctions
        c. Implied Rescission
        d. Cancellation Versus Rescission
    2. Executory Accord, Accord and Satisfaction, Substituted
        Agreement and Unilateral Accord
        a. Executory Bilateral Accord
        b. Unilateral Accord
        c. Accord and Satisfaction
        d. Substituted Contract
    3. Novation
    4. Account Stated
    5. Release and Covenant Not to Sue
        a. Release
        b. Covenant Not to Sue
    6. Acquisition by the Debtor of the Correlative Right

7. *Alteration*
8. *Performance—To Which Debt Should Payment Be Applied?*

A. IMPRACTICABILITY

1. IMPRACTICABILITY IS NOT NECESSARILY A DEFENSE
The general rule is that when a contractual promise is made, the promisor must perform or pay damages for the failure to perform no matter how burdensome performance has become as a result of unforeseen changes. The doctrine of impracticability is an exception to this rule of no-fault liability.

2. WHEN IMPRACTICABILITY IS A DEFENSE
When a performance becomes impracticable because of an event, the non-occurrence of which was a basic assumption on which the contract was made, the duty is discharged, unless the language or situation points to a contrary result.

a. Three Part Test
In determining whether the defense of impracticability applies, three questions are considered. (1) Was there, *contrary to a basic assumption of both parties,* an unexpected contingency? (2) Did this event make performance impossible, or under the modern and U.C.C. view, impracticable? (3) Upon whom should the risk of the unexpected contingency be placed?

1) The Basic Assumption
Certain assumptions are more basic than others. Both parties may assume a stable market, reliable sources of supply, and the continued financial ability of a purchaser of goods and services. Yet sudden market instabilities (unless caused by war or other catastrophe) and loss of financial ability are not deemed to violate basic assumptions. Another approach to some situations is that there are certain understood risks assumed by the contracting parties. Among these risks are market shifts, interruption of sources of supply, and financial capability.

Traditional categories in which basic assumptions have been found to have been violated involve: (1) destruction of the subject matter or of the means of performance; (2) death or illness of a person essential for performance; (3) supervening illegality or prevention by law; (4) reasonable apprehension of danger to life, health or property; and (5) failure of the contemplated mode of delivery or payment.

2) Upon Whom Is the Burden of the Event Placed?
Assuming a basic assumption has failed because of one of these events and has made performance impracticable, is non-performance excused? It is not, if the party claiming the excuse is (a) contributorily at fault for the occurrence of the event or (b) if there is a contractual term allocating the risk to this party. If the contract does not allocate the risk, the court will generally allocate it to the party claiming the

excuse if (c) the event was reasonably foreseeable, if (d) normal business understanding allocated the risk to this party or (e) such an allocation seems fair.

Examples: (1) *D* promised to license to *P* the use of a Music Hall on certain dates. Prior to the time for performance, the Music Hall was destroyed by fire without any fault on *D*'s part. *D* has the defense of impossibility of performance. If the Music Hall had been closed because of a mortgage foreclosure, the result would have been different because the impossibility would be "subjective." This is another way of saying that *D* would have assumed the risk of financial ability to perform.

(2) *S* promised to deliver 2,000 tons of Regent potatoes to be grown upon *S*'s farm. Through no fault of *S*, a pestilence struck the farm and destroyed the potato crop. *S* has the defense of impossibility of performance. The result would be the same even if the particular farm was not mentioned in the agreement, provided both parties assumed that the crop was to be grown on this land. The mere fact that *S* is a potato farmer does *not* prove, without more, that such a basic assumption existed.

(3) *C* (contractor) agrees to construct a building on land owned by *O*, "the building to be completed and delivered by May 5." On April 30, the nearly completed building is destroyed by fire without either party being at fault. Although impossibility or at least impracticability certainly exists, *C* does not have the defense. Some believe this result is proper because it is the contractor who has control of the job site and is best able to guard against accidental fires, negotiate for excuses, and arrange for insurance. Others believe the result is rooted primarily in *stare decisis*, because American cases in the early nineteenth century refused to excuse contractors in this kind of situation on the ground that it is possible for the contractor to start over again.

(4) *C* agrees to repair *O*'s roof. After the repair work is underway, the building is destroyed without fault on the part of either party. *C* is excused. Performance *is* impossible. *O* is liable in quasi contract for *C*'s part performance. The same analysis is made as to the rights of sub-contractors against general contractors.

(5) *S* agrees to transport wheat from Texas to India. The parties contemplate that the vessel will use the Suez route, and freight charges are calculated on that basis. After the vessel was underway, the canal is closed as a result of war between Israel and Egypt. *S* does not have the defense of impracticability because substitute routing around Africa is available, albeit at extra cost. Moreover, the event was foreseeable and its possibility discussed in the press. Foreseeability is an important factor in deciding whether a risk is assumed. The reasoning is that if an event is foreseeable the party should negotiate protective clauses.

(6) *S,* the owner of a factory, agrees to sell its output to *B.* The government requisitions the factory to produce military uniforms. Therefore, *S* is unable to produce the kind of goods that were promised *B.* Prevention by *supervening* domestic law, regulation, court order, or the like is grounds for the successful assertion of the defense of impracticability, unless the court order or requisition is based on the fault of the party. Under U.C.C. § 2–615(a) it is irrelevant whether the requisition was valid or not.

(7) *A* agrees to work for *B* for one year under *B*'s personal supervision. *A* dies. *A*'s estate has the defense of impossibility. (Note the relativity of the criteria. Death of any human is, of course, foreseeable. Foreseeability is down-played in death and illness cases.) If *B* had died, *B*'s estate would have the same defense. The rationales are that *A*'s duties as employee are nondelegable and *B*'s duties of *personal* supervision are also non-delegable. Note, however, that in most cases death of the employer would not discharge the contract.

(8) *A,* a general contractor, agrees to construct a building for *B.* During the course of construction both *A* and *B* die. *A*'s estate is obligated to complete the building and *B*'s estate is obligated to pay. The duties of a general contractor are delegable and duties of payment are also delegable.

(9) *A* agrees to work for *B* for one year in Venezuela. When *A* arrives at the job site from the United States, *A* is informed that an epidemic of a serious contagious disease is in progress. There is no vaccine for this disease, and how long the epidemic will last is impossible

to predict. *A* returns home. *A* has the defense of impracticability based on reasonable apprehension of danger to health.

(10) *S* agrees to sell certain goods to *B* for $100,000. As a result of inflation *S*'s production costs have tripled. Performance of the contract would cause *S* to lose a substantial sum on the transaction. *S* reveals these facts to *B*, stating that delivery will not be made unless *B* agrees to pay an increased price. *B* refuses, and *S* does not deliver. *S* does not have the defense of impracticability. Increased costs are within the scope of the risks assumed by a fixed price contract. If the increased costs were the result of a severe shortage of raw materials or supplies caused by an event such as war, embargo, etc., the defense of impracticability could be sustained if it is not undercut by contributory fault, assumption of the risk or similar arguments. (See U.C.C. § 2–615, Comment 4.)

3. TEMPORARY AND PARTIAL IMPRACTICABILITY

When the impracticability of a performance is temporary or partial, the general notion is that the promisor is obligated to perform to the extent practicable unless the burden of performance would be substantially increased. However, the promisee may reject any delayed or partial performance if the tendered performance is less than substantial.

4. TEMPORARY AND PARTIAL IMPRACTICABILITY UNDER THE U.C.C.

The U.C.C. enacts rules with respect to temporary and partial impracticability that agree with the common law rule stated in the preceding paragraph. The Code is, however, somewhat more specific.

a. Temporary Impracticability Under the U.C.C.

If the seller expects to be late in tendering delivery and *if the lateness is excusable because of impracticability,* the seller must seasonably notify the buyer of any expected delay. The buyer may then cancel any non-installment contract. The buyer may cancel any installment delivery or an installment contract under the criteria for their cancellation discussed in connection with exceptions to the perfect tender rule. On the other hand, the buyer may within a reasonable time, not exceeding 30 days, agree to accept the delayed delivery or deliveries.

b. Partial Impracticability Under the U.C.C.

Allocation is the key concept when the seller, *on grounds of impracticability,* can deliver only part of the promised goods. As in the case of excusable delay, the seller must seasonably notify the buyer of the shortfall and communicate the estimated quota allocated to the buyer. The quota must be fixed in a fair and reasonable manner. In fixing quotas the seller may include allocations for regular customers who are not under contract, and also an allocation for its own needs. The buyer has a reasonable time, not exceeding 30 days, to accept the allocation. Otherwise the seller's duties are discharged. If the contract is an installment contract, the buyer's rights to cancel are subject to the criteria for cancelling installment contracts discussed in connection with exceptions to the perfect tender rule.

5. IMPRACTICABILITY OF MEANS OF DELIVERY OR PAYMENT
a. Delivery
"*Substituted performance*" is the apt caption for the U.C.C. provision that deals with unavailability of an agreed type of carrier, docking facilities, or manner of delivery. Although the method of delivery may be of serious concern, it is not usually at the core of the bargain. Consequently, the U.C.C. requires that a commercially reasonable substitute be employed and accepted, if available (U.C.C. § 2–614(1)).

b. Payment Before Delivery
The same section of the Code deals with the failure of the agreed means or manner of payment because of domestic or foreign government regulation. If the agreed means or manner of payment becomes unavailable, the seller's obligation to deliver is discharged. However, if a commercially reasonable substitute means or manner of payment is available the buyer has the option to use the substitute which reinstates the seller's duty to deliver.

c. Payment After Delivery
If the agreed means or manner of payment becomes unavailable because of governmental regulations after the goods are delivered, the buyer may pay in the means or manner provided in the regulation. The buyer is discharged even when the regulatory means or manner is not a commercially reasonable equivalent as long as it is not "discriminatory, oppressive or predatory." This provision is directed mainly toward foreign government regulations controlling the movement of currency.

6. IMPRACTICABILITY AND CONDITIONS
a. Perspective
The present topic deals with impracticability as a defense to non-performance of a *promise*. Earlier we considered how impracticability relates to excuse of conditions. See p. 247 supra.

B. FRUSTRATION

1. WHAT CONSTITUTES FRUSTRATION
Where the object of one of the parties is the basis upon which both parties contract, the duties of performance are constructively conditioned upon the attainment of the object.

a. Impracticability Compared
In impracticability cases, one party cannot perform or can perform only in a more burdensome way than had originally been contemplated. In frustration cases, performance is practicable, but the purpose of at least one of the parties is frustrated to the extent that the performance contracted-for has become valueless (or nearly so).

b. Elements
The defense of frustration has rarely been allowed. It requires: (1) An event that frustrates the purpose of one of the parties and the occurrence of this event must be the *basis on which both parties* entered into the contract. (2) The frustration must be total or nearly total. (3) The party who asserts the defense must not, expressly or impliedly, have assumed the risk of this occurrence nor be guilty of contributory fault. In addition, the defense will be disallowed if the court determines that community standards would allocate the risk of the event to the party whose purpose has been frustrated.

c. Perspective
Frustration cases closely resemble mistake cases. Frustration arises when the parties are mistaken as to a future event. As in mistake cases the presence of unjust enrichment is often the chief underground factor that points towards relief.

> *Examples:* (1) Krell advertised his apartment as available for use for viewing the coronation procession of King Edward VII. Henry responded, and a contract was agreed upon whereby Henry was to have the use of the apartment for two days in exchange (in today's equivalents) for several thousand dollars. The coronation was cancelled because of the illness of the King. Henry has the defense of frustration. Note that there is no impossibility of performance. Henry can pay, and Krell can let Henry have the rooms. Krell has not breached. He has not promised that the coronation would take place. Yet it is clear that the coronation was the basis on which both parties entered into the contract. The contract was senseless but for the expected coronation and Krell's enrichment was unearned.

(2) *B* was about to be married and ordered a wedding gown from *C,* who made the gown. Before the wedding, *B* died. *B*'s estate does not have the defense of frustration because the occurrence of the wedding was not the basis upon which both parties entered into the contract. This conclusion is bolstered by the fact that *C*'s enrichment is earned by labor and material expended in the ordinary course of business.

(3) *T* was in possession under a lease which provided that: "It is expressly agreed that the only business to be carried on in said premises is the saloon business." A National Prohibition Law was enacted. *T* has the defense of frustration against the landlord's claim for rent. The quoted clause shows the basis on which the parties entered into the contract, and it is totally frustrated.

(4) Lloyd leased to Murphy certain premises for a five year term. The lease was signed four months before U.S. entry into World War II. The lease stated that it was "for the sole purpose of conducting thereon the business of displaying and selling new automobiles (including servicing and repairing thereof and of selling the petroleum products of a major oil company) and for no other purpose . . . except to make an occasional sale of a used automobile." Upon entry by the U.S. into World War II, sales of new automobiles were severely restricted by government regulation. Lloyd told Murphy that he waived the restrictive clause and would allow a sublease. But Murphy vacated, claiming frustration. Lloyd sued. Judgment for Lloyd. The frustration defense fails on two grounds. First, the frustration is not total. Other uses were permissible. Second, entry into the war and the consequent curtailment of civilian auto sales was foreseeable at the time the lease was entered into. Since the event was foreseeable, failure to guard against it indicates an assumption of the risk.

d. Restitution After Discharge for Impracticability or Frustration

When a contract is discharged for impracticability or frustration the executory duties are at an end. Yet, one or both parties may have partly performed. Compensation for part performance is available in the restitutionary action of quasi-contract.

C. RISK OF CASUALTY LOSSES

Perspective:

When goods or real property are in the process of being sold or are under lease or bailment, the question frequently is, which of the parties must bear the risk of damage or destruction of the subject matter? For example, if Vendor and Purchaser enter into a contract for the purchase and sale of real property, which party should bear the loss caused by a fire that occurs after the contract was entered into and before closing of title?

1. REAL PROPERTY

The majority rule places the risk of loss on the purchaser. The theory is based on the theory of equitable conversion; once the contract is made the purchaser is regarded by a court of equity as the owner. The minority view places the risk of loss on the seller until title closes. A third view, embodied in the Uniform Vendor and Purchaser Risk Act, places the risk of loss upon the purchaser only if he or she is in possession or has legal title. The Uniform Vendor and Purchaser Risk Act has been enacted in about ten states.

2. LEASES

The orthodox common law rule placed the risk of loss on the lessee. Today, this view seems to have been largely abandoned in favor of the concepts of constructive eviction and implied warranties.

3. SALE OF GOODS

a. Effect of Risk of Loss

Assume goods have been damaged or destroyed without fault of either party to a contract for sale. If the risk of loss had shifted to the buyer, the buyer is liable to pay the price. Otherwise the seller will be liable for breach of contract unless the breach is cured by tender of replacement conforming goods. In two limited situations the seller may have the risk of loss (the seller won't be paid) but will not be liable for damages. These are (1) impracticability is a defense (see p. 280 below) and (2) where the contract expressly provides "No Arrival No Sale." (U.C.C. § 2–324).

b. "Shipment" Versus "Destination" Contracts—Use of Common Carriers

1) Factual Distinction

Most risk of loss cases involve injury to goods in transit. The U.C.C. seeks to provide clear and certain rules that usually work in tandem with normal insurance practices in commerce. Merchants have long thought in terms of contracts whereby the seller is responsible for shipping the goods—getting them aboard a common carrier in the seller's city, as opposed to the much less usual "destination" contract whereby the seller undertakes the responsibility of getting the goods to the buyer's city or plant.

2) Rule
Under a "shipment" contract the risk of loss passes to the buyer when the goods are delivered to the carrier even if the seller reserves a security interest in the goods. Under a "destination" contract, risk of loss shifts when the goods are duly tendered to the buyer at destination.

c. **Distinguishing "Shipment" From "Destination" Contracts**
If the contract is unclear whether it is a "shipment" or "destination" contract, the rule is that it is a "shipment" contract. It is not a "destination" contract unless it explicitly so provides. There are certain terms, entrenched in commercial usage, which are frequently used to indicate the parties intent. These are:

(1) "F.O.B. (free on board) seller's plant" (or seller's city) indicates a shipment contract. The seller bears the risk and expense of loading goods onto the carrier and not beyond.

Example: A contract between a seller in Mobile and a buyer in New York City provides: "Ship to 140 W. 62nd Street, N.Y.C., F.O.B. Mobile." This is a shipment contract: the risk of loss shifts to the buyer when the goods are loaded aboard a carrier in Mobile.

(2) "F.O.B. buyer's plant" (or buyer's city) indicates a destination contract. The seller bears the risk and expense of transportation until due tender to the buyer.

(3) "F.A.S. (free alongside) vessel" indicates a shipment contract. The seller bears the risk and expense of delivering the goods alongside the vessel or onto a designated dock.

(4) C.I.F. (cost, insurance and freight) and C. & F. (cost and freight) terms indicate shipment contracts despite the fact that the seller must pay transportation charges. Under a C.I.F. contract although the seller must also insure the goods, the insurance is for the benefit of the buyer.

(5) "Ex–Ship" indicates that risk of loss does not pass to the buyer until the goods leave the ship's tackle or are otherwise properly unloaded.

d. **Delivery by Seller's Own Truck or on Seller's Premises**
Where a carrier is not used, as where the seller transports the goods in its own vehicle, or the buyer is to pick up the goods, the seller is in control of the goods and is likely to carry insurance on them. If the seller is a merchant, risk of loss shifts only if and when the buyer takes

possession of the goods. If the seller is a nonmerchant, the risk shifts when the seller tenders delivery.

Example: *B* contracts to buy a customized car from an Aston–Martin dealer. The car arrives at the dealer's premises on time. The dealer repeatedly notifies *B* of its arrival, and *B* neglects to come to the dealer's premises to pick up the car for an unreasonable period of time. *B* is in breach. The car is destroyed by a fire for which neither party is at fault. The risk of loss is on the seller even if *B* had paid in full in advance. The result would be different if the seller were a non-merchant.

e.   Goods Held by a Bailee
At times, goods in the hands of a bailee (such as a warehouseman) are sold with no expectation of a prompt transfer of possession. Risk of loss passes to the buyer in either of three eventualities. (1) If the buyer receives a negotiable document of title that covers the goods. (2) If the bailee acknowledges the buyer's ownership. (3) If the seller gives the buyer a non-negotiable document of title or a written direction to the bailee, risk of loss passes after the buyer has had a reasonable time to present the document or direction to the bailee. If the buyer presents the document or direction, risk of loss does not shift if the bailee refuses to honor it.

f.   The Effect of Seller's Breach on Risk of Loss
The clear rules on risk of loss are suddenly made murky if it can be proved that the seller has breached by tendering non-conforming goods. If the non-conformity is such that the buyer may reject (under the perfect tender rule or the installment contract rules), the risk of loss remains on the seller until the buyer accepts the non-conforming goods or the seller cures. If the buyer revokes acceptance of the goods, it may shift the risk of loss to the seller to the extent that its insurance coverage is inadequate. The buyer, however, must have revoked prior to the casualty for this rule to apply.

g.   The Effect of the Buyer's Breach on Risk of Loss
If the buyer breaches or repudiates prior to the shift of the risk of loss, the breach will itself shift the risk to the buyer provided that (a) the goods are conforming, (b) they have been identified to the contract, and (c) the loss occurs within a commercially reasonable time from the breach. However, the risk of loss passes to the buyer only to the extent that the seller's insurance is inadequate to cover the loss.

4. RISK OF LOSS AND IMPRACTICABILITY

The mere fact that the particular goods the seller intends to deliver are destroyed does not give the seller the defense of impracticability. If the seller does not offer replacement goods, it will be liable, but under appropriate circumstances it may be excused for any unavoidable delay under the doctrine of temporary impracticability. See p. 273 supra. However, under the provisions of U.C.C. § 2–613, if the contract dealt with identified goods (e.g., particular pieces of furniture rather than particular types), the seller is excused if the goods are totally destroyed without its fault prior to the risk being shifted to the buyer. If the loss is partial the buyer has the option to reject the goods or accept them with an allowance.

Example: B orders a living room set that is identical to a set shown in S's showroom. S places such a set on S's truck. Before it arrives at B's home, the truck and its contents are destroyed solely because of the negligence of a third person. S is not excused from performance. The result would be different if B had ordered the floor samples themselves.

5. TWO SPECIAL SITUATIONS: SALE ON APPROVAL AND SALE OR RETURN
a. Sale on Approval

In a "sale on approval," the goods are sent to the buyer for the buyer's use with the understanding that the buyer may return the goods if they do not meet the standard of satisfaction. (See the material on conditions of satisfaction, p. 239 supra). The risk of loss remains with the seller until the buyer "accepts" the goods. Failure to notify the seller of a rejection within a reasonable time is an acceptance. The expense of return is also borne by the seller.

b. Sale or Return

In a "sale or return" (consignment) sale the goods are sent to the buyer primarily for resale. Although the buyer may return conforming goods, the risk of loss passes to the buyer under the ordinary rules that govern the shifting of risk of loss. The risk remains with the buyer until the goods are returned to the seller at the buyer's expense.

6. THE OMNIPOTENCE OF THE CONTRACT

All the rules governing risk of loss are gap fillers based in large part on the probable intention of the parties. The parties are perfectly at liberty, subject to the rule of conscionability, to provide for the allocation of risk of loss in any way they wish.

Example: S contracted to construct a mast for B's yacht. After construction commenced, S asked B if B's insurance covered the mast. After telling S that he would "check it out," B told S he had coverage. Fire destroyed S's boatyard and the incomplete mast. Although there was no express agreement by *B* to assume the risk of loss, *B*'s statement about insurance coverage is the basis for an equitable estoppel. *B*'s statement about insurance forestalled *S* (who had no fire coverage other than on real property), from insuring the mast. This is the equivalent of an express assumption of the risk of loss.

D. ILLEGALITY

1. WHAT IS AN ILLEGAL BARGAIN?
a. Generally
A bargain is illegal, if either its formation or its performance is criminal, tortious or contrary to public policy. Subject to exceptions, an illegal bargain is not enforceable. The courts generally leave the parties where they find them.

Examples: (1) *A* delivers heroin to *B* in exchange for a cash payment of $50,000 and *B*'s promise to pay $50,000 in one week. Neither party is licensed to possess heroin. The bargain is illegal because the Criminal Code prohibits such transactions.

(2) *A* promises to kill *X* in exchange for *B*'s promise to pay him $10,000. The agreement is illegal because its performance is criminal.

(3) *B*, a newspaper reporter, promises *A* $500 if *A* procures certain confidential files from *A*'s employer. *A* performs. The agreement is illegal because it involves commission of the tort of conversion.

(4) *B* service company, promises *A*, an actual or potential competitor, $10,000 a year if *A* refrains from opening an office in *B*'s city. Even in the absence of anti-trust legislation, the agreement is illegal as a restraint of trade. The buying-off of competitors is against public policy.

Comment: The above examples involve obvious kinds of illegality. Under the general rule stated below (p. 284), it is clear that *A* can recover in none of these cases. The difficult cases are those where the illegality is somewhat remote from the agreement. Remoteness will be illustrated by four kinds of situations: (1) bribery, (2) license violations, (3) depositary cases, and (4) instances where one party has knowledge of the illegal purpose of the other.

b.   Bribery Cases

An agreement is illegal if it calls for the payment of a bribe, is procured by a bribe, or is performed by bribery.

Examples: (1) *B* promises *A*, who is purchasing agent of *X* Inc., the sum of $1,000 if *A* purchases certain of *B*'s products for *X*. *A* makes the purchase for *X*. The agreement between *B* and *A* is illegal because commercial bribery is criminal.

(2) *B* pays *A*, who is purchasing agent for *X*, Inc., the sum of $1,000 in exchange for *A*'s agreement to purchase certain goods for *X*. The ensuing agreement between *B* and *X* is illegal because it was *procured* by an illegal act.

(3) *B* hires *A* as *B*'s agent to purchase certain movie rights from *Y*. *A* is to receive a commission if *A* obtains the rights which *A* obtains by bribing an agent of *Y*. *A*'s conduct in *performing* the contract was illegal; therefore the contract between *B* and *A* has become illegal according to some strong modern authorities. Traditionally, the illegal conduct was regarded as too tangential, collateral or remote to infect the contract itself with the taint of illegality.

c.   Licensing Cases

If a license is required to control the skill or moral quality of persons engaged in a trade or profession, an agreement to practice that trade or profession by an unlicensed person is illegal. If the license is solely a revenue raising measure, the agreement is not illegal. If the license is required for other purposes, the courts will decide on a case by case basis.

Examples: (1) *A*, an unlicensed plumber, installs plumbing pursuant to an agreement with *B*. Plumbing licenses are issued only after a difficult examination of plumbing skills. The agreement is illegal.

(2) *A*, an unlicensed plumber, installs plumbing pursuant to an agreement with *B*. In this locality, plumbing licenses are issued to everyone who applies and pays an occupation tax of $500. The agreement is a binding contract.

(3) *A*, an unlicensed milk dealer, sells milk on credit to *B*. Licenses to act as a milk dealer are obtained by a showing of financial ability to pay one's debts. The court will attempt to ascertain the legislative intent of the licensing statute. In all likelihood a court will find that the agreement is legal despite the unlicensed status of *B*, unless the court finds that

the legislative intent was to invalidate agreements made by unlicensed milk dealers.

(4) *A*, an unlicensed liquor dealer, sells liquor to *B* on credit. Liquor licenses are required primarily to screen out organized crime elements from the liquor industry. The court will find that the agreement is illegal.

d. Depositaries
A depositary of the fruits of a crime may not refuse to return the money or goods deposited unless the depositary is a party to the illegal transaction.

Examples: (1) *A*, a swindler, illegally obtains money from *B*. *A* deposits the money with *C*. *C* cannot refuse to repay the money to *A*. The deposit is viewed as remote from the crime.

(2) *B* gives a sum of money to *A* for the purpose of bribing purchasing agents. *A* pockets the money, and *B* seeks restitution. The defense of illegality will be sustained. *A* is not a mere depositary but a participant in an illegal scheme.

e. Knowledge of Illegal Purpose
Knowledge by the seller of goods or services of the illegal purpose of the buyer taints the contract with illegality only if the intended purpose involves serious moral turpitude or if the seller does something to further the illegal purpose of the other.

Examples: (1) *S* sells cigarettes to *B* on credit knowing that *B* intends to smuggle them into a neighboring state where cigarettes are taxed at a much higher rate. The contract is not illegal and may be enforced.

Caveat: Some states make criminal facilitation a crime. Under such a statute knowledge of the illegal purpose would make the contract criminally illegal. The next two examples are decided under the traditional rule which does not outlaw criminal facilitation.

(2) *S* sells a rifle to *B* on credit knowing that *B* intends to kill *X*. The contract is illegal because the intended purpose involves serious moral turpitude.

(3) *S* contracts to sell ammunition to *B*, knowing that *B* intends to export the purchase and also knowing that *B* does not have an export license. *S*, at *B*'s request, packs the ammunition in boxes marked "plumbing fixtures." The

contract is illegal because *S* had gone beyond the point of mere knowledge of the scheme. *S* has assisted it.

2. EFFECT OF ILLEGAL BARGAIN
a. Illegal Executory Agreements
An illegal executory bargain is void so that neither party to the agreement can enforce it.

1) Comment

In each of the examples in the first part of this chapter ("What is an Illegal Bargain") where there was a finding of illegality, the agreement would not be enforced.

2) Exceptions

(a) If a party is justifiably *ignorant of the facts* creating the illegality and the other is not.

Example: *A* enters into a contract of employment with *B*, an insurance company, for a five year term. Unbeknownst to *A*, *B* has not obtained a license necessary to enable it to lawfully do business. *A* can recover compensation for any services rendered before discovery of the illegality and, on establishing that he or she would have been ready and willing to continue had the performance been legal, also for breach of the executory portion of the bargain.

(b) If the illegality is minor and the party who is *ignorant of the law* justifiably relies upon an assumed special knowledge by the other party of the requirements of law, the contract may be enforced by the innocent party.

Example: *O* and *B*, a building contractor, make an agreement for the construction of a building, the contract providing that the building code be followed. *B* had misrepresented to *O*, the owner, minute regulations of the building code. *O* can recover against *B* for breach. This is an exception to the general proposition that a person is responsible for knowing the law. Here *B* has special knowledge that *O* does not have and cannot be expected to have.

(c) Certain statutes, enacted to protect a certain class, mark only one party as the wrongdoer. Contracts in violation of such statutes are enforceable by the protected party.

Example: L and T execute a lease under which T agrees to pay a rental which is illegally high under rent control legislation. The legislation is designed to protect tenants and penalizes landlords who violate its terms. L breaches the lease by failing to maintain and repair the premises as covenanted in the lease. T may enforce the provisions in the lease concerning maintenance and repair.

(d) If an illegal provision does not involve serious moral turpitude and if the parties would have entered into the contract irrespective of the offending provision, the illegal portion of the agreement is severed, and the balance of the agreement is enforceable. The illegal provision must not be central to the party's agreement.

Examples: (1) Over-broad covenants not to compete (pp. 321–322 infra).

(2) Illegal penalties (pp. 309–310 infra).

(e) If an agreement can be interpreted so that either a legal or illegal meaning can be attributed to it, the interpretation giving the agreement a legal meaning will be preferred. An illegal contract can also be *reformed* to make it legal.

Example: A and B agree on a mortgage loan. The documents are drawn up by a title insurance company. The title company uses a printed form which provides for usurious interest in the event of a default. The agreement can be reformed by excision of the illegal clause, provided the parties did not knowingly agree to the usurious interest provision.

b. **Illegal Bargains Executed in Whole or in Part**
Where there has been performance under an illegal bargain the court will not aid either party and will leave the parties where it finds them.

Examples: (1) S pays A, who is purchasing agent for B, the sum of $1,000 in exchange for A's promise to place certain orders with S. A breaches the agreement, and S seeks restitution. Restitution is denied. Also, as discussed above, S cannot successfully sue for breach.

(2) Suppose that the facts in the above example are modified so that A places the orders as agreed. B, upon discovery of

the bribe, refuses to pay for the goods delivered. *S* sues for the price. Recovery denied.

Exceptions:

1)   Reprise
     The exceptions under "Illegal Executory Agreements" also apply here. In addition, where performance has been rendered, there are several additional exceptions.

2)   Divisibility
     If a performance is illegal, but other performances under the agreement are legal, recovery may be had for the legal performance provided that the illegal performance does not involve serious moral turpitude. "Divisibility" is not used in this context in the same sense as it is used in the chapter on performance. Divisibility is not determined according to fixed rules but by the judicial instinct for justice.

   Example: *A,* a licensed plumber, agrees to remodel a bathroom for $2,000. *A* does the entire job, including electrical work, for which *A* has no license, although a license is required in the locality. Although there is no apportioned price for the electrical work, the court will treat the contract as divisible, allowing recovery for the reasonable value of the non-electrical work, but not exceeding the contract rate.

3)   Not in *Pari Delicto*
     A person who has performed under an illegal bargain is entitled to a quasi-contractual recovery if this party is not guilty of serious moral turpitude and, although blameworthy, is not equally as guilty as the other party to the illegal bargain.

   Comment: There are two classes of cases in which the notion of not-in-*pari-delicto* is generally available. In the first kind, the party enters into the illegal bargain under duress or circumstances close to duress. In the second kind, the rule that makes the bargain illegal is designed to protect one class of persons against another.

   Examples: (1) *A,* a refugee, gave *B* jewels to be used to bribe border guards so that *A* could escape Hitler's army. *B* absconded with the jewels. Years later, *A* discovers *B* and sues for the value of the jewels. *A* can recover from *B* as *A* was not in *pari delicto.* A person who makes an agreement in dire necessity and motivated by self preservation has not committted an act of serious moral turpitude.

(2) *A*, a borrower, agrees with *B*, a lender, for a loan at a usurious interest rate. *A*, a member of the class that usury laws aim to protect, may recover the excess interest paid.

4) *Locus Poenitentiae* (Place for Repentance)
Even if a plaintiff is in *pari delicto* and therefore as blameworthy or more blameworthy than the defendant, plaintiff is entitled to avoid the bargain and obtain restitution if plaintiff acted in time to prevent the attainment of the illegal purpose for which the bargain was made, unless the mere making of the bargain involves serious moral turpitude. The plaintiff is generally not permitted to recover if the withdrawal comes after any part of the illegal performance is consummated. Repentance also comes too late if it comes only after the other party to the bargain has indicated that performance will not be forthcoming, or after attainment of the unlawful purpose is seen to be impossible.

Example: *A* gives $1,000 to *B* for the purpose of bribing a public official. Before any attempt is made by *B* to carry out the illegal purpose, *A* demands that *B* return the money. *A* may recover. The result would be different if the public official had rejected the bribe.

c. **Change of Law**
1) Legalization of the Activity
If an agreement is illegal when made and subsequently becomes legal because the law is changed, the change does not validate the agreement except where the repealing statute so provides expressly or impliedly.

Example: *A* borrows money from *B*, promising to pay a usurious rate of interest. Before the time for performing the bargain, a statute is enacted allowing such a rate of interest. The bargain is still illegal unless the statute manifests an intention to validate such bargains.

2) Supervening Illegality
If a contract is lawful when made, but the performance is outlawed prior to full performance, the case is governed by the doctrine of impracticability of performance. (See p. 270 supra).

3) **Supervening Illegality of an Offer**
    If a lawful offer is made, but performance of the proposed contract is subsequently outlawed, the power of acceptance is terminated.

d. **Change of Facts**
    Where the bargain is illegal and a change of facts removes the cause of the illegality, the contract remains illegal. However, the parties with full knowledge of the facts may subsequently ratify the agreement.

    Example: *A,* who is not a member of the bar, is retained by *B* to file a tort claim against *X* on *B*'s behalf. *A* is subsequently admitted to the bar and successfully obtains a recovery against *X* for *B*. *B* need not pay *A*'s fee. The result would be different if, before complete performance, *B,* with full knowledge of the facts, had ratified the contract.

E. DISCHARGE OF CONTRACTUAL DUTIES

Perspective:
Many methods of discharging a contractual duty are discussed elsewhere; for example, non-fulfillment of a condition, anticipatory repudiation, impossibility of performance, disaffirmance for lack of capacity, etc. In this chapter several consensual kinds of discharge will be discussed.

1. **MUTUAL RESCISSION**
    a. **Rescission Requires a Mutual Agreement**
        If A and B enter into a bilateral executory contract, they can rescind it by mutual agreement. The surrender of rights under the original agreement by each party is the consideration for the mutual agreement of rescission.

    b. **Distinctions**
        Within limits, parties to a contract are free to end the obligations of the contract by agreement. The limits are imposed by the doctrine of consideration. One must distinguish three situations: (1) rescission occurring before any performance; (2) rescission occurring after part performance by one or both parties; (3) rescission occurring after full performance by one party. In the first two situations, consideration is found in the surrender of rights under the original agreement by each party. In the third situation the rescission is void for want of consideration.

        Examples: (1) *A* and *B* enter into a contract by the terms of which *A* agrees to work for *B* for a period of one year, and *B* agrees to pay $500 every week. Before performance begins, the parties mutually rescind their duties under the contract. The rescission is effective to discharge the duties under the contract because each party is suffering a bargained for detriment—the surrender of the performance to be rendered by the other party.

(2) In example (1), if *A* works for a week and then the parties mutually rescind, there is no consideration problem for the same reason stated in example (1). The only question is whether *A* should be paid for the work *A* performed. This is a question of interpretation and logically depends upon whether the parties intended to rescind only the executory part of the contract or to discharge all duties under the contract including the duty to pay.

(3) In example (1), if *A* had completely performed and the parties then agreed to mutually rescind, the agreement would be ineffective because *B* would not be suffering any detriment. The result may be different by statute or if a gift has been completed.

c.   Implied Rescission
While rescissions are ordinarily expressed in words they can be implicit in conduct. Some courts call an implied rescission an "abandonment."

Example: *S* and *B* enter into a contract by the terms of which *S* agrees to manufacture and sell to *B* a given machine and *B* agrees to pay $50,000. Neither party has any experience in the design or manufacture of such a machine. The contract provides that preliminarily *B* is obligated to provide more precise specifications, and *S* is to provide preliminary design sketches. Neither party acts. After a reasonable time there is an implied rescission. Both parties' failure to cooperate in its performance is regarded as an abandonment of the contract. From another perspective, if either party sued the other, the plaintiff could not establish due compliance with all conditions precedent.

d.   Cancellation Versus Rescission
In the face of a material breach, the injured party may properly cancel the contract. In cancelling, the aggrieved party may incorrectly use expressions such as "I rescind." According to U.C.C. § 2–720, which restates the sounder common law cases, "unless the contrary intention clearly appears, expressions of cancellation or 'rescission' of the contract or the like shall not be construed as a renunciation or discharge of any claim for damages for an antecedent breach."

Examples: (1) *A* promises *B* that a structure will be completed before January 1 and it is agreed that time is of the essence. Because of certain delays by *A*, it is obvious the structure will not be completed on time. Despite this delay, *B* permits *A* to complete the structure. Because *B* has effectively waived the express condition that *A* perform on time, *B* is required to pay. The question remains whether *B* can successfully sue for the breach based upon late performance or whether *B* has renounced the right to damages. The question is one of interpretation. Did *B* manifest an intent to renounce the right to damages? If *B* did, the renunciation is effective without consideration.

(2) *S* and *B* enter into a contract for the sale of goods. *S* commits a material breach. *B* writes to *S* stating, "I rescind the contract." *B*'s expression effectively cancels the contract but does not amount to a renunciation of the right to damages. It should be noted that, if *B*'s notice manifested an intent to surrender the right to damages, it could have this effect without consideration. U.C.C. § 1–107 provides that a claim to damages may be discharged by a signed writing renouncing the claim and delivered to the breaching party.

2. EXECUTORY ACCORD, ACCORD AND SATISFACTION, SUBSTITUTED AGREEMENT AND UNILATERAL ACCORD

a. Executory Bilateral Accord

A bilateral executory accord is an agreement that an existing claim shall be discharged IN THE FUTURE by the rendition of a substitute performance. Prior to performance or breach the existing claim is suspended. Upon performance, there is an accord and satisfaction that discharges the claim. If, however the debtor breaches, the prior obligation revives and the creditor has the option of enforcing the original claim or the executory accord. If the creditor breaches, the debtor may ordinarily obtain specific performance of the accord.

Comment: The common law did not regard executory accords as binding contracts. Today most states enforce them. New York, by statute, does not enforce them unless they are in writing and signed by the party against whom enforcement is sought.

b. Unilateral Accord

An offer by a creditor or claimant to accept a performance in satisfaction of a credit or claim is known as a unilateral accord.

Comment: At early common law the offeror could, with impunity, refuse the tender of performance even if the performance was tendered prior to any revocation. Under modern law, if tender is refused, the debtor may sue for damages for breach of the accord, or, in a proper case, for specific performance. New York requires that the offer be in writing and signed by the offeror.

c. Accord and Satisfaction
An accord and satisfaction is formed in one of three ways:

(1) Performance of an executory bilateral accord; or

(2) Acceptance of an offer to a unilateral accord; or

(3) Creation of a substituted contract. (See immediately below).

d. Substituted Contract
A substituted contract resembles an executory bilateral accord. The distinction is that the claimant or creditor agrees that the claim or credit is *immediately* discharged in exchange for the promise of a future performance. The prior claim or credit is merged into the substituted contract. Consequently, in the event of its breach, it alone determines the rights of the parties. There would be no right to enforce the prior claim, unless the new agreement is void, voidable, or unenforceable.

Examples: (1) *C* (creditor) writes to *D* (debtor), "I promise to discharge the debt you owe me upon delivery of your black horse if you promise to deliver it within a reasonable time." *D* promises. This is an executory bilateral contract of accord because it is a bilateral agreement that relates to the satisfaction or discharge of a claim at some *future time*—here upon the delivery of the horse. If the horse is delivered and accepted, an accord and satisfaction is formed. If it is not tendered within a reasonable time, *C* may pursue the original debt. *C* may instead sue for damages for breach of contract to deliver the horse. If *D* tenders within a reasonable time and *C* refuses the tender, *D* can resist any action by *C* to collect the debt by counter-claiming for specific performance.

(2) *C* writes to *D*, "If you will promise to deliver your black mare within 30 days, I will immediately treat the debt you owe me as satisfied and discharged." *D* accepts the offer. There is a substituted agreement. The factual difference between this case and case (1) is that here *C* agrees to discharge the claim when *D* makes the promise rather than

when the promise is performed. *C* may enforce only the substituted contract.

(3) *C* writes to *D*, "If you *deliver* your black horse within a reasonable time I promise to discharge your debt." If *D* delivers the horse and *C* accepts, there is a binding accord and satisfaction. If *D* tenders the horse and *C* refuses to take it, *D* may sue for damages for breach of a unilateral contract of accord or, in a proper case, sue for specific performance.

3. NOVATION

A contract is a novation if it does three things: (a) discharges immediately a previous contractual duty or a duty to make compensation and (b) creates a new contractual duty, and (c) includes as a party one who neither owed the previous duty nor was entitled to its performance.

Example: *A* owes *B* $100. *B* and *C* agree that *C* here and now assumes *A*'s duty, and that *B* here and now releases *A* from the obligation to pay $100. There is a novation even though *A* has not suffered any detriment and *A* has not assented to the arrangement. *A* is a third party beneficiary and *A*'s assent is presumed, but *A* is empowered to disclaim the discharge if *A* so desires.

Note: It is necessary to distinguish an executory accord from a novation. A novation is a substituted contract that operates immediately to discharge an obligation. If the discharge is to take place upon performance, the tripartite agreement is merely an executory accord.

4. ACCOUNT STATED

An account stated arises where there have been transactions between debtor and creditor resulting in the creation of matured debts and (a) the parties by agreement compute a balance which the debtor promises to pay and (b) the creditor promises to accept in full payment for the items of the account.

Discussion: An account stated often results from an implied agreement—the sending and retention of the account without objection for more than a reasonable time. But the inference of assent is generally held to be rebuttable. Consideration is *not* necessary to support the account but the promises are enforceable only to the extent of the previous obligation. Thus the main effect of an account stated is to shift the burden of going forward with the evidence to the party who claims the account is incorrect.

Example: *S* made various shipments of seed to *B*. *S* sent *B* monthly statements showing the shipments and the price of each of them.

A February shipment was billed together with other shipments for three successive months. *S* sues, alleging an account stated. *B* alleges that the February shipment was never received. *S* succeeds in the action. It is irrelevant whether *B* received the seed. When there has been a course of dealing, *B*'s failure to object to the item of account for three successive months results in an objective manifestation of assent.

5. RELEASE AND COVENANT NOT TO SUE
a. Release
1) Generally

A release is a writing manifesting an intention to discharge another from an existing or asserted duty. A release supported by consideration discharges the duty. At common law, consideration was not necessary if the release was under seal. Today, the effectiveness of a release of a duty without consideration is largely dependent upon local statutes.

2) U.C.C.

U.C.C. § 1–107 provides that: "Any claim or right arising out of an alleged breach can be discharged in whole or part without consideration by written waiver or renunciation signed and delivered by the aggrieved party."

b. Covenant Not to Sue
A covenant not to sue is a promise by a creditor not to sue either permanently or for a limited period of time. This promise must be supported by consideration to be valid.

Comment: A release is an executed transaction while a covenant not to sue is executory. A covenant not to sue is sometimes used to circumvent the common law rule that the release of one joint obligor releases all of them.

6. ACQUISITION BY THE DEBTOR OF THE CORRELATIVE RIGHT
Acquisition by the debtor of the correlative right in the same capacity in which the duty is owed discharges it.

Example: *A* owes *B* $100. *A* is *B*'s next of kin. *B* dies without a will, so that *A* inherits all of *B*'s personal property. The duty to *B* is discharged by the acquisition by *A* of the correlative right.

7. ALTERATION
A fraudulent alteration of a written contract by one who asserts a right under it extinguishes the right and discharges the obligor's obligation.

1) Waiver
   The aggrieved party may forgive the alteration, thus reinstating the contract according to its original tenor.

2) Negotiable Instruments
   A holder in due course of an instrument altered by a prior holder may enforce it according to its original tenor.   U.C.C. § 3–407.

8. PERFORMANCE—TO WHICH DEBT SHOULD PAYMENT BE APPLIED?

A duty is discharged by performance.   However, a common problem involves a debtor who has several obligations to the same creditor.   When the debtor sends a sum of money to the creditor which debt should be credited?

Where a person owes several debts to a creditor payments are to be applied in the following sequence:

(a)   in the manner manifested by the debtor unless the manifestation violates a duty to a third person such as a surety;

(b)   if the debtor manifests no intention, the payment may be applied at the discretion of the creditor provided it is not applied to a disputed, unmatured or illegal claim, and also provided it is not applied so as to violate a duty of the debtor to a third person of which the creditor is aware, and is not applied as to cause a forfeiture;

(c)   if the creditor manifests no intent on receipt of payment, the law will allocate payment in the manner deemed most equitable.

REVIEW QUESTIONS

A, a producer, hired *B*, an inexperienced actor, to play a minor part.   A license was required to put on the performance.   The license was to protect the public from overcrowding, fire hazards and the like.   At the time of contracting and performing, *B* was unaware that *A* was unlicensed or even that a license was required.   *A* has not paid *B* for his services.

1. T or F   *B* can recover on the contract, because *B* was unaware that *A* did not have a license.

2. T or F   In an action by *B* on the contract it is not relevant that *B* was unaware of the licensing requirement because ignorance of the law would not excuse *B*.

S entered into an agreement with *B*, an agent for an unfriendly foreign power, promising to procure certain governmental documents classified as "Top Secret" and to paint *B*'s house. Each of these performances had a separately apportioned price.

3. T or F The executory bilateral agreement is void.

4. T or F If *B* performed his promises, *B* could recover the price for painting under the doctrine of *locus poenitentiae*.

Brush, a portrait painter, agreed to paint a portrait of Beauty, promising to commence on May 4 and to complete it by June 20, Beauty's birthday. A down payment was paid, and the balance was due on completion. The painting was started and destroyed by fire when half completed.

5. T or F Brush would have the defense of impossibility.

6. T or F If Brush died before starting the painting, Beauty could recover back the down payment.

A agreed to work for *B* for 6 months, and *B* promised to engage *A*'s services for 6 months. After two months of performance, *B* asked *A* if *A* would be willing to rescind their agreement and work for *C* for the remaining 4 months. *A* agreed as did *C*.

7. T or F *B* continued to be liable to *A*.

8. Essay Landlord (*L*) and tenant (*T*) entered into a 25 year written and subscribed lease commencing January 1, 1990, whereby *T* agreed to build facilities at *T*'s own expense on the premises for the sole purpose of operating a drive-in motion picture theater and the sale of popcorn, soda pop, and snacks. No rent was payable until June 1, 1990. From and after this date *T* was to pay rent in the amount of $3,000 a month.

On March 1, 1990, after *T* had diligently commenced and continued construction of the facilities in accordance with the contract, the County Board of Supervisors voted to authorize the condemnation of the parcel for use as a park. *T* immediately stopped construction. The County condemned the land on August 1, 1990.

(a) *L* has commenced an action against *T* for rent for the months of June and July. May *L* recover?

(b) Assume that prior to commencement of the suit, *L* and *T* negotiated as to whether *T* should pay rent, and *L* agreed to take $3,000 in full satisfaction of *T*'s demand for $6,000. However, *L* refused to accept *T*'s tender of $3,000 in cash. May *T* raise these facts as a defense?

(c) Assume that *C*, the construction contractor retained by *T*, was not licensed by the township in which the drive-in theater was being built. A township ordinance required such a license which is granted upon a showing of financial stability, the payment of a $1,000 application fee, and the identification of corporate officers if the applicant is a corporation. In an action by *C* against *T* what is the consequence of *C*'s lack of a license?

VII

CONTRACT REMEDIES

Analysis

A. Damages
   1. Goal of Damages
   2. Foreseeability—General and Consequential Damages
      a. Application
      b. Particular Situations
   3. Certainty
      a. Discussion
      b. Alternatives Where Expectancy Is Uncertain
   4. Mitigation
      a. Discussion
      b. Exception
      c. Non-exclusive Contracts
   5. Present Worth Doctrine
   6. Liquidated Damages
      a. Penalties Distinguished
      b. Formulas Are Acceptable
      c. Shotgun Clauses Are Dangerous
      d. Can't Have It Both Ways
      e. Specific Performance Not Excluded
      f. Additional Agreed Damages—Attorney's Fees

    7. *Limitations on Damages*
      a. *Discussion*
      b. *Failure of Essential Purpose*
    8. *Punitive Damages*
    9. *Mental Distress*
  10. *Nominal Damages*
B. *Restitution*
    1. *Goal of Restitution*
    2. *When Is Restitution Available*
    3. *The Party Avoiding Must Offer to Return Property*
      a. *Equitable Action*
      b. *Worthlessness*
      c. *Consumption or Loss of Possession*
      d. *Divisibility*
    4. *Defendant's Refusal to Accept an Offered Return*
    5. *Measure of Recovery*
    6. *No Restitution After Complete Performance*
    7. *Election of Remedies*
    8. *Specific Restitution*
C. *Equitable Enforcement*
    1. *Inadequacy of the Legal Remedy*
      a. *Uniqueness*
      b. *Affirmative Rule of Mutuality*
      c. *Conjectural Damages*
    2. *Defenses to Specific Performance*
      a. *Validity of the Contract and Value*
      b. *Certainty of the Contract*
      c. *Impossibility*
    3. *Equitable Discretion*
      a. *Difficulty of Supervision*
      b. *Personal Service Contracts*
      c. *Undue Risk*
      d. *Unconscionability*
      e. *Unclean Hands*
      f. *Laches*
      g. *Balancing Hardships*
    4. *Specific Performance With an Abatement*
    5. *Relationship Between Specific Performance and Damages*
      a. *Specific Performance Plus Damages*
      b. *Specific Performance and Liquidated Damages*
      c. *Effect of Denial of Specific Performance*
    6. *Restraining Orders*
      a. *Employment Contracts With Affirmative and Negative Duties*
      b. *Trade Secrets*
      c. *Covenants Not to Compete*

A. DAMAGES

1. GOAL OF DAMAGES
The aggrieved party receives "gains prevented" (expectancy interest) plus "losses sustained" (reliance and restitutionary interests), subject to the limitations imposed by the doctrines of foreseeability, certainty and mitigation.

Discussion: The basic goal of contract damages is to place aggrieved parties in the same economic position they would have achieved had their contracts been fully performed. The aggrieved party is entitled to the "benefit of the bargain."

Example: Purchaser contracts with manufacturer for the production of special machinery and repudiates the contract after production has been started. The manufacturer recovers lost profits (contract price minus what the full cost of production would have been) plus losses sustained (cost of labor and supplies actually expended to the extent such costs are not salvageable).

2. FORESEEABILITY—GENERAL AND CONSEQUENTIAL DAMAGES
Contract damages cannot be recovered unless they are foreseeable to the parties at the time of contracting.

a. Application
"General damages" are those foreseeable to reasonable persons similarly situated. "General damages" are calculated by the standardized rules discussed below. "Special" or "consequential" damages are those which are foreseeable because at the time of contracting the party in breach knows that in the event of breach no substitute performance will be available.

Examples: (1) S contracts to make deliveries of flour to B, knowing that B operates a large bakery and also knowing that because of a severe shortage, flour is almost unavailable on the spot market. S fails to make a scheduled delivery. Because of B's inability to acquire flour in timely fashion, B is forced to shut down the bakery for a week. In addition to "general damages", B may recover for loss of a week's profits.

(2) S contracts to deliver large quantities of sugar to B, knowing B is a wholesaler who sells to large users. The first scheduled delivery is April 1. Unbeknownst to S, B contracts with T for delivery on April 1 of the sugar that S promised to deliver. Also unknown to S, B contracted to deliver "S brand" sugar to T and not just "sugar." S fails to deliver on April 1. B cannot cover because "S brand" sugar is

unavailable. *T* sues *B* for damages and recovers. *B* now sues *S*, claiming lost profits on the resale and reimbursement for the damages paid to *T*. *B* does not recover for these damages. Although *S* knew *B* bought for resale it had no reason to know that this contract of resale allowed so little time between *S*'s delivery date and the date for redelivery. Moreover, it had no reason to know *B* contracted to deliver sugar by brand name and thus had disabled itself from being able to cover.

b.   Particular Situations
1)   Sale of Goods
   a)   Seller's Non-delivery
   Purchaser recovers as general damages the difference between market price and contract price or between cover price (price reasonably paid even if in excess of the "market") and contract price.

   Examples: (1) *B* contracts to purchase sugar from *S* at 17 cents a pound for delivery on April 1. *S* fails to deliver. On April 1, the market price is 22 cents. *B*'s general measure of damages is 5 cents per pound.

   (2) *B* contracts to purchase sugar from *S* at 17 cents per pound for delivery on April 1. On April 1, the market price could be found by a jury to be 22 cents. However, some spot sales were for as much as 29 cents. Supplies were thin and spot prices erratic. *S* failed to deliver, and *B* called a reputable broker who found a spot seller who delivered covering sugar to *B* at 26 cents. *B*, who has acted in a commercially reasonable way, may recover the difference between the cover price and the unpaid contract price. In addition, *B* may recover any broker's fee as "incidental" damages.

   b)   Seller's Breach of Warranty
   Purchaser can recover as general damages the difference between the value the goods would have had if they had been as warranted and their actual value. Value is determined as of the time and place of acceptance.

   Comment: Notice that this rule is a rule of "difference in *value*." Price is *not* a factor.

Example: S, a merchant deciding to close out a line of machinery, advertises a close-out sale. B purchases a new grinding machine for $1,000. Comparable new merchantable machines are valued at $2,000. The machine has a hidden defect which makes it unmerchantable and worthless. Absent an effective limitation of liability or disclaimer, B is entitled to $2,000 in damages. If the defect had reduced the market value of the machine to $500, B would be entitled to $1,500.

c) Buyer's Breach
For total breach by the buyer as to goods the buyer has not accepted, the seller may recover the difference between the contract price and the market or resale price. If the seller has an unlimited supply of the goods involved, however, the seller has lost the profits on the sale, so the seller may instead recover "the profit (including reasonable overhead) which the seller would have made from full performance by the buyer." U.C.C. § 2–708(2).

Discussion: The rule gives three alternative measures of recovery. (In addition, a seller may have an action for the price [see d below].) The last of the three measures applies to a merchant who contracts to sell stock in trade; for example, the automobile dealer. The economic injury done to the seller by the buyer's total breach is that the seller has lost the profit on a sale. Unless the car is unique, its resale to another buyer does not make the seller whole because presumably the seller could have procured another similar car for the second buyer. The contract price-market price formula will not make the seller whole as presumably the sale was at or near the market price. The contract price-resale price formula is most appropriate for contracts for the sale of unique goods and goods that are not part of the seller's stock in trade. The *contract price-market price* measure is most appropriate for contracts for the sale of commodities and other fungible goods for which there is an active market.

d) Seller's Price Action
If the buyer has accepted the goods, or if the goods are destroyed after risk of loss has passed to the buyer, the seller can recover the price. A price action is also available if the goods are

identified to the contract and the seller cannot reasonably resell them.

e) **Consequential and Incidental Damages in Sales Cases**
Consequential damages are available to a buyer if the foreseeability test is met. See p. 299 supra. Sellers *cannot* claim consequential damages (U.C.C. § 1–106), but frequently can get incidental damages. Buyers, too, can claim incidental damages. These include, but are not limited to, brokerage commissions, storage charges, advertising costs, and auctioneer's fees made necessary by the other's breach.

2) **Employment Contracts**
a) **Employer's Breach**
Employees who have been discharged in breach of contract may recover the wages or salary that would have been payable during the contract term minus the income that they have earned, will earn or could with reasonable diligence earn during the contract term. In the case of a long term contract the "present worth" doctrine (see p. 309 below) will be applied.

> *Discussion:* Notice that a contract price minus market price formula is not used in this context. *Prima facie* the employee is entitled to the contract price. This is reduced only if the employer meets the burden of proof that other employment was obtained or could reasonably have been obtained during the contract term (see p. 307 *infra.*)

b) **Employee's Breach**
If an employee quits in breach of contract the employer recovers the difference between the market value of the employee's service minus the contract price.

> *Discussion:* In other words, the employer recovers more than nominal damages only if the employee was underpaid. Although, in theory, consequential damages are available, only a handful of cases have granted consequential damages against a breaching employee.

3) **Construction Contracts**
a) **Contractor's Delay**
Damages for delay are measured by the rental value of the completed premises for the period of delay.

b) **Contractor's Failure to Complete**
Failure to complete is compensated by the additional cost of completion plus delay damages.

c) **Defect in Construction**
If the breach consists of a defect in construction, the damages are the cost of correcting the defect, unless this would constitute unreasonable economic waste.

Examples: (1) *C* (Contractor) promised to comply with each of *O*'s (Owner's) specifications. One of these was the use of Reading pipe. *C* breached by installing Cohoes pipe, a brand of comparable quality. The breach was not discovered until after most of the pipe was walled in by plaster. Correcting the breach would involve economic waste. *O*'s damages are limited to the difference in value between the structure as it should have been built and the value it has as it was built. This is the same rule as for breach of warranty in sales cases.

(2) *C* contracted to build a suburban house for *O* with a garage and driveway. Rather than excavate a rock formation, *D* built the driveway with a 22½% grade, which is so steep the driveway cannot be used safely and conveniently. A 12½% grade is considered the permissible maximum. The cost of redoing the driveway and lowering the garage would be $20,000. The full purchase price was $68,000. The defendant offered evidence to show that the property's value, despite the defect, exceeded the contract price. *O* recovers the cost of curing the defect. The difference in value rule will not be applied where the defect affects the usability and safety of the premises. Normally, it will not be applied where the defect is willful, which also appears to be the case here.

d) **Owner's Breach**
If no work has been done, the contractor recovers the anticipated profit, that is, the contract price minus the projected cost of performance. If the work has been started, the contractor recovers the anticipated profit plus the cost of labor and supplies actually expended.

Perspective: If the contract was an unprofitable one, the contractor will normally prefer to sue for restitution rather than damages. (See p. 314 infra.)

e) Consequential Damages in Construction Cases
If foreseeability is shown, consequential damages are available against a breaching contractor. If an owner's breach is a failure to pay or a repudiation, consequential damages are *never* available to the contractor.

Example: C promised to complete a one family residence for O by September 30. Before contracting, O informed C that O had contracted to convey O's present residence to T by October 1 and would be liable to T for liquidated damages in the amount of $100 a day for any delay in conveying. Consequently, it was urgent that the completion of the new residence be timely. C did not substantially perform until October 15, when O was able to occupy the new house. As a result of the delay, O was liable to T for $1,500. C is liable to O for the sum of $1,500 as consequential damages.

4) Contracts to Sell Realty
a) Vendee's Total Breach
If a contract vendee totally breaches the contract, the vendor may recover the difference between the contract price and the value of the realty.

Perspective: This is the same rule as is applied to breach by a purchaser of goods. Contrast the rule as to vendor's breach, stated below.

b) Vendor's Total Breach
(i) *English Rule. For total breach, the vendee may recover only the down payment plus reasonable expenses of a survey and examination of title.*

Rationale and Comment: The vendee, under this orthodox view, is not entitled to the expectancy interest. The rule originated because land titles in England were often insecure and registry systems were poor. Consequently, many good faith vendors were unable to convey marketable title.

Exception: If the vendor (a) refuses to convey or (b) is aware of the title defect at the time of contracting, the vendor is liable for the difference between contract price and market value. Because the rationale for the English rule is not applicable, the vendee's expectations are protected.

(ii) *American Rule. Under the "American Rule", followed in a bare majority of jurisdictions, no matter what the reason for the breach, the vendor is liable for the difference between contract price and market value.*

Perspective: This is the same as the primary rule of damages applicable where a seller of goods totally breaches.

c) Consequential Damages
Consequential damages against a vendor in default is a strong possibility under both the American rule and the exception to the English rule.

Example: *V* advertised property for sale. *P,* who told *V* that the purchase was for speculation and probable quick resale, entered into a contract with *V* on January 15 to purchase the property for $100,000, conveyance to be on February 28. On February 1, *P* entered into a contract with *T* for the resale of the property for $120,000. *V* repudiated. Because *V,* at the time of contracting, was aware of *P*'s purpose and knew that this purpose could not be accomplished if *V* breached, *V* is liable to *P* for the $20,000 loss of profit.

d) Vendor's Delay
If the breach consists of a delay in conveying, the vendee may recover for the rental value of the premises during the period of delay.

3. CERTAINTY
The fact of loss and its amount must be proved with reasonable certainty.

a.   Discussion

The standard of certainty requires a higher quality of proof on the issue of damages than for other issues in a lawsuit. It is applied with special stringency to lost profits, particularly lost profits as consequential damages.

> *Examples:* (1) *S* agrees to sell sugar to *B,* who, as *S* well knows, operates a bakery. *S* is also aware of a sugar shortage. *S* breaches. *B* is unable to cover and is forced to close the bakery for a week, losing profits. This is the kind of consequential damages claim that is most closely scrutinized. If *B* were operating a new business, almost certainly *B* would be unable to prove these damages. (For an alternative measure of damage, see "Alternatives Where Expectancy Is Uncertain," below.) If *B* had an established business with a relatively stable record of profitability and adequate records, proof could be made with sufficient certainty. Exactness of damages need not be shown but a reasonable basis for computation must be proved.
>
> (2) *A,* a publisher, totally breaks a contract to publish a novel by *B,* a previously unpublished author. *B* was to be compensated strictly on a royalty basis. *B* cannot establish the loss of royalties with sufficient certainty.

b.   Alternatives Where Expectancy Is Uncertain

1)   Protection of Reliance Interest

Where the aggrieved party cannot establish the lost expectancy interest with sufficient certainty, the aggrieved party is permitted to recover expenses of preparation for and of part performance as well as other foreseeable expenses incurred in reliance upon the contract. If it can be shown by the defendant that the contract would have been a losing proposition for the plaintiff, an appropriate deduction will be made for the loss that was not incurred.

> *Example:* Defendant promised to use diligence in marketing, at $1 a box, 90,000 boxes of Christmas cards produced by plaintiff. The cards were of unique designs that related to the events of the year. Defendant totally breached, and plaintiff had no alternative way of marketing them in time for the Christmas season. Because of the "novelty" nature of the designs, plaintiff cannot prove that the 90,000 boxes would have been sold. The salvage value in the following year is trivial. Nonetheless, plaintiff may recover expenditures for labor and material ($17,000) minus the net salvage value of the cards ($2,000). Defendant has the burden of proving that full

performance of the contract would have resulted in a loss to plaintiff and what the amount of that loss would have been. If defendant can show what that loss would have been, the loss would have been subtracted from plaintiff's $15,000 recovery.

2) **Rental Value of Profit–Making Property**
If the breach disables the aggrieved party from using profit-making property, the aggrieved party may recover the rental value of the property.

> ***Example:*** S delivers and installs a defective furnace in B's new glass factory. As S could have foreseen at the time of contracting, the defect prevents the opening of the factory for a prolonged period. Because B's factory is new, it is unlikely that B can prove lost profits with sufficient certainty. Nonetheless, B may recover the rental value of property for the period the factory was closed because of the breach. If rental value is unclear, it can be inferred by calculating the going rate of interest upon the cost of the factory.

3) **Value of an Opportunity**
If a duty is conditioned upon a fortuitous event, and the breach makes it uncertain whether the event would have occurred, the aggrieved party may recover the value of the chance that the event would have occurred.

> ***Example:*** Plaintiff was one of fifty semi-finalists in a beauty contest in which twelve finalists would receive cash prizes, the lowest of which was $4,000. The defendant neglected to notify plaintiff of the time and place of the final competition. A jury verdict for $1,000 is upheld. The plaintiff had roughly a 1 in 4 chance of being selected as a finalist.

> ***Discussion:*** The rule only applies to aleatory contracts, such as contests and policies of insurance.

4. MITIGATION
Damages that could have been avoided by reasonable efforts cannot be recovered. Conversely, the aggrieved party may recover reasonable costs incurred in an effort to minimize damages.

a. Discussion

The aggrieved party need take only reasonable action to avoid damages. Heroics are not required. The notion of mitigation is built into many rules of damages. For example, an aggrieved purchaser cannot recover consequential damages if "cover" is possible; i.e., comparable goods could have been bought in the market at the time of learning of the breach. An employee who has been wrongfully fired should take a comparable job if one is available. In addition, it is a doctrine to be applied to any case where damages could reasonably have been minimized.

Example: Shirley MacLaine contracted with *D* to play the female lead in "Bloomer Girl," a musical to be filmed in California for a minimum agreed compensation of $750,000. *D* decided not to produce "Bloomer Girl." In substitution *D* offered Miss MacLaine the lead in "Big Country," a Western to be filmed in Australia. She declined to play in "Big Country" and sues for $750,000. Because the offer of the substituted role was comparable neither in the kind of role played nor in the location of the filming, she has not acted unreasonably in refusing the role. Note, however, that had she taken the substitute role or accepted any other employment for the contract period, earnings from such employment would have been subtracted from her recovery.

b. Exception

One is not required to enter into another contract with the breaching party even if the offered contract would have minimized damages. This is an alternate ground for the prior illustration.

c. Non-exclusive Contracts

The principle of mitigation is not necessarily applicable in cases where the relationship between the parties is not exclusive. If the aggrieved party is free to enter into other similar contracts, entry into such a contract after breach does not reduce damages.

Example: *A,* the owner of a car rental fleet, contracts to rent a car for one year to *B,* who repudiates. *A* then rents the car that had been earmarked for *B* to *C. C*'s rental payments do not reduce the damages recoverable against *B,* provided that it can be shown that *A* had a sufficient supply of cars to accommodate both *B* and *C.* The basic idea is the same as in the case of an action by an automobile dealer against a repudiating buyer discussed on p. 301 supra.

5. PRESENT WORTH DOCTRINE
Where damages include payments that were required to be made in the future, the value of the payments must be calculated at their present worth.

Example: D repudiates a contract that requires payment to P of $20,000 per year for 20 years. The contract is not exclusively a unilateral obligation to pay a sum of money. (See p. 252 supra.) Consequently, an action for anticipatory breach is available. P sues to recover $400,000—20 years times $20,000: P does *not* recover $400,000. That sum invested at 10% would return $40,000 per year and at the end of 20 years would be intact. Instead, P is entitled to judgment for a sum of money which could purchase an annuity that would yield $20,000 per year for 20 years. The cost of such an annuity depends upon the interest rates in effect at the time of purchase.

6. LIQUIDATED DAMAGES
a. Penalties Distinguished
Liquidated damages clauses are valid. Penalty clauses are void. A clause will be deemed a valid liquidated damages clause if it is a reasonable and good faith attempt to pre-estimate the economic harm that would flow from breach. Penalty clauses are designed to deter breaches by the prospect of punishment.

Comments: (1) Note that the key element in distinguishing a liquidated damages clause from a penalty clause is its *purpose*. (2) Note also that courts are more prone to uphold a provision as a liquidated damages clause if the injury caused by the breach is difficult or impossible to estimate accurately.

Example: P, an oral surgeon, hired D, also an oral surgeon, to work as an assistant in P's Gloversville office. A clause provided that D would not practice oral surgery in Gloversville, except in association with P. It further provided that if D violated this promise, D would pay the sum of $60,000 to P. The clause will be upheld if it seems that the sum realistically deals with the probable financial injury that a breach would cause. This clause is particularly likely to be upheld in a case such as this because actual damages are very difficult to prove with a reasonable degree of certainty.

b. Formulas Are Acceptable
Valid liquidated damages clauses are often expressed in formulas rather than in exact dollar amounts. Such an expression does not affect the validity of the clause.

Example: *V* contracts to sell a residence to *P*. A deed of conveyance and possession are to be delivered on October 1. *P,* who is married and has four children, intends to move into the house on October 1 and explains this to *V* prior to contracting. At *P*'s insistence, the contract provides that for each day's delay in delivery of possession *V* will pay liquidated damages of $200. The sum is reasonable in the light of alternative lodging costs in the area, increased cost of food, storage of furniture, etc. The clause will be upheld.

c. Shotgun Clauses Are Dangerous

A clause providing that "$50,000 will be paid for breach of this contract" may be deemed a penalty because it does not proportion the damages to any particular kind of breach. Notice that in each of the illustrations of valid liquidated damages clauses given above, the clause targets the kind of breach that triggers the liability for liquidated damages. The question is one of interpretation. If it is possible to interpret the clause as targeted solely at a total breach (or other specific kind of breach), then it is *not* a shotgun clause and is *not* invalid under the rule applicable to shotgun clauses.

d. Can't Have It Both Ways

The courts will strike down a clause that attempts to fix damages in the event of breach while giving the aggrieved party the right to obtain judgment for additional actual damages that may be established. Such a clause does not involve a reasonable attempt to definitively pre-estimate the loss.

e. Specific Performance Not Excluded

A valid liquidated damages clause does not give a breaching party an option to pay liquidated damages or perform. Therefore, the presence of such a clause does not preclude a decree for specific performance. However, the aggrieved party cannot normally have both remedies. If the aggrieved party obtains a decree for specific performance, the decree may also quantify such actual damages as may have been sustained between the time of the breach and the time of the decree.

f. Additional Agreed Damages—Attorney's Fees

The award of damages does not ordinarily include reimbursement of the successful party's attorney's fees. However, a contract can provide that, in the event of breach, the aggrieved party may recover reasonable attorney's fees incurred in enforcement of the contract, thereby permitting recovery of an agreed amount in excess of the damages that would accrue by operation of law.

6. LIMITATIONS ON DAMAGES

The U.C.C. and the common law permit the parties to limit damages "as by limiting the buyer's remedies to return of the goods and repayment of the price or to repair and replacement of non-conforming goods or parts." U.C.C. § 2–719(1) (a). The Code further provides that: "Consequential damages may be limited or excluded unless the limitation or exclusion is unconscionable. Limitation of consequential damages for injury to the person in the case of consumer goods is prima facie unconscionable but limitation of damages where the loss is commercial is not." U.C.C. § 2–719(3).

a. Discussion

The general approach of the U.C.C., which is similar to that of the common law, is to uphold agreed upon limitations of liability. The primary restriction on contractual freedom to limit liability is that of conscionability. Normally, limitations on commercial losses are upheld.

> *Example:* A operates a business that is heavily dependent upon the "Yellow Pages" of the telephone directory as a source of customers. The telephone company, in breach of contract, placed A's name and number in the wrong category of listings. This caused a drastic diminution in the amount of business during the year. A's contract with the telephone company provides that A's remedy for breach is limited to restitution of the amount paid for advertising in the directory. The limitation is valid.

b. Failure of Essential Purpose

"Where circumstances cause an exclusive or limited remedy to fail of its essential purpose, remedy may be had as provided in this act." U.C.C. § 2–719(2).

1) Discussion

This rule is statutory and does not exist at common law. It is far less broad than an initial reading might convey. The issue is not conscionability of a limitation clause. Rather, the issue is the *purpose of the limitation clause.*

> *Example:* A contract for the sale of a new car limits the purchaser's warranties to repair and replacement of defective parts. The car has numerous defects. Despite many trips to the dealer's service department for replacement of defective parts, the car does not operate properly. The purpose of the clause limiting the buyer's remedies has failed. It was designed to limit the dealer's liability but also to provide the buyer with a serviceable car for the warranty term. Consequently, the buyer may return the car and

obtain restitution of the purchase price and recover general and consequential damages for breach of warranty. Compare the previous example concerning the "Yellow Pages." There the purpose is solely to limit liability. Assuming the U.C.C. were applicable (it, of course, is not), the clause does not fail of its purpose.

7. PUNITIVE DAMAGES

Punitive damages are not available in a contract action unless the breach involves an independent tort.

Examples: (1) *S* contracts to deliver sugar to *B* on February 1. *S*, out of malice, withholds delivery. *B* may recover general damages and consequential damages (if the test of foreseeability is met). *B* may not recover punitive damages.

(2) *S* contracts to provide services to *B* commencing February 1. *B* no longer desires the services contracted for and prevents *S*'s performance by hiring *S*'s key employees in breach of their contracts with *S*. *B* is liable for punitive damages. In addition to *B*'s breach by prevention, *B* has committed the tort of wrongful interference with the contractual relation between *S* and *S*'s employees.

Comments: (1) Some jurisdictions now grant punitive damages where elements of fraud, malice, gross negligence or oppression "mingle" with the breach as in example (1) above. Although the U.C.C. specifically bars punitive damages except where specifically provided (§ 1–106(1)), this provision is sometimes overlooked in cases such as example (1) above.

(2) Some jurisdictions grant punitive damages against insurance companies in cases where there is a bad faith refusal to settle a claim.

(3) California will also grant punitive damages where there is a bad faith refusal to recognize the existence of a contract.

8. MENTAL DISTRESS

The law does not compensate for mental distress caused by a contractual breach in most contractual contexts. In a few atypical cases; *e.g.,* breach of contract for funeral arrangements, such compensation has been allowed.

9. NOMINAL DAMAGES
Every breach of contract creates a cause of action. If the aggrieved party suffers no economic harm or cannot prove such harm with sufficient certainty, nominal damages can be recovered, *e.g.,* six cents.

B.   RESTITUTION

1.   GOAL OF RESTITUTION
The basic goal of actions at law or in equity for restitution is to place the aggrieved party in the same economic position this party had enjoyed prior to entering into the contract. This is accomplished by requiring the defendant to restore to the plaintiff what defendant has received from the plaintiff. Such restoration will not fully recapture the *status quo ante* if the plaintiff has incurred expenses in reliance upon the contract, but which have not benefited the defendant. A modern but unorthodox trend permits recovery of such expenditures in a restitution action.

2.   WHEN IS RESTITUTION AVAILABLE?
Restitution is available in six principal kinds of contractual situations:

a.   Total Breach of Contract.

b.   Avoidance of a Contract for Incapacity, Duress, Misrepresentation, etc.

c.   The Agreement is not a Contract Because of Indefiniteness, Misunderstanding, Agent's Lack of Authority, etc.

d.   The Agreement is Unenforceable Because of the Statute of Frauds and Certain Kinds of Illegality.

e.   The Agreement is Discharged Because of Impracticability or Frustration.

f.   The Defaulting Party Seeks to Recover for Part Performance.

3.   THE PARTY AVOIDING MUST OFFER TO RETURN PROPERTY
A party who seeks to avoid a contract, as a precondition to an action for restitution, must offer to return any property received. The offer may be conditional on the other party's restitution of what has been received by the other.

Exceptions:

a.   **Equitable Action**
Specific restitution may be decreed in an equitable action despite the plaintiff's failure to offer to make restitution. This is because a decree in Equity can be conditioned upon the plaintiff's restoration. In many states,

judgments at law do not have this flexibility. It must be remembered that there must be grounds for equitable intervention before specific restitution will be granted.

b. Worthlessness
If the property received was worthless or became worthless because of its defects, failure to offer its return will not defeat the plaintiff's action.

c. Consumption or Loss of Possession
If services have been received, they, of course, cannot be returned. If the goods received have been consumed or disposed of, return is not possible. Consequently, the requirement of an offer to return is dispensed with. Instead, the value of the services or goods will be offset from the plaintiff's recovery.

d. Divisibility
If the contract is divisible into several agreed exchanges and the grievance does not relate to all of them, the plaintiff need not offer to return those things received pursuant to a divisible portion about which there is no grievance.

4. DEFENDANT'S REFUSAL TO ACCEPT AN OFFERED RETURN
If a defendant improperly refuses an offer of return, the plaintiff may assert a lien on the goods and may sell what has been received. The price will be credited to the restitution claim.

5. MEASURE OF RECOVERY
The plaintiff receives the reasonable value of services rendered, goods delivered, or property conveyed less the reasonable value of any counter-performance received, irrespective of any enrichment.

Comment: "Unjust Enrichment," the principal philosophical underpinning of the restitution remedy, does not provide the measure of recovery.

Examples: (1) An attorney contracted to try a divorce case for $750. After nearly completing the trial, the client wrongfully fired the attorney. The reasonable value of the services was $5,000. The attorney recovers $5,000.

(2) C contracts to add a porch of rather ugly design on O's house for $5,000. Before the work is completed, O wrongfully orders C to cease performance. C recovers the reasonable value of services rendered although the ugly and incomplete porch diminishes rather than adds to the value of O's realty.

6. NO RESTITUTION AFTER COMPLETE PERFORMANCE
Restitution is not available if a debt has been created.

Example: An attorney contracts to try a divorce case for $750. After completing the trial, the client wrongfully repudiates. The attorney has no restitution action and is limited to an action for $750.

7. ELECTION OF REMEDIES
In the absence of a statute, a plaintiff cannot recover both restitution and damages.   Under the U.C.C., recovery may be had under both headings.

Examples: (1) A seller tenders a defective machine for which the purchaser has paid. The purchaser may reject it, or revoke acceptance of it. The purchaser may then recover the purchase price and, under the U.C.C., recover damages. Damages are usually measured by the increased cost of replacing the machine with a substitute.

(2) *A* assigns a patent to *B* who promises to pay a royalty and to use best efforts to promote the patented invention. *B* totally breaches. *A* may elect to sue for damages or to seek restitution at law for the value of the patent, but cannot have restitution plus damages. A third possibility is a decree in equity for specific restitution of the patent.

8. SPECIFIC RESTITUTION
Specific restitution will be ordered where the legal remedy is inadequate.

Discussion: The typical restitution action at law for the reasonable value of one's performance is a "quasi-contractual" action, a label that appears to be disappearing, and in which the judgment is for a sum of money. In equity, through various devices, such as a decree cancelling a deed, or the imposition of a constructive trust, specific restitution of property transferred or wrongfully acquired may be compelled. The remedy at law is deemed inadequate where property is transferred in exchange for the promise of something other than money, and the exchange will not be forthcoming (Example 1), and also where the contract breacher has acquired money or property in violation of a relationship of trust and confidence (Example 2).

Examples: (1) *A* conveys his or her house and land to *B* in exchange for *B*'s promise to support and take care of *A* for *A*'s life. *B* repudiates. *A* may have specific restitution. *A*'s remedies at law are inadequate. Damages are speculative. Restitution at law for the value of the property is not an adequate remedy as *A* has evinced no intent to convey at market value.

(2) *A* contracts with the CIA to be an intelligence agent and agrees not to publish any material about CIA operations without clearance from the CIA. In violation of the contract, *A* writes and causes to be published a book about CIA activities. A constructive trust is imposed upon *A*'s royalties from the book. Note that normally a plaintiff *cannot* recover the profits that a defendant has made from a breach of contract. Here, however, there is grounds for such relief in equity because of the confidential relationship between the CIA and its agent.

C. EQUITABLE ENFORCEMENT

1. INADEQUACY OF THE LEGAL REMEDY
Equity will enforce a contract by decreeing specific performance or by a restraining order only if the legal remedy of damages or restitution is inadequate.

a. Uniqueness
Equity will order specific performance to a contract purchaser if the subject matter of a contract of sale is unique. The legal remedy is inadequate because the disappointed purchaser cannot replace the subject matter on the market.

Examples: (1) Real property is always deemed unique. Each parcel is deemed to have its individual character.

(2) Heirlooms, works of art, and other one-of-a-kind objects; and

(3) Patents, copyrights, closely held stock, and other intangibles not readily available on the market are deemed unique.

b. Affirmative Rule of Mutuality
If a purchaser could have obtained a decree of specific performance in the event of the seller's breach because the purchaser's legal remedy would have been inadequate, the seller can obtain a decree of specific performance in the event of the purchaser's breach.

Example: *V* contracts to sell a house to *P* for $100,000, payable in cash. *P* repudiates. *V* may obtain a decree of specific performance although there is nothing unique about *P*'s performance—the payment of money.

c. Conjectural Damages
The legal remedy is inadequate if damages are conjectural and restitution does not carry out the ends of the contract.

Examples: (1) *S* contracts to supply *B*'s requirement of natural gas for a ten year term. In the third year, *S* repudiates. *B* sues for specific performance. *B* can obtain equitable enforcement because damages for failure to supply gas for the next seven years are highly conjectural.

(2) Contracts of insurance, annuity contracts based on life expectancy, and contracts to give security are other illustrations of contracts for which damages for breach are highly conjectural. Consequently, they are typical instances in which specific performance is available as a remedy for breach; e.g., a breach by the insurer prior to the happening of the insured event.

2. DEFENSES TO SPECIFIC PERFORMANCE
a. Validity of the Contract and Value
Equity will not enforce a contract that is invalid. Moreover, it requires that the contract be for value. Nominal consideration will not suffice, and a contract under seal without consideration will not suffice. Value consists of any consideration in fact bargained for or the existence of an antecedent debt. For example, a right is exchanged for value if it is given as security for or in total or partial satisfaction of a pre-existing debt.

Exception: An option contract for a nominal consideration or under seal (in those jurisdictions where the seal is still viable) will be specifically enforced, provided that it looks to further performances for a fair exchange.

Example: *V* offers to sell Blackacre to *P* for $20,000, a fair price. *V* also agrees to make the offer irrevocable for 30 days in consideration of $1. The following day, *V* purports to revoke the offer, and *P* thereafter gives *V* a notice of acceptance and brings an action for specific performance. Despite the fact that the consideration is nominal, equity will decree specific performance.

b. Certainty of the Contract
Equity requires that the parties' performances be described in the contract with greater precision than is the case in an action at law. Because the penalty for non-compliance with a decree is punishment for contempt, the parties and the court must know what to do with reasonable certainty.

c.   Impossibility
Equity will not order a defendant to render a performance that is impossible even where impossibility will not excuse a breaching party in an action for damages.

Example: *V* contracts to sell Blackacre to *P*. Subsequently, *V* breaches the contract by conveying to *T*, a bona fide purchaser for value. Because the impossibility is self-induced, *V* does not have the defense of impossibility of performance in an action at law. Nevertheless, the court will not order specific performance, because *V* no longer has the capability of performing.

3.   EQUITABLE DISCRETION
Specific performance is never a matter of pure entitlement. The court has wide power of discretion in determining whether or not to grant the remedy. The factors to determine whether the discretion should be exercised against enforcement are reducible to certain doctrines, such as "difficulty of supervision," discussed below.

a.   Difficulty of Supervision
Equity, in its discretion, will refuse to order specific performance of contracts where supervision of performance by the court will be unduly burdensome.

Discussion: Only rarely will a court specifically enforce a contract to build or repair a structure. Yet, the court will do so where the "injustice from refusal to enforce outweighs the probable burden of supervision." For example, a court has ordered specific performance of a railroad's contractual promise to a city to elevate its tracks. In other special circumstances, specific enforcement of a contract to build has been ordered, especially where the performance is to be on the *defendant's* land. In such cases the plaintiff cannot hire a contractor to do the job and sue for damages.

b.   Personal Service Contracts
Employment contracts are not specifically enforced against the *employee*. Such decrees would reek of involuntary servitude and possibly would run afoul of the Constitution. At times, however, an employee may be *enjoined* against working for another, resulting in indirect enforcement (see p. 321 below.) Enforcement against an *employer* is normally denied because of the difficulty of supervision, or because of the adequacy of the legal remedy. But arbitration awards of reinstatement have been enforced.

c.   Undue Risk
If performance of the contract would impose an undue risk that the counter-performance will not be received, specific performance will be denied.

Discussion: It used to be the general rule that if for any reason specific performance could not be decreed against one party (e.g., difficulty of supervision), it could not be decreed against the other. This negative rule of "mutuality of remedy" has been abandoned and the undue risk doctrine is what remains of it.

Example: *V* contracts to sell Blackacre to *P*. *V* is to convey title on *P*'s making of a down payment, and *P* is to make further payments in installments over a ten year period. *V* repudiates, and *P* seeks a decree of specific performance. The court may condition a decree for specific performance on *P*'s executing a mortgage to secure *V*'s right to payment.

d.   Unconscionability
Under the doctrine of unconscionability, equity has refused to enforce contracts that are valid at law. Inadequacy of consideration coupled with any sharp practice, non-disclosure, overreaching, abuse of confidential relationship, etc., will result in a refusal of specific performance even where the inequitable conduct would not enable the party to avoid the contract.

e.   Unclean Hands
Specific performance will be denied if the plaintiff is guilty of any inequitable conduct with respect to the transaction, even if in concert with the defendant so that no unconscionability exists.

Example: *D*, a professional athlete of extraordinary skill, entered into a voidable contract to play baseball for *T* while under the age of majority. *P* induced him to play for *P* at a higher salary. *D* disaffirmed his contract with *T*, and after attaining the age of majority, entered into a binding contract with *P*. *T* then induced *D* to breach the contract with *P* to play for *T*. *P* sues *D* to enjoin him from playing with *T*. *D* sets up the defense of unclean hands. Injunction denied. *P* who inequitably interfered with *D*'s contract with *T*, cannot equitably complain of *D*'s similar behavior at a later time in concert with *T*.

Perspective: "Unclean hands" is related to illegality, but conduct short of illegality may give rise to the doctrine.

f.   Laches
Even if the statute of limitations has not run, specific performance will be denied if the plaintiff's failure promptly to commence a law suit prejudices the defendant as by causing the defendant to change position or where the plaintiff has remained inactive until the subject matter has risen in value.

g.   Balancing Hardships
Specific performance will be denied where the hardship to the defendant or to the public will be greatly in excess of any benefit to the plaintiff.

Examples: (1) A railroad breached its contract to erect a private railroad crossing which had little or no value to the plaintiff and would involve considerable cost to the defendant. Specific performance was denied.

(2) A defendant railroad breached its contract to share trackage. The defendant's employees threatened to strike if the contract were to be performed. Hardship to the defendant and to the public were cited as grounds for denial of equitable relief.

4. SPECIFIC PERFORMANCE WITH AN ABATEMENT
When a vendor's title to real property is encumbered so that the vendor is unable to convey the interest specified in the contract, the vendee may obtain a decree of specific performance with an abatement in price. In essence, this decree involves specific performance with an offset for damages for a partial breach. In rare cases, specific performance will be refused if only a radically different kind of estate can be conveyed from that contracted for.

Examples: (1) *V* contracts to sell a farm to *P*. A title search reveals the land is encumbered by easements that had not been disclosed by *V*. These easements diminish the value of the land by 15%. The court may order specific performance with an appropriate abatement in price.

(2) *V* contracts to sell a farm to *P* for $100,000. A title search reveals that *V* only has a life estate. Because *V*'s life expectancy is limited, the value of *V*'s interest is $20,000. *P*'s action for specific performance with an abatement will be denied.

5. RELATIONSHIP BETWEEN SPECIFIC PERFORMANCE AND DAMAGES
a.   Specific Performance Plus Damages
A decree for specific performance is often accompanied by an award of damages. Often this will be an award of damages for delay in performing, say, a contract to convey real property. In other cases it may be an award of damages for partial breach of, say, an output contract.

b.   Specific Performance and Liquidated Damages
The presence of a liquidated damages clause does not preclude an award of specific performance (see p. 310 supra).

c.   Effect of Denial of Specific Performance
If specific performance is denied because of the adequacy of the legal remedy or because of the exercise of equitable discretion, the plaintiff may thereafter commence an action for damages or restitution at law. The denial of specific performance on equitable grounds does not deprive the plaintiff of the legal remedy. Under modern practice, in many jurisdictions, plaintiff may join the equitable action with the law action in one law suit. In such a suit, if the equitable remedy is denied, the legal remedy may be granted.

6.   RESTRAINING ORDERS
Specific relief, of a sort, is often obtained by a restraining order. While these are most often sought in personal service contracts, they are not limited to such contracts.

Example: S contracts to sell S's entire output to B. For breach of this contract a court can enjoin S from selling to others. Such a negative order frees the court from the need to supervise sales to B.

a.   Employment Contracts With Affirmative and Negative Duties
Where an employee promises to work exclusively for an employer for a given period, although equity will not compel the employee to work, it will enjoin the employee from working for another if the employer can show irreparable harm from breach of the express or implied negative covenant not to work for another.

>   *Example:*   An opera singer breaches a contract to sing with plaintiff's company and signs on with a competing company in the same city, which draws on the same clientele. An injunction, restraining the singer from performing for the competitor, may be granted. A contrary result will be reached if the singer signs up with a company from a distant city because there would be no injury from breach of the negative covenant.

b.   Trade Secrets
A covenant not to divulge trade secrets will be enforced by injunction. Even in the absence of such a covenant, a duty not to divulge will be implied and enforced by injunction.

c.   Covenants Not to Compete

An agreement not to compete, unconnected with another transaction, is void. An ancillary covenant connected with the sale of a business, an employment contract, a lease, and certain other transactions may be valid, if reasonable. If unreasonable, the orthodox view was that the entire covenant fell. The modern cases allow partial enforcement, limiting the injunction to a reasonable time and area.

1)   **Ancillary to Sale of Business**
Reasonableness is judged by whether the duration and territorial area of the restraint is in excess of the area in which the seller enjoyed good will or of the period of time the good will can reasonably be expected to continue.

2)   **Ancillary to Employment**
Covenants of this kind are tested by stricter criteria. Equity will enforce such a covenant (1) to the extent necessary to prevent an employee's use of trade secrets and confidential customer lists or (2) where the employee's services are "special, unique and extraordinary." An injunction will be limited to the area and time necessary to protect the employer's interests.

> ***Example:***   *P*, a nationwide firm specializing in advising businesses on how to minimize unemployment insurance costs, hired *D* eleven years ago. *D*'s employment contract provided that if *D* left *P*'s employ, *D* would refrain for three years from entering any competing business in seven named counties, one of which was the place of employment. *D* became vice-president in charge of operations and was thoroughly conversant with all aspects of the operation but had little involvement with sales. *P*'s services were sold to major companies listed in industrial directories. After eleven years, *D* resigned and set up a competing business in the same community. *P* seeks an injunction: (1) prohibiting *D* from operating a competing business, and (2) permanently enjoining *D* from soliciting *P*'s customers. All relief is denied. *D* may solicit *P*'s customers as there is no secret customer list. *D* may compete. Under the orthodox view, still widely followed, the covenant is over-broad in its geographical range and therefore is void in its entirety. While the modern view permits limited enforcement of an over-broad covenant, there must be a substantive basis for enforcement. Here, there are no trade secrets, nor are *D*'s services "unique and extraordinary," despite the fact *D* is a talented and skilled professional.

REVIEW QUESTIONS

On April 15, Vendor contracted to sell to Vendee, a wholesaler, 10,000 yards of satin, delivery to be made on September 15 of the same year at a price of $5.00 a yard, which amount was paid in full on signing the contract. Payment before delivery enabled Vendee to purchase at a price lower than the market.

On April 16, Vendee contracted to sell 5,000 yards of the satin to Shrunk, Inc., at the price of $9.00 per yard and 5,000 yards to Shriek, Inc. at $7.00 a yard. Vendee promptly notified Vendor of the resale contracts and instructed Vendor to deliver the satin directly to Shrunk and Shriek who were retailers in the trade.

Because of a series of business misfortunes, Vendee's liquid assets became dangerously short, and Vendor became aware of this. Vendor, whose son was jilted by Vendee's daughter, maliciously and with intent to injure Vendee, failed to deliver the satin.

On the evening of September 15, Vendee demanded that if the satin were not delivered, Vendor should immediately make restitution of the $50,000 paid and begin negotiations on the issue of additional damages. Vendor replied that he would consider it "when I have time, maybe when I get back from Acapulco in February."

On September 15, the market price of satin was $8.00 a yard. Shrunk agreed with Vendee to rescind their contract and they exchanged releases. Shriek demanded immediate delivery of the satin or payment of damages. With the proceeds of a loan, Vendee was able to satisfy Shriek and other creditors. Vendee went out of business and has ulcers and hypertension proximately caused by Vendor's breach.

1. T or F   Because Vendor's breach was malicious, Vendee may recover punitive damages.

2. T or F   Because Vendor's breach was malicious, Vendee could have successfully brought an action for specific performance.

3. T or F   Vendee is not entitled to restitution of the payment because Vendee's damages remedy is adequate.

4. T or F   Vendee's general damages against Vendor are measured by the difference between contract price and the market price on September 15.

5. T or F   Vendee is not entitled to damages for the medical problems caused by the breach.

6. T or F   Because Vendor was unaware of the resale price, Vendee cannot recover for loss of profits on the resale to Shrunk.

7. T or F   Because the resale price to Shrunk was above the market price, Vendee cannot recover from Vendor his full loss of profits on the resale contract to Shrunk.

8. T or F   Assuming Shriek had sued Vendee instead of settling, Shriek would have been entitled to the difference between the contract price and the market price even if Shriek had not covered.

9. T or F   Because Vendee and Shrunk voluntarily exchanged releases, Vendee is not entitled to damages from Vendor for lost profits on the resale contract with Shrunk.

10. Essay: Edwards secured a patent on a converter for transforming black and white television sets into color television sets. The invention had worked in laboratory tests and was believed to be capable of mass production at moderate cost. Lacking funds for development, Edwards entered into an agreement with Uncas. The latter provided a substantial capital investment and received 100% of the stock and the position of President in a newly formed corporation called Colorvideo. Edwards assigned the patent to Colorvideo and received a contract to serve as general manager of the corporation for twenty-five years at a salary of $50,000 per year plus 5% of the net profits of the corporation during the life of the patent. All these arrangements were made in October 1989. It was anticipated that a plant would be built and production under way in one year. Contracts were let for construction of the plant and for the purchase of raw materials. In particular, Colorvideo contracted on October 30, 1989, with International Metals for the purchase of 10,000 linear yards of standard wire such as is generally used in electronic circuitry. International Metals was told of the use to which the wire would be put and of the fact that Colorvideo had contracted with Titanic, Inc., for delivery of 100,000 converters provided that in Titanic's sole discretion the converters would satisfactorily perform their function. In early 1990, a shortage of wire of this type developed because of explosive growth of microcomputer production. Realizing that it would be unable to meet its commitment to Colorvideo from its own plants, International Metals contracted with Japan Metals, Inc., which agreed to manufacture the wire and deliver it directly to Colorvideo.

Japan Metals failed to perform its agreement. As a result, Colorvideo, which had acquired a plant and all necessary personnel and materials, was forced to delay production for one year. Uncas, who wrongfully suspected that Colorvideo's failure to obtain the wire was due to Edwards' incompetence, fired him. Edwards decided, instead of seeking other employment, to build a home laboratory and to develop a practical water desalinization process.

(a) What remedies are available to Edwards?

(b) What is the extent of the liability of International Metals to Colorvideo?

(c) What is the extent of the liability of Japan Metals to International Metals?

*

VIII

AVOIDANCE OR REFORMATION FOR MISCONDUCT OR MISTAKE

Analysis

A. Duress
   1. What Constitutes Wrongful Conduct
      a. Violence or Threats of Violence
      b. Imprisonment or Threat of Imprisonment
      c. Wrongful Seizing or Withholding of Property,
         Including the Abuse of Liens or Attachments
      d. The Abuse of Legal Rights or the Threat Thereof
      e. Breach or Threat to Breach a Contract
   2. Coercion by a Third Person
   3. Voidable or Void?
      a. Does It Make a Difference?
      b. When Does Duress Make a Transaction Void?
B. Undue Influence
   1. What Is Undue Influence?
C. Misrepresentation
   1. Requirements
      a. Scienter Is Not a Requirement
      b. Deception
      c. Reliance
      d. Justification
      e. Injury Not Usually a Requisite

       f.   The Misrepresentation Must Be of Fact and Not Opinion or Law
       g. Promissory Fraud and Statements of Intention
       h. Non-disclosure
       i.   Misrepresentation by a Third Person
   2. Cure of a Misrepresentation
   3. Merger Clauses
   4. Election of Remedies
   5. Restoration of Status Quo Ante
   6. Fraud-in-the-Factum: A Rarity
D. Mistake
   1. Perspective
   2. Mistake of Fact Versus Mistake in Judgment
   3. Mutual Mistake
   4. Mistake Versus Uncertainty
   5. Mutual Mistake as to Injuries
   6. Mutual Mistake as to Acreage
       a. Avoidance
       b. Restitution
       c. Perspective
   7. Unilateral Palpable Mistake
   8. Unilateral Impalpable Mistake
   9. Mistake of Law
 10. Mistake in Performance
 11. Defenses to Avoidance or Recovery for Mistake
E. Reformation for Mistake, Misrepresentation or Duress
   1. Reformation for Mistake
       a. The Prior Agreement
       b. The Agreement to Reduce to Writing
       c. The Variance
   2. Reformation for Misrepresentation
   3. Reformation for Duress
   4. Reformation and the Parol Evidence Rule
   5. Defenses to Reformation
       a. Bona Fide Purchaser for Value
       b. Equitable Defenses
       c. The Effect of Negligence
F. Unconscionability
   1. Unconscionability in Equity
   2. Unconscionability at Law
   3. What Constitutes Unconscionability
       a. Unfair Surprise (Procedural Unconscionability)
       b. Oppression (Substantive Unconscionability)
       c. The Hybrid—Surprise and Oppression
   4. Judge Versus Jury
   5. The Irrelevance of Hindsight
   6. Consumer Protection
   7. Termination Clauses and Sales of Goods
   8. Limitation on Consequential Damages—Personal Injuries

G. "Duty" to Read
    1. Rule
    2. Exceptions
        a. If the Document or Particular Provision Is Not Legible
        b. If the Provision Is Placed In Such a Way That It Is Not Likely to Come to the Attention of the Other Party
        c. Fraud
        d. Mistake
        e. Unconscionability
H. Affirmance or Ratification
    1. Discussion
    2. Affirmance by Conduct
        a. Exercise of Dominion
        b. Delay
    3. The Party Avoiding Must Offer to Return Property Received

A. DURESS

Any wrongful act or threat that is the inducing cause of a contract constitutes duress and is grounds for avoiding the contract. Where the coercion involves economic pressure rather than a threat of personal injury or the like, however, duress is usually not present unless the party coerced can show that there was no reasonable alternative but to assent.

1. **WHAT CONSTITUTES WRONGFUL CONDUCT**
    a. **Violence or Threats of Violence**
        Example: A threatens B with physical injury unless B signs an acceptance of A's offer. A's threat would not coerce a person of ordinary firmness, but does induce B, who is easily susceptible to threats. The contract is voidable. A subjective test is used to determine whether B's acceptance was induced by the threat.

    b. **Imprisonment or Threat of Imprisonment**
        Examples: (1) An employer discovers that an employee has been embezzling money. The employer threatens the employee with criminal prosecution unless the employee makes restitution. The employee is induced to sign a promissory note in the amount of $5,000 payable to the employer. According to the Restatement, Second, the note is voidable. The cases, however, are in disarray and often deny contractual relief on grounds of illegality rather than duress if part of the consideration is the employer's promise not to prosecute. Even if the note is voidable, the employer's claim for restitution of the amount embezzled is not barred.

        (2) A is arrested as a result of mistaken identity. After the mistake has been ascertained, the prosecutor tells A that charges will be dismissed if A signs a release of claims for false arrest and false imprisonment. A signs. Subsequently, A sues for false arrest and false imprisonment. The release is voidable because of the implicit threat of continued wrongful imprisonment.

    c. **Wrongful Seizing or Withholding of Property, Including the Abuse of Liens or Attachments**
        A wrongful threat to detain or the wrongful detention of property of another amounts to duress if it coerces the assent of the other to an unfair transaction and the coerced party had no reasonable alternative but to assent.

Examples: (1) An attorney who has been fired by his or her client exercises a retaining lien on documents for a corporate merger and agrees to release them only on payment of an outrageous fee. Because of the urgency of the situation and because there is insufficient time to obtain judicial relief the fee is paid. The fee may be recovered to the extent it is excessive.

(2) A foreign traveller's baggage is attached in order to coerce a settlement in excess of what is owed. This is done despite the traveller having other attachable assets in the jurisdiction. The excess may be recovered if the court is convinced that the traveller had no reasonable alternative but to assent to the settlement. This illustration is based upon an old case which found duress. In today's world of international credit cards and electronic funds transfers, a factual finding that there was no reasonable alternative is more doubtful.

d. The Abuse of Legal Rights or the Threat Thereof
Rights exist to protect certain interests. At times rights are exercised or threatened to be exercised to attain ends other than for which they exist. If used for illegitimate ends, the rights are abused and a transaction coerced by such an abuse may be set aside if the coerced party was induced to consent because of such coercion. The Restatement, Second, takes the position that duress does not exist if the coerced party had any reasonable alternative; but the cases in this category seem to consider that factor as just one circumstance to determine whether coercion was the inducing cause of the consent.

Examples: (1) An employer threatens to fire an employee whose hiring is at will unless the employee sells certain shares of stock to the employer. The shares are recoverable, subject to the plaintiff's repayment.

(2) A husband threatens a custody battle on grounds of the wife's adultery unless the wife surrenders shares of stock owned by her. She surrenders them. The shares or their value are recoverable.

e. Breach or Threat to Breach a Contract
Recent cases hold that a threatened breach of contract constitutes duress if the breach would result in irreparable injury because of an absence of an adequate legal or equitable remedy or other reasonable alternative such as a substitute supplier. In addition, however, the breach or threatened breach must be a violation of the duty of good faith and fair dealing.

Example: S, a supplier of component parts to B, a radar manufacturer acting under a Navy contract, threatens not to deliver components promised under a contract except at a greatly increased price and only if it is awarded a second contract to supply similar components to B under a second government contract that has been awarded to B. No other supplier of similar components can make delivery for eight months. Failure to agree would expose B to damages for breach of its contract with the Navy and would prejudice its ability to get future government contracts. Duress exists. The excess payments can be recovered, and the second contract avoided. Note that the threat to breach unless the second contract were signed is clearly a breach of the duty of good faith and fair dealing. The threat to breach unless the price is raised is not necessarily such a breach. According to the Restatement, Second, a party may insist upon a price rise if there is economic justification for it. However, if, as in this example, the purchaser is known to be committed to a third party, under a fixed-price contract, it would seem that the threat to breach unless more money is paid is a violation of the duty of fair dealing, even if there were some economic justification for the price rise. At any rate, everyone would agree that the threat not to deliver unless the second contract was awarded is an outrageous violation of the duty of good faith and fair dealing.

Perspective: Courts will first look to see if the renegotiated contract lacks consideration, but the U.C.C. has abolished the requirement of consideration for contract modifications.

Example: D owes C a debt of $5,000 that is overdue and uncontested. C desperately needs cash. D, who knows of C's needs, offers C $4,000 in full satisfaction of the debt, threatening not to pay until a judgment is entered. C agrees and signs a release that is not under seal. C can sue for the balance under the rule of Foakes v. Beer (supra p. 156) as there is no consideration for the release. In a jurisdiction where a signed release is effective without consideration, C can avoid the release on grounds of duress if C can show there was no reasonable alternative but to sign the release.

2. COERCION BY A THIRD PERSON
If the wrongful pressure is applied by a third person, the transaction can be avoided if the other contracting party knows of the coercion, or the other party does not give value. If the other party gives value without notice of the wrongful conduct, the coerced party cannot avoid the contract.

Perspective: This is a variation upon the bona fide purchaser for value rule of property law.

3. VOIDABLE OR VOID?
a. Does It Make a Difference?
Throughout the discussion of duress we have been presupposing a valid transaction and its possible avoidance. The general run of duress cases involve voidable transactions. Just below we will point out one situation where duress renders a transaction void. There are several consequential differences between voidable and void transactions. (1) Good title to property that is acquired in a voidable transaction can be transferred to a bona fide purchaser for value. (2) A voidable transaction can be ratified.

b. When Does Duress Make a Transaction Void?
A transaction is void if it is in no sense the consensual act of the party. A contract signed because a shotgun is pointed at one's head is consented to if one has a general idea of what one is signing. The contract is voidable. If one does not have any idea of the contents of the writing, one is in no sense consenting. The document is void. These cases are rare, if they exist at all.

Perspective: Compare the rule concerning fraud-in-the-factum p. 343 infra.

B. UNDUE INFLUENCE

1. WHAT IS UNDUE INFLUENCE?
The gist of undue influence is unfair *persuasion* rather than coercion. Persuasion is unfair in two classes of cases. First, where a person uses a position of *trust and confidence* to convince the other to enter into a transaction that is not in the best interests of the party who is the subject of the persuasion. Second, it is also unfair where a person uses a *position of dominance* to influence a transaction against the best interests of the subservient party. The foremost indicator of undue influence is an unnatural transaction resulting in the enrichment of one of the parties at the expense of the other.

Examples: (1) Plaintiff, an elderly and financially inexperienced housemaid, inherited a good deal of money and property. Harold and Faye, an elderly couple experienced in business, promised her a home with them for life if she would advance them money for the construction of a motel to be repaid without interest. She relied totally on Harold, advancing him money without keeping records or even recollection of the amounts. She was forced to leave because of conflicts with Faye. Thereafter she entered into a settlement agreement relying on Harold's figures as to the amount he had received. These figures considerably understated the amounts received. The settlement was set aside. Plaintiff's trust and confidence in Harold was total. He exerted his influence in a manner inconsistent with her interests and enriched himself. She is entitled to an accounting and an equitable lien on the premises.

(2) Confidential relations include cases such as example (1), but typically involve husband-wife, parent-child, trustee-beneficiary, guardian-ward, attorney-client, administrator-legatee, physician-patient, clergyman-parishioner, and fiance-fiancee.

(3) *A* is old, infirm, and bedridden and lives in the home of *B*, one of his children. *B* threatens to cease supporting and caring for *A* unless *A* deeds his real property to *B*. *A* does so and soon thereafter dies. *A*'s estate may successfully sue to set aside the deed unless it can be shown that the value of the property is not greatly in excess of the value of the services. Note that, in addition to the confidential relationship of parent-child, *B* was in a position of dominance.

C. MISREPRESENTATION

If a misrepresentation constitutes an actionable tort, avoidance is allowed, but all of the elements of tortious misrepresentation are not required for avoidance.

1. REQUIREMENTS
a. Scienter Is Not a Requirement

A misrepresentation is an assertion that is not in accord with existing facts. Avoidance may be based on a negligent or even an innocent misrepresentation. However, an *intentional* misrepresentation *need not be material,* while an *unintentional* misrepresentation *must be material.* A representation is material if (a) it would influence the conduct of a reasonable person or (b) the person using the words knows that it would likely influence the conduct of the other party even if it might not influence a reasonable person. *Rationale:* If the misrepresentation is intentional, the wrongdoer has accomplished his or her intended purpose even if the statement was immaterial whereas one who innocently or carelessly misstates a seemingly unimportant fact has no reason to know that the statement will cause action.

Example: *V,* a seller of farmland, tells *P,* a prospective purchaser, that the land was once the site of the principal lodge of the Delaware Indians. *V* had been told this story in his youth and believed it to be true, but it is false. The representation is not material to the reasonable purchaser and will not give grounds for avoidance unless V is aware of any special influence this story might have upon P's decision to contract to purchase at the price P did. If V was aware of the inaccuracy of the statement or knew that the story was of dubious veracity, P could avoid the contract of purchase provided the other elements of avoidance (deception, reliance and justification) are made out.

b. Deception
The party must have been deceived. If the party did not believe the representation, it cannot later be used as a basis for avoidance.

c. Reliance
The party must have relied upon the representation in the sense that the party regarded the representation as an important fact and that it influenced the decision to enter into the contract.

d. Justification
The old idea that a party could not avoid a contract for fraud unless there was a "right to rely" has largely been superseded by the idea that avoidance will be allowed even "to the simple and credulous." The law is in flux on the question, but if the representation is purely factual (as opposed to a representation of fact and opinion or fact and intention) the modern law regards reliance as justified in almost every case. A party is justified in relying even if the party is negligent in investigating the facts or in not investigating the facts.

Example: V advertised certain real property for sale. V described it as having 580 feet of road frontage and that an engineering report showed that the land had a gravel content of 80,000 cubic yards. V believed these representations, both of which were based on representations made to V by the prior owner. P, relying on the advertised facts, purchased and subsequently sought to avoid the purchase after discovering that the gravel bed was exhausted after 6,000 cubic yards were removed and that the road frontage was only 415 feet. V was successful in this action to avoid the purchase despite the fact that, prior to purchasing, V did not have the land surveyed and did not check out the engineering report. The court points out that the misrepresentations, although innocent, were material. As in sale of goods cases, the rule of caveat emptor is dead. Even a negligent purchaser need not offer justification for relying on the seller's statements of fact.

e.   Injury Not Usually a Requisite
Even if a party gets something as valuable as, or more valuable than, the performance promised, a party may avoid the contract. The rationale is that the party's autonomy has been tinkered with when given false information that prevents the exercise of the party's own best judgment.

> *Example:*   *B*, negotiating a purchase of a fur coat for his lady friend, told the seller, *S*, that he would pay no more than $4,000 for a particular coat. The lady friend secretly told *S* she would pay the balance of *S*'s $5,000 asking price. *S* then told *B* that he could have the coat for $4,000, and an agreement was reached with *B* for the sale at that price. The lady friend made the secret payment of the balance. *B* was permitted to avoid the sale despite the fact that *B* received a $5,000 coat for only $4,000 out of his pocket.

> *Exception:*   Most cases hold that where a purchaser of land misrepresents the purpose for which the purchase is being made, avoidance is not permitted unless the seller owned adjacent land the value of which will decrease because of the intended use.

> *Example:*   Purchaser buys a farm at fair market value, representing the intention to farm it. Instead the purchaser is acting on behalf of a power company that is assembling a site for a power plant. Seller is upset because had the seller known the facts, a much higher price could have been obtained. Avoidance will not be permitted.

f.   The Misrepresentation Must Be of Fact and Not Opinion or Law
A party is not justified in relying on a statement merely of opinion such as "buy an umbrella today; tomorrow it's likely to rain." Nonetheless, many statements of opinion also imply a factual assertion. "It's uncomfortably hot and muggy today," expresses an opinion but does imply certain facts about the temperature and humidity. An assertion of law is sometimes a statement of fact; e.g., "Iowa has adopted the U.C.C.," but more usually is a statement of opinion, as when the person making an assertion prognosticates how the Iowa courts will solve a "battle of the forms" case. Although one may not rely on what is merely an opinion, one may rely on the implied facts contained in an opinion if it is reasonable to do so. The following are categories of cases in which such reasonableness is likely to exist. In each case it is assumed that the other elements of avoidance (deception, reliance and justification) exist.

(1) *The Representor Is or Claims to Be an Expert.*

Example: "This car is in excellent condition," spoken by an auto dealer is a representation of fact. When spoken by a non-expert owner, it is not, unless it falls into category (iv) below.

(2) *The Representor Has Superior Access to the Facts Upon Which the Opinion Is Based.*

Examples: (1) "This is an original engraving by Paul Revere and has been in our family since 1770." Normally a statement of authorship of an antique work of art is treated as a statement of opinion. In this case, however, the opinion is ostensibly based upon family tradition and is a factual representation.

(2) A franchisor of a chicken raising system advertises that the franchise would "return to the careful broiler raiser an income roughly equal to half as much as is obtained on an average size farm in the midwest—and it will do so for about 6 hours of one person's attention daily." The statement is treated as a representation of fact because the franchisor quite clearly has unique access to facts upon which it is based. Note also that this case fits under the expertise category as well.

(3) *There Is a Relationship of Trust and Confidence Between the Parties.*

Example: *A*, who has been *B*'s trusted advisor in financial matters, offers to buy Blackacre from *B* for $100,000, stating, "in my opinion that is a fair price." *B* accepts the offer without making any inquiry as to Blackacre's value. *A* soon thereafter resells Blackacre for $150,000. Statements of value are at the very core of the opinion rule and are generally *not* treated as representations, but in this instance, because of the relationship of the parties, *B* is justified in relying upon *A*'s statement of value. Alternatively, this could be viewed as a case of undue influence.

(4) *The Opinion Intentionally Varies Radically From Reality.*

Examples: (1) *S*, the owner of a car, has recently had major unrepaired difficulties with his transmission and clutch. *S* tells *B*, a prospective purchaser, that the car is in A–1 condition. *B*, who is deceived, makes the purchase. *S*'s statement clearly varies radically from reality. It is intentional. It is treated as a misrepresentation. Consequently, *B* can avoid the sale.

(2) Plaintiff, an elderly widow seeking new interests in life, enrolled in defendant's school for ballroom dancing lessons. Although she had no dance aptitude and little sense of rhythm, she was repeatedly the target of "a constant and continuous barrage of flattery, false praise, excessive compliments, and panegyric encomiums" inducing her to enter into a number of contracts for an aggregate of 2,302 hours for lessons for a cash outlay of $31,000 (1961 dollars). The court indicates she is entitled to avoid the contracts. Note that this case smacks also of undue influence.

(5) *The Representation Is of the Law of Another Jurisdiction.* If the person making an assertion of law is a lawyer, that assertion can be treated as a factual representation under the expertise category. If the representor is not an attorney, the assertion is treated as merely an opinion unless the case falls under a different exceptional category. If, however, the assertion, whether or not made by a lawyer, relates to a law of another jurisdiction, it is treated as a representation of fact.

g. **Promissory Fraud and Statements of Intention**
The making of a promise without an intention to carry it out is a misrepresentation of fact, as is a statement of intention when one has no intention to carry it out.

(1) *Discussion.* "The state of a man's mind is as much a fact as the state of his digestion." Consequently, if the promisor does not intend to carry out the promise the promisor is lying. Similarly, a non-promissory statement of intention is a representation.

Example: A developer of tract housing tells a prospective purchaser of a house in the tract that the development company intends to install tennis courts and a golf course nearby. The company has no such intention. The developer has made an intentional misrepresentation. If the other elements (deception, reliance, and justification) are present, the purchaser may avoid the contract of sale. The same result is reached if the contract expressly promised that such sports facilities would be installed and it can be proved that there was no intent to carry it out.

(2) *Where Promise Is Unenforceable.* There is no consensus whether the promissory fraud rule can be applied to a promise that is void or unenforceable on grounds of lack of consideration, the parol evidence

rule, the Statute of Frauds, etc. Some courts have refused to apply the rule to such promises on the belief that such application would subvert the rules with respect to the validity and enforceability of promises. Many courts and the Restatement, Second, take the view that the promissory fraud doctrine does apply to such cases. In other words, if a contracting party makes a promise that cannot be enforced because it is barred by the parol evidence rule and does not intend to keep the promise, the contract can be avoided for misrepresentation.

(3) *Mere Non–Performance Does Not Prove Misrepresentation.* It is important to note that mere non-performance of a promise does not prove that the promisor never intended to perform. It must be proved that there was a lack of intent to perform at the time of promising.

h. Non-disclosure

We start with a general rule that there is no duty to disclose facts that would tend to discourage the other party from entering into a proposed deal. This general rule is being eroded by a group of exceptions.

Exceptions:

(1) *Statutory disclosure rules, such as S.E.C., Truth-in-Lending, etc.*

(2) *Concealment (Positive Action to Hide) Is the Equivalent of a Misrepresentation.*

Example: Prior to offering a machine for sale, the owner paints over a crack on the engine block. This is a misrepresentation of fact, and if the other elements (deception and reliance) are present, the purchaser, can avoid the contract.

(3) *Where Partial Disclosure Is Misleading.* In the law, silence is better than a half-truth. A truthful statement that omits important qualifying facts is a misrepresentation.

Examples: (1) *A,* a hospital, offers *B,* who is in the Phillipines, a position in Oregon. *B* is aware that the hiring is at will, but is unaware that the Board of Trustees has before it a proposal to abolish the position. Upon arrival in Oregon, *B* is told that the position has been abolished. *B* has a tort action for deceit because of the non-disclosure of the full facts. Whenever there is a right of action for deceit, there is alternatively a right to avoid the contract.

(2) *A* reads to *B* a proposed contract, omitting certain material clauses. *B* assents and signs the document. *B* can avoid the contract even though *B* was negligent in not reading it. Note that if *A* had read none of the contract to *B*, *B* would be bound under the "duty to read" concept and would have no power of avoidance.

(4) *Changing Circumstances and New Information.* *S* makes a true assertion, but changing circumstances cause the assertion to no longer be true. *S* has a duty to inform the other of the change. Similarly, if *S* honestly but incorrectly makes an assertion and discovers the error, what had been an innocent misrepresentation has now become intentional.

(5) *Where a Party Becomes Aware That the Other Is Operating Under a Mistake as to a Vital Fact.* This rule is similar to and, to a large extent, coextensive with the doctrine of unilateral palpable mistake. See p. 346 infra. The duty to disclose does not run to all kinds of vital facts. Certainly, there is a duty to disclose latent defects such as termite infestation where the seller knows that the buyer is unaware of such infestation. On the other hand, a party need not disclose superior information about market trends. The ethics of the community are the ultimate resource to determine where to draw the line. The rule requiring disclosure is but an emanation of the obligation of good faith and fair dealing. The Restatement, Second, points this out in the two illustrations given below.

Examples: (1) *P* learns from published government surveys that *V*'s land contains valuable minerals and knows that *V* does not know this. *P* offers to purchase the land without disclosing this information. *V* accepts. The contract is not voidable because *P*'s conduct is not a breach of the obligation to act in good faith. The discretionary remedy of specific performance may, however, be denied. See p. 351 infra.

(2) *P* learns of the valuable mineral deposits on *V*'s land by trespassing. *P*'s failure to disclose is the equivalent of a representation that the land contains no valuable mineral deposits. The contract is voidable if the other elements (deception, reliance, justification) for avoidance are present.

(6) *Where There Is a Confidential Relation.* Where there is a confidential relationship (e.g., husband and wife, mother and son, priest and penitent, etc.) that falls short of a fiduciary relationship, there is nevertheless a duty to disclose all *material facts* that bear on the transaction. This duty is not limited to vital facts and includes the

disclosure of publicly available information as well as privately obtained information about market trends and land values that bear on the transaction. Compare this rule with the last two examples above and with the doctrine of undue influence (pp. 333–334 supra).

(7) *Where There Is a Fiduciary Relation.* If the relationship is a fiduciary one in the strict sense (trustee-beneficiary, attorney-client, executor-beneficiary), the duty of disclosure is more stringent than in a confidential relation. Fiduciaries must reveal all relevant facts that they know or *should know.* Beneficiaries must be aware of their legal rights. Even if these requirements are met, the transaction can be avoided if it is not on fair terms.

(8) *Suretyship, Marine Insurance, Partnership and Joint Ventures.* In each of these kinds of contracts, broad disclosure rules have been laid down by the courts. These rules are generally akin to those governing *confidential relationships.*

(9) *Where Specific Performance Is Sought.* Where the remedy sought is specific performance, relief will be denied because of non-disclosure of material facts even if there is no special relationship between the parties.

Non–Disclosure in Perspective: In sale of goods cases, non-disclosure by a seller is often irrelevant because, unless warranties have been excluded, relief can be had on an implied warranty.

i. Misrepresentation by a Third Person

If a misrepresentation is made by an agent of a party acting within the scope of the agency, the party is chargeable as if the party had made the statement. If a party, prior to contracting, has received false or otherwise incorrect information from a third person who is *not* an agent of the other party, that party cannot avoid a contract induced by this information unless the other party learned of the misrepresentation prior to contracting. This is a variant of the bona fide purchaser for value principle.

2. CURE OF A MISREPRESENTATION

If after a misrepresentation is made but before the deceived party has avoided the contract, the facts are brought into line with the representation, the contract is no longer voidable.

Example: V, seeking to induce P to purchase V's land, falsely informs P that the land is zoned for light industrial use. V knows that this is incorrect but a proposed change is pending. P contracts to purchase the land. Before P learns of the deception, the zoning ordinance is changed so that the land is now zoned for light industrial use. The contract is no longer voidable by *P*.

3. MERGER CLAUSES

Despite a "merger" clause, or a "there are no representations" clause, parol evidence is admissible to show that a misrepresentation was made. An "as is" clause excludes warranties, but does not exclude evidence of representations.

Rationale: It will be remembered that the parol evidence rule does not exclude evidence tending to show that a contract is void or voidable.

4. ELECTION OF REMEDIES

If the misrepresentation and ensuing deception, reliance and injury constitute a tort, the deceived party must elect between either a tort action or the exercise of the power of avoidance followed by a restitutionary action.

Exception: Under the U.C.C., both remedies are available but items of recovery cannot be duplicated.

Example: *S* sold a horse to *P*, representing it to be a stallion although *S* knew it to be a gelding. Before discovering the deception, *P* incurred costs for caring and feeding the horse. Upon discovering the deception and in the absence of a statute, *P* may offer to *return the gelding*, avoid the contract and sue for return of the purchase price; thereby forgoing the ability to recover other expenses. Alternatively, *P* could sue for breach of warranty but must *keep the gelding* and recover the difference between the value of the horse as warranted and its actual value plus consequential damages. A third possibility is an action for deceit. This requires *P* to *keep the gelding* and obtain tort damages. Under the U.C.C., *P* need not choose among these three options but may pursue all three. *P* may return the horse, get restitution of the purchase price, and collect damages as well. Thus, *P* should end up with the purchase price, the costs of care and feeding, and the additional cost of obtaining a stallion of the kind represented minus the value (if any) of the use of the horse. Remember, however, that the common law still governs if the contract is not for the sale of goods.

5. RESTORATION OF STATUS QUO ANTE

Where restitution is sought at law in a quasi-contractual action, the plaintiff must, before suing, offer to restore any tangible benefits received under the contract. Plaintiff need not have done so if what has been received has perished because of its defects, is worthless, or consists of money that may be offset. However, in an equitable action no prior offer to restore is required, but the equitable decree can be conditioned upon such restoration. An equity action is available if something other than, or in addition to, a money judgment is sought; e.g., cancellation of a deed.

6. FRAUD–IN–THE–FACTUM: A RARITY

Where a party signs a document that is radically different from that which the party was led to believe was being signed and the circumstances are such that a reasonable person similarly situated would have signed it, the document is void.

Discussion: In almost all cases of legally cognizable misrepresentation, the contract, at most, is voidable. The kind of misrepresentation discussed up to this point has been called "fraud in the inducement." In rare cases, fraud renders a transaction void. This is quaintly known as "fraud-in-the-factum" (or execution). The chief consequence of this kind of fraud is that a bona fide purchaser for value from the fraud-feasor does not take good title. In the usual case of fraud, (fraud in the inducement), a bona fide purchase for value from a fraud-feasor acquires good title.

Example: A husband asks his wife to sign a document and represents to her that the document is a property division solely for the purpose of saving on income taxes. She has habitually trusted him in all financial affairs. She signs, without reading, what purports to be a separation agreement. The agreement is void.

Perspective: Compare the case where duress makes a contract void rather than voidable (p. 333 supra).

D. MISTAKE

1. PERSPECTIVE

Certain kinds of mistakes may prevent the formation of contracts. These include misunderstandings (See p. 203 supra) and mistakes in transmission (See p. 112 supra). Here, however, the discussion centers on mistake as a ground for avoiding a transaction.

2. MISTAKE OF FACT VERSUS MISTAKE IN JUDGMENT

For avoidance the mistakes must relate to a basic assumption as to *vital existing facts*. Risks as to *changing facts* are governed by the rules of *impracticability* and *frustration*. Risks of mistakes in *judgment* are quintessential contractual risks from which the court will not relieve a party. These include, for example, risks regarding the profitability of a stock purchase or the number of labor hours required to complete a task.

3. MUTUAL MISTAKE

Where the parties are mistaken about a basic assumption upon which they base their bargain, the transaction can be avoided. However, it can only be avoided if a substantially different exchange of values occurs because of the mistake, and the risk of the mistake is not otherwise allocated by agreement of the parties or by the court because such other allocation is reasonable.

Examples: (1) A pregnant cow of excellent breeding stock is mistakenly believed by both parties to be sterile and is sold at a price far below what she otherwise would bring. The sale can be avoided because "A barren cow is substantially a different creature than a breeding cow. There is as much difference between them as there is between an ox and a cow." This case treated the facts as a mistake of subject matter.

(2) A charity and a landowner work out a transaction whereby it is believed that the landowner will be able to receive a large charitable deduction. But for the deduction the transaction would be of no interest to the owner, and both parties know this. Existing regulations barred charitable deductions of this kind. The transaction may be avoided. Notice that the vital fact about which they had a mistaken assumption does *not* relate to the identity or quality of the subject matter. Older cases insisted that the mistake had to relate to the subject matter, as in example (1).

(3) *A*, a 55 year old man, purchases an annuity contract from *B*, an insurance company, whereby *B* is to pay a fixed sum monthly to *A* for life. At the time of contracting, unknown to *A* and undetected by a medical examination required by *B*, *A* has a terminal illness that causes death six months later. Before dying, *A* purports to avoid the contract. The transaction cannot be avoided. Despite the existence of a mutual mistake as to a vital fact, the court will determine that it is reasonable that *A* assume the risk of mistake. Both parties to an annuity contract should understand that it is an aleatory contract; that is, a contract of hazard.

4. MISTAKE VERSUS UNCERTAINTY

Where the parties are uncertain or consciously ignorant of a vital fact there is no right of avoidance.

Example: A woman found a stone that appeared to be a gem. She took it to a jeweller who honestly stated his ignorance of its nature and offered her $1 for the stone. She agreed and made the sale. The stone was an uncut diamond worth $700. Avoidance was not permitted because the parties were uncertain rather than mistaken.

5. **MUTUAL MISTAKE AS TO INJURIES**
    The orthodox view is that a release of a personal injury claim can be avoided if there are unknown injuries but not if there are unforeseen consequences of known injuries.

    Discussion: Diagnosis is distinguished from prognosis. However, some jurisdictions allow avoidance if there is a vital mistake as to the nature and effect of known injuries also.

    Example: Plaintiff suffers a blow to the head in an automobile collision. The injury appears slight. Plaintiff releases the claim against the negligent driver for $100. Subsequently, it appears that serious permanent injuries were caused by a blood clot on the brain that resulted from the blow. Even under the stricter view, plaintiff may set aside the release. Knowledge of a blow to the head is not knowledge of injury to the brain.

6. **MUTUAL MISTAKE AS TO ACREAGE**
    a. **Avoidance**
        If the number of acres contracted to be conveyed or actually conveyed are discovered to be materially different from what the parties believed, the aggrieved party may avoid the contract or conveyance. Avoidance is permitted whether the sale is on a per acre basis or in gross.

    b. **Restitution**
        If the contract or conveyance is on a per acre basis, the purchaser may have restitution of the purchase price for any shortage of acres. The seller has a restitution action for payment for additional acres. If the purchaser has not paid, the remedy is an abatement in price rather than restitution.

        Discussion: If a sale is in gross, the only available remedy is avoidance. If the sale is on a per acre basis, the aggrieved party may have restitution (or abatement) as an alternative to avoidance. However, in a per acre sale, the discrepancy is not always material. In such a case only restitution (or abatement) is available.

        Examples: (1) *V* contracts to sell a farm to *P*. The price is calculated on the basis of $3,000 an acre. The acreage is assumed to be 220 acres because a property description prepared for *V*'s ancestor so states. After paying the price, receiving a deed of conveyance, and taking possession, *P* orders the land surveyed. The survey reveals that the land contains 190 acres. Because there was a mutual mistake as to quantity, and the price was set on a per acre basis, *P* can obtain restitution of $3,000 for each "missing" acre. Because the discrepancy is large enough to be deemed material, *P*, alternatively, can avoid the deed and obtain restitution of the entire purchase price.

(2) *V* advertised the XYZ ranch for sale for $250,000, describing it as containing 900 acres, a grazing permit on federal land, and some horses and equipment. Some of the land was nearly worthless. *P* contracted to purchase the ranch for $250,000 after *V* agreed to throw in additional equipment. *P* had the land surveyed. The survey showed a deficiency of 70 acres. *P* demanded an abatement for the deficiency. When *V* refused, *P* purported to avoid the contract. *P* sues for restitution of the down payment, and *V* sues for damages. *V* receives judgment for damages. The sale is *not* on a per acre basis since it includes goods and a grazing permit on other land. In addition, the land was of uneven quality, some acres being worth much less than the rest. Consequently, *P* is not entitled to a reduction in price. The less than 10% deficiency in area is not deemed material enough to justify avoiding the contract. *P*'s unjustified attempt to avoid the contract is a repudiation.

c.   Perspective

These cases are treated under mistake despite the fact that the vendor has made a misrepresentation of fact. The reasons are historical.

7.   UNILATERAL PALPABLE MISTAKE

A mistake by one party of which the other is, or ought to be, aware is grounds for avoidance. Cases of this kind are sometimes treated, with the same result, as cases of fraudulent non-disclosure. (See p. 340 supra).

8.   UNILATERAL IMPALPABLE MISTAKE

Avoidance is allowed for unilateral impalpable mistake if (a) the mistake if computational, clerical or something of that sort rather than a mistake in judgment, (b) enforcement of the contract would be oppressive, resulting in an unconscionably unequal exchange of values and (c) avoidance would impose no substantial hardship on the other.

Example: A construction company enters its bid for constructing a building, making a computational error that would result in doing the job at a substantial loss. It discovers its mistake the day its bid is accepted. It may avoid the contract, but the result would be different if the mistake were not vital or if the discovery of the mistake came significantly later so as to prejudice the other party. Note that loss of the expectancy engendered by a favorably low bid is not deemed prejudicial for purposes of this rule.

9. MISTAKE OF LAW

The orthodox view is that a mistake of law (except for mistake of the law of another jurisdiction) is not grounds for avoidance, but the modern trend and the Restatements take the position that relief will not be denied merely because the mistake is one of law. However, mistake of law is not, in all respects, treated as mistake of fact. If the mistake relates to something other than the legal consequences of words or conduct, the mistake, if vital, may be grounds for avoidance. Generally, a person is bound by the legal consequences of his or her acts such as making an offer, an acceptance, a waiver etc., whether or not the person knows the legal consequences of the act.

Examples: (1) *V* contracts to sell a parcel of land to *P*, who intends to construct a health club on the premises, and *V* knows this. Both parties think this is a lawful use of the land. However, several days before contracting, the zoning ordinance is amended to prohibit such use. Because of the revision of the ordinance, the market value of the land is substantially diminished. The contract is voidable by *P* for mutual mistake.

(2) *S* contracts to sell goods to be delivered to *B* on January 2. *S* tenders delivery on January 3 when the market price has fallen well below the contract price. *B*, in total ignorance of the perfect tender rule, accepts delivery. This act of acceptance cannot be avoided.

10. MISTAKE IN PERFORMANCE

Recovery may be had for payments, overpayments, deliveries of returnable goods, and conveyances of excessive land made in the mistaken belief that the performance was owed under a contract with another, even if the mistake is negligent and unilateral, but there must be a mistake rather than uncertainty.

Examples: (1) An insured under a life insurance policy disappears under circumstances that make it probable but not certain that the insured perished. The policy amount is paid to the beneficiary. The insured is later found alive suffering from amnesia. The payment cannot be recovered because there was conscious uncertainty rather than mistake. The result would be different if a corpse had mistakenly been identified as the insured; the parties would have been certain, but mistaken.

(2) A commercial tenant because of its own computer programming error pays rent twice a month rather than monthly and does so for two years. The excess payments may be recovered.

Exception: If the parties who mistakenly pay have a moral obligation to do so, restitution is not allowed.

Example: *X* pays money to *Y* although, unknown to *X, Y*'s claim is unenforceable or barred by the statute of limitations. The payment may not be recovered.

Perspective: The rule stated for mistake in performance refers to money, returnable goods and land but makes no reference to services. Services rendered by mistake cannot be returned. Consequently, there is no duty to pay for such services.

11. DEFENSES TO AVOIDANCE OR RECOVERY FOR MISTAKE
1. Change of position.

A contract cannot be avoided or the value of a performance recovered for mistake if the other party has detrimentally changed position in reliance upon the contract or performance.

Example: Defendant asks plaintiff broker to sell defendant's shares of XYZ Company. The broker mistakenly assumes the shares to be of XYZ Co. of America, a valuable listed security. Instead the shares are of XYZ of Colorado, an unlisted security of little value. Because of the mistake, the defendant is paid $30,000 in excess of the value of the shares and uses the sum to pay off a mortgage loan on defendant's house. The plaintiff can recover the money. Paying off the mortgage or keeping the money in a bank equally enrich the defendant unjustly. Consequently, the change of position is not detrimental.

2. Affirmance of the transaction after discovery of the mistake. (See p. 356 infra.)

3. Failure to avoid the contract with reasonable promptness after discovery of the mistake. (See p. 357 infra.)

E. REFORMATION FOR MISTAKE, MISREPRESENTATION OR DURESS

1. REFORMATION FOR MISTAKE
Reformation of a writing for mistake is available if three requisites are met. (1) There must have been a prior agreement. (2) There must have been an agreement to put the agreement in writing. (3) Because of a mistake, there is a variance between the prior agreement and the writing.

a. The Prior Agreement

The prior agreement may have been oral or written. An indefinite or tentative agreement suffices. If by error, rather than by modification, clauses earlier agreed upon are misstated or omitted, the writing may be reformed.

b. The Agreement to Reduce to Writing

Reformation is not available if the parties intentionally omit or misstate a term. If *one party,* without the consent of the other, intentionally omits a term that has been agreed upon, reformation is available on grounds of misrepresentation.

c. The Variance

Frequently the variance is an arithmetical error. Sometimes it is a misdescription of the subject matter, as a typist's error in a metes and bounds description of real property. At times, the parties mistake the legal effect of their writing. Reformation is available in each of these circumstances.

Examples: (1) *V* agrees to sell Blackacre to *P.* It is agreed that *V* can remove a mill, but *V* fails to tell *V*'s lawyer about the mill agreement. *V*'s lawyer prepares a deed conveying Blackacre and "all improvements" thereon. *V* signs without reading the document or, alternatively, reads but does not comprehend that the legal effect is to transfer the mill. Under either alternative, *V* can obtain reformation.

(2) *A* contacts an insurance company (*I*) and asks about "term" life insurance and is quoted accurate rates for "term" insurance and agrees to purchase a "term" policy. *I*'s secretary mistakenly takes a form for a "whole life" policy, types *A*'s name and beneficiaries thereon as well as the term insurance premium. A whole life policy is far more expensive than term insurance and builds up a cash value while a "term" policy does not. *I*'s agent delivers the policy to *A.* Some years later *A* asks *I* for the cash value of the policy. *I* can obtain reformation of the policy.

(3) *V* contracts to convey Blackacre to *P.* Blackacre is agricultural land consisting of 100 acres and the going rate for farm acreage in this vicinity is $3,000. The contract price is $300,000. Neither party is aware that the land is zoned for industrial use making it worth $900,000. Reformation is *not* permitted because the mistake does not go to the transcription of their agreement. The mistake may be grounds for avoidance unless the court allocates the risk to *V.*

2. REFORMATION FOR MISREPRESENTATION
If one party misrepresents the content or legal effect of a writing to the other, the other may elect to avoid the contract or to have it reformed to express what was represented.

> *Example:* C, a construction company, bargains for the right to deposit demolition waste on O's land. They reach agreement whereby permission is granted in exchange for a sum of money. In addition, C promises O that before depositing the waste, the topsoil will be removed and then replaced onto the waste. C prepares a writing, representing to O that it contains their entire agreement. The promise with respect to the topsoil removal and replacement is not contained in the writing. O signs the writing without reading it. The writing may be reformed. Alternatively, as the misrepresentation goes to a vital existing fact—the contents of the writing as to a material term—O may avoid the contract.

3. REFORMATION FOR DURESS
Cases of reformation for duress are few. The remedy requires that (1) there is a binding contract preliminary to entering into a more formal contract; (2) one party is coerced into agreeing to a more formal contract that is at variance with the original agreement.

> *Example:* B, a bank, makes a binding commitment to A to provide specified financing at 12% interest to be secured by a mortgage loan on premises A has contracted to purchase. On the day prior to the date set for closing the bank informs A that the loan will not be made unless A signs a bond and mortgage calling for 15% interest. Because of the surrounding circumstances, A has no reasonable alternative but to yield. A's suit for reformation will be successful.

4. REFORMATION AND THE PAROL EVIDENCE RULE
The parol evidence rule is inapplicable in an action for reformation. However, a decree for reformation must be based on "clear and convincing" evidence, a higher standard than is normally required in a civil suit.

5. DEFENSES TO REFORMATION
a. Bona Fide Purchaser for Value
Reformation will not be granted if the effect of the decree would infringe on the rights of a bona fide purchaser for value or other third persons who have justifiably relied upon the document as written.

b. Equitable Defenses

Reformation is an equitable action. Consequently, it is subject to equitable defenses such as unclean hands and laches. (See p. 318 supra.) A decree for reformation may be withheld in the sound discretion of the court.

c. The Effect of Negligence

Negligence is no bar to reformation. Refer back to the previous examples. In a number of them the plaintiff committed multiple acts of carelessness. It is important to note, however, that reformation is not available if one party carelessly believes that a writing will contain a particular provision. Unless this belief was shared or induced by the other, no proper case of reformation is made out. This is not because of negligence. Rather, it is because the writing is not at variance with the agreement.

F. UNCONSCIONABILITY

1. UNCONSCIONABILITY IN EQUITY

For centuries, equity has refused to grant specific performance of contracts that were unconscionably obtained or unconscionable in content. Such decisions do not necessarily invalidate contracts but leave the parties to their legal remedies.

Example: V had an oil lease on federal land with one poorly producing well on it. P, by checking public records ascertained that oil in large amounts had recently been found in the vicinity of V's leasehold. V was unaware of these recent discoveries. P telephoned V and asked him if he would sell the lease. V said yes, stating that his price was $5,000. The parties executed a document giving P, in exchange for $100, a 90 day option to purchase an assignment of the leasehold for $5,000. In light of the recent discoveries, this was considerably less than the value of the leasehold. P exercised the option, but V repudiated. Specific performance is denied. Equity *does* consider the adequacy of the consideration. Note that the price was set by V. The information possessed by P was publicly available. Nonetheless, the imbalance between price and value is deemed unconscionable especially in view of P's non-disclosure.

2. UNCONSCIONABILITY AT LAW

Since enactment of the U.C.C. § 2–302, courts in sales cases and in non-sales cases have exercised the power to strike down or limit contracts or contract clauses on grounds of unconscionability. Prior to enactment of the U.C.C., courts sometimes reached similar results by indirection, particularly by spurious interpretation.

3. WHAT CONSTITUTES UNCONSCIONABILITY

The Code comments indicate that there are two kinds of unconscionability. First, "unfair surprise," termed by some as "procedural" unconscionability. Second, "oppression," termed by some as "substantive" unconscionability.

a. Unfair Surprise (Procedural Unconscionability)

A burdensome clause that does not come to the attention of a party adhering to a contract will be struck down if a reasonable person would not expect to find it in the contract and the reason it was not noticed was its burial in small print, or the inability of the adhering party to comprehend the language.

Examples: (1) *A* checks a coat in a hotel checkroom and is given a plastic token that bears an identification number. On the reverse is language purporting to limit the hotel's liability to $25. The limitation of liability is ineffective unless it can be shown that *A* was aware of the language on the token. Traditionally, this result has been based on lack of mutual assent. This result is correct, because normally *A* would have no reason to know that contractual terms had been proposed. Today, similar analysis is applied to specific clauses in what a party understands to be a contract. Although a party may have given blanket assent to a contract by signing it, the party can be relieved from the burden of one-sided clauses that one would not reasonably expect to be in the contract.

(2) A franchise agreement between a petroleum company and a filling station operator contains a clause whereby the latter agrees to indemnify the petroleum company against liability for the negligence of the petroleum company's employees on the premises. An employee of the company negligently loses control of a tank truck hose while filling the filling station's tank, spraying the operator and others. The indemnity provision is unexpected and constitutes "unfair surprise" because of the shift of the normal risks. The court rules that, unless the operator is made aware of the provision and actually assents to it, it is invalid. The provision, although perhaps one-sided, is not necessarily oppressive. If the operator was aware of the clause, perhaps the risk could have been insured against.

b. Oppression (Substantive Unconscionability)

Provisions of a contract that are assented to but are grossly one-sided may be voided or modified by the court. A contract that suffers from total overall imbalance; that is, one that is grossly one-sided, may be voided.

Examples: (1) A poor non-English speaking consumer promises to pay $1,145 for a $348 appliance. The court limits recovery to a reasonable price.

(2) A homeowner agrees to pay $2,500 for home improvements worth $1,000. Little work is done before the homeowner repudiates. The court permits no recovery by the contractor.

c. The Hybrid—Surprise and Oppression

Analytically, the surprise and oppression cases can be distinguished. However, where unconscionability has been found, the facts generally contain a mixture of lack of knowledgeable assent and a clause or contract that unduly benefits the party who has drafted the contract.

Example: *B*, a welfare mother of limited education, has purchased furniture on the installment plan from *S*. While still indebted to *S*, she purchases a stereo set on credit. The purchase agreement provides: "all payments now and hereafter made by *B* shall be credited pro rata on all outstanding leases, bills and accounts due *S* at the time each such payment is made." The effect of this "cross-collateral clause" is to give *S* a security interest in all the goods sold by *S* to *B* until her debt is reduced to zero. *B* defaulted, and *S* moves to replevy all the goods ever sold to *B* by *S*. Replevin denied. The clause is "procedurally" suspect because it is not readily comprehensible, even to a college graduate. Moreover, it is substantively suspect because the cross-collateral clause is, or may be, unreasonably favorable to *S*. This combination has led at least one court to rule that unconscionability exists.

4. JUDGE VERSUS JURY

Unconscionability is a question of law for the court, not for the trier of fact. The court must allow evidence of the commercial setting and purpose of a provision prior to ruling on the question. Consequently, it is almost always impossible to read a contract and decide that it, or any part of it, is unconscionable. Extrinsic evidence is necessary prior to deciding.

5. THE IRRELEVANCE OF HINDSIGHT

Unconscionability must be judged by looking at the circumstances existing at the time of contracting without reference to future events. Supervening oppressiveness is governed by the doctrine of impracticability.

6. CONSUMER PROTECTION

In the great majority of cases in which unconscionability has been found, the party protected by the finding has been a consumer. Generally, business organizations are expected to protect themselves. There have been a few cases protecting a small business against a corporate giant. See example 2 under Unfair Surprise, above, and see the next paragraph, below.

7. TERMINATION CLAUSES AND SALES OF GOODS

Under § 2–309(1) of the U.C.C., a contract for the sale of goods that is indefinite in duration is not terminable except on reasonable notice. The Code's focus is on retail franchises and wholesale distributorships which envisage a continuing, often exclusive, relationship. But other relational contracts are also included; e.g., a requirements contract of indefinite duration. U.C.C. § 2–309(3) goes on to provide that an agreement dispensing with reasonable notice is invalid "if its operation would be unconscionable."

Example: B was the exclusive dealer in Northern New Jersey for aluminum siding produced by S and had so acted for 8 years. After S had decided to terminate the agreement, but before notifying B of its intention, B, with the knowledge and encouragement of S, leased additional land and expanded its warehouse. The court finds that 20 months notice of termination is appropriate under the circumstances. A contract provision dispensing with a reasonable period of notification would have been unconscionable.

8. LIMITATION ON CONSEQUENTIAL DAMAGES—PERSONAL INJURIES

Another provision of the U.C.C. (§ 2–719) that makes specific reference to unconscionability deals with limitations on consequential damages. Although the Code permits limitations on damages and permits the exclusion of consequential damages, it indicates that the exclusion is subject to the rule of conscionability. "Limitation of consequential damages for injury to the person in the case of consumer goods is prima facie unconscionable but limitation of damages where the loss is commercial is not." U.C.C. § 2–719(3). Of course, it is possible to have a finding of unconscionability in the case of the exclusion of commercial losses based on the general doctrine of unconscionability. However, this would be most unusual.

G. "DUTY" TO READ

1. RULE

Assent to a document that purports to be a contract or other consensual transaction implies assent to the terms contained therein.

Perspective: The material discussed here repeats rules stated elsewhere, but this general discussion may help crystallize the effect of not reading a document to which one assents.

Example: B negotiates with S for the purchase of a new car, for its financing and for its insurance. After shaking hands on the dickered price, payment terms, insurance coverage and fees, *S* presents *B* with a mass of documents for signature. These documents faithfully contain all of the terms discussed. But they also contain considerably more terms. The additional terms protect the interests of *S,* as dealer, as well as the interests of the manufacturer, the finance company, and the insurer. *B* signs at the places indicated by *S.* Other unsigned documents, labelled "limited warranty" and "Automobile Insurance Policy" are handed to *B.* *B* is bound by the terms of the documents unless one of the exceptions mentioned below applies.

2. EXCEPTIONS

a. If the document or particular provision is not legible.

b. If the provision is placed in such a way that it is not likely to come to the attention of the other party.

Example: A limitation of liability is printed on a box containing goods sold. The limitation is not binding on the purchaser unless it can be shown the buyer was aware of the limitation.

c. Fraud

(i) *Fraudulent Inducement.* Where one party materially misrepresents the contents of a writing, the modern cases permit the defrauded parties to avoid such contracts despite a failure to read, if they were deceived and relied upon the representations. Alternatively, the contracts may be reformed to conform to the representations.

(ii) *Fraud-in-the-Factum.* A contract is void where the misrepresentation (1) goes not only to the content of the document but also to the nature of the document, and (2) the document is radically different from the kind represented and (3) it was not unreasonable for the party to sign it. (See p. 343 supra.)

d. Mistake

(i) *Unilateral Mistake.* If only one party assents to a document under the mistaken belief that it contains, or does not contain, certain provisions, this party is generally bound by the document. In two situations, however, relief may be available.

(a) *Palpable Mistake.* If the other party is, or ought to be, aware of the mistaken belief, the mistaken party may avoid the contract or have it reformed to conform to what the mistaken party thought the document contained.

(b) *Impalpable Mistake.* If the other party has no reason to know of the mistake, the mistaken party cannot have reformation but may avoid the contract, provided enforcement of the contract would result in an unconscionably unequal exchange of values, and avoidance would impose no substantial hardships on the other.

(ii) *Mutual Mistake.* If both parties share the same mistake as to the contents of a writing, it will be reformed to conform to their belief. (See p. 348 supra.)

e. Unconscionability.

As indicated earlier, for analytical purposes, two kinds of unconscionability are distinguished: unfair surprise and oppression. The second category is unrelated to "duty" to read because even if an oppressive clause is read and comprehended it can be invalidated by a court. The first category goes to the heart of this topic. Modern cases scrutinize, and sometimes hold void, burdensome, unexpected clauses that have not been read by, or explained to, a party adhering to a form contract.

H. AFFIRMANCE OR RATIFICATION

1. DISCUSSION

Affirmance and ratification are equivalent terms. Upon discovering a misrepresentation or mistake, and on escaping duress or undue influence, a party has choices. One of these choices is to continue to accept the obligations of the contract. A manifestation of intent to continue with the transaction is an affirmance. No consideration is required for an affirmance. After affirmance, the power of avoidance and the right to seek reformation are lost.

2. AFFIRMANCE BY CONDUCT
a. Exercise of Dominion
After a party's power to choose between affirmance and avoidance ripens, the continued exercise of dominion over property received under the contract or continued acceptance of benefits under the contract affirms the contract.

Examples: (1) Plaintiff, a salesman under contract for one year's service, agreed to a new contract at considerably diminished pay. He agrees to this new contract as a result of threats made by his employer of being fired and deported. These threats constitute duress. He continued in his employ for nine months. At no time during this period did he protest the new terms and conditions. His many communications with his employer (who usually was in a distant city) were friendly. By accepting benefits of the coerced contract, after the coercion has been removed, he has ratified the contract.

(2) *B* purchases land from *A*. The deed is voidable for mutual mistake. "On discovery of the mistake, *B* tenders a deed back to *A*, who refuses to accept it. *B* continues to occupy and use the land. *B*'s conduct amounts to affirmance and he is precluded from avoiding the contract." Restatement, Second, Contracts § 380, ill. 4.

b. Delay
An affirmance occurs if a party fails within a reasonable time to avoid the contract after the power to do so has ripened.

Discussion: What is a reasonable time is normally a question of fact. If the party seeking to avoid has received no benefits under the contract, and the other has not taken any action in reliance on the first party's silence, a reasonable period of time can be long indeed. If the aggrieved party has received speculative securities, anything more than slight delay would constitute affirmance. It would be inequitable to allow even a defrauded party to speculate at the other's risk. Fault is also a factor. The more odious the duress or misrepresentation, the longer a period of reasonable time the party has to avoid. On the other hand, the negligence in discovering the grounds for avoidance by the party who seeks to avoid is grounds for abbreviating the period. In short, three factors dominate the determination of reasonableness of time to avoid: (1) reliance by the other; (2) speculative benefit gained by stalling; (3) fault.

3. THE PARTY AVOIDING MUST OFFER TO RETURN PROPERTY RECEIVED
This requisite and its exceptions is discussed in connection with the remedy of restitution. See p. 342 supra.

REVIEW QUESTIONS

B, a lawyer, asked *S*, Inc., a lumber yard, for a price quote for 5,000 linear feet of pressurized 2″ × 4″ lumber. *S* quoted a price of $625, whereupon *B* placed the order for 5,000 linear feet. The lumber was delivered with a bill for $625 which *B* paid. At *S*'s regular selling price the bill should have been $1,250. The error in the price quote and bill resulted from a mistake in calculation by *S*'s clerk. *B* used the lumber to construct a deck. Upon discovery of the mistake, *S* demanded payment of an additional $625.

1. T or F *S* can recover because the mistake should have been obvious to *B*.

2. T or F *S* cannot recover because the mistake was unilateral.

3. T or F *S* cannot recover because the mistake was caused by negligence.

4. T or F *S* cannot recover because *B* changed position.

5. Essay   Mrs. Klaus, a property owner and a Lutheran, was greatly interested in furthering her church and particularly in healing conflicts among the several organizational groups, known as synods, of the church. A group of leaders of various Lutheran synods came up with a proposal to erect an intersynodical Lutheran high school and to further this purpose organized the Lutheran High School Association of Jefferson County. In 1980, Mrs. Klaus signed an agreement turning over possession of a 20 acre wooded tract of land to the Association. In return the Association agreed to pay a total of $40,000, in 40 equal annual installments, without interest. ($40,000 was the fair market value for a cash sale.) Concurrent with the last payment Mrs. Klaus was to execute a conveyance of the tract to the Association.

The Agreement provides that "no part of said land shall be developed and used by said purchaser, its successor or assigns, for any other than religious and educational purposes for a period of 40 years from the date of this agreement."

The Association made all payments called for by the agreement, but was unable to raise sufficient funds for a high school until 1989 when a large cash grant made it feasible to start construction. The Association, however, determined to build the school on a more centrally located tract of land. In 1989, the Association has announced its plan to assign the contract with Mrs. Klaus to the Alliance, a non-Lutheran Protestant group, which has immediate plans for constructing a seminary on the still undeveloped Klaus tract. We do not know the price paid by the Alliance, but the fair market value of the tract is now $200,000. Mrs. Klaus died in 1988 and her heirs have varying mixtures of religious piety and economic hunger. They feel that the Association has taken advantage of their ancestor who, they assert, was not interested in furthering the religious work of non-Lutheran religious groups. They offer evidence in this regard. They have asked you what are the remedial possibilities and the prospects of success as to each of them. What will you tell them? Explain.

IX

THIRD PARTY BENEFICIARIES

Analysis

A. Types of Beneficiaries
    1. Operative Concepts and Categories
        a. Privity
        b. Intended Beneficiary
        c. Who Is the Promisor?
        d. Incidental Beneficiary
        e. Creditor Beneficiary
        f. Donee Beneficiary
        g. Promises of Indemnity
        h. The Municipality Cases
        i. The Surety Bond Cases
B. Promisor's Defenses
    1. Defenses From the Third Party Beneficiary Contract
    2. When Rights Vest
        a. Omnipotence of the Contract
        b. Creditor Beneficiaries
        c. Donee Beneficiaries
        d. Perspective
    3. Counterclaims
    4. Promisee's Defenses Against the Beneficiary

C. Cumulative Rights of the Beneficiary
    1. Creditor Beneficiary
    2. Donee Beneficiary
D. Rights of the Promisee Against the Promisor

A. TYPES OF BENEFICIARIES

Except for intended beneficiaries, persons not in privity may not recover on a contract.

1. OPERATIVE CONCEPTS AND CATEGORIES

a. Privity
A person is not in privity unless a contracting party has made a promise to the person.

b. Intended Beneficiary
A person for whom a promisee extracted the benefits of a promisor's promise is an intended beneficiary.

> *Discussion:* There is a wide variety of tests to determine who is an intended beneficiary. The most commonly used tests are: 1) to whom is the performance to run (if it is to run directly to the third person, this person is an intended beneficiary), and 2) whether the promisor reasonably understood that the promisee intended to benefit the third person; that is, whether the third person was an ultimate intended beneficiary of the promisor's performance. The parties' intentions are but one factor used to determine if a beneficiary is intended or not. The courts have also openly and covertly employed policy considerations.

c. Who Is the Promisor?
Throughout this chapter there are references to the "promisor" and the "promisee." In a bilateral contract there are at least two promisors. Under the test of the previous paragraph, "promisor" refers to the party who is to render the performance that most directly inures to the beneficiary. Normally it is the "promisee" who is bargaining for the other party's promise to benefit the third party.

> *Example:* B owes $300 to C. B promises to lend $300 to A in exchange for A's promise to pay $300 to C. Although A and B have both made promises, for purposes of third party beneficiary analysis, A is the promisor, because A's promised performance is to deliver money to C, a person not in privity.

d. Incidental Beneficiary
A party who receives benefits from a promisor's performance, but who was not intended to be a beneficiary is an incidental beneficiary and therefore has no rights in the contract. (See, *e.g.,* examples (4) and (9) below.)

e. **Creditor Beneficiary**
If a promisee extracts from the promisor a promise to render a performance to a third person because the promisee is indebted to the third person, then the third person is a creditor beneficiary.

Comment: Motive should not be confused with intent. For instance, in example (3) below, *B* wants *A* to pay *C*. *B*'s motive is not likely to be affection or benevolence. *B* wants the creditor to be paid so as to be free of the debt. *B* seeks to accomplish this by having *A* pay *C*. While the motive is not benevolence, it is accomplished by a payment to *C*, which is a benefit to *C*.

f. **Donee Beneficiary**
If the promisee's purpose in extracting the promise is to confer a gift upon the third person, the third person is a donee beneficiary. (See examples (2), (5), (10) and (12) below.)

Comment: The distinction between donee and creditor beneficiaries is not ordinarily important on the issue of intent to benefit but may be important on other issues, such as when rights vest (see below).

g. **Promises of Indemnity**
The promise of an indemnitor against liability or an indemnitor against loss does not ordinarily give rise to a third party beneficiary situation because the intent to benefit is deemed to run to the promisee. An exception appears to have been made in the case of public contracts. (See examples (6), (7) and (8) below.)

h. **The Municipality Cases**
Municipal contracts that create enforceable rights in third persons are of three types. These are: (1) where a contractor agrees to perform a duty that the municipality owes to individual members of the public and the breach of which would create tort liability against the municipality; (2) where the contractor promises the governmental body to compensate members of the public for injuries done them despite the absence of a governmental duty; and (3) where the governmental body enters into a contract to gain advantages for individual members of the public.

i. **The Surety Bond Cases**
Laborers, suppliers, and subcontractors are not third party beneficiaries of a performance bond because the purpose of this type of bond is to assure payment of damages to an owner in the event of a contractor's non-performance. They are generally held to be third party beneficiaries of a payment bond. While the motive of a promisee in procuring a payment

bond is to protect itself from mechanics' liens, the intent is also to benefit the laborers, suppliers, and subcontractors by seeing to it that they are paid. It is presumed that these third parties are not intended beneficiaries of a joint performance-payment bond. If a joint bond were not deemed to solely benefit the promisee, the bond might be dissipated in paying third parties without paying the promisee.

Examples: (1) *B* owes *C* $300. *B* sells a quantity of hay to *A* who promises *B* and *C* to pay $300 for the hay to *C*. All three parties are present at the time *A*'s promise is made. *C* is a promisee, in privity with the promisor, *A*. Consequently, the concepts peculiar to third party beneficiary contracts, such as the concept of vesting, are inapplicable to these facts.

(2) A son promised his father to pay $1,000 to his sister if the father would forbear from selling certain property. The father forbore. The sister, a person not in privity, is an intended donee beneficiary. Intended, because the performance of the promise (payment) runs directly to her; donee, because the promisee-father intended to confer a gift upon her.

(3) *B* owes $300 to *C*. *B* then lends $300 to *A* in exchange for *A*'s promise to pay $300 to *C*. *C* is an intended creditor beneficiary. Intended, because the performance (payment) is to run directly to *C*; creditor, because *B*'s purpose in entering into the contract is to discharge an obligation which *B* owed to *C*.

(4) *A*, a bank, promises *B* a loan with which to pay *B*'s creditors. The creditors are incidental beneficiaries because the performance (payment) by *A* runs to *B* and not to *B*'s creditors. As incidental beneficiaries, *B*'s creditors have no rights against *A*.

(5) *A*, a lawyer, drafts a will for *B*. *C* is a beneficiary under the will. Because the will was improperly drawn, *C* received less under the will than the testator had intended. Although the promised performance (drawing a will) runs to *B*, the promisor understood that the promisee's ultimate intent was to benefit *C*, a beneficiary of the will. Therefore, under the second test given above for intended beneficiaries, *C* is an intended beneficiary of the contract between *A* and *B*. If the first test were employed, *C* would not be an intended beneficiary.

(6) *A* promises *B* to reimburse *B* in the event that *B* is compelled to pay *C*. *B* is compelled to pay *C*. *A* is an indemnitor against loss. *A*'s performance (payment) runs to *B*. Therefore, *C* is an incidental beneficiary.

(7) *A* promises *B* to discharge *B*'s legal liability in the event *B* becomes liable to *C*. *B* incurs a liability toward *C*. *A* is an indemnitor against liability. Despite the fact that performance of the promise runs directly to *C*, the cases mostly hold that *C* is not an intended beneficiary of *A*'s promise. These cases have often been decided on policy grounds.

(8) *B*, a municipality, owes a duty to the public to keep its streets in repair. *A*, a street railway, contracts with *B* to maintain the streets and to indemnify *B* if *B* is compelled to pay damages because of *A*'s improper performance. *C* suffers damages as a result of *A*'s breach. Although *A* is an indemnitor against loss, and therefore *C* would not ordinarily be considered a third party beneficiary [see (6) above], the results in municipality cases are generally different. It should be noted that the duties owed by municipalities to the public are defined by tort law.

(9) *B*, a city, entered into a contract with *A*, a water company, whereby *A* agrees to furnish water at a specified pressure in *B*'s fire hydrants. The house of *C*, located in *B*, was destroyed by fire because *A* failed to provide water at the specified pressure. *C* is not an intended beneficiary because the performance of the promise—supplying water at specified pressure in *B*'s hydrants—runs to *B* and not to *C*. Policy considerations lead to the same result. If *A* were liable, it would be a crushing burden not factored into its water rates. Also, most property owners carry fire insurance. If *A* were liable, it would essentially be a reinsurer (an entity that insures insurance companies).

(10) *B*, a city, entered into a contract with a contractor whereby the latter agreed to lay certain sewer lines. The contractor promised *B* to be liable to members of the public for damage done to private property. *C*'s property was damaged as a result of the contractor's construction work. *C* is an intended donee beneficiary because the promised performance is a promise of compensation and runs directly to members of the public.

(11) *B*, a city, entered into a contract with *A*, a water company, which provides a maximum schedule of rates to be charged to users. *C*, a property owner, is billed for water at a rate in excess of the contract rate. *C* need not pay more than the contract rate. The rate limitation was intended to benefit individual members of the public.

(12) *X* owns real property and, in exchange for a loan, mortgages it to *C*. *X* sells the property to *B* who takes "subject to" the mortgage which means that, although the land is encumbered by the mortgage, *B* accepts no personal liability for the debt. *B* subsequently sells the property to *A* who "assumes" the mortgage, which means that *A* promises *B* to pay the debt. Although *A*'s promised performance runs directly to *C* and by the usual test *C* is an intended beneficiary, there is substantial authority to the effect that *C* has no rights in the contract. Because *B* had merely taken subject to the mortgage and was not *C*'s debtor, *C* cannot be classified as a creditor beneficiary. Because it is unlikely that *B* had any donative intent, many courts have refused to treat *C* as a donee beneficiary. Others have, however, recognized *C* as an intended donee beneficiary.

B. PROMISOR'S DEFENSES

1. DEFENSES FROM THE THIRD PARTY BENEFICIARY CONTRACT
In the absence of agreement to the contrary, the promisor can assert against the beneficiary any defense the promisor has against the promisee.

Examples: (1) *B* promises not to cut down certain timber in exchange for *A*'s promise to pay *C* $100. *B* is not obligated to *C* and intends that the $100 be a gift. *B*, contrary to agreement, cuts down the timber. Although *C* is an intended donee beneficiary who may sue, *C* does not prevail in an action against *A* because *A* has the defense of non-performance against *B* which can be used against *C*.

(2) *B* promises to do certain carpentry for *A* in exchange for *A*'s promise to pay $1,000 to *C*, a creditor of *B*. *B* fails to substantially perform the carpentry. Although *C* is an intended creditor beneficiary of *A*'s promise to *B*, *C* cannot recover against *A*, because *A* has the defense of failure of constructive condition (non-performance) against *B*, which is also available against *C*.

Exceptions:

(1) *Where the parties agree that the beneficiary will have enforceable rights despite any defense that the promisor might be able to assert against the promisee.*

Example: Fire insurance policies purchased by homeowners often cover the interests of both the homeowner and the mortgagee. These frequently provide that the mortgagee (as third party beneficiary of the policy) may recover despite the failure of the owner to pay the premium. In the event a fire occurs after the owner's failure to make timely payment, and before any notice of cancellation is received by the mortgagee, the mortgagee may recover on the policy although the owner may have no right to recover for injury to the owner's interest in the property.

(2) *Where the rights of the beneficiary have vested, the rights may not be varied by subsequent agreement between the promisor and the promisee.*

Discussion: Re-examine examples (1) and (2) on page 365. In each of them, the beneficiary's rights have been effectively destroyed by the promisee's material breach of the contract. This destruction of rights occurs whether or not the rights of the beneficiary have vested. If we vary the examples so that *A* and *B mutually agree* to curtail *C*'s rights, the agreement is ineffective against *C*.

2. WHEN RIGHTS VEST

a. Omnipotence of the Contract

The parties may provide as they wish with respect to vesting. For example, the contract may validly provide that rights of third parties are always divestable or that they vest immediately.

b. Creditor Beneficiaries

The rights of a creditor beneficiary vest, at the latest, when the beneficiary brings an action to enforce a contract or otherwise materially changes position in reliance on the contract. The tendency today is to hold that rights vest as soon as the beneficiary learns of the promise and assents to it.

c. Donee Beneficiaries

According to the original Restatement, the rights of a donee beneficiary vest immediately upon making the contract, but the Restatement, Second, and much case law has indicated that the same rule that applies to creditor beneficiaries should be applied to donees.

Example: *B* promises not to cut down certain timber in exchange for *A*'s promise to pay *C* $100. Before *C* learns of the agreement, *B* and *A* enter into a substituted contract, discharging *C*'s rights. *C*'s rights are effectively discharged if *C* is a creditor beneficiary. If *C* is a donee beneficiary, *C*'s rights are effectively destroyed under the modern view incorporated in the Restatement, Second.

d.   Perspective
Vesting has a very limited role. It does not give the beneficiary the equivalent of a fee simple absolute in the promise. It only insulates the beneficiary from a curtailment of rights by mutual agreement of the promisor and promisee. It does not insulate the beneficiary from defenses such as failure of constructive condition. (See p. 365 supra.)

3.   COUNTERCLAIMS
The promisor can effectively raise against the beneficiary a counterclaim that the promisor has against the promisee only if it is in the nature of a recoupment; that is, if it arises out of the same transaction upon which the promisor is being sued. The recoupment may be used only as a subtraction from the beneficiary's claim and not for affirmative relief.

4.   PROMISEE'S DEFENSES AGAINST THE BENEFICIARY
Suppose after the promisor, *A*, makes the promise to *B* for the benefit of *C*, a supposed creditor of *B*, *A* discovers that *C* is not a creditor because *B* has a valid defense against *C*. The availability of this defense to *A* depends upon the interpretation of the contract. If the promisor promises to pay irrespective of any such defense, it is not available. If *A* promises merely to perform to the extent *B* is obligated, the defense may be raised. If the promise is to pay a specific debt, it is generally held that the promise is to pay irrespective of such a defense.

Example: *C* sold an oil burner to *B* on credit. When *B* sold the house, *A*, the purchaser, agreed to assume the payments still due on the oil burner contract. These amounted to $800, and *A* received a credit of that amount against the purchase price. *A* failed to make the payments, alleging that *C* materially breached a warranty made to *B*. *C* is a third party beneficiary of *A*'s promise to assume the debt. *A* may not raise the defense of breach of warranty, because *A* has assumed a specific debt and the preferred interpretation is that *A* has promised to pay irrespective of *B*'s defense against *C*. This interpretation is preferred because (1) *A* has received a credit from the promisee for the assumption and (2) *B* does not want to be involved in litigation with *C* over an oil burner in which *B* has no further interest. (As indicated below, *A*'s assumption of the debt does not discharge *B*'s liability.)

C. CUMULATIVE RIGHTS OF THE BENEFICIARY

1. CREDITOR BENEFICIARY
A creditor beneficiary has rights against both the promisor and the promisee and may obtain judgment against both. The beneficiary may only receive one satisfaction.

Novation Contrasted: If a creditor beneficiary releases the promisee in exchange for the promisor's assumption of the obligation, the substituted contract between promisor and beneficiary is called a novation. No novation occurs in a normal third party beneficiary contract, because the beneficiary does not impliedly release the debtor when the beneficiary assents to, or even attempts to enforce, the promisor's assumption. The beneficiary may obtain judgment against the promisee on the original debt and against the promisor on the third party beneficiary contract. Although entitled to judgment against both, the beneficiary is entitled only to one satisfaction.

Examples: (1) *B* is indebted to *C* in the amount of $10,000. *A*, for a consideration, agrees with *B* to assume *B*'s obligation to *C*. *A* fails to pay. *C* may obtain judgment against *B* on the original debt. *C* may also obtain judgment against *A* on the contract of assumption. However, *C* is entitled to collect only the sum of $10,000 plus interest and costs.

(2) *B* is indebted to *C* in the amount of $10,000. *A*, *B*, and *C* work out a three-party substituted contract whereby *C* agrees to *discharge B*, and *A* agrees to pay the $10,000 to *C*. This three-party arrangement is a novation. *C* has rights only against *A*. (See p. 292 supra.)

2. DONEE BENEFICIARY
Although a donee beneficiary has rights against the promisor, the donee has no rights against the promisee unless after the donee's rights have vested, the promisee has received a consideration to discharge the promisor. The donee's remedial rights are limited to the value of the consideration.

Example: *B* promises not to cut down certain timber in exchange for *A*'s promise to pay *C* $1,000. *C* is not a creditor of *B*, and *B*'s motive is to confer a gift on *C*. *C*'s rights subsequently vest. *A* and *B* subsequently agree that in consideration of $200 *A* will be discharged from the obligation to *C*. *C*, as a donee beneficiary, ordinarily would have no rights against *B*, but because *B* received it as consideration for discharging A, C is entitled to recover $200 from B.

D. RIGHTS OF THE PROMISEE AGAINST THE PROMISOR

In addition to the promisor's liability to the beneficiary, the promisor is under an obligation to the promisee for performance of the contract.

Discussion: Although this chapter has focused on the rights of the beneficiary, it should not be forgotten that the promisor's contract is with the promisee. In the case of a donee beneficiary contract, the promisee usually suffers no damages by a promisor's breach, and restitution may not be a satisfactory remedy. In such a case the legal remedy may be inadequate and, if so, an action for specific performance will be entertained. In a creditor beneficiary contract, breach by the promisor can cause substantial harm to the promisee. If such damages occur, they are recoverable.

Examples: (1) B owes C $10,000. For a consideration A assumes the duty to pay. Because A breaches, B is forced to pay C. B has an action against A for $10,000.

(2) In a separation agreement, the husband promised his wife that he would leave, by will, certain specified legacies to their children. He died without complying with the promise. The children, as intended third party donee beneficiaries, can enforce the promises made for their benefit against their father's estate. Alternatively, the wife has an action for specific performance against the estate of the husband. Note, because she suffered no economic injury, the wife's remedy at law is inadequate, and therefore she is entitled to specific performance.

REVIEW QUESTIONS

B purchased a tractor from C, financing the purchase by signing a note and giving a security interest in the nature of a chattel mortgage in the tractor. Subsequently, B sold the tractor to A who in writing stated: "I hereby assume and promise to pay off the note you owe to C for the purchase of this tractor."

1. T or F In an action by C, A may raise as a defense facts tending to show that B misrepresented the condition of the tractor.

2. T or F In an action by C, A may properly raise as a defense facts tending to show that the tractor was defective when C sold it to B.

3. **T or F** If the agreement between *B* and *A* contained an additional clause stating, "*C* shall have no right to enforce this agreement," *C* would be barred from recovering judgment against *A*.

4. **Essay** Starr, Inc., a manufacturer, was losing money. It owed $100,000 to State Bank. Starr sold its business to Enterprise, Inc., representing falsely that its annual gross sales had averaged $15,000,000. In fact, they had averaged about $8,000,000. Enterprise paid $500,000 in cash for the assets of the business and agreed to pay $100,000 to State Bank and also agreed to honor existing warranties on products Starr had sold. Neither Enterprise nor Starr notified State Bank or holders of warranted products of this contract. After six months of operation Enterprise learned of the falsity of Starr's representation. About the same time, one of Starr's products failed to operate properly. It caused an explosion that resulted in personal injuries and property damage to a warranty holder. The damage was evaluated at about $1,000,000. The failure that occurred involved a defect in manufacture that was expressly warranted against. State Bank and holders of the warranty learned of the Starr–Enterprise deal only after they unsuccessfully tried to reach Starr's officers or directors. They managed to find a former employee who had a vague recollection of the contract. State Bank has brought an action against Enterprise for the $100,000 debt owed by Starr. The persons injured by the explosion have sued Enterprise for damages. A copy of the Starr–Enterprise contract was produced in pre-trial discovery proceedings. Decide the cases. Explain.

5. **Essay** Mr. B contracted with Mrs. S to purchase her house for $210,000, making a down payment of $21,000. The contract provided that closing would take place in 60 days and that title would be conveyed by Mrs. S to Ms. T, Mr. B's sister. A week after the contract was signed, Mr. B was killed in an accident. Ms. T has asked Mr. B's executor to pay the balance and complete the purchase. The executor refuses. Ms. T has asked Mrs. S to sue Mr. B's executor for specific performance. Mrs. S refuses, stating that she is content to keep the down payment, cancel the contract, and forget the whole thing. The closing date has passed with no further action by the parties. What are the rights of Ms. T? Explain.

X

ASSIGNMENT AND DELEGATION

Analysis

A. *Assignment of Rights*
  1. *What Is an Assignment*
  2. *U.C.C. Coverage*
  3. *U.C.C. Exclusions*
  4. *Deviants From the Norm*
     a. *Gratuitous Assignment*
     b. *Voidable Assignment*
     c. *Assignment of Future Rights*
  5. *Formalities*
  6. *Attachment and Perfection of Security Interests in Accounts*
     a. *Attachment*
     b. *Perfection*
  7. *Priorities*
     a. *Comment*
     b. *Unperfected Assignments*
     c. *Non-code Cases*
  8. *Floating Lien*
     a. *Comment*
     b. *Prior Law*
  9. *Non-assignable Rights*
     a. *Standing to Complain*

        b.   Contractual Prohibition of an Assignment
        c.   Contractual Authorization of an Assignment
        d.   Option Contracts
   10. Defenses and Counterclaims of the Obligor Against the Assignor
        a.   Defenses
        b.   Counterclaims
        c.   Circumventing Rule
   11. Rights of the Assignee Against the Assignor
        a.   Express Warranties or Disclaimers of Implied Warranties
        b.   Implied Warranties
B. Delegation of Duties
   1. What Is a Delegation?
   2. Liability of the Delegant
   3. Liability of the Delegate
   4. Non-delegable Duties
        a.   What Duties Are Non-delegable?
        b.   Delegation in Sales Contracts
        c.   Effect of Improper Delegation

A. ASSIGNMENT OF RIGHTS

1. WHAT IS AN ASSIGNMENT?

An assignment is a manifestation of intent by the owner of a right to effectuate a present transfer of the right. The manifestation of intent must be addressed to the assignee or someone on the assignee's behalf.

> ***Perspective.*** An assignment's closest analogy is to a sale of goods or a conveyance of land. It is an executed transaction. Consequently, words of promise do not create an assignment. An order communicated to the debtor alone is not an assignment.

> ***Examples:*** (1) *D* owes *C* $1,000. *C* gives a writing to *A* which states that *C* transfers *C*'s credit against *D* to *A*. *C* has assigned the right to payment to *A*.

> (2) *D* owes *C* $1,000. *C* promises to assign this credit to *A*. No assignment is created. Assuming the promise is enforceable, *A* has rights similar to those of an assignee of future rights discussed below.

> (3) *D* owes *C* $1,000. *C* writes to *D*, "Please pay the balance due me to *A*." This is an order to pay. No assignment is created.

> (4) *D* owes *C* $1,000. *C* owes *A* $500. *C* writes *A*, "I will pay you out of money that *D* owes me." *A* is not an assignee of a portion of *C*'s right against *D*. This is merely a promise to pay out of a fund.

2. U.C.C. COVERAGE

In its simplest form an assignment is an outright transfer, but an assignment is frequently made as a security device. The right is transferred for security only. It is similar to a mortgage of real property rather than the conveyance of a fee simple. Although Article 9 of the U.C.C. focuses primarily upon security devices, it governs the assignment of an "account" whether the assignment is an outright transfer or the creation of a security interest. An account is "any right to payment for goods sold or leased or for services rendered not evidenced by an instrument or chattel paper whether or not it has been earned by performance." U.C.C. § 9–106 (1972 Amendment).

3. U.C.C. EXCLUSIONS

Although Article 9 of the U.C.C. governs assignments of accounts regardless of the purpose of the assignment, specific exceptions are enumerated in the code. These include:

(a)   Wage assignments;

(b)   Assignments of accounts in connection with the sale of a business from which they arose;

(c)   An assignment of rights under a contract coupled with the delegation of the assignor's duties to the assignee;

(d)   Rights to receive rents from a lease of real property.

Where the transaction is not governed by Article 9, the common law rules apply. In some instances, other legislation will apply. For example, most states have statutes regulating or outlawing wage assignments. Article 2 of the Code has several provisions that govern the assignment of rights in contracts for the sale of goods.

4.   DEVIANTS FROM THE NORM

There are three types of assignments that deviate from the norm and create problems which do not exist in the case of an ordinary assignment.

a.   Gratuitous Assignment

The fact that the assignor makes a gift of a right against the obligor is not a defense available to the obligor. An assignment, as an executed transaction, requires no consideration. But, as between the assignor and the assignee, the gift must be complete. If it is not complete, the assignee's rights can be terminated by the death of the assignor, by a subsequent assignment of the same right or by a notice of revocation communicated to the assignee or to the obligor. Since a right cannot be physically delivered, the gift can be completed by other substitute delivery methods such as: by the receipt of payment by the assignee, by delivery of the assignment in writing, by delivery to the assignee of a symbolic writing that incorporates the debt, or by application of the doctrine of promissory estoppel. An assignment given for a pre-existing debt is for "value" and is not deemed to be gratuitous.

b.   Voidable Assignment

An assignment may be voidable by the assignor because of infancy, insanity, fraud, duress, etc. The same rules that apply for avoiding a contract also apply here.

c.   Assignment of Future Rights

An assignment of a future right is the assignment of a right which will arise under a contract that has not yet been made. The generally accepted common law rule is that an assignment for value of a future right is an equitable assignment. At common law such rights were generally considered to be superior to those of the assignor. But they were considered inferior to those of a subsequent assignee for value of the same right without notice, and to the rights of a subsequent attaching creditor of the assignor who is without notice of the claim of the assignee provided the attachment is made before the right comes into being. Generally speaking, under the Uniform Commercial Code, if the assignee of future rights complies with the perfection requirements of the Code, the assignee will prevail. (See U.C.C. §§ 9–204 and 9–402).

Examples: (1) *C* enters into a contract with *D* whereby *C* is to construct a building for *D* and is to be paid as the work progresses. *C* borrows money from *A* bank and to secure repayment of the loan, assigns the rights to payment to *A*. *A* receives a valid legal assignment even at common law. The right to payment is a present conditional right, not a future right.

(2) *C*, an unemployed school teacher, assigns to *A* the salary that *C* hopes to make with a new employer. *C* subsequently obtains a teaching job with *D*. The assignment violates no wage assignment statute and is not governed by the U.C.C. *A* has an equitable assignment that is subordinate to the rights of *C*'s attaching creditors.

5. FORMALITIES

In the absence of statute an assignment may be oral. Under Article 9 a writing is required unless the assignee is in possession of the collateral involved. Possession of an account is not possible; consequently, if the assignment of the account is governed by Article 9, a writing is required. If there is no writing, the assignment is not enforceable against anyone. An assignment or promise of assignment of rights that is not governed by Article 8 or 9 is not enforceable unless it is in writing if the remedy sought is in the amount or value of $5,000 or more. (U.C.C. § 1–206.)

6. ATTACHMENT AND PERFECTION OF SECURITY INTERESTS IN ACCOUNTS

a. Attachment

"Attachment" relates to the relative rights of the assignor and assignee. Once the rights of an assignee attach, the assignee's rights are superior to those of the assignor. Unless there is an agreement to the contrary, the rights of the assignee attach as soon as (1) there is an agreement that it attach, (2) value has been given, and (3) the account in which the assignee has rights is identified. It is important to remember that if Article 9 governs, the assignment must be in writing for the assignee's rights to attach.

b. Perfection

"Perfection" relates to the rights of the assignee against third parties. Perfection cannot occur until the assignment attaches. Under Article 9, perfection occurs when the assignor takes possession of the collateral. However, in the case of accounts, possession is not possible. With accounts it is the filing of a notice of assignment (financing statement) in a public record office which is the normal method of perfecting the assignment. Filing is not required to perfect a security interest in an account where the assignment (either by itself or in conjunction with others) does not constitute a significant part of the accounts of the assignor. In this case the rights of the assignee are perfected on attachment.

7. PRIORITIES
Under the U.C.C., an assignee who has perfected the security interest in an account has priority over a party whose rights are subsequently perfected, including lien creditors, secured creditors and a trustee of the assignor's bankrupt estate.

a. Comment
The business purpose of taking assignments of accounts as security for loans is to give the lender priority over other creditors of the assignor, just as a mortgagee has priority in a mortgagor's real property. In the event that the assignor becomes unable or unwilling to pay debts as they mature, the assignee can insist that the obligor pay the assignee rather than the assignor or the unsecured creditors of the assignor. The Code permits the realization of this business purpose provided the assignee's rights are perfected.

b. Unperfected Assignments
A subsequent secured creditor, and a subsequent lien creditor will prevail over the rights of an assignee who has not perfected the assignment. (U.C.C. § 9–301 as amended 1972). A lien creditor is an unsecured creditor who has acquired a lien by attachment, levy or the like and includes a trustee of the assignor's estate in bankruptcy.

c. Non-code Cases
1) Assignee Versus Attaching Creditor

At common law, the priority between an assignee and a creditor who had obtained an attachment on the right assigned is governed by the rule: "prior in time, prior in right." Consequently, priority depended on the relative time of the attachment and of the assignment. However, the assignee may be estopped from asserting this priority. For example, it is often held that the assignee loses this priority if the *obligor* has not received notice of the assignment in sufficient time to call the assignment to the attention of the court in the attachment proceedings. The more modern view deprives the assignee of priority only if the assignee fails to give notice of the assignment prior to payment by the obligor to the attaching creditor.

2) **Successive Assignees**
At common law there are three competing rules to determine priority among successive assignees of the same obligation:

(a) New York Rule. Prior in time is prior in right.

(b) English View. The first assignee to notify the obligor prevails provided this assignee has taken the assignment for value and without notice of any prior assignment.

(c) Four Horsemen Rule (Rule of the Restatements and the Prevailing Rule). Prior in time is prior in right unless a subsequent assignee who pays value in good faith (1) obtains payment from the obligor; or (2) recovers judgment from the obligor, or (3) enters into a substituted contract with the obligor; or (4) receives delivery of an instrument that incorporates the debt.

3) **Latent Equities**
An assignment to a bona fide assignee for value without notice destroys any latent equities third persons may have in the right. The older view was to the contrary.

> ***Example:*** *D* owes *C* $1,000. *T* induces *C* to accept $100 to assign the right to $1,000 by misrepresenting material facts. *T* subsequently assigns the right to *X* who takes in good faith, for value, and without notice of *C*'s right to avoid the assignment to *T*. *C* has no rights against *D* or *X*. Although *C* may have a tort claim against *T*, *C* has lost all rights in the account against *D*.

8. FLOATING LIEN
U.C.C. § 9–205 expressly validates a floating lien on a shifting stock of goods or accounts.

a. Comment
This rule permits a debtor to grant to the creditor a security interest in the shifting stock in trade and a security interest in shifting accounts. This permits the debtor to dispose of the goods and collect the accounts without being required to account to the creditor for the proceeds. The agreement may provide that the creditor's lien or interest automatically attaches to newly required stock in trade and to newly created accounts.

b. Prior Law
Prior to the U.C.C., the law had difficulties with the floating lien. Under the rule of *Benedict v. Ratner,* the lien was regarded as void because the

creditor's failure to police the debtor was considered to be a fraud on other creditors. The U.C.C., however, takes notice of the practice of lenders to allow free rein to debtors until such time as the debtor's financial status appears shaky. Another difficulty was that the floating lien purported to cover goods and accounts not yet in existence. Under the Code, if the creditor files a financing statement that identifies the assigned rights, the assignment of future rights is treated as if it were the assignment of present rights.

9. NON–ASSIGNABLE RIGHTS

A right is assignable except where the assignment: (1) would materially change the duty of the other party; (2) would materially vary the burden or risk of the other party; (3) would impair materially the other party's chance of obtaining return performance; or (4) would be contrary to public policy.

Examples: (1) *D* owes *C*, $1,000. *C* is in San Francisco. *C* assigns the right to payment to *A* who is in Chicago. Although *D*'s duty is varied to a slight extent, the right is assignable. Sending a check to Chicago is not materially different from sending it to San Francisco.

(2) *D* agrees to paint *C*'s portrait for a fee. *C* purports to assign the rights to *A* intending for *D* to paint *A*'s portrait. The purported assignment is ineffective. The assignment would materially change *D*'s duty.

(3) *D* insures a house owned by *C*. *C* sells the house to *A* and purports to assign its insurance coverage to *A*. The house is destroyed by fire. Neither *C* nor *A* can recover from *D*. *C* no longer has an insurable interest in this house and the assignment to *A* is ineffective. *D*'s risk would be materially changed if the assignment were valid. *D*'s risk is affected by the identity of the owner of the premises.

(4) *C* has a yearly retainer contract with *D*, an attorney. *D* assigns the rights and delegates the duties to *A*, another attorney. The assignment is ineffective. Although *D*'s *right* to receive payment is assignable, the *duty* to perform legal services is non-delegable (see p. 385 below for non-delegable duties). Because the duty is non-delegable, the purported delegation impairs *C*'s chance of obtaining return performance. Therefore, the assignment with which it is coupled is ineffective. To generalize, an assignment that is coupled with a delegation of non-delegable duties is ineffective.

(5) *A,* a public officer, purports to assign a portion of a yet unearned salary. The assignment is against public policy. The same rationale forbids assignments of government pension rights and alimony and support payments.

a. Standing to Complain

An assignor cannot effectively complain that the assigned right is non-assignable. Only the obligor may complain. If the obligor expressly or tacitly consents to the assignment there is an effective waiver.

b. Contractual Prohibition of an Assignment

1) Common Law Rule

At common law a provision in a contract prohibiting an assignment of rights was generally sustained as valid under the general principle of freedom of contract, although several courts did strike down such provisions as illegal restraints on alienation. If, however, the court was able to find that the provision was not drafted with sufficient clarity to accomplish the purpose of voiding the assignment, the anti-assignment clause was treated as a promise not to assign. An assignment would breach the promise and give the obligor an action for breach, but the assignment was valid. Because damages for breach of the provision are ordinarily nominal, the anti-assignment clause was frequently of no practical value.

2) The U.C.C. Rule

Under U.C.C. Article 9 an anti-assignment clause is ineffective to prohibit the assignment of an "account." Also Article 2 permits the assignment of the right to damages for total breach or of a right arising out of the assignor's due performance of the assignor's entire obligation, despite a clause purporting to prevent assignment.

Comment: In the clash between freedom of contract and freedom of alienation, the Code comes out strongly in favor of freedom of alienation. All accounts covered by Article 9 are freely alienable. In addition to accounts, in a sale of goods situation, the rights to receive delivery of goods that have been paid for and the right to damages for total breach are also freely alienable despite a restraint on alienation.

3) Interpretation Under Article 2

Article 2 of the Code provides (and the Restatement, Second, agrees) that general language purporting to prohibit "assignment of the contract" should be construed as barring only the delegation of duties, unless the circumstances indicate the contrary.

Comment: Although assignment and delegation are two distinct legal concepts, the Code recognizes that contracting parties do not always make the distinction. It also takes note of the probability that the primary concern of a party drafting an anti-assignment clause is that the performance of the other party not be delegated.

c. Contractual Authorization of an Assignment

A contract provision that authorizes an assignment will be honored (even if the rights are not otherwise assignable), but a merely routine clause to the effect that the contract "shall inure to the benefit of heirs and assigns" will not have that effect.

d. Option Contracts

The offeree's rights in an option contract are assignable provided the rights are otherwise assignable and the duties otherwise delegable and any promise expected to be made by the offeree has been made.

Comment: Option contracts are offers but are also contracts. While offers are not assignable, option contracts generally are.

Examples: (1) *D*, for a consideration, offers to sell Blackacre to *C* for $50,000 cash, the offer to be irrevocable for 60 days. *C* assigns the right to purchase to *A* who tenders $50,000 to *D* within the 60 day period. *D* refuses the tender. *A* can successfully pursue a claim for specific performance.

(2) *D*, for a consideration, offers to sell Blackacre to *C* for $50,000, payable $20,000 in cash and $30,000 by a purchase money bond and mortgage executed by *C*, the offer to be irrevocable for 60 days. *C* assigns the right to purchase to *A* who tenders $20,000 in cash and a bond and mortgage executed by *A*. *D* refuses the tender. *D* properly refused the tender. The offer looked to the credit of *C*, not *A*. If *A* had tendered $20,000 cash and a bond and mortgage executed by *C*, then *D* would be obligated to convey.

10. DEFENSES AND COUNTERCLAIMS OF THE OBLIGOR AGAINST THE ASSIGNOR

a. Defenses

The obligor may assert against the assignee any defense which the obligor could have asserted against the assignor. The same general rule applies to a sub-assignee. The maxim is that the assignee stands in the shoes of the assignor.

Example: D contracts to pay $5,000 to C in exchange for carpentry work which C promises to perform. C assigns the right to payment to A. C does not perform the work. D may successfully resist A's claim to payment because there is a failure of the constructive condition that work be performed before payment is due.

Comment: Defenses that can be raised may run the entire gamut of the defenses to a contract, including formation problems such as lack of consideration or fraud, and supervening defenses such as impracticability.

Exception: When the rights of the assignee have vested, they may not be discharged or curtailed by a *subsequent agreement or other voluntary transaction between the obligor and assignor.* Vesting occurs when the assignee notifies the obligor of the assignment.

Example: D promises to pay C $5,000 for certain carpentry work. C assigns his rights to A who notifies D of the assignment. C performs the carpentry and subsequently purports to release D from the duty to pay. The release is ineffective because it is a voluntary transaction between D and C purporting to discharge A's rights. If C had failed to perform the work, A could not compel D to pay even though A's rights had vested.

Qualification of the Exception: Under Article 9 of the U.C.C., even after notice to the obligor, the assignor and obligor have a limited right to curtail the rights of the assignee. If the assigned right to payment has not yet been earned by performance, the assignee and obligor may, in good faith and in accordance with reasonable commercial standards, modify or substitute for the contract. When this occurs the assignee has rights under the new agreement.

Example: Raintree County contracts with C for the construction of a new county courthouse for $25,000,000. C assigns the rights to payment to A, a bank, which extends C a line of credit to be drawn upon as C purchases supplies and meets the payroll. Many citizens denounce the project as extravagant. In response to these criticisms, county officials have the architects redesign parts of the building so as to cut the cost. The county renegotiates the contract with *C* resulting in a smaller courthouse at a reduced contract price of $18,000,000. *A*'s rights are effectively curtailed. Note that *A* is not injured by the change except as it may have to locate other creditworthy borrowers.

b. Counterclaims

To what extent may an obligor raise as a counterclaim against an assignee a claim that the obligor has against the assignor? Under Article 9 of the U.C.C., this depends in part, on whether or not the counterclaim stems from the same transaction.

1) Same Transaction (Recoupment)

If the obligor's counterclaim arises out of the same contract from which the assignee's rights stem, the obligor may raise the counterclaim by way of defense. This defense, known as recoupment, cannot be used for affirmative relief against the assignee but only by way of subtraction.

Example: D purchases a printing press from C for $100,000, paying $20,000 down. The balance is to be paid in 60 days. C assigns the right to payment of the $80,000 balance to A. Because the press contained a defect that breached the implied warranty of merchantability, D suffered consequential damages of $250,000. A's action for $80,000 will be defeated. D may recoup $80,000 from A but cannot get a judgment for money damages against A.

2) Different Transactions (Set–Off)

If the obligor's counterclaim arose from a different transaction with the assignor, this counterclaim may be raised against the assignor only if it accrues before the obligor receives notice of the assignment. This defense, known as set-off, cannot be used for affirmative relief against the assignee but only by way of subtraction.

Comment: The rule focuses on when the obligor receives notice of the assignment. The obligor does *not* receive notice when the assignee files a financing statement. Filing gives constructive notice to subsequent creditors, but it does not give constructive notice to the obligor.

c. Circumventing Rule

To circumvent the rule that an assignee stands in the shoes of the assignor, a waiver of defense clause is frequently employed. Sellers who sell on credit often use credit instruments drafted by the bank or finance company to whom they will assign the credit instrument. These instruments frequently provide that the assignee shall not be bound by any defense or claim that the obligor has against the assignor. Such a clause lends to the instrument some of the traits of a negotiable instrument.

1) U.C.C. Rule
Under Article 9 of the U.C.C., waiver of defense clauses are valid provided the assignee takes the assignment in good faith, for value, and without notice of the claim or defense, except that such a clause cannot effectively prohibit the raising of a real defense. (§ 9–206.) Real defenses are: voidability for infancy, voidness for total incapacity, illegality or fraud in the factum, and discharge in insolvency proceedings.

2) Exceptions for Consumer Paper
The U.C.C. provision validating waiver of defense clauses subordinates the rule to "any statute or decision which establishes a different rule for buyers or lessees of consumer goods . . ." Many states have invalidated such clauses in consumer protection legislation, as has the Federal Trade Commission. The general rule validating waiver of defense clauses continues to be viable in non-consumer transactions.

11. RIGHTS OF THE ASSIGNEE AGAINST THE ASSIGNOR
a. Express Warranties or Disclaimers of Implied Warranties
Within broad limits, the assignee and assignor may agree as they wish as to warranties. Thus, the assignor will be held to any express warranty that is made. A warranty disclaimer is similarly upheld where the parties agree to the disclaimer.

b. Implied Warranties
In the absence of an express agreement to the contrary, an assignor warrants that:

(1) *the assignor will do nothing to defeat or impair the value of the assignment;*

(2) *the right exists and is subject to no defenses or limitations not stated or apparent; and that*

(3) *any document delivered is genuine and what it purports to be.*

The implied warranties do not run to a sub-assignee (an assignee of an assignee).

Comment: The assignor does not impliedly warrant that the obligor is solvent or that the obligor will perform; that is, the assignor is not a guarantor.

B. DELEGATION OF DUTIES

1. WHAT IS A DELEGATION?

A delegation occurs when an obligor (delegant) appoints another person (delegate) to render a performance that is owed to a third person. There are many kinds of delegations and delegates. At the simplest level an employee who is told to deliver a package of goods owed to a third person is a delegate. Somewhat more complex is the status of a construction subcontractor to whom a portion of the work is delegated. More complex yet is the status of a person to whom the entire performance of the obligations of a contract, including the duty of supervision of the performance, is delegated.

2. LIABILITY OF THE DELEGANT

Delegants cannot free themselves from liability by delegating duties.

Comment: This is perhaps the only immutable rule in the law of contracts. There is no way an obligor can be freed from liability other than by consent of the obligee, the decree of a bankruptcy court, or passage of the statute of limitations. The delegant can be discharged from liability by a novation. A novation is a three party agreement whereby the delegate assumes the duties of the obligor and the assumption is accepted by the obligee in substitution for the original obligor's liability. A novation is not an exception to the rule. The discharge occurs only by consent of the obligee.

3. LIABILITY OF THE DELEGATE

The delegate becomes liable to the third party only if the delegate makes a promise that is deemed to be a promise that is for the benefit of the third person.

Examples: (1) *D* agrees to build a house for *C*, pursuant to certain plans. *D* subcontracts the plumbing work to *A*. *A* fails to complete the work within the time provided for in the original contract. *C* seeks to hold *A* liable for delay damages. *C* has no cause of action. The promise of the subcontractor is not deemed to be for the benefit of the owner but solely for the benefit of the delegant. Based on *stare decisis* it is generally held that the owner is only an incidental beneficiary of a construction subcontract.

(2) *D* owes *C* $10,000 secured by a mortgage on Blackacre. *A* purchases Blackacre from *D* who delegates to *A* the duty to pay *C*. *A* promises *D* to pay $10,000 to *C*. *C* is a third party beneficiary of *A*'s promise. *A*, a delegate of *D*, has also "assumed" an obligation to *C*. There is no novation because *C* has not agreed to discharge *D*. *C* may obtain judgment against

both *D* and *A*, but is entitled to only one satisfaction. In other words, when *A* "assumed" the mortgage, *C* became a third party intended creditor beneficiary of *A*'s promise to pay.

(3) In the prior illustration assume that, in exchange for *A*'s assumption of *D*'s obligation, *C* discharged *D*. The result would be a novation. Only *A* would be liable to *C*.

(4) *C* and *D* enter into a bilateral contract. *D* delegates the duty to *A* who agrees to assume the duty. *D* informs *C* of the delegation and assumption and states that because of the assumption *C* no longer should look to *D* for performance or liability in the event of nonperformance. Thereafter *C* accepts *A*'s performance. There is substantial authority to the effect that when *C* deals with *A* in the face of *D*'s repudiation an implied novation occurs. The new Restatement, however, follows the lead of the U.C.C. and rules that the obligee can prevent an implied novation by notifying the delegant or delegate that performance will be accepted under protest.

(5) *D* and *C* enter into a bilateral contract. *D*'s duty is non-delegable but *D* delegates it to *A* who agrees for a consideration to assume the obligation. *C* deals with *A* knowing of the delegation. Because *C* has dealt with *A*, the non-delegability has been waived, and *C* may no longer complain that the duty was non-delegable.

Perspective: The above illustrations duplicate in part those given in the section of this outline on third party beneficiaries. We are now adding a new dimension to our study of these illustrations by considering the delegation of duties that appear in these cases.

4. NON–DELEGABLE DUTIES
a. What Duties Are Non-delegable?
Certain duties are delegable; others are not. The test is whether performance by the original obligor or under the obligor's personal supervision is required by the contract. Such a requirement may be expressed in the contract. If it is not, such a requirement will be implied in two kinds of cases:

(a) Where the contract is predicated on the unique skills of the obligor, and

(b) Where the contract is predicated on the trust and confidence that the obligee has placed in the obligor.

Examples: (1) *D* agrees to paint *C*'s portrait. Subsequently, *D* delegates the duty to paint to *A*, an able and better known portrait painter. The delegation is ineffective. *C*'s selection of an artist is presumptively based on *C*'s judgment of the artist's style. *C*'s exercise of taste, even if idiosyncratic, is given effect.

(2) *C* retains *D*, a lawyer in a distant city, to defend a lawsuit. *D* delegated the retainer and assigned the right to payment to *A*, who was successful in causing the case to be dismissed. *C* need pay neither *A* nor *D*. The duties were improperly delegated to *A*. The relationship of attorney and client is based on the trust and confidence of the client. Although the attorney may delegate a substantial part of the duties of preparing a defense to law clerks, associates, partners and even outside counsel, the attorney cannot delegate the duty of overall management and supervision of the case.

(3) *C* contracts with *D* to have an addition built onto a house. *D* delegates the plumbing work to *A*. The delegation is proper. The skills are mechanical. *D* could have performed the contract by hiring a crew of plumbers, each of whom could have been changed on a day to day basis. When this can happen, the contract duties are delegable.

(4) *C* contracts with *XYZ*, Inc., a small specialized company that does applied scientific research, and which had a reputation for excellence. The contract looked to the development of a prototype of a battery operated furnace. *XYZ*, Inc., assigned its rights and delegated its duties to *A*, Inc. The delegation is proper. The delegant is a corporation and its scientists could be changed at any time. Nothing in the contract required the personal performance of any given person.

b.   Delegation in Sales Contracts

In general, the delegation rules of the U.C.C. are the same as the common law. It will be recalled that, under the U.C.C., a general clause prohibiting assignment of the contract has the effect of prohibiting the delegation of duties. Also, under the Code, unless the language or circumstances point to a contrary intention, an assignment in general terms is treated as doing three things: (1) assigning the rights, (2) delegating the duties, (3) and creating an assumption of duties. The U.C.C. also authorizes the obligee to demand assurances from the delegate whenever the other party assigns rights and delegates duties to a third person.

c. Effect of Improper Delegation
An attempted delegation of a non-delegable duty is ineffective. It is also a breach. If persisted in, the breach is material.

REVIEW QUESTIONS

S, a distributor of footballs, and *B*, a sporting goods retailer, entered into a contract whereby *S* agreed to sell and *B* agreed to buy 1,000 Brand X footballs of an agreed model at $25 per football, payment to be made 90 days after delivery. The contract provided that any assignment of rights in the contract would be void. Before delivery of the footballs, *S* purported to assign *S*'s rights to *C*.

1. T or F   The purported assignment to *C* was ineffective.

2. T or F   My answer to the previous question would be different if the purported assignment was made after delivery of the footballs.

Assume that there is no anti-assignment clause, and that *S* made a second assignment to *D* who paid value and took without notice of the first assignment, and that *D* gave notice of the assignment to *B* who paid *D* before learning of the assignment to *C*.

3. T or F   Under none of the competing common law rules can *C* recover from *D*.

4. T or F   The result in question 3 today may depend on a factor or factors not mentioned in the facts.

Assume hereafter that the assignments previously mentioned had not been made by *S*. Instead, before delivering the footballs, *S* had, for a valuable consideration, signed and delivered a writing that read "I hereby assign my contract with *B* to *X*."

5. T or F   This would be interpreted as only a delegation of duties.

Assume hereafter that there was only an attempted delegation of duties from *S* to *X* with an agreement by *X*, for a consideration, to assume the duties of *S*.

6. T or F   *B* may treat the delegation as creating reasonable grounds for insecurity.

7. T or F   The duties attempted to be delegated were non-delegable.

8. T or F   Assume the duty was delegable and that upon delegating the duty *S* stated to *B* that *S* no longer considered itself obligated by the contract and that *B* should look solely to *X* for performance. If *B* deals with *X* thereafter, there would be a novation.

9. Essay   On January 2, 1990, Abel contracted in writing subscribed by both parties to sell to Baker 1,000 bales of cotton on or before May 1, 1990 at the price of $50,000, payable $20,000 cash on delivery. On delivery of the cotton, Baker was to execute a promissory note in the amount of $30,000 payable in one year. The contract also stated that "this contract is non-assignable." On March 1, 1990, Caleb bought Baker's business. At the bottom of the contract with Abel, Baker wrote, "I hereby assign this contract to Caleb." This document was delivered to Caleb. Abel was notified by letter of this transaction. Abel in reply, on March 6th, wrote to Baker and Caleb saying "Since you have wrongfully assigned, I regard the contract as terminated and am selling the cotton elsewhere."

(a)   Assume that Caleb sued on March 7, 1990, without tendering anything. What are the rights of the parties?

(b)   Assume that no action has been commenced and on April 15, 1990, Abel wrote Caleb and Baker, "I retract my letter of March 6th. I will make delivery on May 1st." What are the liabilities of Caleb and Baker if Caleb refuses to accept delivery?

ANSWERS TO REVIEW QUESTIONS

I. MUTUAL ASSENT—OFFER AND ACCEPTANCE

1. **True.** The answer is supplied by the statement that a reasonable person in P's position would conclude that A was not serious. Under the objective theory of contracts and the reasonable person approach, there is no contract.

2. **True.** The parties here clearly agreed that this was a sham arrangement and therefore intended that no legal consequences would attach to the writing.

3. **False.** If a doctor promises to follow a certain procedure, the doctor has made an enforceable commitment. On the facts, the doctor appears to have made such a promise. If so, she has a cause of action. The most that can be argued on the other side is that this is a question of fact.

4. **False.** This is similar to the cases involving ads for the sale of goods. First, it is doubtful if there is language of commitment. The fact that the Tribune will refuse certain types of advertisements does not mean that it will accept all others. In any event, there is no statement of quantity. Thus, an offer was not made.

5. *True.*   As a common law proposition an announcement that an auction will be held is deemed to be a statement of intention. Under the Uniform Commercial Code, even after the goods have been put up for sale, the auctioneer may withdraw the goods from sale except where the auction is "without reserve" and a bid is received within a reasonable time.

6. *False.*   P's first communication was only an inquiry. D then asked for an offer. When P named a sum P made an offer. But this was rejected by D. P then made an additional inquiry. D's statement is not language of promise or commitment. Rather D is saying that an offer for less than $56,000 would not be considered. Thus, the only offer that is made is P's offer to pay $56,000 which was made when P said "I accept". This offer was not accepted.

7. *False.*   Although B may have been legally bound to return the watch so that there is no consideration, there is an additional reason why B may not recover. B did not know of the offer or intend to accept.

8. *False.*   B clearly knew of the offer. The issue is intent to accept. Under one view, the offeree may testify to his or her state of mind. If B testifies to having a subjective intent to accept and is believed, B will prevail. Under a second view, there is a presumption that B intended to accept, and B is not permitted to testify as to subjective intention. The presumption is rebuttable. On the facts, whether the presumption is rebutted is probably a question of fact.

9. *False.*   Although a reasonable person could conclude that this was an offer looking to a series of unilateral contracts, it could also be concluded that the act called for was the discontinuance of publication and that there was one unilateral contract with a series of performances. In either event, abstaining from publication for a week is a condition precedent to A's obligation to pay $10 each week. The main difference is that if A's words amounted to an offer looking to a series of unilateral contracts, A would be free to revoke prospectively. This is not true under the second analysis.

10. *False.*   A is not contractually bound under the rules of acceptance by silence because A did not have a reasonable opportunity to reject the services. In addition under the rules of property law A would not be guilty of an act of wrongful dominion by occupying the house because the structure is A's.

11. *False.*   Since A was unconscious, A did not expressly or impliedly agree to anything. B is entitled to a quasi-contractual recovery measured by the reasonable value of B's services.

12. ***Depends.*** It depends upon whether a reasonable person in the position of A would conclude that B expected to be paid for the work to be done prior to the contract or that B was doing the preliminary work in hopes of obtaining the contract. The custom of the trade might supply the answer.

13. ***False.*** Although there seems to be an offer and an acceptance by an act of dominion, the Restatement, Second, states that the offeree is not bound by the offered terms where, as here, they are manifestly unreasonable. If there is no contract there is a conversion and A should have the option of suing in contract, tort, or quasi-contract, but nevertheless the Restatement takes the position that A should be limited to a reasonable value recovery in this contractual action.

14. ***True.*** Because the counter offer is effective when it is received, and was lost, it does not act as a rejection. The letter of acceptance is authorized (reasonable) and is effective when sent (2 P.M.) even though it was lost. Under the majority view, a revocation is effective when it is received. Therefore, there is a contract. Under the minority view that a revocation is effective when sent, the result would be different.

15. ***True.*** Despite the quoted language, the offer is revocable. There is no consideration to support the promise of irrevocability. U.C.C. § 2–205 does not apply, because the case involves real property. The rejection terminated the revocable offer as did the revocation.

16. ***False.*** Because no time period is stated, the offer is open for a reasonable time. Because the offer is to sell at a fixed price in a fluctuating market, it is clear that the offer should be open for a relatively short period—long enough to give the offeree a reasonable opportunity to consider the offer. This time had long since elapsed when the attempted acceptance occurred.

17. ***False.*** The manifest purpose of the offeror is the conviction of the criminal. This can happen until the statute of limitations expires. When this happens depends upon the law of a particular jurisdiction, but under the facts it is clear that it had not.

18. ***False.*** The offeror may stipulate in the offer that the power of acceptance shall terminate upon the happening of a certain event. If the event happens before the acceptance, the power of acceptance lapses even though the offeree is not informed that the event has occurred.

19. ***True.*** When an offer is made in a face to face or telephone conversation or in any situation where there are direct negotiations, the offer is

deemed, in the absence of a manifestation of a contrary intention, to be open only while the parties are conversing.

20. *False.* A revocable offer looking to a series of contracts may be terminated prospectively. Under the majority view, an adjudication of incompetency followed by the appointment of a guardian terminated the offer even though B was unaware of what transpired. Under this view, A is liable only for the first delivery.

21. *False.* The "equal publicity" doctrine does not apply because A knew of B's existence and address. A was bound to personally notify B.

22. *True.* The payment of $100 makes the offer irrevocable. Under the modern view, the counter offer does not terminate the original offer. Therefore it can still be accepted by B.

23. *True.* Whether the 7 days are measured from Jan. 2 or Jan. 3, an acceptance sent on Jan. 9 is timely if sent in an authorized (reasonable) manner, which is the case here. In computing 7 days, the day from which the computation is made is not ordinarily considered.

24. *False.* Under the provisions of U.C.C. § 2–311 there is a contract.

25. *False.* The traditional common law rule is that an agreement to agree as to a material term renders the agreement too vague and indefinite to be enforced (void). But here the quoted words indicate that the parties have agreed to make a good faith effort to reach agreement. A breach of that promise will amount to a breach of contract.

26. *(a)* (1) Thompson's call was undoubtedly an inquiry.

(2) Case's reply amounted to an offer. There is language of commitment (I will sell to you). The offer was sufficiently definite (subject matter, price and delivery). It was made to one person. The phrase "or to anybody else for that matter", is best understood as a comment to Thompson indicating an intent to sell to someone else if Thompson did not accept. (See 6 below).

(3) Did the offer lapse? (a) Because the parties were face to face, the offer presumably lapsed after the conversation. But the words "upon an agreement" could indicate the contrary. (b) Was the acceptance within a reasonable time? Probably not, but essentially this is a question of fact.

(4)(a) Proper mode of acceptance. As a common law proposition, the words "upon an agreement" indicate an offer looking to a bilateral contract and, even if the offer is considered ambiguous, it would still be deemed to look to a bilateral contract. (b) Under the U.C.C. if the offer "unambiguously" looks to a bilateral contract, it must be accepted by promise. If the offer is ambiguous or indifferent, it may be accepted by any reasonable means including promise, performance or the commencement of performance. Thompson, however, has not performed because Thompson has not paid. At most, picking up the tractor is the beginning of performance in which case the offeror may treat the offer as having lapsed if the offeror does not receive notification within a reasonable time. (Is notification after two weeks reasonable?) (See 3b above). But the offeror may treat the situation as if a contract was formed.

(5) Alternatively, Thompson may be viewed as having accepted by an act of wrongful dominion. The act of dominion would be wrongful if Thompson could accept only by promise and failed to make one, or if the offer had lapsed. In the event that there is a wrongful act of dominion, Case would have the option given by U.C.C. § 2–606; i.e., he could hold Thompson to an acceptance of the offer or, at Case's option, as a tortfeasor.

(6) Was an offer made to Petersen? (i) The offer to Case is not transferable to Petersen. (ii) There was no general offer to the public. The offer was communicated to Thompson alone. (See 2 above). The only way in which it can be said that there was an offer to Petersen would be if Case had made Thompson Case's agent for this purpose. This seems unlikely on the facts presented.

(b) If (a) is answered thoroughly, there is little to say here. If you eliminated the quoted language, then the offer is indifferent (ambiguous) as to the manner of acceptance.

(c) At common law, the sentence relating to the arbitration clause would appear to make the communication a counter offer. (Could it be a mere comment on the terms?) Under the U.C.C., the first question is whether there is a definite and seasonable expression of acceptance. This seems to be the case and the acceptance is clearly not conditional. Thus, there is a contract. The additional term does not become part of the contract whether or not the parties are merchants. The offeror did not assent to the term and the additional term is a material alteration under most of the cases decided on this issue. Therefore, there is a contract but it does not include the arbitration clause.

27. (1) The first paragraph merely provides factual background and raises no legal issues.

(2) In the next paragraph, plaintiff invited defendant to give the plaintiff a 60 day option on terms suggested by the plaintiff. No legal relations have been affected.

(3) The reply by defendant does not make the requested offer. Does it make any offer? Although it contains detailed terms and comes in reply to a letter requesting an offer, it lacks language of commitment and contains language that demonstrates a lack of present commitment.

"We would be willing to sell . . . *if such an offer were made today,*" either indicates a lack of commitment or, at best is an offer open for a day. The phrase "letter of intent" also normally shows a lack of commitment. More conclusively, there is a further reference to an offer to be made by plaintiff that will be a "firm and binding one." Perhaps contradictory is language that: "you are assured . . . we will enter into a contract . . ." Such language appears promissory. Nonetheless, taken as a whole, the communication is at best ambiguous as to its legal effect. Offers are not construed from weak language. They must be clear expressions of commitment.

(4) Even if it were deemed to be an offer, the letter contains terms that are indefinite. "Suitable assurances" unless fleshed out by usage in this type of case appears vague as to what such assurances might be and what personnel are involved. "Mutually satisfactory arrangements" is also quite indefinite. Even if this language is construed as requiring bargaining in good faith by plaintiff, Conroy is not a contracting party and Conroy would be under no such obligation.

(5) The large sums of money spent by plaintiff was doubtless in reliance upon defendant's manifestation of intention to enter into the contract. Recently, courts have protected the reliance interest of a party who in good faith expends money in reliance upon continued good faith negotiations. The cases involve an extension of the doctrine of promissory estoppel. The facts do not indicate whether defendant broke off negotiations in bad faith.

(6) Plaintiff's letter of April 1 is conceivably an acceptance of defendant's offer, if one deems defendant's letter of February 28 to be an offer. It is a manifestation of willingness to enter into the contract on defendant's terms. However, plaintiff labels its communication as an offer. One would suspect that a court would hold an apparently sophisticated business to its own conclusion as to the nature of its communications.

(7) The reference to the formal agreement to be drafted by General Counsel may well be found, as a factual question, to indicate that plaintiff had no intention to be bound until such an agreement were entered into. We are dealing with an apparently sizable corporate acquisition and it is unlikely that there was an intent to be bound until the details were worked out.

II. CONSIDERATION AND ITS EQUIVALENTS

1. ***True.***   All three elements of consideration are present. The mother suffered detriment in naming the child as desired by the putative father. This was clearly bargained for by the father. The mother in turn knew of the offer and intended to accept.

2. ***True.***   P suffered detriment in delivering the goods. This was bargained for by D. P knew of the offer and intended to accept. The fact that D promised to pay for past deliveries is not important because of the rule that one consideration will support many promises.

3. ***False.***   D's promise is not enforceable because under the law of Guardian and Ward P in returning etc., was only doing what P is legally obligated to do and did not suffer detriment. Thus, there is no consideration to support D's promise. The duty discussed here is not imposed by the law of contracts.

4. ***True.***   When D promised to guarantee payment, D made an additional promise and there was no consideration because P never did anything other than what P was legally obligated to do. Thus there was no consideration for this promise.

5. ***True.***   Under the majority view, plaintiffs were only doing what they were legally obligated to do. There was no consideration to support the promise of D to pay an additional sum.

6. ***True.***   Under the First Restatement, D's promise to pay more would not be enforceable because there was no impossibility of performance. Under the Restatement, Second, the promise is binding even though not supported by consideration "if the modification is fair and equitable in view of circumstances not anticipated when the contract was made." Before this rule can be applied, additional facts must be known. In any event, the applicable rule is U.C.C. § 2–209(1) which provides that a modification is binding without consideration even though it is oral. Under the U.C.C., D would be required to pay the additional sum provided P is acting in good faith and has a legitimate commercial reason for seeking a modification.

7. ***False.***   The common law rule is that the agreement may be modified despite the contrary provision in the initial agreement. U.C.C. § 2–209(2) could not change the result because it relates only to a contract for the sale of goods.

8. ***True.***   B's promise to pay A a fair share of the profits is too vague and indefinite to be enforced and the result is a void bilateral contract

under the doctrine of mutuality of consideration. Although *A* complies with the two minimum rules for forging a good unilateral contract out of a bad bilateral contract *A* is still not able to enforce the contract, because despite *A*'s performance *B*'s promise is too vague and indefinite to be enforced. Thus *A* is not entitled to a contractual recovery but may recover in quasi contract.

9. ***True.*** *D* has made alternative promises. In such a case the rule is that for detriment to exist each alternative must be detrimental. On the facts, *D* must either sell or give 5 days notice. Each alternative is detrimental. Under U.C.C. § 2–309, there may be a question of unconscionability.

10. ***True.*** Here *B* has made only one promise (to buy 12 carloads) and *S* has made two promises (to sell 12 carloads and give *B* the option of buying 13 more carloads). The rule is that one consideration (*B*'s buying) will support many promises. Thus, *B*'s promise is consideration for *S*'s promise to sell an additional 13 carloads. As to these 13 carloads, *S* has made an irrevocable offer (option contract). *S* is not free to revoke this offer. *B* is entitled to receive the additional 13 carloads.

11. ***True.*** Because the work is requested, it is clear, under modern law, that in the absence of a promise to pay a specific sum, *B* would be entitled to the reasonable value of the services. The issue is whether, under the law relating to moral obligation, *B* is entitled to $7,200 or $10,000. According to most, *B* may recover $10,000. Corbin would limit the enforcement to an amount not disproportionate to the value of the services. The Restatement, Second, is unclear.

12. ***True.*** It is clear that there was substantial injurious reliance on the part of *D* on the gift promise made by *F*. Thus the doctrine of Promissory Estoppel applies. Under the First Restatement, where a court could choose either a contractual recovery or nothing, it is possible that $17,000 would be awarded. Under the notion of flexibility of remedy espoused by the Restatement Second, *D* would probably be limited to reliance damages—$2,000.

13. ***True.*** This is a case of gratuitous agency under the doctrine of promissory estoppel. Despite the fact that all of the elements for a promissory estoppel exist, under the traditional approach in a gratuitous agency situation, the promise will be enforced only where there is misfeasance—negligent performance. Here, there is only non-feasance—failure to perform. Thus *P* will not recover under the traditional rule.

14. (1) It is clear on the facts that there was no consideration for *A*'s promise. *B*'s "kindnesses" amounted to past consideration. *A*'s reference to "friendship," etc., indicates a gift making state of mind. *A* apparently was not bargaining for *B* to come to the United States or for *B* to work in the business.

(2) The next question is moral obligation. Receipt of unrequested benefits does not, as stated above, create a legal obligation. If a subsequent promise is made to pay for these benefits, the majority of cases hold that the promise is unenforceable. A minority view would permit enforcement of the promise. The Restatement, Second, would take the same position with respect to benefits received in an emergency. Recovery would also be permitted under the California statute mentioned in the text.

(3) "Permanent employment", standing alone, amounts to a hiring at will in the absence of a consideration over and above the employment. Here under the conclusions reached in (a) above there was no such consideration.

(4) However, *B* took substantial action in reliance upon *A*'s promise. It would appear that *B* may recover under a theory of promissory estoppel if it can be established that the action involved injury to *B*. The question is, how his damages should be computed? Should he be limited to reliance damages or should he obtain a full contractual recovery?

Full contractual recovery would entitle *B* to the value of *A*'s promise. Assuming the promise means *B* will have a job for his working life, *B* would be entitled to wages for that period of time, minus what *B* earns or reasonably could earn at substitute employment. (Wages as a truck-driver appears to be a proper standard because the parties defined "employment" by practical construction, i.e., course of performance.) Reliance damages would likely be more appropriate here. *A* generously extricated *B* from his difficulties abroad, paid *B*'s travel expenses and gave *B* a start in a trade. Justice might dictate some small, if any, recovery for what *B* gave up when he left Poland, to the extent that these exceeded the benefits *B* received under the contract.

III. LEGAL CAPACITY

1. *True.*   The infant may disaffirm an executed transaction for a reasonable time after reaching majority. Here *A* disaffirms immediately after reaching maturity. The action is timely. Since *A* seeks restitution *A* must account for the consideration received. *A* should tender return of the money.

2. *True.*   Here the contract is executory at least as far as the adult is concerned. The youth has obtained no benefit under the contract, and there is no injustice to the adult in allowing the youth to disaffirm. The only other question is whether *A* ratified the contract after majority by telling the seller that another payment would be made. A statement that payment will be made is not generally a ratification.

3. *False.*   Normally, if the incompetent's executed contract is on fair terms and the other party has no reason to know of the incompetence, the transaction cannot be disaffirmed unless the status quo ante can be restored.

4.   Despite a misrepresentation of age the majority view allows the infant to disaffirm.   On disaffirmance the infant must return any consideration received which the infant still has or anything traceable to the consideration.   An interesting question is whether the grandfather's reimbursement falls into this category.   If so, it would appear that the airline would be entitled to only $150, the value of the flight, rather than $200 or $300.

Another question is whether the flight is a necessary.   It is questionable whether a college education at a distant location is a necessary.   If the education is a necessary, however, it would seem to follow that the flight is also.   If it is, Janice is liable for the reasonable value of the flight.

IV.   PROPER FORM (WRITING) AND INTERPRETATION

1. *False.*   Since there is a total integration the writing may not be contradicted or supplemented.   But this rule does not apply where there is an express condition precedent to the formation of a contract.   This appears to be the situation here.

2. *True.*   If it is assumed that there is a total integration, the writing may not be contradicted or supplemented.   If there is a partial integration, the writing may not be contradicted but it may be supplemented by a consistent additional term.   The offered term appears to be contradictory and therefore it would not make any difference if the integration is total or partial.   In either event the term is inadmissible.

3. *False.*   Whether or not the requirements contract is a total integration the evidence is admissible because the stock agreement has its own separate consideration on each side.   Thus, there is at most a partial integration and the only issue is whether this agreement contradicts the main agreement.   Since it is clear that there is no contradiction, the evidence is admissible.

4. *False.* The case relates to the one year section of the Statute of Frauds. Logically, the contract is not within the Statute, as the severance could legally occur the same day. Since the day of contracting is disregarded as a fraction of a day, the contract is performable within one year.

5. *False.* The one year section of the Statute of Frauds is not violated if the promise by its terms may be performed within one year, however unlikely or improbable that may be. Here, it is possible that the plaintiff may not need the switch, for example, after six months. Therefore, the defendant's promise is not within the one year section of the Statute of Frauds.

6. *False.* Under one view the promise not to compete for two years is within the Statute of Frauds. But under another view, since the essential purpose of the promise would be attained by the death of the promisor, the promise is not within the Statute of Frauds.

7. *False.* It is clear that the agreement cannot be performed within one year from the *making* thereof. However, the court permitted a contractual recovery on the theory of promissory estoppel because "unconscionable injury" should not be permitted. Here, contrary to many other cases, *P* was not limited to reliance damages.

8. *False.* *D*'s promise is not within the one year section of the Statute of Frauds because *P* could die within one year from the making of the promise. In a few jurisdictions, the Statute is supplemented by a lifetime or a testamentary disposition provision. Under these statutes, restitution would be available.

9. *False.* As soon as the memorandum was signed, the Statute was satisfied. Delivery is not needed.

10. *False.* An oral acceptance of a written offer to a contract that is within the Statute of Frauds results in a contract enforceable against the offeror.

11. *False.* The oral rescission is effective, despite the fact that the original agreement was within the Statute of Frauds and in writing.

12. *True.* The oral modification is enforceable, because the new agreement is not within the Statute of Frauds.

13. *False.* The oral modification is unenforceable, because the agreement, as modified, is within the Statute. As a result, the written contract stands unmodified.

14. *False.* Even though one of the writings containing an essential term is not signed, under the majority rule, if the documents by internal evidence refer to the same subject matter or transaction, the memoranda are sufficient to satisfy the Statute of Frauds.

15. *True.* The executor is orally promising to be personally liable for a debt of the estate. The executor is therefore promising to answer for the debt, default, or miscarriage of another, and has a defense under the suretyship Statute of Frauds.

16. *True.* The amount involved is clearly for an amount in excess of $500. *B* is not a merchant and the written memorandum is not effective against *B*. The result would be different if *B* were a merchant. See U.C.C. § 2–201(2).

17. *True.* Here, both parties are merchants, and the confirmatory memorandum is sufficient to satisfy the U.C.C. Statute of Frauds. But, in addition, there is a problem with the one year section of the Statute of Frauds. The more stringent requirements of that Statute's rule with respect to a memorandum must be met. *B*'s letter incorporates the confirmatory memorandum and satisfies the Statute of Frauds.

18. *False.* Although marriage is a contemplated condition of the contract it is not the consideration. The agreement is, therefore, not within the section of the Statute of Frauds that relates to an "agreement made upon consideration of marriage."

19. *True.* If *F* is bargaining for them to marry, marriage is the consideration and a writing is needed. If marriage is not consideration then the Statute is not involved, but in that event there is no consideration to support the promise.

20. *True.* The real property Statute of Frauds is not applicable to a brokerage contract which is a service contract. The real property aspect is only incidental. In a number of jurisdictions, a separate statute requires a broker's retainer to be in writing.

21. *False.* Although, in most instances, the agent's authority need not be in writing, under a number of statutes, the authority of the agent must be in writing in a case involving real property.

22. *False.* If the vendor of the property conveys the property to the vendee, the promise of the vendee will be enforced even though it is oral.

23. Because *C* was obliged to pay *E* $90,000 in fifteen monthly installments, it seems clear that the agreement, by its terms, may not be performed within

one year from the making thereof. Thus, the one year section of the Statute of Frauds is involved. It is not clear from the question whether the parties had signed the instrument and whether the writing mentioned contained all of the essential terms necessary to satisfy the Statute.

In addition to the Statute of Frauds problem, there is a parol evidence rule problem. This stems from the fact that during negotiations (presumably prior to the writing) the parties had agreed (it is not important if the agreement was reached during prior negotiations in writing or orally) "that if overtime became necessary it should be added on a time-and-a-half basis." Whether this evidence is admissible depends upon whether the writing was an integration (which it undoubtedly was) and if so whether it was a total or a partial integration. If it is a total integration, it may not be contradicted or supplemented. If it is partial, it may not be contradicted but it may be supplemented by consistent additional terms. Here, it is debatable whether the term offered is consistent or contradictory. In addition, under the various views discussed in this outline, different conclusions as to whether the integration was partial or total could be reached. For example, under Williston's view, it would appear that it would be natural to have included this term in the writing and so the integration would be total with the result that this term would be excluded. The U.C.C. parol evidence rule would not apply because the agreement does not relate to sale of goods.

This question arises in another form because a later oral agreement of the parties provided, in part, that C would pay E "a time-and-a-half for all worker hours worked over forty hours per week." (Presumably overtime started after 40 hours). Here, we are not dealing with the parol evidence rule, because this agreement was subsequent to the writing and the parol evidence rule does not apply to subsequent agreements. The issue is one of consideration. Was there consideration for C's promise to pay E $6,000 per month until the job was completed, plus time-and-a-half for overtime? If the time-and-a-half provision was in the original agreement this would not be a problem but the problem would still exist as to the promise to pay $6,000 per month. At first blush, it would appear that E is not suffering any detriment. U.C.C. § 2–209(1) does not affect the problem because it relates only to sale of goods. However, it could be argued that if the original agreement was unenforceable, E would be free to terminate the obligation under the original agreement and thus would not be burdened by pre-existing duty. However, before doing this E may be required to demand a sufficient memorandum from C.

The validity of the modification is not affected by the clause in the original agreement that recited "this contract may be amended only in a signed writing." Under the common law rule, the agreement may be modified by a subsequent agreement despite the existence of such a clause. There is a contrary U.C.C. provision (U.C.C. § 2–209(2)) (but see also subdivisions 4 and 5) which does not apply because the agreement does not relate to the sale of goods.

The subsequent agreement does not appear to contravene the Statute of Frauds because *by its terms* it may be performed within one year, however unlikely or improbable that may be. The result is the same whether the arrangement was unilateral or bilateral. Because the new agreement is not within the Statute of Frauds, it is enforceable, even if the prior arrangement was within the Statute of Frauds and satisfied by a sufficient writing. Under the majority rule the new agreement is not only enforceable without a writing but also serves to discharge the prior written agreement. Thus, the subsequent agreement would appear to be binding if it is in fact supported by consideration.

There are a number of additional questions that could be considered. (1) There was no duress with respect to the modification agreement because there was no threat to breach the contract. If there were such a threat there would still not be duress under the modern view because the threatened breach would probably not be a breach of the duty of good faith and fair dealing. (2) *C*'s explanation that it had not paid the bills because it "was short of cash" would appear to be an admission of liability. (3) When *E* paid $2,000 and refused to pay more, this could arguably be looked upon as the basis of an accord and satisfaction. If *C*, as indicated above, is bound by an apparent admission, then the claim is liquidated and there is no basis for an accord and satisfaction. If *C* is not, there may still be an accord and satisfaction if *C* has sufficiently manifested that intention. (4) *C*'s estimate, mentioned at the beginning of the contract, does not appear to affect the problem particularly since *E* was undoubtedly as expert as *C* in determining the time required for a performance and, thus, there is no basis for any reliance.

V. CONDITIONS, PERFORMANCE AND BREACH

1. *False.* The condition is excused by *U*'s prevention. An action for damages is available to *N*.

2. *False.* The offer ripened into a bilateral contract by *N*'s promise. While an offer can be revoked, a contract is not revocable.

3. *False.* Handsome must make the determination in good faith. This requirement is a sufficient restraint on his freedom so that his commitment is genuine.

4. *False.* The appropriate doctrines are prospective failure of condition and anticipatory repudiation.

5. ***False.*** The contract is not divisible. Although the payout is on a per mile basis, it is apparent that a major part of the price is allocated to the tunnel.

6. ***True.*** In a service contract, absent agreement to the contrary, the rendition of services is a constructive condition precedent to payment.

7. ***True.*** The doctrine of anticipatory breach does not apply to a case where the repudiating party is under an obligation solely to pay money at a fixed time or fixed times.

8. ***False.*** The insurer's installment obligations are not apportioned exchanges for agreed installment obligations by the insured.

9. ***True.*** *A* appeared totally unable to perform and *A* was unable to provide assurances. *Z*'s conduct in hiring a substitute was permissible.

10. ***False.*** In view of the response to the prior question, *B*'s contract with *Z* is clearly binding upon *B* and *Z*.

11. ***False.*** Under any view of the matter cancellation is too precipitous. Under the new Restatement, *B* may suspend any performance and demand assurances. Under the old Restatement the inquiry would include the question of whether *S* had a right to prepay the mortgage or a justifiable expectation that the mortgagee will accept prepayment.

12. ***False.*** Even if *B* had the right to cancel, there would be no right to sue for anticipatory breach. *S* has not taken any act, after contracting, that is inconsistent with the obligations of the contract.

13. ***True.*** The waiver made on March 1 may be retracted until such time as there has been a change of position in reliance upon it. No such change of position is stated.

14. ***True.*** A clause that makes time of the essence creates an express condition that performance be rendered at the stated time.

15. ***False.*** Because it is an express condition, it cannot be a constructive condition.

16. ***False.*** It is both. *S* has a duty to tender title on June 1 and *S*'s rights are conditioned on such tender.

17. ***False.*** See the discussion of the answer to the preceding question.

18. As a general rule a date specified in a contract for completion of performance is not of the essence; that is to say, failure to complete on time is not, standing alone, a material breach. Consequently, the aggrieved party cannot treat such delay as a failure of condition. Cancellation is not a permissible response.

The cancellation took place almost three weeks after the scheduled completion date. About two-thirds of the work remained to be done. It would appear from this that on July 16, X was in material breach. Although failure to complete on that date was not *per se* a material breach, substantial lack of completion would be a material breach. If so, Constructor waived the constructive condition of substantial performance by the due date, resulting in an obligation by X to complete within a reasonable time. Whether August 2 is the end of a reasonable period of time is basically a question of fact. It would have been better for Constructor to have fixed a new reasonable completion date on July 16, stating that this new date was of the essence. If Constructor justifiably cancelled it has an action against X for total breach. If, however, the cancellation is unjustified, X has an action for total breach against Constructor.

X's breach may be excused. Delays caused by weather are, however, seldom excused. Barring extreme and unforeseeable conditions, a construction contractor assumes the risk of weather. [See Chapter VI on Defenses]. Delays caused by delays of other subcontractors were specifically made excuses by the contract, but conditioned on filing a timely notice of claim. X's evidence that a representative of Constructor waived the condition of timely written notice is relevant and admissible. As it is subsequent to the making of the contract it is not barred by the parol evidence rule. Waiver of a condition that is not a material part of the agreed exchange is effective without consideration. The condition of timely notice is not part of the agreed exchange which essentially is a trade of money for masonry. If a substantial part of X's delay was excusable on this ground, X would be absolved of any charge of material breach.

The bringing in of Y raises a number of problems. If X was not materially in breach when Y commenced work, Constructor repudiated the contract by bringing in Y, unless the bringing in of Y was justified because of the prospective inability of X to substantially perform. In all likelihood, however, when X acquiesced in the bringing in of Y there was a modification of the contract by conduct. There is no indication that X protested. At any rate, the existence of this modification is a question of fact.

Y's conduct in offering a higher rate of pay gives X no rights against Y. There is no privity between subcontractors. [Chapter X on Third Party Beneficiaries]. It is doubtful whether Constructor is responsible for Y's actions. X will argue that the paying of higher wages to masons hindered X's performance, excusing the resulting delay. Yet Constructor is not responsible for such hinderance unless, as discussed in the previous paragraph, the bringing in of Y was wrongful and the hinderance is a proximate result of that wrong. This seems doubtful because there would appear to have been an implied modification of the contract.

VI. DEFENSES

1. *True.*   Ignorance of facts making a contract illegal insulates a party from the charge of illegality.

2. *False.*   In the law of contracts ignorance of the law insulates one from the charge of illegality when one relies on the presumed expertise of the other party. The inexperienced actor can rely on the presumed expertise of the producer.

3. *True.*   The illegal provision is central to the agreement.

4. *False.*   The doctrine of *locus poenitentiae* is engaged when one party withdraws from an illegal agreement.

5. *False.*   It was not impossible to complete the portrait prior to the fire and it is not impossible to start again.

6. *True.*   The death of the artist discharges the contract because the performance is personal. Generally, the law attempts to restore the status quo ante when such discharges occur.

7. *False.*   A novation has been formed. Note that B consented to a discharge of the agreements B had with A.

8. (a) The question boils down to the issue of whether T may successfully raise the defense of frustration of purpose. T's performance (paying money) is surely not impossible to perform. Nonetheless, once condemnation became imminent it would have been senseless for T to continue with the construction of the theater facilities. T's basic purpose in entering into the lease appears to have been frustrated. This is the starting point for the defense to be considered, but it is not sufficient in itself.

Was the ability to operate a theater a basic assumption shared by both parties? The lease was for a long term and for a restricted use. It would appear that L shared with T the assumption that a theater could be operated on the site as a long term proposition. Nonetheless, we must ask whether the risk was assumed by T. This in part turns on whether the condemnation was foreseeable as a possibility. If it was foreseeable, then T will be held to have assumed the risk. A foreseeable risk is assumed when a party fails to negotiate an exemption from it.

Was the frustration total? Frustration is not a defense unless the event totally or almost totally frustrates the purpose of the contract. It seems clear that the drive-in theater was frustrated in its totality, but we do not know if the land could have been used for any other purpose during July and August. The lease permits the selling of snack food. Absent further facts it is difficult to gauge whether this was a viable use or whether the selling of snacks (clearly intended as accessory to the use of the land as a drive-in theater) at the location would be so impracticable as to be equated with total frustration. Moreover, we do not know if other uses (e.g., a parking lot) could have been made of the land with the consent of L. The burden is on T to prove the defense. If the facts given are all T has proved, the defense should not be allowed.

Thus far this essay is written on the assumption that the lease does not allocate the risk of condemnation. To the extent that it does, the lease itself provides the answer to our question.

(b) T's second defense is that of discharge by accord and satisfaction. T will argue that the settlement was a substituted contract resulting in the discharge of the rent claim and its substitution by the settlement agreement. The new agreement acts as an accord while at the same time it acts as a satisfaction of L's claim. The consideration for L's agreement is T's surrender of T's good faith and not unreasonable defense of frustration.

L may prefer to view the settlement agreement as an executory accord. This kind of an agreement is unenforceable at common law and is still unenforceable in some jurisdictions. For example, in New York an executory accord is enforceable only if it is in writing.

The distinction between an executory accord and a substituted contract is that the latter is intended to discharge immediately the pre-existing claim. In an executory accord the intention is to discharge the claim upon performance of the accord. Consequently, the classification of the agreement is a question of interpretation. If the parties have not made themselves clear, the greater the deliberateness and formalization of the agreement, the more likely we are dealing with a substituted contract. Of course, under the modern view it would make no difference on these facts into which class the agreement fell.

(c) C's lack of a license is not necessarily fatal to its claim against T. When a licensing requirement is based upon a legislative determination to control the moral fitness or skills of a licensee, it is generally held that the lack of a license is a bar to recovery of fees allegedly earned by the practice of the unlicensed activity. Because the practice of the activity without a license is illegal, contracts made in direct connection with the activity are deemed illegal. This is based upon a presumed legislative intent to bar the collection of fees wrongfully earned.

When, however, the licensing requirement serves other ends, the law is less clear. In searching for legislative intent, the courts have generally held that if the purpose of the statute is to impose an occupation tax, a contract entered into by an unlicensed practitioner is not invalid. Where the purpose, as here, is less clear, each case must be decided on its own facts.

In the case at bar, revenue is being raised but there is some control exercised over the licensee by requiring financial stability and requiring disclosure of the corporate officers. [Because of the last two requisites, it is obvious that the police power is being engaged. Consequently, the case is closer to the cases where the licensing requirement is designed to control the fitness of the licensee. *C* may not recover from *T*.] [Alternative conclusion: Because no effort is made to weed out applicants who lack professional skills or who are morally unfit, the licensing requirement is far removed from the class of cases that hold that unlicensed professionals, such as lawyers, doctors and plumbers cannot recover from their clients. *C* may recover from *T*.]

VII. CONTRACT REMEDIES

1. *False.*   The weight of authority disallows punitive damages for contractual breaches.

2. *False.*   The precondition for specific performance is the inadequacy of the legal remedy. Malice is not usually relevant on this question.

3. *False.*   Restitution at law (quasi-contractual recovery) is one of the options a party aggrieved by a breach has, whether or not the damages remedy is adequate.

4. *True.*   The buyer's general damages are measured by the difference between market price and contract price on the day the buyer learns of the breach.

5. *True.*   Damages for breach of contract are limited to economic losses.

6. *False.*   The seller is liable for consequential damages if the seller knows the buyer's needs and that the buyer is unable to cover. The seller knew that Vendee had contracted to resell to Shrunk. It is not relevant that Vendor did not know the resale price.

7. **False.** Vendee's expectation of making a profit somewhat greater than other sellers may be making is entitled to protection.

8. **True.** There is no requirement that an aggrieved buyer cover.

9. **False.** Once again, Vendee's expectation of making resale profits is protected. The fact that Shrunk released Vendee should not inure to the benefit of Vendor.

10. (a) The firing of Edwards was wrongful. Consequently, Edwards has an action for breach of contract. Specific performance is not an available remedy as courts will not order an employer to reinstate an employee for breach of contract. The rationale is that due performance is too difficult for a court to supervise and that a court is unwilling to force continuation of a personal relationship.

Edwards must opt for either restitution or damages. Because Edwards has transferred a unique thing—rights to a patent—to Colorvideo in exchange (in part) for a percentage of the profits from its exploitation, the remedy at law is less than adequate. Consequently, an action in equity for specific restitution is available. In such an action the court can decree the revestment of the patent. In addition, the court can order the payment of damages for breach of the employment aspects of the relation. The identical measure of damages as is applied in a court of law (see below) would be applied.

Another restitutionary remedy would be a quasi-contractual action. In this action Edwards can receive judgment for the reasonable value of the patent. This is likely to be an undesirable choice. Although Edwards receives the value of the patent—assuming it can be established by expert witnesses—Edwards cannot receive damages for breach of the expectations engendered by the employment aspects of the contract. One cannot get contractual and quasi-contractual relief for the same breach, except as modified by statute.

The third option is an action for damages. Normally, this is measured by the value of expectations—the benefit of the bargain. As for loss of salary, Edwards is entitled to the promised salary less what is earned or reasonably should be earned by exercising reasonable diligence during the term of the contract. Whether the choice of activities was reasonable raises essentially questions of fact. The value of the research services to himself or herself may be deducted from the salary. The recovery will also be reduced by application of the present worth doctrine.

In the action for damages Edwards would also be entitled to the expected 5% of profits. The difficulty however, is whether this amount can be proved with reasonable certainty. The converter is new and has never been mass produced, much less marketed. Whether it would be a success, and whether it would be profitable, is unknown. To assess 5% of unknown profits would be speculative. Should Colorvideo before trial develop a history of profitability, however, this fact may remove the uncertainty.

(b) Generally, a seller in default is made to pay the difference between the market price (or cover price) and the contract price. In a seller's market the market price generally exceeds the contract price and Colorvideo is entitled to damages on this basis. But here, Colorvideo's economic loss doubtless exceeds this by far. Because it was unable to cover, (assuming it proves there was no reasonable way to cover), it suffered serious consequential injury. Damages for such injury are available if the seller had reason to know of the needs of the buyer and the buyer cannot minimize the loss by cover. International knew seller's needs and Colorvideo apparently could not cover. Consequently, International is liable for Colorvideo's lost profits. As discussed in (a) these may be too speculative. Alternatively, Colorvideo's reliance damages can be redressed. These would include the rental value of the plant, wasted salaries, unsalvageable materials and the like. It would also include damages Colorvideo may have to pay to Titanic, but not damages payable to Edwards, because the breach with Edwards was not proximately caused by International's breach.

(c) Although International may recover for breach against Japan Metals and may recover market price minus contract price damages, it may not recover consequential damages. There are no facts indicating that Japan Metals knew the particular needs of Colorvideo.

VIII. AVOIDANCE OR REFORMATION FOR MISCONDUCT OR MISTAKE

1. *False.* The answer might be "True" if *B* were a carpenter, but absent a specific showing that *B*, a lawyer, was knowledgeable about lumber prices, it cannot be said that the mistake was obvious to *B*.

2. *False.* Today, relief from mistake is not denied merely because the mistake is unilateral.

3. *False.* Negligence is not a bar to relief for mistake.

4. *True.* *B* has changed position by building the deck. The case is different from the XYZ stock case used in the illustration. Although *B* is enriched by having a deck at a cheap cost for lumber, there is no practical way for *B* to restore the lumber. In the XYZ case, money can be paid back.

5. The heirs would be unsuccessful if they sought to set aside the contract on grounds of unconscionability. Because of the interest-free financing, there is a

great disparity between the value of the property ($40,000) and the present value of a promise to pay that sum over 40 years. Although such disparity can be circumstantial evidence of unconscionable conduct, it is rebutted by the circumstances that indicate a partially donative intent by Mrs. Klaus.

The evidence may well tend to show that Mrs. Klaus intended to benefit "*Lutheran* religious and educational purposes" rather than religious and educational purposes *in general*. Nonetheless, the contract does not so state. This evidence would be admissible in an action for reformation where the parol evidence rule is inapplicable. For the action to succeed, however, it is not sufficient to prove Mrs. Klaus' lack of interest in furthering the work of non-Lutheran groups, nor is it sufficient to prove that Mrs. Klaus affirmatively intended to benefit only Lutheran groups. It must be shown that it was *agreed* between the parties that the use of the land would be limited to Lutheran organizations. It must also be shown that the writing failed to reflect this agreement because of the misconduct of the Association or because of mistake. Did the Association deliberately palm off the writing as reflecting the agreement (if there was one) to limit the land to Lutheran uses? If so, reformation will be granted. Similarly, if it can be shown that both parties were under the mistaken belief that the contract limited the use of the land in accordance with the still hypothetical agreement, reformation would be available. The prospects for success appear minimal based on the summary of the evidence given in the problem. There is no reference to the essential fact—that there be an agreement that, because of fraud or mistake, was not incorporated into the writing. It should be pointed out that if such evidence were to be found, say, by discovery, there would be no economic benefit to the heirs by a decree of reformation. The intent of their ancestor, would, however, be carried out.

A remedy that would produce economic benefits to the heirs would be the avoidance of the contract and recovery of the land. If the contract is recorded with the registry of deeds (or its local equivalent) a decree of cancellation would be required. It is again doubtful whether this remedy is available to the heirs. There is nothing to indicate that the Association misrepresented any fact to Mrs. Klaus or that it misrepresented the content or legal effect of the writing. If so, there would be a basis for avoiding the contract. The mere fact that Mrs. Klaus mistakenly assumed that the land would be used solely by Lutheran organizations is not a sufficient basis for avoidance. Her mistaken belief (if indeed it can be proved she had this belief) that the contract restricted the use to such organizations is not grounds for rescission unless it can be proved that this belief was induced by the Association or shared by the Association.

Assuming there were grounds for rescission or reformation, there is a possible affirmative defense. Neither remedy will be allowed on grounds of mistake (as opposed to misrepresentation) if there is a change of position by the

Association. The announced deal with the Alliance may be such a change of position. Indeed, if a contract has been entered into with the Alliance, these remedies would be unavailable to the Klaus heirs even if misrepresentation were proved, providing the Alliance is a good faith purchaser for value and without notice of the equities of the heirs.

IX. THIRD PARTY BENEFICIARIES

1. *True.* C's rights against A derive from the contract between B and A. Defenses that A has against B may be raised by A against C, the beneficiary.

2. *False.* Generally a promisor may not raise defenses that the promisee has against the beneficiary.

3. *True.* C's rights against A are dependent upon the intent of B and A to benefit C. Such intent is excluded by the quoted term.

4. When Enterprise promised Starr to pay $100,000 to State Bank to satisfy Starr's obligation to the Bank, the Bank became a third party intended creditor beneficiary of the contract between Enterprise and Starr. Performance of Enterprise's promise to pay directly to the Bank would clearly benefit the Bank and is intended by the contract. Similarly, the warranty holders are intended creditor beneficiaries inasmuch as the contract requires Enterprise to honor justified warranty claims presented by them.

   The absence of notification is of no relevance. The absence of knowledge of the contract is equally irrelevant on the facts. Notice of the existence of the promise for the benefit of the third party is not needed. Notice is relevant on the issue of whether Starr and Enterprise could have modified or rescinded the agreement by mutual agreement, but that issue does not arise under the facts.

   In the action by State Bank, Enterprise can raise against the State Bank any defense it has against Starr, based on the general rule that the promisor may raise against the beneficiary any defense it has against the promisee. The obvious potential defense is that of avoidance of the contract on the ground of Starr's material misrepresentation of fact. Enterprise, however, can use this against Starr only by way of defense. State Bank is not liable for any damages suffered by Enterprise beyond the amount of Starr's obligation to State Bank.

   For the same reasons, Enterprise can raise against the warranty holders the same defenses it has against Starr and State Bank.

5. Ms. T is clearly an intended beneficiary of Mrs. S's promise to convey the real property, as performance runs directly to her. She is apparently a donee beneficiary as the facts fail to indicate any obligation owed by Mr. B to Ms. T. Her rights have vested as she knows of the contract and has assented to it, but this fact is not relevant under the circumstances.

If Ms. T would pursue her action against Mrs. S, the promisor, Mrs. S would have the defense of non-payment. Clearly, as a constructive concurrent condition to her duty to convey, payment must be tendered and the facts indicate this has not and will not happen.

If Ms. T were to pursue an action against B's estate, the estate can point out that Mr. B's intention was to provide Ms. T with a gift. Delivery of the gift never was effected and there is no obligation for the estate to complete a gift.

X. ASSIGNMENT AND DELEGATION

1. *False.* There is some common law authority to the effect that an anti-assignment clause can nullify a purported assignment. This transaction is now governed by Article 9 of the U.C.C. which invalidates any term that purports to restrain the assignability of a right to the payment of money ("account") whether earned or expected to be earned.

2. *False.* See explanation to the previous question.

3. *False.* The New York view is "first in time, first in right."

4. *True.* Under the U.C.C. a filing system has been inaugurated. If the assignee has received an assignment of a significant part of the outstanding accounts of S, the first assignee who has given value and who has filed prevails.

5. *False.* An assignment is created by words of present transfer. (Do not confuse this rule with the notion that an anti-assignment clause is construed, unless the circumstances indicate to the contrary, as merely forbidding delegation.)

6. *True.* Whenever one party to a sale of goods contract delegates all his or her duties, the other contracting party has reasonable grounds for insecurity and may demand assurances of both the delegant and the delegate.

7. *False.* The duty is to deliver footballs of certain specifications. B has no substantial interest in having S personally perform.

8. *True.* If *B* deals with *X*, without protesting *S*'s repudiation, *B* is deemed to have agreed to a novation.

9. (a) The initial question is the effect of the anti-assignment clause. Article 2 of the U.C.C., which applies because the contract is for the sale of goods, provides that unless the contrary intention is manifested, an anti-assignment clause is to be construed as barring only the delegation of duties. Consequently, the assignment is not barred by the anti-assignment clause.

Under the Code, as at Common Law, rights are not assignable if the assignment would materially change the duties of the obligee. Abel's duties are not changed. Non-assignability also exists if the obligee's burden or risk is materially changed or if the obligee's chances of getting return performance are materially impaired. None of these rules affects the case at bar. Abel is still entitled to cash and Baker's note. This last credit risk is one Abel voluntarily undertook.

Under the Code, an assignment in general terms is deemed to be an assignment coupled with a delegation and assumption of duties. Here the delegation is barred by the anti-assignment clause. Therefore the delegation is ineffective, but is not a material breach unless persisted in. Abel's remedy for the uncertainty created by the transaction between Baker and Caleb would be to demand assurances of each of them. Consequently, Abel's letter of March 6th was an over-reaction and a repudiation, entitling Caleb to bring an immediate action for anticipatory breach.

In such an action the plaintiff's tender of performance is excused, but plaintiff must show that but for the repudiation plaintiff would have been ready, willing and able to perform on the date performance was due. Caleb thus may recover on a showing of the source from which the cash payment was to come and that Baker's note would have been tendered.

(b) Abel's retraction is timely. There is no indication that either Caleb or Baker changed position in reliance upon the repudiation or stated that the contract was at an end. Consequently, Abel may retract, reinstating the duties of all parties.

Both Caleb and Baker would be liable. Baker is liable on the original contract. It is simply impossible for an obligor to transfer or divest an obligation except with the consent of the obligee.

Caleb's liability is less clear. As stated earlier, general words of assignment also carry with it a delegation and assumption of duties. Such delegation is barred by the anti-assignment clause. Arguably, however, when Abel retracts, Abel is waiving the non-delegability of the duties and more likely the nonassumability of the duties. Since an assumption of liability can only benefit Abel, such a waiver is probably in accord with Abel's real intent.

Of course, Caleb's refusal of delivery was a material breach. In contracts for the sale of goods, refusal to accept delivery within the contract term is a material breach which justifies cancellation of the contract and triggers a right to demand damages for total breach.

PRACTICE EXAMINATION

MULTISTATE QUESTIONS

For the purposes of this test, you are to assume that the Uniform Commercial Code has been adopted. No other statute except the Statute of Frauds is in effect.

Questions 11–13 are based on the following fact situation.

Brill saved the life of Ace's wife, Mary, who thereafter changed her will to leave Brill $1,000. However, upon Mary's death she had no property except an undivided interest in real estate held in tenancy by the entirety with Ace. The property had been purchased by Ace from an inheritance.

After Mary died, Ace signed and delivered to Brill the following instrument: "In consideration of Brill's saving my wife's life and his agreement to bring no claims against my estate based on her will, I hereby promise to pay Brill $1,000."

Upon Ace's death, Brill filed a claim for $1,000. Ace's executor contested the claim on the ground that the instrument was not supported by sufficient consideration.

11. In most states, would Brill's saving of Mary's life be regarded as sufficient consideration for Ace's promise?

(a) Yes, because Ace was thereby morally obligated to Brill.

(b) Yes, because Ace was thereby materially benefited.

(c) No, because Ace had not asked Brill to save her.

(d) No, because the value of Brill's act was too uncertain.

12. With respect to the recital that Brill had agreed not to file a claim against Ace's estate, what additional fact would most strengthen Brill's claim?

(a) Brill's agreement was made in a writing he signed.

(b) Brill reasonably believed he had a valid claim when the instrument was signed.

(c) Mary had contributed to accumulation of the real property.

(d) Brill paid Ace $1 when he received the instrument.

13. On which of the following theories would it be most likely that Brill could recover?

(a) Ace and Brill have made a compromise.

(b) Ace must give restitution for benefits it would be unjust to retain.

(c) Ace is bound by promissory estoppel.

(d) Ace executed a binding unilateral contract.

Questions 55–59 are based on the following fact situation.

Paul and Daniel entered a contract in writing on November 1, the essential part of which read as follows: "Paul to supply Daniel with 200 personalized Christmas cards on or before December 15, 1970, bearing photograph of Daniel and his family, and Daniel to pay $100 thirty days thereafter. Photograph to be taken by Paul at Daniel's house. Cards guaranteed to be fully satisfactory and on time." Because Daniel suddenly became ill, Paul was unable to take the necessary photograph of Daniel and his family until the first week of December. The final week's delay was caused by Paul's not being notified promptly by Daniel of his recovery. Before taking the photograph of Daniel and his family, Paul advised Daniel that he was likely to be delayed a day or two beyond December 15 in making delivery because of the time required to process the photograph and cards. Daniel told Paul to take the photograph anyway. The cards were finally delivered by Paul to Daniel on December 17, Paul having diligently worked on them in the interim.

Although the cards pleased the rest of the family, Daniel refused to accept them because, as he said squinting at one of the cards at arm's length without bothering to put on his reading glasses, "The photograph makes me look too old. Besides, the cards weren't delivered on time."

55. In an action by Paul against Daniel, which of the following would be Daniel's best defense?

    (a) The cards, objectively viewed, were not satisfactory.

    (b) The cards, subjectively viewed, were not satisfactory.

    (c) The cards were not delivered on time.

    (d) Daniel's illness excused him from further obligation under the contract.

56. Which of the following statements is most accurate?

    (a) Payment by Daniel of the $100 was a condition precedent to Paul's duty of performance.

    (b) The performances of Paul and Daniel under the contract were concurrently conditional.

    (c) Payment by Daniel of the $100 was a condition subsequent to Paul's duty of performance.

    (d) Performance by Paul under the contract was a condition precedent to Daniel's duty of payment of the $100.

57. Assuming that a proper interpretation of the contract required that the Christmas cards be personally satisfactory to Daniel, which of the following arguments would be of LEAST help to Paul?

    (a) Paul did not have sufficient time to produce cards of a quality satisfactory to Daniel.

    (b) Daniel did not make an adequate examination of the quality of the cards.

    (c) Daniel's dissatisfaction with the cards was the result of delivery after December 15 rather than of any lack of quality in the cards.

    (d) Daniel's dissatisfaction with the quality of the cards was not genuine.

58. Which of the following statements with regard to the taking of the photograph is LEAST accurate?

(a) An implied condition of Paul's duty of performance was that Daniel reasonably cooperate with Paul in arranging for the taking of the photograph.

(b) Daniel was under an implied duty to cooperate reasonably with Paul in arranging for the taking of the photograph.

(c) By entering the contract as written, Paul assumed the risk that Daniel would fail to cooperate in arranging for the taking of the photograph.

(d) A refusal by Daniel to cooperate reasonably in arranging for the taking of the photograph would excuse Paul from further obligation under the contract and also give Paul a right of action against Daniel for breach of contract.

59. Which of the following statements regarding the legal effect of Daniel's illness is LEAST accurate?

(a) Daniel's illness and the related developments excused Paul from his obligation to deliver the cards on or before December 15.

(b) Prompt notice by Daniel to Paul of Daniel's recovery from his illness was an implied condition of Paul's duty under the circumstances.

(c) Paul was under a duty of immediate performance of his promise to deliver the cards, as of December 15, by reason of the express language of the contract and despite the illness of Daniel and the related developments.

(d) Daniel's conduct after his illness constituted a waiver of the necessity of Paul's performing on or before December 15.

60. Baker, the seller, authorized Smith in writing to sign a contract for the sale and purchase of land for him. Arthur, the buyer, orally authorized Thomas to sign the contract for him. Smith and Thomas signed the contract: "Baker by Smith, his agent" and "Arthur by Thomas, his agent." Arthur refuses to complete the purchase. Baker sues Arthur who pleads the Statute of Frauds. Baker will

(a) win, because the sales contract was in writing

(b) win, because his agency contract was in writing

(c) lose, because he did not sign the contract personally

(d) lose, because Arthur's agency contract was not in writing

Questions 79–82 are based on the following fact situation.

In 1965, Insured took out a life insurance policy, Insurer promising, on condition that Insured paid an annual premium until death, to pay $50,000 to Insured's wife. The policy stated that Insured had power to change the beneficiary and to assign the policy.

In 1966, Insurer, deeming its insurance risks excessive, entered into a contract with Reinsurer which provided that, in exchange for Insurer's promise to pay an annual premium, Reinsurer promised to perform the duties of Insurer under the policy with Insured.

In 1969, Insured changed the beneficiary from his wife to his son. Upon receiving notice of this, the son wrote a letter to his father expressing appreciation and sent notes to Insurer and Reinsurer stating how fortunate he was that his father had named him the beneficiary under the policy with Insurer and Reinsurer, and advising that, in light of this information, he had purchased a lot on which to build a house.

Later in 1969, Insured, being in need of funds, borrowed $5,000 and assigned the policy to Assignee as security.

In 1970, Insurer's financial condition improved. Consequently, Insurer and Reinsurer rescinded the contract of reinsurance.

Later in 1970, Insured died, the premiums on the policy with insurer having been paid for the years 1965 through 1970 and the policy being in force.

79. Insured's wife sued Insurer to collect the proceeds of the policy. How would the court hold?

   (a) Judgment on Insured's wife's suit for the proceeds is denied, because the wife is an incidental beneficiary and an incidental beneficiary has no protected rights.

   (b) Judgment on Insured's wife's suit for the proceeds is denied, because insured reserved the power to change the beneficiary and exercised the power.

   (c) Judgment is given to Insured's wife for the proceeds, because the wife is a donee beneficiary and her right vested when the policy was issued to Insured.

   (d) Judgment is given to Insured's wife for the proceeds, because the wife is a creditor beneficiary and bringing suit on the policy was a change of position in reliance.

80. Insured's son sued Insurer to collect the proceeds of the policy. How would the court hold?

(a) Judgment in Insured's son's suit for the proceeds is denied, because the son should have sued Reinsurer before proceeding against Insurer.

(b) Judgment in Insured's son's suit for the proceeds is denied, because the son should have sued Reinsurer and Insurer jointly.

(c) Judgment is given to Insured's son for the proceeds, because the son has a right against Insurer and Reinsurer and may elect to bring action against Insurer.

(d) Judgment is given to Insured's son for the proceeds, because the son is subrogated to Insurer's right against Reinsurer.

81. Insured's son, not having collected from Insurer, sued Reinsurer on the contract of reinsurance. How would the court hold?

(a) Judgment for Insured's son is denied, because the son is an incidental beneficiary of the reinsurance contract.

(b) Judgment for Insured's son is denied, because the change of beneficiary clause in the insurance contract prevented the son's right under the reinsurance contract from vesting prior to Insured's death and Insured and Reinsurer rescinded their contract.

(c) Judgment is given to Insured's son, because the son is a creditor beneficiary of the Reinsurer's promise, notice was given to the son and he assented and changed his position in reliance.

(d) Judgment is given to Insured's son, because the son is a donee beneficiary of the Reinsurer's promise and assent is presumed.

82. Assignee, not having been paid the $5,000 that he lent to Insured, sued Insurer for $5,000. Insured's son intervened, alleging that Assignee did not have a right to any sum under the insurance policy. How would the court hold?

(a) Judgment in Assignee's suit is denied, because Insured's son was named beneficiary before Insured made the assignment, and the beneficiary, being first in time, prevails over the assignee.

(b) Judgment in Assignee's suit is denied, because Insured's son is a donee beneficiary and the promisee cannot discharge any part of a donee beneficiary's right.

(c) Judgment is granted to Assignee for $5,000, because consideration was given for the assignment.

(d) Judgment is granted to Assignee for $5,000, because Insured reserved power to change the beneficiary and to assign the policy.

Questions 96–99 are based on the following fact situation.

Barnes had been a beekeeper for many years, making a modest living selling honey in the area surrounding his farm. When he became aware of a sudden demand for beeswax for use in the manufacture of candles and certain types of exotic soaps sold in specialty shops, he built a plant to manufacture these items. The candle and soap business developed so rapidly that Barnes found it profitable to sell his bee farm to Stevens for $50,000. The sale contract provided that "Barnes reserves the right to purchase all of the beeswax produced by Stevens during the next five years at the current market price at time of delivery, delivery and payment to be made at weekly intervals, and Stevens agrees to supply in any event a minimum of 100 pounds of beeswax per month during that period." When the sale was closed, Barnes's lawyer handed Stevens' lawyer a letter stating: "This is to notify you that I will take all of your beeswax production until further notice."

For one year, Stevens delivered to Barnes and Barnes paid for all of the beeswax produced by Stevens. During that year, Stevens, who was an expert beekeeper, increased his beeswax production by 100 per cent by increasing the number and productivity of the bees. Stevens then proposed to Barnes that, since he had doubled production, it would only be fair that he supply Barnes with half of his new total, but in any event a minimum of 100 pounds per month, leaving Stevens free to sell the remainder of the wax at higher prices for new uses being made of beeswax. Barnes, in a signed writing, agreed to the proposal by Stevens for the remaining period of the original contract. During the following year, Stevens delivered to Barnes and Barnes paid for one-half of all of the Beeswax produced by Stevens.

As the first year of the new contract ended, Stevens was stung by a bee and due to an allergy became so seriously and permanently ill and impaired as to be unable to attend to bees. From that time on he never made another delivery to Barnes.

96. The original agreement between Barnes and Stevens was

(a) enforceable in all respects

(b) unenforceable, because there was no consideration for Stevens' promise to sell all of his production to Barnes

(c) unenforceable, because of failure to fix a definite price

(d) unenforceable, because of the unreasonable period of time involved

97. Assuming that the original agreement was a contract, the modification reducing the contractual amounts by 50 per cent was

(a) enforceable in all respects

(b) enforceable only to the extent of beeswax tendered by Stevens

(c) unenforceable, because there was no consideration for Barnes' promise to take only one-half of the production.

(d) unenforceable, because of the indefiniteness as to the quantity of the goods

98. Assuming that contractual obligations existed between Barnes and Stevens, Stevens' refusal to perform was

(a) justifiable because he had not promised to produce any beeswax

(b) justifiable because his performance was excused because of his permanent disability

(c) justifiable only if he gave Barnes reasonable notice so that Barnes could buy beeswax elsewhere

(d) not justifiable and constituted a breach of contract

99. Assume that Stevens had not been permanently disabled, but that at the end of the first year of the new arrangement sold his farm to Taylor, and that Stevens thereafter produced no beeswax. By selling his bee farm to Taylor, Stevens did which of the following?

(a) Discharged his obligation to Barnes by full performance.

(b) Became liable to Barnes if Taylor did not sell beeswax to Barnes.

(c) Was excused from delivering beeswax to Barnes.

(d) Breached his contract with Barnes.

Questions 117–120 are based on the following fact situation.

Able and Baker entered into a contract relating to a motion picture, *Squaring the Circle.* Baker promised to compose the music and transfer the copyright to Able, on condition that Charles be engaged to write the lyrics; and Able promised to produce and to direct the motion picture and to pay Baker 5 per cent of the box office receipts.

Soon after the contract was executed, Baker delivered to Dodge a letter which stated, "In appreciation of your dedicated service as my secretary, I intend to give you, in installments as received, 10 per cent of the monies paid to me under the contract with Able for composing the music for *Squaring the Circle*." Dodge sent a copy of the letter to Able.

Able engaged Charles to write the lyrics. The musical score and lyrics were completed on schedule, and Baker assigned to Able the copyright to the music.

Baker, encountering financial difficulty, assigned to Easy the contract with Able for $200,000. To save Baker embarrassment, Easy did not notify Able of the assignment. Baker's financial condition worsened. Hence, Baker assigned to Fox the contract with Able for $250,000. Fox did not inquire of Able whether he had been notified of a previous assignment, but Fox promptly notified Able of the assignment to him.

Prior to completion of *Squaring the Circle,* Able received a long-desired opportunity to direct the motion picture *Our Lovely Ladies.* Unable to direct two pictures simultaneously, Able assigned the contract with Baker to George. George promptly notified Fox of the assignment. Fox protested that Able was a more artistic director than George. George completed the picture, critics noting that the artistry diminished after Able relinquished direction.

At the end of the first month of exhibition of *Squaring the Circle,* George entered on his account book a credit of $5,000 to the contract between Able and Baker. The following day, Howe, a creditor of Baker, served garnishment process on George in an action against Baker. A day later, George received claims from Dodge, Easy, and Fox, each stating that he was assignee under the contract between Able and Baker. To avoid possible multiple payment, George refused to pay anyone.

117. Dodge, as assignee of Baker, sued George, as assignee of Able. What would the court hold with respect to Dodge's action?

    (a) Judgment is denied, because a letter is not an accepted commercial symbol for property and, thus, is not an appropriate form of assignment.

    (b) Judgment is denied, because Baker's letter to Dodge did not include words of present transfer, an essential element of an assignment.

(c) Judgment is granted, because Baker's letter to Dodge constituted an assignment of a portion of Baker's right under the contract between Able and Baker, and Dodge gave notice to the obligor.

(d) Judgment is granted, because Baker's assignment to Dodge was first in time and, thus, the subsequent assignments, even though for value, cannot defeat it.

118. Easy and Fox, as assignees of Baker, sued George as assignee of Able. Assuming the absence of assignment perfection statutes, what would the court hold with respect to Easy's action?

(a) Judgment is granted, because Easy was the prior assignee and Fox's giving notice of the assignment was not sufficient to give priority over Easy's assignment.

(b) Judgment is denied, because Easy, being the prior assignee, contributed to the deception against Fox by failing to give notice of the assignment.

(c) Judgment is denied, because Easy, although the prior assignee, did not give notice of the assignment, while Fox, the subsequent assignee did give notice.

(d) Judgment is denied, because the contract between Able and Baker was subject to a condition and, thus, the assignment was not effective.

119. In the garnishment proceeding by Howe, the creditor of Baker, what would the court hold?

(a) The creditor prevails over the assignee, because the obligor (George, as successor to Able) had a good defense against the assignment.

(b) The creditor prevails over the assignee, because the right of a creditor is superior to that of an assignee and the creditor filed suit before the assignee recovered the monies allocated to the contract.

(c) The assignee prevails over the creditor, because the assignment left nothing for the creditor to attach and the obligor had notice of assignment in time to assert the assignment as a defense to the attachment proceeding.

(d) The status quo is maintained, because in a contest between a creditor and an assignee, the obligor (George, as successor to Able) is protected against double liability by permitting the obligor to pay either party.

120. Fox sued Able, alleging that the contract was not assignable by Able and that substitution of George as producer and director had decreased box office receipts. The court would hold that the obligor (Able) is

(a) not liable to the obligee (Baker) or his assigns, because the delegation of duty was neither contrary to public policy nor prohibited by the contract

(b) not liable to the obligee (Baker) or his assigns, because the production and direction of the picture do not constitute a performance having a personal character

(c) liable to the obligee (Baker) or his assigns for such damage as may be proved, because, although an obligor may delegate any duty, he remains responsible for any default of the delegate

(d) liable to the obligee (Baker) or his assigns for such damage as may be proved, because the obligor's duty involved personal skill and discretion and the obligee had a substantial interest in having him perform the duty

121. Arthur owns a 500–acre farm on which his dwelling is situate. He enters into the following written agreement:

I, Arthur, agree to sell Walter my dwelling and a sufficient amount of land surrounding the same to accommodate a garden and lawn. Price: $20,000. Received: $1.00 on account.

> Signed: "Walter"
> _____
> "Arthur"

Walter refuses to perform the agreement. Arthur sues for specific performance. Judgment for

(a) Arthur, because he has a written agreement signed by the party to be charged therewith

(b) Arthur, because the agreement satisfies the Statute of Frauds

(c) Walter, because the agreement is ambiguous

(d) Walter, because $1.00 constitutes a nominal consideration which will not support a contract

Questions 135–138 are based on the following fact situation.

Peter and Don entered into a written contract pursuant to which Peter agreed to manufacture for Don, and Don agreed to buy, 1,000 whirligigs at a price of $10 per whirligig, "it being expressly agreed and understood that Don shall be under no liability under this contract unless 1,000 whirligigs are delivered to Don at his place of business no later than May 1, 1970." Nine hundred whirligigs, meeting Don's specifications, were tendered by Peter on May 1, 1970. The remaining 100 whirligigs were tendered on May 3, 1970. Don refused to accept any of the whirligigs.

135. In an action by Peter, which of the following defenses of Don would best resist a demurrer (motion to strike)?

    (a) Time was of the essence.

    (b) Peter had not substantially performed as of May 1.

    (c) The market value of whirligigs had decreased by 90% between the time the contract was made and May 1.

    (d) Lightning had struck Don's place of business on May 1 and utterly demolished it.

136. The provision in quotation marks is

    (a) a promise but not a condition

    (b) neither a promise nor a condition

    (c) an express condition

    (d) an implied condition

137. The contract is

    (a) divisible

    (b) entire

    (c) neither divisible nor entire

    (d) partially divisible and partially entire

138. In an action by Peter against Don, which of the following contentions of Peter would best support Peter's case, assuming each contention to be factually sustainable?

    (a) Don had orally agreed, just prior to the time the written contract was executed, to accept and pay for partial deliveries of the whirligigs.

    (b)   Whirligigs are a unique product produced only by Peter and in a size and tolerance that varies with the needs of each purchaser.

    (c)   Delivery of the 100 whirligigs on May 1 was delayed by the shipper, and was not Peter's fault.

    (d)   A drop in Don's credit rating from "good" to "fair" had caused Peter not to produce and tender the full 1,000 whirligigs on or before May 1.

153. Jones, as seller, and Williams, as buyer, orally agreed for the purchase and sale of a dwelling. Williams' wife moved into the dwelling and spent substantial sums for repairs. Jones refused to convey. Williams sued Jones and Jones pleaded the Statute of Frauds. The decision will be controlled by

    (a)   the doctrine of part performance

    (b)   the fact that Williams, personally, has not performed

    (c)   Mrs. Williams' knowledge of the contract

    (d)   whether Jones had knowledge of Mrs. Williams' acts

Questions 154–159 are based on the following fact situation.

Bond, the president of Bond Snowmobile Company, was advised by a consumer consulting firm that within 18 months virtually every state will have enacted laws requiring that all snowmobiles be outlawed unless they can be operated noiselessly. After an extensive search, Bond discovered that Sanders, who was in the business of building engines, had developed a quiet gasoline engine which could be adapted for snowmobile use.

Bond contracted in writing with Sanders to purchase 100 engines at $250 each, freight prepaid to Bond's warehouse. Bond realized that prospective snowmobile purchasers demand high-speed performance, and tests of Sanders' engines showed that they had difficulty in developing sufficient horsepower to sustain the required speed. Therefore, the contract of sale expressly provided that each engine would develop 32 horsepower.

The contract also provided that the engines would be delivered in lots of 25 per month beginning June 1, that Bond should pay for each lot of 25 engines as delivered, and that Bond would make payment within 24 hours after delivery.

Immediately upon delivery of the first lot of 25 engines on June 1, Bond forwarded to Sanders a check for $6,250, but upon testing each of the 25 engines, Bond determined that none of them would develop more than 15 horsepower. Proper testing of the engines required at least 72 hours and cost Bond $2,500.

Bond decided that, despite the lack of sufficient horsepower, he would install 5 of the engines in snowmobiles to determine how fast they would travel. On June 10, Bond notified Sanders that he was rejecting all of the engines delivered and would reject all future deliveries because of the horsepower insufficiency.

154. Which of the following statements is correct with respect to Bond's right to inspect the engines?

    (a)   He retained the right to inspect.

    (b)   He forfeited the right to inspect by failing to inspect the engines before he paid for them.

    (c)   He forfeited the right to inspect by failing to inspect the engines before they arrived at his warehouse.

    (d)   He forfeited the right to inspect by not providing for such right in the contract of sale.

155. By installing 5 engines, how many engines did Bond accept?

    (a)   0

    (b)   5

    (c)   25

    (d)   100

156. Assuming that the value of the 5 engines was $100 each, and that engines with 32 horsepower have a value of $250 each, what is the maximum Bond can recover on the 5 engines installed?

    (a)   Nothing

    (b) $500

    (c) $750

    (d) $1,250

157. With respect to the 20 delivered but uninstalled engines, Bond can recover

    (a)   nothing

(b)   two-thirds of the $5,000 paid for them

(c)   the entire $5,000 paid for them, but cannot resell the engines for Sanders' account

(d)   the entire $5,000 and resell the engines for Sanders' account

158. In addition to recovery, if any, on the 20 delivered but uninstalled engines, Bond can also recover

(a)   inspection costs plus any costs for the care and custody of the engines

(b)   punitive damages for an additional $5,000

(c)   damages for his mental suffering

(d)   the amount he can prove he lost due to the delay in placing 20 snowmobiles on the market

159. In regard to the 75 undelivered engines, Bond can "cover," which means that he can

(a)   buy waterproof tarpaulins in order to protect Sanders' engines

(b)   purchase 75 engines from someone else in substitution for those due from Sanders

(c)   place a sufficient amount of money in an escrow account in a bank to cover the cost of purchasing the 75 engines from someone else

(d)   purchase a letter of credit to cover the cost of purchasing 75 engines from someone else

177. Allen, as seller, and Barnes, as buyer, enter into an oral agreement for the sale and purchase of land. Barnes refuses to complete the transaction and Allen sues Barnes. Barnes fails to file an answer to Allen's complaint. Allen wins because

(a)   the agreement is not within the Statute of Frauds

(b)   of the state of the pleadings

(c)   there was no fraud

(d)   the Fourteenth Amendment to the United States Constitution guarantees every litigant a day in court

Questions 183–187 are based on the following fact situation.

On November 1 the following notice was posted in a privately operated law school:

> The faculty, seeking to encourage legal research, offers to any student at this school who wins the current National Obscenity Law Competition the additional prize of $500. All competing papers must be submitted to the Dean's office before next May 1.

(The National Competition is conducted by an outside agency, unconnected with any law school.) Student read this notice on November 2, and thereupon intensified his effort to make his paper on obscenity law, which he started in October, a winner. Student also left on a counter in the Dean's office a signed note saying, "I accept the faculty's $500 Obscenity Competition offer." This note was inadvertently placed in Student's file and never reached the Dean or any faculty member personally. On the following April 1, the above notice was removed and the following substituted therefor:

> The faculty regrets that our offer regarding the National Obscenity Law Competition must be withdrawn.

Student's paper was submitted through the Dean's office on April 15. On May 1, it was announced that Student had won the National Obscenity Law Competition and the prize of $1,000. The law faculty refused to pay anything.

183. Assuming that the faculty's notice of November 1 was posted on a bulletin board or other conspicuous place commonly viewed by all persons in the law school, such notice constituted a

(a) preliminary invitation to deal, analogous to newspaper advertisements for the sale of goods by merchants

(b) contractual offer, creating a power of acceptance

(c) preliminary invitation, because no offeree was named therein

(d) promise to make a conditional, future gift of money

184. As to Student, was the offer effectively revoked?

(a) Yes, by the faculty's second notice

(b) No, because it became irrevocable after a reasonable time had elapsed

(c) No, because of Student's reliance, prior to April 1, on the offer

(d)   No, unless Student became aware of the April 1 posting and removal before submitting his paper

185. The offer proposed a

(a)   unilateral contract only

(b)   bilateral contract only

(c)   unilateral contract or bilateral contract, at the offeree's option

(d)   unilateral contract which ripened into a bilateral contract, binding on both parties, as soon as Student intensified his effort in response to the offer

186. How was the enforceability of the promise affected by Student's winning of the National Obscenity Law Competition?

(a)   It became enforceable through the happening of a condition precedent to the faculty's duty of performance.

(b)   It was unenforceable as an unexecuted promise to make a gift.

(c)   It was unenforceable, even if effectively accepted by Student, because the outside agency conducting the National Competition was under a pre-existing duty to award its announced prize to the winner.

(d)   It was accepted by the act of the outside agency in awarding the National Competition prize to Student.

187. The promise of the faculty on November 1 was

(a)   enforceable on principles of promissory estoppel

(b)   enforceable by Student's personal representative even if Student had been killed in an accident on April 16

(c)   not enforceable on policy grounds because it produced a noncommercial agreement between a student and his teachers, analogous to intramural family agreements and informal social commitments

(d)   not enforceable because Student, after entering the National Competition in October, was already under a duty to perform to the best of his ability

SAMPLE ANSWERS

11. c. D should be eliminated at the outset as the worst answer, for if there were consideration for the promise the parties would be free to agree on the value of the service however uncertain its market value might be. A and B are variants of the moral obligation concept. Ordinarily receipt of unrequested benefits creates no obligation and a subsequent promise to pay for such benefits is not supported by consideration. Even under the liberal minority and Restatement, Second, view, the benefit must have been received by the promisor and not, as here, a third party.

12. b. The claim is invalid and therefore the question is whether the surrender of an invalid claim constitutes detriment. Reasonable belief that there is a valid claim is important under the various rules governing the question. A should be excluded. A signed writing substitutes for consideration only in a few states and even in these only in limited circumstances. C appears to be totally irrelevant as we are dealing with a contractual claim against Ace, not with a restitution claim against Ace or the wife. D introduces the question of nominal consideration, a weak foundation for any claim and worse involves the exchange of one sum of money for the promise of another sum.

13. a. We would begin by excluding C and D. There is no injurious reliance to trigger promissory estoppel. Ace made no unilateral contract which would involve a promise on his part asking for a performance by Brill. We are left with A and B. The choice involves a rehashing of questions 11 and 12. If Brill can show good faith and reasonableness of his claim, the parties have entered into an accord and satisfaction even though his claim is invalid. The word "compromise" is a poor choice of words to describe an accord and satisfaction, but it is so used with some frequency. B restates the restitution theory which as indicated above is weak even under the more liberal minority view.

55. b. Subjective satisfaction is called for by the contract as the subject matter calls for gratification of personal taste. The late delivery is excused by Daniel's illness and waiver.

56. d. At last an easy question! It is clear that Paul is to perform before Daniel is to pay and therefore Paul's performance is a condition precedent. If you answered c, read C & P §§ 11–5, 11–6, and 11–7 carefully.

57. a. Each of the other arguments has merit on the question of whether Daniel in good faith was dissatisfied with the quality of the cards. A is of no help to Paul since he assumed the risk that he would produce cards of satisfactory quality, and the assumption of risk includes the amount of time necessary to complete the performance properly. In any event there is nothing to indicate that the time factor was in any way related to the quality of the work.

58. c. It is clear that the taking of the photographs requires the cooperation of both of the parties. Consequently there is an implied promise by Daniel to cooperate and Paul's performance is impliedly conditioned on Daniel's cooperation. Paul certainly did not assume the risk of Daniel's failure to cooperate.

59. c. The illness and Daniel's failure to give prompt notice and the waiver excused the lateness. (See 55 supra). Thus, the time for performance was extended by the actions of the other party. Therefore A and D are essentially accurate. B reflects Daniel's duty of cooperation (see 58 supra).

60. a. An agent may generally sign for his principal. The agent's authority to bind his principal need not be in writing. A number of states, however, require written authority if the contract is within the real property Statute of Frauds. There are twenty-five such states. Past multi-state examination instructions require that you ignore local statutes and answer under "general law." "General law" would appear to include the classical Statute of Frauds, but not local variations. Read the instructions on your examination carefully to see if this instruction appears on it.

79. b. Since payment of the policy in the event of death is to be made to the wife she is an intended third party beneficiary. Since the facts do not indicate any creditor-debtor relation between husband and wife, she is a donee beneficiary. Because the insured reserved the power to change his beneficiary, the rights of the beneficiary could not vest against this power.

80. c. When Reinsurer promised to perform the duties of Insurer, the son became a third party creditor beneficiary of this assumption of duties. The son may obtain a judgment against either or both but is entitled to only one satisfaction.

81. c. The son is an intended creditor beneficiary, because the promisee, Insurer, was under a conditional obligation to the son. Although his right was divestable if Insured changed his beneficiary, this does not mean he had no vested rights in the separate contract between Insurer and Reinsurer. When he assented and changed his position his rights became vested except as provided by the contract. There was nothing in the contract between Insurer and Reinsurer which allow Insurer and Reinsurer to divest his rights.

82. d. The change of beneficiary clause prevents the rights of the son from vesting as against the power of Insured to change beneficiary or to assign the policy. C is incorrect because no consideration is required for an assignment. At any rate, the assignment is for value and so the death of the assignor does not terminate the assignment which would be the case if the assignment were gratuitous. B is incorrect. See 79 supra. A attempts to confuse you with a rule governing successive assignments, which does not apply to third party beneficiaries.

Some students have been concerned with the insurable interest problem which may lurk in this question. Ignore the issue. The multi-state does not test on insurance law.

96. a. There is consideration for the promise. One consideration will support many promises. The price set in terms of current market price is sufficiently definite. Even though this is an exclusive dealing arrangement (and therefore a restraint of trade) under the circumstances a five year term is not unreasonable.

97. a. Contracts for the sale of beeswax relate to the sale of goods and therefore are governed by Article 2 of the U.C.C. which permits modification of contracts without consideration. (§ 2–209(1)). Output contracts are not deemed indefinite. A contract for 50% of output is therefore not indefinite. This disposes of C and D. B appears to be pure delirium.

98. d. A is incorrect. See the material on requirement and output contracts. B is not correct because this is not a contract for personal services but for the sale of beeswax. Disability of a promisor is not an excuse for non-performance unless the duties are non-delegable. There is nothing in the contract requiring Stevens to attend to the bees personally. C introduces a point that would be relevant only if Stevens were excused by his disability. Some commentators on this question have regarded B as the correct answer on the grounds that Stevens is an expert beekeeper and therefore his duties are non-delegable. However, U.C.C. § 2–210, comment 4 indicates that under the Code duties under output contracts are generally delegable. Assuming that this is an exceptional case because of Stevens' expertise, therefore excusing him, the correct answer would then be C, because U.C.C. § 2–615(c) requires seasonable notification of any excuse by virtue of impracticability.

99. b. A and C are incorrect. The contract is for a five year term so there was not full performance. There was no excuse by impossibility as any impossibility of performance was caused by his own affirmative act. D is incorrect. The sale is not per se a breach as the duties are delegable and Taylor may have assumed the duties. If Taylor assumed the duties, Barnes would be liable if Taylor did not perform the obligations of the contract. If the contract is considered to be personal (see 98 above) the correct answer is D.

117. b. As you read this fact pattern your first reaction may be that horribly difficult questions will be asked. But the questions asked are really rather basic. In this question A is plainly wrong as a letter may create an assignment and C and D are irrelevant because there was no assignment. An assignment requires words of present transfer, which are not present here (e.g., "I assign," "I transfer," "I grant").

118. a.   D is wrong.   A present conditional right may be assigned.   B and C express the English rule, which is a minority rule.   A is correct under both N.Y. rule and the four horsemen rule.

119. c.   The rule is that an assignment which precedes an attachment has priority so long as the obligor has notice of the assignment in time to assert it as a defense in the attachment proceedings.   B is wrong as an assignment transfers the rights and if the necessary formaligies are undertaken an assignee has priority over the assignor's creditors.   A is obscure.   What defense could George possibly have against the assignment?   D is wrong and simply concocts a preposterous rule of law.

120. d.   It is clear that the "assignment" by Able was not just an assignment but also a delegation of duties.   D is a good statement of the rule of law with respect to delegation of duties and fits the facts.   A and C do not accurately reflect legal principles.   B, like D, is based on a correct statement of law, but misapplies it.   The obligation to direct a motion picture is clearly a personal one.

121. c.   As to A & B both are superficially correct inasmuch as the Statute of Frauds appears to be satisfied, but one must do more than satisfy the Statute to win a case.   D is wrong.   There is plenty of consideration in the implied promise to pay the price.   The problem here is the clause stating, "sufficient amount," etc.   It is vague and indefinite and presumably the examiners are using the word "ambiguous" in this sense.   The agreement is too vague and indefinite to allow a court to order specific performance.

135. a.   The quoted clause clearly makes time of the essence.   Delivery on the stated date was made an express condition to Don's duties, which is but another way of stating that time is of the essence.   Moreover, the perfect tender rule would produce the same result.   C is a weak defense as change in market values is a normal business risk assumed by fixed price contracts.   D is not a sufficient defense in itself, as demolition of the premises does not necessarily excuse performance unless its continued existence was the basis on which the parties contracted.   Could not delivery be taken anyway?   B is a tempting answer, but why a defense of lack of substantial performance when perfect performance is required by the contract?

136. c.   The words condition Don's duty to accept and pay for the goods.

137. b.   It is entire because all of the whirligigs are to be delivered at the same time.

138. a.   This is a tough one as all of the contentions are difficult to make out.   A is a parol evidence problem.   There are cases sustaining such precontractual waivers of written contracts, but mostly insurance contracts.   It should also be remembered that the U.C.C. has liberalized the parol evidence rule. B is based on the idea that insistence on exact compliance with the contract will result in a forfeiture. Yet there is nothing in the U.C.C. which specifically adopts this approach and the general rule of "perfect tender" would seem to disavow it. Moreover, although there is hardship there is no forfeiture in a strict sense as Don doesn't keep the goods. C is not normally a good excuse. This is a destination contract and risk of shipment delays is on the seller short of impossibility caused by a shipping strike or the like. D is the least plausible excuse. The facts could have triggered a demand for assurance but do not justify partial delivery.

153. a. All of the facts given in B, C, and D are relevant in determining whether the purchaser's part performance will take the contract out of the Statute of Frauds. Other facts are also relevant, including the relationship between Mrs. Williams' conduct and the contract.

154. a. The right to inspect is not normally lost by payment in accordance with the contract. Payment was due within 24 hours of delivery and inspection required 72 hours.

155. b. By installing the goods with knowledge of their non-conformity, Bond did an act inconsistent with the seller's ownership and so accepted the goods. U.C.C. § 2–606(1)(c). The Code goes on to say (§ 2–606(2)) that "Acceptance of any commercial unit is acceptance of that entire unit." Here each engine is a commercial unit. The engines are not inter-related as, for example, the machinery components of a car wash. Consequently, Bond accepted 5 rather than 25 or 100 engines.

156. c. For breach of warranty the measure of damages is the difference between the value of the goods accepted and the value they would have had if they were as warranted. Applying the formula, $250 − $100 = $150 damages per engine times five engines yields $750.

157. c. Resale for the account of another is a seller's remedy; not a buyer's. An attempted resale by the buyer would be an acceptance of the goods (U.C.C. § 2–606) unless the buyer is not repaid the $5,000. The buyer can hold the goods for the seller and get restitution. The buyer can also get damages, but none of the choices present this possibility.

158. a. These are incidental damages, recovery for which is permitted under U.C.C. § 2–715(1). Mental suffering damages and punitive damages are rarely given in contract cases and never in transactions between merchants. D can possibly be claimed as consequential damages but there are insufficient facts to prove liability for such damages.

159. b. This question is simply one of nomenclature.

177. b. The agreement is within the Statute of Frauds. However, the Statute of Frauds can only be raised by pleading it as an affirmative defense.

183. b. This is a typical offer to a unilateral contract, similar to an offer to a reward. The language is clear.

184. c. B is clearly wrong. Offers do not become irrevocable by lapse of time. A and D deal with the equal publication rule, and would be difficult to deal with but for choice C. (As to the equal publication rule did the faculty have notice that Student was acting on the strength of its offer?) It is by now well established that part performance of the act requested by an offer to a unilateral contract makes the offer irrevocable.

185. a. The offer looks to acceptance by performance only. A promise to submit a prize winning essay is not asked for nor could it be implied. Consequently the contract could not be deemed bilateral except under the much criticized California rule alluded to in D.

186. a. In a unilateral contract situation the performance of the act requested is the condition precedent to the promisor's duty of performance. B is incorrect as the faculty is attempting to stimulate activity on the part of the students rather than to be benevolent. C is deceptive. The pre-existing duty of the outside agency is not relevant. Neither the faculty nor the student were under pre-existing duties. Consequently, their contract is not affected by the pre-existing duty rule. D is incorrect. The performance was the entry into the competition. Winning was an additional condition precedent to the faculty's obligation.

187. b. Student had fully performed before his death. Therefore his estate may recover although the condition precedent of winning had not occurred. In other words death did not terminate the power of acceptance because student had fully performed. C raises the gift question again. Look at the terms of the offer. D is incorrect. A contest entrant is under no duty to do his or her best or even to complete the contest. Student was free to withdraw. Answer A is plausible but contracts are not enforced on promissory estoppel grounds if there are more conventional grounds for enforcement.

COMPREHENSIVE EXAMINATION QUESTIONS

QUESTION 1

Owner retained Broker to find a buyer who would purchase a designated house and lot. The written and subscribed contract between Owner and Broker provided that a commission of $1,400 would be payable in 14 monthly installments to commence "when the broker produced a purchaser who is ready willing and able to purchase." Broker succeeded in finding a purchaser who entered into a written contract of sale with Owner and who had sufficient funds to make the purchase. Broker brought an action for $1,400 and moved for summary judgment.

Owner submitted an answering affidavit that stated in substance (1) that the parties orally agreed that the commission would be paid on the closing of title in a lump sum; (2) that title failed to close because the purchaser refused to proceed upon learning of a cloud on title; (3) that the contract authorized Broker to search title but Broker did not search title and neither party was aware of the cloud on title; and (4) that the house was destroyed by fire between the time the contract was signed and the closing of title.

Rule on the motion for summary judgment, discussing the issues involved.

QUESTION 2

Special Interests, Inc., (SI), a duly registered lawful lobbying organization, conducted a fund raising drive, soliciting pledges from those who shared its views. It received this signed pledge from Pledgor: "In consideration of SI's valuable services to the nation, heretofore and in the future, I pledge $5,000 to SI, payable in six months."

Pledgor owned a grinching machine. Lessee orally offered to lease the machine. Pledgor was receptive, saying: "I'll let you have the machine for five years if you agree to pay me $500 a month and pay SI the $5,000 that I pledged last week." Lessee said, "Okay, but I want the right to cancel if I'm not satisfied with the machine. I'll take it on a trial basis for 3 months." Pledgor said nothing further, and helped Lessee load the machine onto Lessee's truck.

After a week, Pledgor told Lessee not to pay the $5,000 to SI, but to pay it directly to Pledgor. Lessee agreed.

Several weeks later, after Lessee put the machine into operation, Lessee angrily told Pledgor that the machine "doesn't grinch worth a darn." Pledgor replied that the only problem was that Lessee didn't know the first thing about the art of using finely calibrated machinery. At the end of this stormy telephone conversation Lessee said that only as much rent as the machine proved to be worth would be paid. Pledgor then went to the site of the machine, repossessed it, and sued immediately for damages. SI subsequently brought suit against Pledgor and Lessee. The actions have been consolidated and will be tried together.

What are the rights of the parties? Discuss.

QUESTION 3

This question is based on a question appearing on the New Jersey Bar Examination.

H owns Hotel and Tee owns an adjacent 18 hole Golf Course.

H desired to arrange golfing privileges at Tee's golf course for Hotel's guests. In December 1980 H told Tee that if Hotel's guests were permitted to use Golf Course free of charge, H would pay Tee $2,500 per month during the season. Tee replied that this would be acceptable "if it is for a five year term and if you purchase all of Hotel's meat requirements from my brother-in-law, Butcher." H agreed. The two men wrote out and subscribed the following

"Agreed: Guests at Hotel may use Golf Course free of charge.

H shall pay Tee $2,500 per month. Duration as per verbal agreement.

H shall purchase Hotel's meat requirements from Butcher."

The parties operated under the agreement during 1981. In December 1981 Tee told H that the monthly payments would be increased to $3,000, "because your guests are overcrowding the course and my lawyer says our deal isn't binding. You have 10 days to decide or I will cancel." Five days later Sport, the proprietor of a sporting goods store located in Hotel, wrote Tee: "I hear you are considering cancelling your deal with H. If you do, it will hurt my sales of golf equipment. If you agree not to cancel during the life of the agreement, I'll pay you $300 per month." Tee wrote back: "I accept"; and in January 1982 Sport commenced paying Tee $300 per month. H continued to pay $2,500 per month to Tee.

On April 15, 1982 Tee announced plans to erect a large resort hotel on land presently occupied by 9 of the 18 holes on Golf Course. H was upset at the announcement and H and Sport refused to make any further payments and H told Butcher that H no longer would buy meat from Butcher. Butcher had recently spent $10,000 expanding refrigeration capacity to provide Hotel with better services.

What are the rights of the parties at each stage of the events set out above? Discuss.

CALIFORNIA BAR EXAM COMPREHENSIVE QUESTION

Katy and Mike operated a motorcycle dealership under the name K & M. In May 1980, Cycles orally agreed to supply motorcycles to K & M for resale at a price 5% less than Cycles' factory list prices. The term of the agreement was for the succeeding five-year period but could be terminated at any time by either party. Cycles immediately sent a written signed confirmation of the agreement which, however, omitted the 5% discount provision. K & M never received the written confirmation.

In November 1980, Katy and Mike terminated their business relationship. They executed a document by which Mike assigned all his rights in K & M contracts to Katy, and by which Katy agreed to be solely liable for all of K & M's business obligations. A copy of the signed document was delivered to Cycles. Cycles continued to ship motorcycles to K & M.

A year after receiving the copy of the document, Cycles sent Katy a statement for $40,000, the factory list price for the latest shipment of motorcycles accepted by Katy. Katy sent Cycles a check for $30,000 with a letter stating that the check was sent in full payment of the statement because Cycles had billed her at prices which were too high. Cycles deposited the check and immediately sent protest letters to Katy and Mike demanding payment of $10,000 and cancelling the agreement to supply motorcycles on the ground that the agreement was not binding and, alternatively, that it was invalidated because Mike had left the dealership.

1. To what relief, if any, is Katy entitled against Cycles? Discuss.

2. To what relief, if any, is Cycles entitled against:

   (a) Katy? Discuss.

   (b) Mike? Discuss.

SAMPLE ANSWERS TO COMPREHENSIVE QUESTIONS

ANSWER 1
Summary judgment denied. Resolution of the dispute hinges upon question of fact.

Item 1 of the affidavit does not indicate whether the oral agreement was made before or after the written contract was signed.

   (a) If the oral agreement was prior to, or contemporaneous with, the written contract, it would be ineffective and barred by the parol evidence rule. The oral agreement is directly contradictory to the written contract.

   (b) If the oral agreement was made subsequent to the written contract, it would have effectively modified the contract. The parol evidence rule does not bar evidence of agreements made subsequent to the writing. The modification is supported by consideration, as there is new detriment on each side. Broker's payments rights are postponed. Owner's payment duty is changed inasmuch as payment must be in one lump sum rather than in installments. The Statute of Frauds presents no obstacle to enforcement, except in those few states that require a brokerage contract to be in writing. The contract, originally not performable within one year, as modified, is performable within a year. Although it relates to real property, it is not a contract for the conveyance of any interest in real property. Therefore, it is not within the real property Statute of Frauds.

Consequently, the motion cannot be granted without knowing when the oral agreement was allegedly made.

Item 2 indicates that seller's title is unmarketable. As between seller and buyer whether buyer was justified in refusing to proceed depends on whether title is curable or not. This question of fact also has an impact upon the Broker's rights. If the written contract stands as written, Broker has complied with all conditions precedent to Broker's right to a commission. When a purchaser, with sufficient financial ability to purchase, signs a contract of sale the purchaser's ability and willingness to perform are established. If the brokerage contract was modified to postpone payment until closing of title, a different condition is imposed. It has been held that time-of-payment clauses in brokerage contracts ("when clauses") create conditions to the broker's right to payment. Unless the condition is excused, the broker's right to payment has not become absolute under the allegedly modified agreement. The condition would be excused, however, if the cloud on title were curable and seller failed to cure. Even if the title were incurable, the condition may be excused on the theory that the seller when listing the property for sale impliedly warranted marketable title. However, this implied warranty may have been negated by facts alleged in item 3 of the affidavit.

Item 3 alleges that Broker was authorized to search title. On the face of it this is not a condition to Broker's rights nor a promise on Broker's part. Its legal effect is ambiguous. Only by a process of interpretation involving parol evidence can it be determined whether the authorization was intended to expressly or impliedly condition Broker's rights on making a search to determine the marketability of Owner's title.

Item 4 describes the destruction of the building by fire. If the written contract stands unmodified, this allegation does not affect Broker's rights. Broker's rights became absolute. The rights of Broker are not discharged by impossibility as it is not impossible for Owner to pay. Frustration of purpose is no defense as Broker has fully performed. If the contract had been modified as alleged in Item 1, and assuming Owner was not at fault in causing the fire, the purpose of the parties may have been frustrated by an event the non-occurrence of which was a basic assumption of the parties. Whether this is the fact can only be determined after a full evidentiary hearing.

Assuming it is determined that the broker is entitled to judgment on the original written contract Broker would only be entitled to the sums due at the time of trial. When a party has fully performed and is entitled to payments at fixed times in the future the law only permits recovery of payments due up to time of trial. A material breach does not accelerate the due dates of debts.

ANSWER 2

The first question presented is whether the pledge is binding. If it is, SI may recover from Pledgor regardless of any assumption by Lessee. The promise to pay must be supported by consideration or its equivalent. Past valuable services are not consideration, because they were not bargained for in exchange for the promise. The services "in the future" could serve as consideration if SI has promised to continue to render its services. The facts do not so indicate. Nonetheless, SI's acceptance of the pledge may well be taken as an implied promise to continue its services. The implication of such a promise may depend upon further information concerning SI's handling of the pledge. For example, if SI drafted the pledge document such an implication would be almost irresistable.

If no promise is implied, the pledge may possibly be upheld under the doctrine of promissory estoppel. Under the rule of the Restatement, Second, of Contracts, a charitable pledge is enforceable without consideration and without proof of reliance by the promisee on the promise. This rule is, in part, founded on a recognition of the important societal role of private charities in this country. However, SI is not a charity. It is doubtful whether SI could successfully invoke the Restatement rule here discussed.

Another approach to the pledge is to look at it as an offer that requests a performance (future service to the nation). If SI has performed any service subsequent to, and with knowledge of, the pledge, the offer becomes irrevocable. This approach has been taken by courts that do not accept the doctrine of promissory estoppel. Again, however, the context has been the charitable pledge and SI is not a charity, but the principle could be applicable to non-charitable pledges.

The lease is valid. Lessee's counter-offer was accepted on the spot. Although Pledgor did not reply in words to Lessee's counter-offer, Pledgor's conduct in assisting Lessee to move the machine is implicitly an expression of assent.

There is, however, a division of authority as to whether this valid lease is enforceable. A five year lease of personalty is within the one year provision of the Statute of Frauds. However, this lease gives Lessee an option to terminate upon dissatisfaction within three months. Many courts would rule that exercise of this option would result in a discharge of the contract rather than its full performance. Under this view, the contract would be unenforceable for want of a writing. Many courts would instead rule that the exercise of the option to terminate would be one of the alternative ways full performance could take place. In these jurisdictions, no writing would be required.

By the end of the telephone conversation Lessee had repudiated the contract, justifying Pledgor's cancellation of the contract. If Lessee was dissatisfied with the machine, Lessee had the option to terminate, but this does not carry with it the right to state dissatisfaction and to reduce the price. The statement was an unequivocal repudiation of duties under the contract. Consequently, subject to the possible defense of the Statute of Frauds, Lessee is liable to Pledgor for total breach.

SI's rights against Pledgor have been discussed. SI's relationship with Lessee is analytically more complex. When Lessee promised Pledgor to pay the $5,000 to SI, SI became a third party beneficiary of Lessee's contract. When Pledgor and Lessee agreed to modify the contract so that SI's rights would be destroyed, this was permissible unless SI's rights had vested. There is no indication that SI even knew of the assumption of the obligation. Knowledge of the promise by the third party beneficiary is minimum standard of vesting, according to most authorities, for anyone other than an infant.

Even if the rights of SI have vested, they are subject to any defenses that Lessee has against Pledgor. This includes Lessee's possible Statute of Frauds defense and any defenses that Lessee may have based on the alleged unsatisfactory quality of the leased machinery.

A last and, difficult, question is whether Lessee can raise against SI the contention that Pledgor was not bound by its pledge to SI because SI supplied no consideration. Leading cases, such as Rouse v. United States, indicate that the promisor may not usually raise defenses against the beneficiary that the promisee could raise against the beneficiary. Such defenses are available only when the contract can be interpreted as containing a provision that the promisor's obligation is conditioned on the promisee being liable to the beneficiary. There is no basis for such an interpretation in the case at bar.

ANSWER 3

1. H made an offer. Tee made a counter-offer which H accepted on the spot, forming an oral contract. It is not a problem that Tee's single promise to allow the use of the golf-course by H's guests is exchanged for two promises by H. One consideration can support multiple promises.

2. The oral contract is within the Statute of Frauds and thus unenforceable unless it is sufficiently memorialized. The written memorandum must contain all of the essential terms agreed upon. Although there is a reference to duration and parol evidence is admissible to clarify vague or indefinite terms, it seems doubtful that a term that merely refers to "as per oral agreement" has sufficient content to satisfy the Statute. Parol evidence would supply the term, not clarify it.

3. Tee's demand of December 1981, even if it were unjustified, was perhaps not a repudiation because it was conditional. There is authority, however, to the ef-

fect that a demand conditioned on an act that goes beyond the contract constitutes a repudiation. In any event, Tee retracted in timely fashion.

4. There is a consideration problem with respect to the agreement between Sport and Tee. Assuming Tee was bound by the contract with H, the traditional rule is that a promise to perform a preexisting duty owed to the other party or to a third person is not consideration. (The Restatements disagree.) Nonetheless, Tee may have provided consideration by retracting the threat to cancel. Assuming Tee's lawyer advised Tee that the contract was unenforceable, his good faith is established and, in view of the Statute of Frauds problem, the contention is not unreasonable. That the course is overcrowded is a foreseeable risk assumed by Tee and not even plausibly a ground for cancellation.

5. The contract between Sport and Tee suffers from the same Statute of Frauds difficulty as does the original writing between H and Tee. Since Sport's letter refers to the original contract, the original memorandum can be treated as part of the memorandum between Sport and Tee. Arguably, the duration term is not sufficiently reduced to writing.

6. Assuming Tee does not have a Statute of Frauds defense, Tee's announcement of April 15, 1982 is not yet a repudiation, nor is it a sufficient expression of prospective unwillingness to perform to justify cancellation by H. Tee has not announced when the hotel is to be built. Depending on the tenor of the announcement, H may be justified in suspending performance and demanding assurances from Tee.

7. Because the original contract between H and Tee called for performances that would be rendered directly to Butcher (paying for meat or, at a minimum, not buying meat from others). Butcher is an intended third party beneficiary of the contract between H and Tee. (Since the contract gives Butcher rights but no duties, it is an option contract.) As a third party intended beneficiary, Butcher's rights have vested. Butcher knows of the contract and has relied upon it. Nonetheless, despite vesting, Butcher's rights against H are subject to any defense that H has against Tee other than those arising from voluntary agreements between H and Tee. Potential defenses are the Statute of Frauds and Tee's prospective unwillingness to carry out the contract.

8. Butcher has no contractual rights against Tee. From all appearances, Butcher is a donee beneficiary, inasmuch as we are not informed of any obligor-obligee relationship between these brothers-in-law. Under the contract, Butcher was the beneficiary of orders and payments from H, not Tee. Butcher was only an incidental beneficiary of Tee's promised performance. It is also clear that a donee beneficiary has no cause of action against Tee in Tee's capacity of promisee.

MODEL ANSWER TO CALIFORNIA BAR EXAMINATION QUESTION

What follows is a "model answer," slightly edited for this edition. This model is beyond what an examiner expects from a student for a grade of A+. It does, however, illustrate the goal against which an examinee's paper is graded. Matter within square brackets has been added for this edition.

Point One: The agreement is not binding for a five year term on Cycles. It is, however, not terminable except on a reasonable period of notice.

As a common law proposition, the agreement would likely be held void for lack of consideration. A promise terminable at the will of a promisor has been regarded as illusory. *Miami Coca–Cola Bottling Co. v. Orange Crush Co.,* 296 F.2d 693 (5th Cir.1924). Under U.C.C. § 2–309(3), however, "termination of a contract by one party except on the happening of an agreed event requires that reasonable notification be received by the other party and an agreement dispensing with notification is invalid if its operation would be unconscionable." The parties did not agree to dispense with reasonable notification; consequently, the question of unconscionability need not be addressed. Therefore, reasonable notification is required. "Reasonable notification" means "a reasonable period of notice." *McGinnis Piano & Organ Co. v. Yamaha Int'l Corp.,* 480 F.2d 474 (8th Cir.1973). Since reasonable notice was not given by Cycles, *absent other defenses,* it is liable for damages suffered by Katy for a reasonable period of time after notice of termination. Reasonableness depends primarily on factors unknown to us, such as the period of time needed to make alternative business arrangements and to recoup one's investment in the dealership. See generally, Gellhorn, *Limitations on Contract Termination Rights,* 57 Duke L.J. 465 (1967).

Section 2–207 of the U.C.C., dealing with additional or different terms contained in a written confirmation, is not relevant to this set of facts as that section presupposes receipt of the confirmation. U.C.C. § 2–207(2)(c).

Point Two: As to the claim of Katy and Mike, Cycles' written confirmation satisfies the writing requirement of the Sales, and can satisfy, under certain circumstances, the One Year Provision of the Statute of Frauds.

The agreement is for the sale of goods and must satisfy the Sale of Goods Statute of Frauds. It is within the One Year Provision of the Statute of Frauds as well. Thus, the transaction would have to meet the terms of both provisions. *Restatement of Contracts* § 178, Comment b; *Restatement (Second) of Contracts* § 110, Comment b.

The Sales Provision is clearly met. The confirmation meets the test of U.C.C.— Sales § 2–201(1) that there be "some writing sufficient to indicate that a contract for sale has been made between the parties and signed by the party against whom enforcement is sought. . . ."

The Statute is satisfied even though an important term (5% discount) is omitted. "A writing is not insufficient because it omits or incorrectly states a term agreed upon." U.C.C. § 2–201(1).

The contract cannot be performed within a one year term and is, therefore, within the One Year Provision of the Statute of Frauds. Although either party can terminate within the year, under the majority view, termination discharges the contract so that it cannot be said that the contract is fully performed if the hypothetical termination takes place. *Restatement (Second) of Contracts* § 130, Comment b. *J. Calamari & J. Perillo, The Law of Contracts* [*3d*] § 19–21. Unlike the U.C.C. Statute of Frauds, the One Year Provision requires that all material terms agreed upon be included in the memorandum. The omission of the 5% discount provision would appear to be a fatal omission. However, the omission can be rectified in two ways. First, if the omission was accidental, under the majority view, the writing can be reformed to reflect the true agreement of the parties. *J. Calamari & J. Perillo, The Law of Contracts* [*3d*] § 19–28. Second, since the clause unilaterally benefits the buyers, they may cure any Statute of Frauds problem by renouncing the benefit of the clause. *Restatement of Contracts* § 221; *Restatement (Second) of Contracts* § 147. The One Year Provision requires a signature "by the party to be charged." The signed confirmation meets this test. It is enforceable against Cycles despite the fact it was not signed by any other party. *Restatement, Contracts* § 211; *Restatement (Second) of Contracts* § 135. The Statutes are satisfied although the only writing that can be found is the copy in Cycles' own files and although the other parties were unaware of the writing. *Transit Advertisers Inc. v. New York, N.H. & H.R.R.*, 194 F.2d 907, 31 A.L.R.2d 1102 (2d Cir.), cert. denied, 344 U.S. 817 (1952).

Point Three: *As to the claim of Cycles against Katy and Mike, the confirmation does not satisfy the Statute of Frauds, but Cycles' claim for payment of goods received and accepted takes the case out of the writing requirements of the Statute of Frauds.*

Under U.C.C. § 2–201(2), a non-signing merchant party loses the defense of the Statute of Frauds if he or she fails to contest a written confirmation within 10 days of receipt. Since K & M never received the confirmation, they have not lost the defense in this way. However, U.C.C. § 2–201(3) provides that, despite the absence of sufficient written evidence of a contract, the contract is enforceable "with respect to goods . . . which have been received and accepted."

As for the One Year Statute of Frauds, full performance takes the contract out of the Statute of Frauds. *Restatement (Second) of Contracts* § 130 and Comment d. Full performance by one party of a divisible portion of a contract permits contractual recovery of the corresponding price for the performance. *Blue Valley Creamery Co. v. Consolidated Products Co.*, 81 F.2d 182 (8th Cir.1936); see Note, 71 A.L.R. 479, 492. Since Cycles seeks payment for a divisible portion of the contract—a discrete delivery of goods for an apportioned price (*Gill v. Johnstown Lumber Co.,* 151 Pa. 534, 25 A. 120 (1892)) the Statute of Frauds is not a defense.

Point Four: *Mike's "assignment" to Katy carried with it an improper delegation of duties. Cycles, however, has lost the power to object to the delegation by waiver.*

According to the U.C.C. § 2–210(4), general language of assignment carries with it a delegation of duties unless other language or the circumstances dictates a contrary interpretation. Mike's general language of assignment coupled with his leaving the business clearly indicates an intent to delegate.

The delegation is, however, improper. Under U.C.C. § 2–210(1) a delegation is improper if the obligee has a substantial interest in having the original contracting parties perform. It is clear that in a franchising (albeit non-exclusive) arrangement such as is present here, Cycles has a substantial interest in determining the individuals who will operate a Cycles dealership. *Paige v. Faure,* 229 N.Y. 114, 127 N.E. 898 (1920) (pre-code but good law); *J. Calamari & J. Perillo, The Law of Contracts 2d* § 18–10 [*3d* § 18–31 p. 766].

Despite the impropriety of the delegation, Cycles, with notice of the delegation, dealt with Katy. Consequently, it waived the non-delegability of Mike's duties. *Seale v. Bates,* 145 Colo. 430, 359 P.2d 356 (1961).

Point Five: *Despite Katy's agreement to be solely liable for contract obligations, Mike remains liable on the Cycles contract.*

Although Katy agreed to be solely liable on K & M contracts, it is fundamental that such an agreement could have no effect on the rights of Cycles against Mike. Consequently, assuming a valid cause of action, Cycles may obtain judgment against both Katy and Mike. *Copeland v. Beard,* 217 Ala. 216, 115 So. 389 (1928); *Erickson v. Grande Ronde Lumber Co.,* 162 Or. 556, 94 P.2d 139 (1929). The fact that Katy is primarily, and Mike secondarily, liable is of interest but of no relevance to the resolution of any problem in this lawsuit.

Point Six: *Cycles did not enter into an accord and satisfaction when it cashed Katy's check under protest.*

At common law it was the general rule that when a debtor tendered a check for less than the amount claimed by his creditor, clearly indicating that it was tendered in full satisfaction of the creditor's claim, the depositing of the check acted as an acceptance of the debtor's offer to an accord and satisfaction. "Protest will then be unavailing if the money is retained." *Hudson v. Yonkers Fruit Co.,* 258 N.Y. 168, 179 N.E. 373 (1932) (Cardozo, C.J.). The creditor is estopped from claiming that the check was tortiously cashed. Despite the absence of assent, estoppel creates the fiction of mutual assent. However, for a valid accord and satisfaction, another element—consideration—is also needed. In cases such as this, the consideration is often the compromise of a good faith dispute. Nothing in the facts clearly indicates such a dispute. Dissatisfaction with the prices charged under the contract is not a bona fide dispute unless, perhaps, if the prices are fixed in bad faith. U.C.C. § 2–305(2).

All of the above, however, is preamble to the U.C.C. which drastically changes the common law. U.C.C. § 1–207 permits the creditor to accept the debtor's conditional check under protest, reserving rights, and permitting the cashing of the check without accepting the offer to an accord and satisfaction. [It is now controversial whether U.C.C. § 1–207 applies to a "full payment check." Although the literal meaning of § 1–207 would indicate that it applies, many courts have now reached a contrary conclusion.]

APPENDIX C

CORRELATION CHART

Contract Law Black Letter Series	Calamari, Perillo & Bender 2d ed.	Dawson, Harvey & Henderson 5th ed.	Farnsworth & Young, 4th ed.	Fessler & Loiseaux	Fuller & Eisenberg 5th ed.	Kessler, Gilmore & Kronman, 3d ed.	Murray, 2d ed.	Arthur Rosset, 4th ed.	Murphy & Speidel, 3d ed.
Chapter I Offer and Acceptance	1–145	314–448	127–252	245–326	359–526 596–627	111–278, 315–418	19–234	434–534	92–330
Chapter II Consideration and Its Equivalents	146–277	185–313	1–126	26–145, 522–541	1–189	279–314, 419–752	235–446	13–44, 167–249	1–91, 331–488
Chapter III Legal Capacity	313–325	529–553	289–301	201–203, 209–211	not covered	not covered	305–308	97–111	558–586
Chapter IV Proper Form, Writing and Interpretation	278–312, 757–801	449–528, 941–957	253–288, 544–647	327–401, 829–830	328–358, B–1 through B–39, 527–594, 628–652	753–859	447–554	249–281, 44–64, 261–264, 272–274	723–781, 489–558
Chapter V Conditions, Performance and Breach	379–537	720–851	648–808	543–759	847–1027	973–1059	853–1021	535–556, 592–653	782–888
Chapter VI Defenses	538–587, 802–846	629–668	440–470, 809–873	460–522	696–742	920–971, 60–61, 97–98	633–666	557–592, 71–80	889–961, 673–721
Chapter VII Remedies	588–687	1–184	471–543	644–759	191–326	1061–1328	667–852, 1173–1258	282–433	962–1228
Chapter VIII Avoidance or Reformation	326–378	553–629, 669–719	301–440	146–244, 402–459	653–695	861–920	554–633	94–166	587–673
Chapter IX Third Party Beneficiaries	688–721	852–901	874–923	760–822	744–796	1329–1439	1023–1090	654–681	1296–1365
Chapter X Assignment and Obligation	722–756	901–940	924–995	822–828	796–847	1441–1558	1091–1172	682–723	1229–1295

APPENDIX D

GLOSSARY

A

Account Stated An "account stated" arises where there have been transactions between debtor and creditor resulting in the creation of matured debts and where the parties by agreement compute a balance which the debtor promises to pay and the creditor promises to accept in full payment for the items of account.

Aleatory Contract An "aleatory contract" is where the performance on one or both sides is made to depend upon a fortuitous event. Examples include insurance contracts and wagers.

Anticipatory Repudiation Restatement, Contracts, § 318 lists three actions which constitute "repudiation":

a. positive statement (to promisee or other person having a right under the contract) indicating the promisor will not or cannot substantially perform;

b. transfer (or contracting to transfer) to a third person of anything essential for substantial performance by promisor;

c. voluntary affirmative act which renders substantial performance impossible or apparently impossible.

A repudiation is "anticipatory" if the repudiation takes place before the time for performance.

Assignment (compared with "Delegation" and "Assumption")

a. Assignment (of Rights). An "assignment" is a manifestation of intent by the owner of a contractual right to effectuate a present transfer of an interest in the right to the assignee. An assignment extinguishes the right in the assignor, unless the assignment is intended to create merely a security interest.

b. Delegation (of Duties). A "delegation" involves the appointment by the obligor of another to render performance on obligor's behalf. A delegation does not eliminate the

451

original contractual obligations of the delegant unless the promisee by a "novation" (see infra) discharges the delegant from the duty to see to it that the promised performance is rendered.

c. Assumption (of Duties). Not every delegation involves an "assumption" of duties by the delegate. Such an assumption occurs if the delegate makes a promise which is intended to benefit the person to whom the duty is owed. An assumption does not affect the delegant's continuing duty of seeing that the performance is rendered.

B

Bilateral Contract (compared with Unilateral Contract)

a. "Bilateral" Contract. Exists if both parties have made promises to render specified performances.

b. "Unilateral" Contract. Exists if one party has promised to perform (offer) and the other party completes the contract (acceptance) by rendering the requested performance rather than by making a return promise.

C

Capacity When a party to an agreement is deemed to lack the "capacity" to enter into a binding contract, the agreement is void or voidable. Classes which have historically been deemed to lack capacity include: (1) infants; (2) persons mentally infirm; (3) spendthrifts.

Consideration While an encompassing definition of this requirement for a valid contract is perhaps impossible, the essence of "consideration" is a legal detriment which has been bargained for by the promisor and exchanged by the promisee for the promise in question.

Condition (compared with Promise)

a. Condition. An act or event, other than the lapse of time, which qualifies a duty to render a promised performance. A condition may be "precedent," "concurrent" or "subsequent."

b. Promise. Defined in Restatement, Second, Contracts, § 2 as a manifestation of in-

tention to act or refrain from acting in a specified way. A promise is said to be "absolute" (independent or unconditional) if nothing but a lapse of time is necessary to make its performance due immediately.

Constructive Conditions (Implied in Law) As opposed to "express" conditions which are either spelled out or implied in fact (by being gathered from the contract terms as a matter of interpretation), "constructive" conditions are imposed by law to meet the ends of justice.

Contract "A contract is a promise, or set of promises, for the breach of which the law gives a remedy, or the performance of which the law in some way recognizes as a duty."

Counter Offer An offeree may decide not to accept the original offer and to instead make an offer on different terms, as to which the original offeree then becomes the offeror and the original offeror becomes the offeree. The effect of a counter offer is to terminate such counter offeror's right to subsequently accept the original offer.

Creditor Beneficiary See Donee Beneficiary.

Delegation (of Duties) See Assignment.

Divisible Contracts A "divisible contract" exists if: (1) performance by each party is divided into two or more parts; and (2) the performance of each party by one party is the agreed exchange for a corresponding part by the other party.

Donee Beneficiary If the promisee (in a third party beneficiary situation) enters into a contract with the purpose of having a gift conferred upon the third party, such third party is called a "donee beneficiary." The third party is called a "creditor beneficiary" if the purpose of the promisee in extracting the promise from the promisor is to discharge an obligation which the promisee owes or believes is owed to the third party beneficiary.

E

Enforceable Contract When a promisee is entitled to either a money judgment or specific performance because of a breach, the contract is said to be "enforceable."

Executory Accord An "executory accord" is an agreement embodying a promise, express or implied, to accept at some future time a stipulated performance in satisfaction or discharge, in whole or in part, of any present claim, cause of action or obligation, and a promise, express or implied, to render such performance.

Express Contract When the parties manifest their agreement by words, the contract is said to be "express."

F

Foakes v. Beer, Rule of Under the rule of *Foakes v. Beer,* a debtor's part payment of a total amount indisputably due is not consideration to support a contract based on the creditor's promise to discharge the remaining amount due after such part payment. One exception to this rule, stated in dictum in *Pinnell's Case* (1602), is that a slightly different performance (e.g. payment one day earlier) is sufficient detriment to support a finding of consideration for the creditor's promise to cancel the debt. This has been called the "hawk, horse or robe" rule because of the use of these items in Pinnell's Case as examples of added items which would constitute sufficient detriment.

Frustration of Purpose (Venture) Where the object of one of the parties is the basis upon which both parties contract, the duties of performance are constructively conditioned upon the attainment of such object. This doctrine, which arose in the "coronation cases" (involving contracts to license the use of various premises to view a coronation procession which was cancelled), is called "frustration of purpose" or "frustration of the venture."

H

Hadley v. Baxendale, Rule of Under the rule of *Hadley v. Baxendale,* "special" or "consequential" damages (as opposed to "general" damages which so obviously result from a breach that all contracting parties are

deemed to have contemplated them) will only be awarded if they were in the parties' contemplation, at the time of contracting, as a probable consequence of a breach of contract.

I

Implied in Fact Contract When the parties manifest their agreement by conduct, the contract is said to be "implied in fact."

Implied in Law (Quasi–Contract) A contract implied in law is not a contract at all, but an obligation imposed by law to do justice even though it is clear that no promise was ever made or intended.

Impossibility of Performance The doctrine of "impossibility of performance" is an exception to the general rule that the promisor must either perform, or pay damages for failure to perform, no matter how burdensome performance has become because of unforeseen circumstances. While the doctrine has evolved around various specific categories, one basic part of the doctrine is that the impossibility of performance must be objective rather than merely subjective.

Incidental (Third Party) Beneficiary A person who is a donee or creditor (third party) beneficiary of a contract is entitled, under certain circumstances, to enforce the contract. Since there will often be many people indirectly or even directly benefited by any given contractual performance, the term "incidental beneficiary" is used to describe those persons who would benefit by the performance but who were not intended by the parties to be benefited and who thus cannot enforce the contract.

Liquidated Damages Clause If a clause determines in advance what the damages for breach will be is upheld, it is called a "liquidated damages clause"; if such a clause is struck down, it is usually then called a "penalty clause." The traditional criteria of a liquidated damages clause are: (1) injury caused by the breach must be difficult or impossible to estimate accurately; (2) parties must have intended that the agreed payment be for the loss, rather than as a deterrent to breach; (3) the stipulated amount of damages must be a reasonable estimate of the probable loss.

Locus Poenitentiae, Doctrine of While a court will usually leave the parties to an illegal contract where it finds them, the doctrine of "locus poenitentiae" permits a party, even one in pari delicto (see infra), to rescind an illegal contract and obtain restitution if the party acts in time to prevent the illegal purpose for which the bargain was made and if the mere making of the illegal bargain does not itself involve serious moral turpitude.

M

Mitigation of Damages A party who is entitled to recover for a breach of contract may not recover for those damages which could have been avoided by a reasonable effort without undue risk, expense or humiliation. This is called the "mitigation of damages" doctrine.

N

Novation A contract is a "novation" if it: (1) discharges immediately a previous contractual duty or a duty to make compensation; and (2) creates a new contractual duty; and (3) includes as a party one who neither owed the previous duty nor was entitled to its performance.

O

Offer An offer is a promise to do or refrain from doing some specified thing in the future. The offer creates a "power of acceptance" which permits the offeree by accepting the offer to transform the offeror's promise into a contractual obligation.

P

Pari Delicto, Doctrine of Under the doctrine of "pari delicto," a party who has performed under an illegal bargain is entitled to a quasi-contractual recovery if this party is not guilty of serious moral turpitude and, although blameworthy, is not equally as guilty as the other party to the illegal bargain.

Parol Evidence Rule Under the "parol evidence rule," prior and contemporaneous oral expressions and prior written expressions are not admissible to vary or contradict the terms of a writing which both parties intended to be the final and complete integration of their agreement. This rule is subject to many exceptions and involves a complex series of pronouncements about intention, integration, etc.

Penalty Clause See Liquidated Damages Clause.

Pre-existing Duty Under the "pre-existing duty" rule, a party who merely does or promises to do something he or she is already legally obligated to do or who refrains from doing or promises to refrain from doing something he or she is already legally obligated to refrain from doing has incurred no detriment for purposes of determining whether his or her act or forbearance constitutes sufficient consideration.

Promise See Conditions.

Promissory Estoppel Section 90 of the Restatement of Contracts, Second, states "A promise which the promisor should reasonably expect to induce action or forbearance on the part of the promisee or a third person and which does induce such action or forbearance is binding if injustice can be avoided only by enforcement of the promise." This is the doctrine of "promissory estoppel."

R

Rescission A "rescission" is an agreement between the parties to cancel the contract; a "termination" is the discharge of duties by the exercise of a power granted by the contract; a "cancellation" is one party's putting an end to the contract by reason of a breach by the other party.

Release A "release" is a writing or an oral statement manifesting an intention to discharge another from an existing or asserted duty. Releases frequently raise problems of consideration.

S

Satisfaction (Accord and,) A "satisfaction" in the context of an "accord and satisfaction" is the performance of an executory accord (see Executory Accord) or the making of a substituted contract.

T

Temporary Frustration or Impossibility A "temporary frustration" (of purpose) or "temporary impossibility" merely suspends the duty of performance until the impossibility or frustrating event ceases. However, the duty of performance is discharged if, after cessation of the temporary frustration or impossibility, the burden of the promised performance would be substantially different than if there had been no such temporary frustration or impossibility.

U

Unconscionable Inadequacy of Consideration While courts will usually not look into the adequacy of consideration (thus permitting great differences between the value of the promise made and the detriment incurred), the U.C.C. has borrowed an equity concept in stating that enforcement of a contract or part thereof may be refused "if the court as a matter of law finds the contract or any clause of the contract to have been unconscionable."

Unenforceable Contract When a contract has some legal consequences but may not be enforced in an action for damages or specific performance in the face of certain defenses such as the Statute of Frauds or a statute of limitations, the contract is said to be "unenforceable."

Unilateral Contract See Bilateral Contract.

V

Void Contract When a purported contract produces no legal obligation upon the part of a promisor, it is sometimes said to be a "void" contract; it is more exact to say that no contract has been created.

Voidable Contract When one or more of the parties has the power to elect to avoid the legal relations created by the contract or the power by ratification to extinguish the power of avoidance, the contract is said to be "voidable." Voidable contracts include:

a. contracts involving minors, and

b. contracts involving fraud, mistake or duress.

*

APPENDIX E

INDEX

ACCEPTANCE
Generally, 99
Act of dominion, 107
Bilateral contracts, 97–102, 105–113
By conduct, 107–108, 124
Conditional, 121
Confirmation, 125
Definite expression of, 120–122
Intent to accept, 101–102, 133
Irrevocable offers, 126–127
Knowledge of offer, 100–101
Lost or delayed, 111, 114
Methods of, 108–109
    Authorised means, 109, 129
    Unauthorised means, 109
Performance, 130
Power of, 99–100, 118
Revocable offers, 113
Series of contracts, offer, 104–105
Silence, 105–107, 133
Terms of, 120–123
U.C.C. and Restatement, Second, 98–99, 109–110, 120–126
Unilateral contracts, 98, 103

Withdrawal of, 112

ACCORD AND SATISFACTION
Definition of, 157
Discharge, 290–291
Duress, 161–162
Executory bilateral accord, 290
Formation of, 291
Substituted contract, 291
U.C.C. Section 1–207, p. 162
Unilateral accord, 290–291

ACT OF DOMINION
Acceptance by, 107

ADVERTISEMENTS
Offer in relation to, 95–96

AFFIRMANCE AND RATIFICATION
Affirmance by conduct, 356
Delay, 357

AGREEMENT
Contemporaneous, 199

In writing, 92–93
To agree, 135–136
U.C.C., 136

AMBIGUITY
See Interpretation

ASSIGNMENT
Attachment, 375
Contractual authorization, 380
Contractual prohibition, 379
Counterclaims, 382
Defenses, 380–383
Definition of, 373
Floating liens, 377
Formalities of, 375
Future rights, 374–375
Gratuitous assignment, 374
Non-assignable rights, 378
Option contracts, 380
Perfection, 375–376
Priorities, in, 376–377
Successive assignees, 377
U.C.C.,
    Coverage & exclusion, 373–374
    Liens, 377–378

Warranties, 383

AUCTIONS, 97

BENEFICIARIES
See Third Party Beneficiaries

BILATERAL CONTRACTS
Acceptance, 97
  By conduct, 107–108
  By silence, 105–106
Ambiguous offer, 98
Communication in, 102
Consideration, 163
Intent to accept, 101
Knowledge of offer, 100–101
Mutuality of obligation, 163
Revocation, 131
U.C.C. & Restatement, Second,
  129, 131
Unilateral v. bilateral contracts,
  97, 128–129

BREACH OF CONTRACT
Improper delegation, 387
Material breach v. substantial
  performance, 235–237
Materiality of, 237
Recovery despite, 240–241
Repudiation, 247
U.C.C., 130

CERTAINTY
Damages, 305–306
Definiteness & indefiniteness of
  terms, 131–133
Sales contracts, 136–138
Silence, 133
U.C.C., 136–138
Void contracts, 131–132

CLAIMS
Liquidated and unliquidated, 157
Validity of, 152–153

**COLLATERAL CONTRACT
RULE,** 196

COMMUNICATION
Interpretation, 202
Construction, 202

**CONDITIONAL ACCEPT-
ANCE,** 121

CONDITIONS
Breach of promise, 235–237
Classification of, 232

Concurrent, 232
Condition precedent, 232
Constructive, 235
Express v. implied, 235, 240
Definition of, 232
Delay, 238–239
Excuses of, 242–247
Failure of, 232, 235, 249
Performance, 237–238
Satisfaction, 239

CONFIRMATION
As acceptance, 125
Confirmatory memorandum, 197–
  198

CONSIDERATION
Adequacy of detriment, 150–151
Bilateral contracts, 163
Duress, 161–162
Elements of, 148–150
Invalid claims, 152–153
Moral obligation, 171
Motives, 150
Nominal, 151–152
Past, 150
Promises, 161–167
Separate, 198
Sham, 151–152
Unilateral contracts, 163–164
Validity of, 170

CONTRACTS
Bilateral and unilateral, 97–98
Modification, 160–161
Objective theory of, 90, 100–102
Option contracts, 126
Output contracts, 169
Requirements contracts, 169
Right of termination, 165–166
Sources of law of,
  Common law, 120
Subjective theory of, 90, 100–102
Substituted contracts, 291
Torts, 107
Void and voidable, 164, 168

CONTRACTS UNDER SEAL,
181

**CORBIN'S RULE OF INTER-
PRETATION,** 204–205
See also Interpretation

COUNTER INQUIRY, 119–120

COUNTER OFFER, 118–119
See also Offer, termination of revocable; Rejection

COURSE OF DEALING, 206
See also Interpretation

COURSE OF PERFORMANCE,
206
See also Interpretation

DAMAGES
Generally, 299
Certainty, 305–307
Conjectural, 317
Consequential damages, 302, 304–
  305
Construction contracts, 302–303
Employment contracts, 302
Equitable enforcement, 316
Foreseeability, 299–300
Inadequacies of legal remedy,
  316–319
Limitations on, 311–312
Liquidated damages clauses, 309–
  310
Mental distress, compensation for,
  312
Mitigation, 307–308
Nominal, 313
Non-exclusive contracts, 308
Present worth doctrine, 309
Punitive, 312
Realty contracts, 304, 307
Sales of goods contracts,
  Breach by buyer, 301
  Breach by seller, 300
  Non-delivery by seller, 300
Value of opportunity, 307

DEATH
Effect on offer and acceptance,
  114–115, 118

DEFENSES
See also Discharge
Discharge, 288
Frustration, 275–276
Illegality of bargain, 281
Impracticability of performance,
  270–274
Risk of loss, 277
Specific performance, 317–318

**DEFINITENESS OF ACCEPT-
ANCE** 120–122
See also Certainty

DEL CREDERE AGENT, 212

DELEGATION
Generally, 384
Improper delegation, 387
Liability, 384–385
Non-delegable duties, 385–386
Sales contracts, 386

DETRIMENT
See Legal Detriment

DISAFFIRMANCE OF IN-FANTS, 187

DISCHARGE
Accord and satisfaction, 290–292
Account stated, 292
Alteration, 293–294
Cancellation, 289–290
Correlative rights, 293
Convenant not to sue, 293
Novation, 292, 368
Release, 293
Rescission,
    Implied rescission, 288
    Mutual rescission, 289

DISMISSAL, 133–134

DIVISIBLE CONTRACTS, 240

DRUG USERS
See Intoxication; Mentally Infirm Persons

DRUNKENNESS
See Intoxication

DURESS
Generally, 330
Abuse of rights, 331
Breach, 331–332
Coercion, 332
Reformation for, 350
Undue influence, 333–334
Wrongful conduct in, 330–331

DUTY OF INQUIRY, 103

DUTY TO READ, 354–356

EMPLOYMENT OFFER, 134

EQUAL PUBLICITY IN REVO-CATION, 116

EQUITABLE ENFORCEMENT
See also Damages

Restitution, 316–317

EQUITABLE ESTOPPEL
See Estoppel in Pais

ESTOPPEL IN PAIS, 244

FACE TO FACE OFFER, 114

FOAKES v. BEER DOCTRINE, 160–161
See also Consideration; Pre-existing Duty Rule

FORFEITURES, 246

FOUR CORNERS RULE, 196

FRUSTRATION
See Defenses

GIFTS, 148–179

ILLEGALITY OF CONTRACTS
Generally, 281, 287–288
Bribery, 282
Licensing statutes, 282–283
Depository defenses, 283
Locus Poenitentiae, 287

INCAPACITY
Adjudication of, 115
Effect on offer and acceptance, 115

INDEFINITENESS
Silence, 133
Terms of, 131–133, 136

INDEPENDENT PROMISES, 241

INFANTS
Avoidance, 187–190
Definition of, 187
Disaffirmance, 187–188
Liability,
    For benefits received, 189
    For necessaries, 188–189
Misrepresentation of age, 190
Torts concerning, 189–190
Voidable promises, 174–175, 187

INSOLVENCY, 251

INSTALLMENT CONTRACTS
See Sales Contract

INTENT TO ACCEPT
See Acceptance; Intent to Contract

INTENT TO CONTRACT
See also Certainty
Intent to accept, 101–102
Intention of legal consequences, 91–92, 135
Manifestation of, 90–91, 130
Objective theory of, 90
Performance, 130
Promise, 93
Reasonable man test, 90–91
Subjective theory of, 90

INTENTION OF LEGAL CON-SEQUENCES
See Intent to Contract

INTERMEDIARY
Liability for mistake, 112–113

INTERPRETATION
Ambiguity of, 202
Course of dealing, 205–206
Course of performance, 206–207
Extrinsic evidence, 202, 205
Rules of,
    Corbin's rule, 204–205
    Plain meaning rule, 202, 205
    U.C.C., 204–205
Williston's rule, 203
Usage of trade, 206

INTOXICATION
See also Mentally Infirm Persons, 191
Effect on contract, 191
Exploitation of intoxicated persons, 191

INVALID CLAIMS
See Claims

IRREVOCABLE OFFERS
See Option Contracts

JEST
See Offer

KNOWLEDGE OF OFFER
See Acceptance

LAST SHOT PRINCIPLE, 120, 124

LATE ACCEPTANCE, 114

LEGAL DETRIMENT
Adequacy, 150–151
Pre-existing duty rule, 153–156
Promise induced by, 148–150

LOCUS POENITENTIAE
See Illegality of Contracts

MAILBOX RULE, 109–111, 128–129
See also Acceptance

MAIN PURPOSE RULE, 210, 211
See also Statute of Frauds

MENTALLY INFIRM PERSONS
Avoidance and ratification, 191
Exploitation of, 191
Liability for necessaries, 191
Promise by, 190
Test of mental infirmity, 190

MIRROR IMAGE RULE, 120

MISREPRESENTATION
Generally, 334
Deception, 335
Fraud-in-the-factum, 343
Intentional and unintentional, 334
Merger clauses, 342
Non-disclosure, 339–341
Partial disclosure, 339
Promissory fraud, 338
Reformation for, 350
Reliance, 335
Remedies for, 341–342

MISTAKE
By intermediary, 112–113
In performance, 347
Mistake of fact v. mistake of judgment, 343
Mutual, 344–345
Recovery for, 348
Reformation for, 348
Unilateral, 346

MODIFICATION OF CONTRACTS, 160–161
See also Consideration

MORAL OBLIGATION
Enforceability of promise, 171–173

MUTUAL ASSENT
Nature of, 90
Objective and subjective, 90

MUTUALITY OF OBLIGATION
Bilateral contracts, 163
Definition of, 163
Unilateral contracts, 163–164

NOTICE OF PERFORMANCE
See Performance

NOVATION
See Discharge

NULLITY
Void contracts, 168

OFFER
Generally, 93–97
Advertisements, 95–96
Ambiguous, 98
Auction, 97
Counter, 118–119
Employment, 134
Face to face, 114
Intent of, 93
Irrevocable offers, 126–128
Jest, 91
Knowledge of, 100
Opinions, 93–94
Preliminary negotiations, 97
Price quotations, 96–97
Revocable offers, 113–119
Revocation of, 115–116
Sale of goods, 108, 129
Statements of intention, 94–95
Termination due to death, 114–115
U.C.C., 128–131

OPTION CONTRACTS
Generally, 126–128
Acceptance of, 128
Nominal consideration in, 152
Termination of, 127–128

OUTPUT CONTRACTS, 169

PAROL EVIDENCE RULE
Integration,
Collateral contract rule, 196
Confirmatory memoranda, 197–198
Corbin's rule, 196–197, 204
Total or partial, 195, 199, 203

Williston's rule, 196, 203
Reformation, 350
U.C.C., 197–198, 204

PAST CONSIDERATION
See Consideration

PERFECT TENDER RULE, 253

PERFORMANCE
Beginning of, 130–131
Delay, 129
Impracticability as defense of, 270–274
Mistake in, 347
Notice of, 103, 130–131
Substantial performance v. material breach, 235–238
U.C.C. & Restatement, Second, 130

PLAIN MEANING RULE, 202, 205
See also Interpretation

PRE-EXISTING DUTY RULE, 153–156, 160–161

PRELIMINARY NEGOTIATIONS, 97

PRICE QUOTATIONS
In relation to offer, 96–97

PRIVITY, 361

PROMISE
Aleatory, 167
Alternative, 171
Condition v. promise, 232–237
Conditional, 166
Conjunctive, 170
Consideration, 148–150
Enforceability, 151
Express, 97
Gift, 179
Illusory, 164–165
Implied, 97, 167
Independent, 241
Intent to offer, 93
Lifetime employment, 134
Moral obligation, 171
Permanent employment offer, 134
Unconscionability, 151
Voidable, 164

PROMISSORY ESTOPPEL
Generally, 118, 176–178

Bargain, 179–181
Employment offer, 134
Gratuitous promise, 148, 177–178

QUASI–CONTRACTUAL RE-
  COVERY, 242
See also Recovery

RATIFICATION
See Affirmance and Ratification

RECOUPMENT, 382

RECOVERY
Divisibility of contract, 240
Independent promises, 241
Quasi-contractual, 242, 286
Statutory relief, 242

REFORMATION
Defenses to, 350–351
For duress, 350
For misrepresentation, 350
For mistake, 348
Parol evidence rule, 350

REJECTION
Counter offer as, 118
Sent with acceptance, 111

REMEDIES
See Damages; Restitution

REPUDIATION
Anticipatory repudiation, 252
Definition of, 247
Insolvency, 251
Retraction of, 249–250
U.C.C., 250–251

REQUIREMENT CONTRACTS
Consideration of, 169–170

RESCISSION OF CONTRACTS
See Modification of Contracts

RESPONDEAT   SUPERIOR
  DOCTRINE, 190

RESTATEMENT, SECOND
See U.C.C. and Restatement, Second

RESTITUTION
  Generally, 313–314
Equitable enforcement, 316–317
Inadequacies of legal remedy,
  316–319

Recovery, 314–315
Specific restitution, 315–316
U.C.C., 242, 315

RESTRAINING ORDERS
See Specific Performance

REVOCABLE OFFER
Termination of, 113–119

REVOCATION
Counter offer, 118
Direct, 115
Equal publicity, 116
Face to face offer, 114
Indirect, 116–117
Rejection, 118
Restatement, Second, 131

RISK OF LOSS
Leases, 277
Sale of goods, 277–280
Sale of property, 277

SALES CONTRACT
Acceptance, 255, 258
Inspection, 258
Installment contracts, 255–256
Perfect tender rule, 253, 257
Performance, 253
Rejected goods, 259
Revocation, 256
Tender, 258
Warranties, 259
  Disclaimer of, 262
  Implied warranties, 260

SATISFACTION
See Accord and Satisfaction

SEAL
See Contracts Under Seal

SHAM, 151

SIGNATURE, 219

SILENCE
Acceptance by, 105–107, 133–134
Intent to contract, 133–134

SPECIFIC PERFORMANCE
Abatement, 320
Covenant not to compete, 322
Damages, 320–321
Defenses to, 317–318
Laches, 320
Mutual assent, 316

Restraining orders, 321

STATUTE OF FRAUDS
Del credere agent, 212
Estoppel,
  Estoppel in Pais, 222, 244
  Promissory estoppel, 221–222
Indemnity, 211
Main purpose rule, 210–211
Marriage, 217
Memorandum, 218
  Parol evidence, 219
  Signature, 219
  Sufficiency, 218–219, 220–221
  U.C.C., 220
Modification, 222–223
Non-compliance, 221
One-year provision, 213–217
Rescission, 222
Sale of goods, 217–218
Sale of land, 212
Suretyship, 209
Voidable promise, 164–165

STATUTE OF LIMITATION
Bankruptcy, 173
Voidable promises, 164

STATUTORY RELIEF, 242

TENDER
See Sales Contract

TERMINATION OF OFFER
See Offer

TERMS OF ACCEPTANCE
  Generally, 120–123, 131–133
Additional, 122–123
Different, 123
Material, 131–133

THIRD   PARTY   BENEFI-
  CIARIES
Counterclaims, 367
Cumulative rights of, 368–369
Defenses, 365–367
Types of, 361–365
  Creditor beneficiary, 362
  Donee beneficiary, 362
  Intended beneficiary, 361
  Municipality contracts, 362
  Promise of indemnity, 362
  Surety bonds, 362–363
Vesting of rights, 366–367

TIME OF ESSENCE, 238

TORTS
Conversion, 107–108
Infants, 189–190
Wrongful discharge, 134

U.C.C. AND RESTATEMENT, SECOND
Acceptance, 98–99, 109–110, 120–126
Agreement, 135–136
Certainty, 136–138
Confirmation, 125
Mailbox rule, 109–110
Offer, 98–99, 113–114, 122–123, 128–131, 136–138
Option contract, 152
Parol evidence rule, 197–198, 204
Performance, 130–131
Promise and consideration, 152
Repudiation, 250–251

Restitution, 242, 315
Statute of Frauds, 220

UNCONSCIONABILITY
Doctrine of, 151, 191, 351
Equity, 351
Oppression, 352
Procedural, 352
Substantive, 352–353

UNIFORM COMMERCIAL CODE
See U.C.C. and Restatement, Second

UNILATERAL CONTRACTS
Acceptance of offer, 98
Bilateral contracts distinguished from, 97, 128–129
Intent to accept, 101

Knowledge of offer, 100–101
Mutuality of obligation, 163–164
Notice of performance, 103–104
Revocation of, 117
U.C.C. Section 2–206, p. 129

USAGE OF TRADE, 206

WAIVER
Failure of condition, 244–245
Repeated waiver, 246
Retraction of, 160–161

WARRANTY OF MERCHANTABILITY, 124

WILLISTON'S RULE OF INTERPRETATION, 203
See also Interpretation

†